Lecture Notes in Artificial Intell

Edited by J. G. Carbonell and J. Siekmann

Subseries of Lecture Notes in Computer Science

Springer
Berlin
Heidelberg
New York
Hong Kong
London
Milan
Paris
Tokyo

Michael G. Hinchey   James L. Rash
Walter F. Truszkowski   Christopher Rouff
Diana Gordon-Spears (Eds.)

Formal Approaches to Agent-Based Systems

Second International Workshop, FAABS 2002
Greenbelt, MD, USA, October 29-31, 2002
Revised Papers

 Springer

Series Editors

Jaime G. Carbonell, Carnegie Mellon University, Pittsburgh, PA, USA
Jörg Siekmann, University of Saarland, Saarbrücken, Germany

Volume Editors

Michael G. Hinchey
James L. Rash
Walter F. Truszkowski
NASA Goddard Space Flight Center
Mailstop 588.0
Greenbelt, MD 20771, USA

Christopher Rouff
SAIC
1710 SAIC Drive
McLean, VA 22102, USA

Diana Gordon-Spears
University of Wyoming
Computer Science Department
Laramie, WY 82070, USA

Cataloging-in-Publication Data applied for

A catalog record for this book is available from the Library of Congress.

Bibliographic information published by Die Deutsche Bibliothek
Die Deutsche Bibliothek lists this publication in the Deutsche Nationalbibliografie;
detailed bibliographic data is available in the Internet at <http://dnb.ddb.de>.

CR Subject Classification (1998): I.2.11, I.2, D.2, F.3, I.6, C.3, J.2

ISSN 0302-9743
ISBN 3-540-40665-4 Springer-Verlag Berlin Heidelberg New York

Springer-Verlag Berlin Heidelberg New York
a member of BertelsmannSpringer Science+Business Media GmbH

http://www.springer.de

© Springer-Verlag Berlin Heidelberg 2003
Printed in Germany

Typesetting: Camera-ready by author, data conversion by PTP-Berlin GmbH
Printed on acid-free paper   SPIN: 10928011   06/3142   5 4 3 2 1 0

Preface

The idea of a FAABS workshop was first conceived in 1998 at the NASA Goddard Space Flight Center, while the Agent Technology Development Group in the Advanced Architectures and Automation Branch (Code 588) was developing a prototype agent community to automate satellite ground operations.

While developing this system, several race conditions arose within and between agents. Due to the complexity of the agents and the communications between them, it was decided that a formal approach was needed to specify the agents and the communications between them, so that the system could be checked for additional errors.

A formal model of the inter-agent communications was developed, with the expectation that this would enable us to find more errors. Success in this convinced us of the importance of using formal methods to model agent-based systems. To share our own experiences and to learn how others were approaching these issues, we decided to hold a workshop on formal methods and agent-based systems.

The response was overwhelming. The result was the first FAABS workshop, which was held at the NASA Goddard Space Flight Center. Posters, paper presentations, panels, and an invited talk by J Moore stimulated much discussion and subsequent collaboration.

This proceedings contains papers from FAABS-II, the second workshop held at the Greenbelt Marriott Hotel (near the NASA Goddard Space Flight Center) in October 2002 and sponsored in conjunction with the IEEE Computer Society. Participants from around the world joined together to present papers and posters, participate in panels, and hear an enlightening invited presentation by Prof. Sir Roger Penrose.

We would like to express our sincere thanks to all those who attended the workshop, presented papers or posters, and participated in panel sessions and both formal and informal discussions. Our thanks to NASA Goddard Code 588 and Code 581 (Software Engineering Laboratory), the Naval Research Laboratory, and CTA, Inc. for their financial support and to the IEEE Computer Society for their sponsorship of this event. Thanks also to Springer-Verlag for once again publishing the proceedings.

We trust that the reader will find this compilation to be of interest, and we look forward to welcoming some of you to FAABS-III, tentatively planned for early 2004.

Greenbelt, MD
May 2003

Organizing Committee

Mike Hinchey, *NASA Goddard Space Flight Center*
Jim Rash, *NASA Goddard Space Flight Center*
Walt Truszkowski, *NASA Goddard Space Flight Center*
Chris Rouff, *SAIC*
Diana Gordon-Spears, *University of Wyoming*

Table of Contents

"What Is an Agent and Why Should I Care?" 1
Tim Menzies, Adrian Pearce, Clinton Heinze, Simon Goss

Organising Logic-Based Agents 15
Michael Fisher, Chiara Ghidini, Benjamin Hirsch

A Statechart Framework for Agent Roles that Captures Expertise
and Learns Improved Behavior 28
Bahram Kimiaghalam, Abdollah Homaifar, Albert C. Esterline

Formal Specification of Interaction in Agent Societies 37
Virginia Dignum, John-Jules C. Meyer, Frank Dignum, Hans Weigand

Formal Verification for a Next-Generation Space Shuttle 53
Stacy D. Nelson, Charles Pecheur

Automated Protocol Analysis in Maude 68
Jeffrey Van Baalen, Thomas Böhne

Towards Interaction Protocol Operations for Large Multi-agent
Systems 79
Joaquín Peña, Rafael Corchuelo, José Luis Arjona

Formal Modeling and Supervisory Control of Reconfigurable Robot
Teams 92
Kiriakos Kiriakidis, Diana F. Gordon-Spears

Computational Models for Multiagent Coordination Analysis:
Extending Distributed POMDP Models 103
Hyuckchul Jung, Ranjit Nair, Milind Tambe, Stacy Marsella

Bounded Model Checking for Interpreted Systems: Preliminary
Experimental Results 115
A. Lomuscio, T. Łasica, W. Penczek

Verifiable Middleware for Secure Agent Interoperability 126
Ramesh Bharadwaj

Distributed Implementation of a Connection Graph Based on
Cylindric Set Algebra Operators 133
Silvana Zappacosta Amboldi

Using Statecharts and Modal Logics to Model Multiagent Plans and
Transactions 146
Albert C. Esterline

Qu-Prolog: An Implementation Language for Agents with Advanced
Reasoning Capabilities... 162
   Peter J. Robinson, Mike Hinchey, Keith Clark

A Model for Conformance Testing of Mobile Agents in a MASIF
Framework 173
   Mikaël Marche, Yves-Marie Quemener

Analysis of a Phase Transition in a Physics-Based Multiagent System.... 193
   Diana F. Gordon-Spears, William M. Spears

You Seem Friendly, But Can I Trust You?........................... 208
   Tim Menzies, David Owen, Bojan Cukic

Taking Intelligent Agents to the Battlefield......................... 220
   Jeffrey Hicks, Richard Flanagan, Plamen Petrov, Alexander Stoyen

Panel Session on "Applications"

Naval Applications of Secure Multi-agent Technology 235
   Ramesh Bharadwaj

Challenges Arising from Applications 236
   Charles Pecheur

Agents Applied to Autonomous Vehicles 239
   Craig Schlenoff

Using XML for Interprocess Communications in a Space Situational
Awareness and Control Application 241
   Stuart Aldridge, Alexander Stoyen, Jeffrey Hicks,
   Plamen Petrov

Panel Session on "Asimov's Laws"

Asimov's Laws: Current Progress 257
   Diana F. Gordon-Spears

Asimov's Laws.. 260
   James P. Hogan

On Laws of Robotics 264
   Yoji Kondo

Panel Session on "Tools and Education"

Challenges Arising from Applications of Agent-Based System 269
   Walt Truszkowski

Tools and Education towards Formal Methods Practice 274
  John-Jules C. Meyer

Poster Presentations

Evaluating Agent-Based Modeling as a Tool for Economists 283
  Margo Bergman

Modeling Traffic Control through Deterrent Agents................... 286
  Michel Rudnianski, Hélène Bestougeff

Towards a Formal Representation of Driving Behaviors 290
  Craig Schlenoff, Michael Gruninger

Formal Analysis of an Agent-Based Medical Diagnosis Confirmation
System 292
  Alexander Hoole, Issa Traore, Michael Liu Yanguo

Agent Programming in Dribble: From Beliefs to Goals with Plans 294
  Birna van Riemsdijk, Wiebe van der Hoek, John-Jules C. Meyer

Author Index 297

"What Is an Agent and Why Should I Care?"

Tim Menzies[1], Adrian Pearce[2], Clinton Heinze[3], and Simon Goss[3]

[1] Lane Department of Computer Science, West Virginia University,
PO Box 6109, Morgantown, WV, 26506-6109, USA, tim@menzies.com
[2] Department of Computer Science and Software Engineering The University of Melbourne,
Victoria, 3010, Australia, pearce@cs.mu.oz.au
[3] Air Operations Division, Aeronautical & Maritime Research Laboratory, Melbourne,
Australia, clinton.heinze|Simon.Goss@dsto.defence.gov.au

Abstract. A range of agent implementation technologies are reviewed according to five user-based criteria and via a comparison with object-oriented programming. The comparison with OO shows that some parts of object technology are a candidate implementation technique for some parts of agent systems. However, many other non-object-based implementation techniques may be just as useful. Also, for agents with mentalistic attitudes, the high-level specification of agent behavior requires numerous concepts outside the object paradigm; e.g. plans, communication, intentions, roles, and teams.

Keywords: Evaluation, agent-oriented, object-oriented.

1 Introduction

Is there anything really new in agent-oriented software? Are agents a bold step forward into the future of software? Or is agency just "new wine in old bottles"?

Our users demand answers to these questions, and others. One gruff user always asked "what are agents and *why should I care*?". To such users, the issue in italics is the key question. Agent technologies are interesting to users *only* if those technologies address issues of interest to the users.

After explaining agents to this gruff user, this users next comment was "this sounds just like OO to me; what's new here?". Such comments motivate this article. Our response to these comments is in three parts:

1. We carefully define the core concepts of agent-oriented software and object-oriented software.
2. Next, we review the diverse range of software labelled "agents".
3. This software is then assessed these concepts with respect to certain user-oriented issues.

The user issues used in this article come from the Australian Workshops on Agent-Based systems. Those workshops have debated the relative merits of the agent implementation technologies shown in Figure 1. In those debates, the technologies were assessed with respect to the problem of building agents for the Air Operations Division (AOD) of the Australian Defense Science Technology Division.

M.G. Hinchey et al. (Eds.): 'FAABS 2002, LNAI 2699, pp. 1–14, 2003.

Name : Notes	Introduced in...
OO : Object-oriented	§2.1
Standard BDI : BDI= beliefs, desires, intentions	§2.2
FORTRAN : How we used to build agents	§3.1
dMARS : A commercial agent-oriented BDI tool	§3.1
Command agents : Heinze and Pearce's extension to dMARS	§3.1
Behavioural cloning : Machine learning to build agents	§3.1
Petri nets :	§3.3
TACAIR/ SOAR/ PSCM : The problem space computational model (PSCM) is how the rule-based system called SOAR implements TACAIR, an agent system.	§3.4
G2 : Gensym's rule-based expert system shell: includes powerful interface tools.	§3.5
MBD-based : The model-based diagnosis system used in NASA's remote agent experiment (RAX).	§3.6

Fig. 1. Agent implementation technologies discussed in this article

For several years, the Australian Defense Forces have been using agent-oriented software to assess potential new hardware purchases. Buying planes and helicopters for the Air Force implies a major commitment to a particular platform. AOD uses operational simulation for answering specific questions about very expensive equipment requisitions, component capabilities and rehearsing dangerous tactical operations. In pilot-in-the-loop flight simulation, intelligent pilots (agents) interact with each other in the computer simulation, as well as the human pilot in the virtual environment. These dynamic, interactive multi-agent simulations pose a challenge for the integration of valid pilot competencies into computer controlled agents. This involves modeling pilot perception through recognition of actions and events that occur during simulation. Such simulators are often used after purchase as training tools. Hence, a core task within DSTO is the construction and maintenance of agent-oriented systems. These AOD agent simulations push the state-of-the-art:

- AOD agents interact at high frequency in a dynamic environment with numerous friendly and hostile agents. For example, AOD agents engage in complex aerial maneuvers against hostile high-speed aircraft.
- AOD agents co-ordinate extensively to achieve shared goals. For example, a squadron of fighters may collaborate to shepherd a cargo ship through enemy lines.
- AOD agents may change their roles at runtime. For example, if the lead of a fighter formation is shot down, then the wing-man may assume the role of fighter lead. As roles change, agents must dramatically alter their plans.

After discussions with AOD users, the following concerns were identified. These concerns are the basis for our user-oriented discussion of the merits of different agent technologies:

- Easy of construction/ modification.
- Provable reliability.

– Execution speed.
– Easy of explanation of agent behaviour.
– Support for *teaming*. Teaming is a special AOD requirement which is described below and may not be widely relevant.

The rest of this article debates the merits of the agent implementation technologies of Figure 1 for AOD applications. After that debate, we will see that agent-oriented systems requires much that does not exist in standard software engineering methods:

– AOD agent programmers do not spend their time fretting about encapsulation, classification, etc.
– Instead, they concern themselves with concepts such as plans, communication, perception, intentions, roles, and teams.

This is not to say that standard methods such as (e.g.) object-oriented are irrelevant to agent construction. At the end of this article we will briefly describe how objects are used within AOD agents for building environments in which we specify agent behavior.

2   Agents versus Objects

Before proceedings, we digress for a brief introduction to agents. In order to simplify the reader's introduction to agents, we will stress the similarities and differences of agent technology to object technology. In what the literature calls *weak agents* maps neatly into object technology. However, object technology is incomplete for implementing what the literature calls *strong agents*.

2.1   Weak Agency

A spectrum of agents types is offered by Woolridge and Jennings [22]. Within that spectrum we say that AOD's agents are at least *weak agents* since they are *autonomous, social, reactive* and *proactive*. They are *autonomous* since, while the simulations execute, AOD agents act within intervention by a human operator. They are are also *social* in the sense that AOD's agents interact extensively with other agents. Also they are *reactive* since AOD analysts develop different scenarios for their agents. Within each scenario, AOD's agents must react to changing circumstances. Further, they are *proactive* since AOD agents can take the initiative within a simulation.

Woolridge and Jennings comment that concurrent object-oriented languages provide much support for weak agents. According to the UML community (e.g. Booch [1]), OO technology consists of at least *identity, state, behavior, classification, inheritance, polymorphism* and *encapsulation*. These terms, and there relations to agents, are described below.

An object is something that can be clearly distinguished from other concepts in the design. Agents can use this *identity* to distinguish themselves from other agents.

Objects are repositories of data. Synonyms for this *state* include attributes or data.

Objects are also repositories of pre-defined *behaviour*. Synonyms for behaviour include methods, functions, procedures, or code. Agents can use state and behaviour to model their beliefs and actions on the world. Further, identity-specific behaviour lets us implement agent *pro-activeness*; each agent-object can carry with itself an agenda of tasks to be performed.

Each object can be categorized into exactly one class. This *classification* defines the state and behaviour that is valid for that object. Agents can use classification to simplify their reasoning about other objects in the domain. For example, if an agent recognizes that the object LauraBush belongs to the Person class, then they can access default knowledge about LauraBush from Person.

Objects can be defined via extensions to parent objects. Services and invariants of such parent objects can be relied on within all the parent's children since parent properties are *inherited*. Agents can use classification to simplify their own internal implementation as well as extending their classification knowledge.

Behaviors can be implemented in different objects using the same name. This *polymorphism* implies some kind of message-passing system; i.e. the results of a particular message is computed from the name of message and the nature of the receiver of that message. The same message sent polymorphically to different objects may generate different responses. Agents can use polymorphism to group together the services offered by other agents. For example, an agent might assume that all other agents in their domain respond to messages such as "position" or "velocity". Polymorphism means agents can assume simple and common interfaces to other agents; i.e. polymorphism simplifies the implementation of agent *social ability*.

Clients of an object should not need access to the internal details of that object. Such clients can ask an object to perform a named service without needing to know the details of how such services are implemented. Agents can use this *encapsulation* to ensure that, when they run *autonomous*ly and asynchronously, their internal knowledge is not mixed up with the knowledge of other agents.

2.2 Strong Agency

According to Wooldridge and Jennings, *strong agents* may possess mentalistic attitudes or be emotional or animated. AOD agents lack emotion but are mentalistic. AOD agents are based on the *beliefs*, *desires* and *intentions* (BDI) paradigm of [17]. The current state of entities and environment as perceived by the agent (abstract labels or percepts) are the agent's *beliefs*. A *desire* is some future states agent would like to be in (a.k.a. goals). *Intentions* are some commitment of an agent to achieve a goal by progressing along a particular future path that lead to the goal (a.k.a. a plan). One advantage with using intentions is that the effort associated with creating them need not be repeated every time they are required. Intentions can be pre-computed and cached. Each intention can be tagged with a trigger describing some situation in which this intention should be accessed and applied.

In this BDI paradigm, deliberation is done through the selection of a goal, selection of a plan that will be used to form an intention, selection of an intention, and execution of the selected intention. All these decisions are based on the beliefs the agent has about the current state of the environment. The process of selecting the forming plan is known as means-end reasoning.

The BDI means-end reasoning approach has proven very beneficial to the AOD, particularly the OPERATOR AGENT that is used to simulate military operations, it is used in support of multi-billion dollar requisitions [20]. This is partly reflected in the maturity of BDI, and the fundamental limitations it overcomes [17]. This includes ways of relaxing the need to have perfect knowledge of opponents' plans.

The BDI approach has made it easier for DSTO to codify tactics and build simulations, and importantly, to get explanations out of them of what happens. The DSTO has found it easier to construct and modifying scenarios, as the Operator Agent is a generalized agent capable of simulating different entities, aircraft, ships etc. Implemented using the dMARS procedural reasoning language [4]), BDI improves abstraction for representation of declarative and procedural knowledge. This allows for improved explanation, as the success of these operational simulations is measured in terms of what all stakeholders receive, whether experts or operators.

The BDI approach has also scaled up for large scale operational simulation-the Operator Agent at the Air Operations Division (AOD) has been used to run operational simulations involving 32 pilots, 400 plans, 10 goals, 25 intentions concurrently, each receiving 8 contacts every 50ms [20].

3   A Range of Agent Technologies

In this section, we explore a range of agent implementation technologies considered at AOD. All our implementation options are compared to some mythical ideal AOD agent system in the *repertory grid* of Figure 2. Figure 2 shows various implementation options (e.g. G2) ranked on different dimensions (e.g. easy/hard to modify). Repertory grids are a knowledge acquisition technique extensively explored by Shaw and Gaines [19, 5]. Their key benefit is that superfluous comparisons between examples are ignored. Dimensions are only added to a repertory grid if they help to distinguish examples. That is, dimensions with no information content are excluded. A side-effect of this approach will be that we will not define in detail different agent implementation technologies. Instead, we will just discuss how these technologies differ according the repertory grid dimensions. However, we do provide references for each method so the interested reader can explore further.

The rest of this section defines the dimensions of Figure 2. The desired end of each dimensions will be shown as headings while the opposite, and undesirable, end of each dimension will be shown in italics.

3.1   Easy to Build/Modify

Opposite= Hard to Build/Modify

AOD's agents are used to handle specialized what-if queries. What-if queries are notoriously ad hoc. Ideally, we should be able to quickly change our agents to accommodate new what-if queries.

Originally, AOD ran its agent simulations using standard procedural languages to implement the decision logic of a human operator. In procedural systems (e.g. FORTRAN) such decision logic may comprise less than 20% of the total system. However,

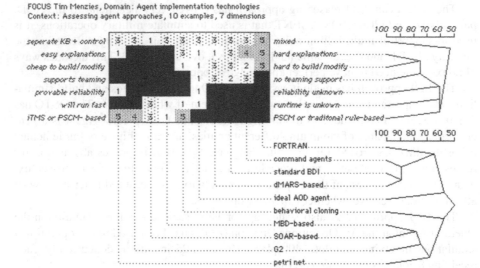

FOCUS Tim Menzies, Domain: Agent implementation technologies
Context: Assessing agent approaches, 10 examples, 7 dimensions

A repertory grid maps examples *into a range of* dimensions. *For any row in the table, if an example scores "5", it is near the right-hand end of a dimension. If it scores "1", it is near the left-hand end of a dimension. For example, bottom left, petri nets scores a "5"; i.e. it is more a rule-based system than a iTMS or PSCM-based system. Black areas denote "don't know". Trees on far right show distances between each example and dimension; e.g. standard BDI and dMARS-based systems are very similar.*

Fig. 2. A comparison of implementation issues for agents. Generated from the web-based repertory grid server at http://gigi.cpsc.ucalgary.ca/.

such code can consume up to 80% of the maintenance effort. For example, new programmers working on a FORTRAN simulator could take up to one year before be able to modify the decision logic.

In response to this maintenance cost, AOD turned to high-level BDI-based agent-oriented languages. Agent-oriented software such as dMARS [4] offers a succinct and high-level representation of the decision logic. Using such agents, AOD has been very successful in reacting to customer "what if" queries from their customers. With the FORTRAN systems, in might have taken weeks before AOD could report simulation results from different operator actions. With the agent systems, such reports can be generated in days or even hours.

Standard BDI is a conceptual framework that must be supported by a tool such as dMARS in order to be practical for real-world practioners. dMARS offers high-level support for BDI and extensive graphical facilities. dMARS reduced the cost of creating AOD agents. However, even though costs were significantly reduced, AOD still finds agent design to be very expensive. Two technologies that address the cost issue are *command agents* and *behavioral cloning of agents*, discussed below.

Command Agents. Pearce and Heinze added another layer on top of dMARS to process the patterns of standard agent usage seen at AOD [14,7]. Their *command agents* divide reasoning into the following . Firstly, *situation awareness* extracts the essential features from the environment. Next, the *assessment* layer ranks the extracted features. These ranking represents a space of options explored by *tactic selection:*. lastly, in the *selection of operational procedure* layer, the preferred option is mapped onto the available resources.

In repeated applications of this framework, Pearce and Heinze report that the command agents framework offers a significant productivity increase for AOD personnel over standard dMARS.

Behavioral Cloning of Agents. *Behavioral cloning* is a machine learning technique. A qualitative model of a domain is generated. The qualitative model is imprecise and so contains areas of uncertainty. A scenario is described. This scenario serves to restrict the ranges of some of the uncertain values within the model. The model is now executed within the constraints offered by the scenario. Where uncertainty exists, the simulator either picks one option at random or backtracks over all options (if such backtracking is tractable). This simulation generates an experience base: a file of examples of the operation of the model. The experience base is then classified according to some domain criteria; e.g. we never ran low on fuel. A machine learner then generates some summary of the classified examples. This technique has been used to generate knowledge of cardiac function [2], satellite electrical systems [15], how to fly a plan [18], and how to run a software project [11].

Behavioral cloning often throws the intermediaries between inputs and outputs. Hence, a disadvantage of behavioral cloning is that the learnt theory can't queried for a rich description for *how* some output was reached. Hence, behavioral clones may be hard to explain.

On the other hand, behavioral cloning scores highly on the "easy to build/modify" scale. Once the background qualitative model has been built, the knowledge required for a new agent can be generated automatically merely by adopting new scenario constraints.

Easy to Modify: Summary. Clearly FORTRAN scores the lowest on this dimension and behavioral cloning, theoretically anyway, scores the highest. dMARS is mid-range on this scale and command agents are easier to modify than standard dMARS systems.

3.2 Supports Teaming

Opposite= No Teaming Support
Teams are a natural means of modeling collaborating defense forces. Teams act as if they share a belief set even though sometimes team members may have subtlety different beliefs. While team member A may not know everything known by team member B, some abstract co-ordination agent knows everything that the team members know.

The current generation of agent software used at AOD is designed for modeling the interaction of solo agents in a shared environment. Coding such tools gets complex when teams co-ordinate and share beliefs. In particular, every exception case where the team believes X while the team member believes Y must be encoded.

At present, AOD makes little use of team-based agent simulations: i.e. most of its systems are at the first-person singular level. Consequently, the spaghetti sections are not large. However, it is anticipated that in the near future, AOD will be making extensive use of team-based simulations.

Some initial experiments have been performed with implementing teaming in a dMARS framework [21]. These initial studies may also supply command agents with a teaming ability (since command agents are built on top of dMARS). Apart from that, the AOD experience is that most agent systems have very little support for teaming.

3.3   Provable Reliability

Opposite= Reliability Unknown
Currently, AOD's agents are only used in the research labs. However, this may change. Each simulator stores extensive tactical knowledge that could be usefully applied in the field. However, before a research prototype can be deployed into the field, its reliability must be certified. In the context of this article we say that reliability is some probability that, after watching the system run and seeing some errors, that in for future time T we will see N errors.

Within AOD there has been some discussions on using petri nets to implement agents. A petri net [16] is a directed graph interconnecting nodes of different types on which multiple tokens are permitted to travel. There are two types of nodes: places and transitions. Arcs connect places to transitions and transitions to places; transitions are never connected to transitions, and places are never connected to places. While Petri nets consist of a small number of elements and the algorithms for evaluation can be expressed very simply, they are sufficiently formal to allow mathematical analysis. These tend to be both detailed and complex. A large suite of reliability results exist for petri nets (as used in Markov chains [10, p759-765]) or otherwise [9]. Agents based on petri-nets/markov models have been used in domains as complicated as Robocup[6] (though Pearce, Heinze and Goss comment that such single state systems do not adapt well when there are multiple entities operating in the simulation [14,7]).

Petri nets are a convenient tool for reasoning about concurrent systems. Unlike a state transition diagram, where execution is sequential, traversing one state after another, with petri nets execution is fully concurrent. Hence, it has been argued that petri nets are a sound basis for constructing reliable agents.

On balance, it is doubtful that AOD will adpot the petri net approach, due to the next point.

3.4   Separate KB and Control

Opposite= Mixed
AOD has a strong commitment to cognitive modeling; i.e. generating human-like behaviour from explicit high-level symbolic representations. Hence, an ideal AOD agent uses such representations.

Different approaches to agent-based systems take a different approach to their representations. General BDI is a conceptual framework, not a specific implementation. Hence, it makes no commitment to levels of control flexibility. Procedural languages like FORTRAN mix domain knowledge and inference knowledge like spaghetti. Recall that it was the maintenance effort associated with such spaghetti code that drove AOD away from FORTRAN. Knowledge based systems take a separate approach: inference and domain knowledge are distinct and can be modified separately. All the non-FORTRAN agent systems being discussed here can be divided up according to how flexible is their control knowledge.

At one end of the control flexibility-scale are agents based on the SOAR architecture (e.g. TACAIR [8]). A SOAR knowledge base has two distinct parts: a standard declarative rule section and a second section describing the control knowledge in rule-based terms. In SOAR, agents seek operators which might take them closer to their goals. Conflict resolution is used to resolve conflicts between competing operators. Conflict resolution is SOAR, the operators, and the domain rule knowledge are all implemented in the same uniform rule-based manner. This means that the knowledge engineer can customize not only the rule base but also the control of how the rules are fired. Rules in SOAR are organized into problem spaces: zones within the kb that discuss the same sets of operators. If a SOAR problem space can't resolve operator clashes, then a *impasse* is declared and SOAR forks a nested problem space with the task of resolving that conflict. Hence, at runtime, a SOAR system conducts a recursive descent through the problem spaces. This is called the problem space computation model (or PSCM [23]). Recursive descent is only an approximation of PSCM. Each problem space is an autonomous group of rules that might "wake-up" and execute if their pre-conditions are ever satisfied. The authors of TACAIR use this feature extensively. TACAIR views its knowledge as an intricate goal hierarchy. Problems spaces act like min-agents; each with their own autonomous agenda that sleep till some trigger condition makes them execute.

At the other end of the control flexibility-scale are petri nets and the decision trees generated by behavioral cloning. Petri nets and decision trees permit no meta-level control of the inference net. In marked contrast to SOAR, inference is via inflexible local propagation rules. It would be a simple matter to add a meta-interpreter to (e.g.) petri nets that could customize the propagation rules. However, such meta-level control would change the runtime properties of a petri net and invalidate all the petri net reliability results.

Halfway between the total flexibility of SOAR and the rigid inflexibility of petri nets/decision trees lies the BDI support systems (dMARS, command agents). These system restrict the knowledge engineer into creating planning systems. However, within that restriction, considerable flexibility is offered.

3.5 Easy Explanations

Opposite= Hard Explanations
Defense personnel audit AOD agent knowledge bases to see if they reflects current Australian defense tactical maneuvers. Hence, it is important that the inner workings of agents can be explained to a domain expert.

Explaining the behaviour of a agent generated from behavioral cloning is difficult. The learnt theory is a mapping of inputs to outputs with all internal connections thrown away. Such internal connections are useful in building rich explanation structures. Still, the simplicity of the decision tree generated from behavioral cloning makes cloned agents easier to understand than those written in some procedural language (e.g. FORTRAN).

AOD supports at least two methods for generating intricate explanations. Firstly, they claim that the agents knowledge base is close in concept to how human operators control defense hardware. At AOD, agency is not merely some implementation trick. Rather, by explicating agent knowledge, AOD is hoping that it is also explicating human knowledge at a comprehensible level of abstraction. Further, the command agents paradigm sits well with standard operational practice within the Australian defense forces. Hence, AOD argues, explaining an BDI/command agents tool is fundamentally simpler than browsing some other conceptual model (e.g. FORTRAN code).

Secondly, AOD uses explanations via graphical visualizations. The dMARS tool makes extensive use of graphical interfaces. Another implementation tool of note is the G2 system. Clancey et.al have used G2 to build elaborate agent systems in which the behaviour of an organization is emergent from the behaviour of the agents representing the workers in that environment [3]. G2 offers extensive support for a traditional rule-based execution paradigm. G2 is also a powerful tool for building elaborate graphical interfaces (e.g. Figure 3).

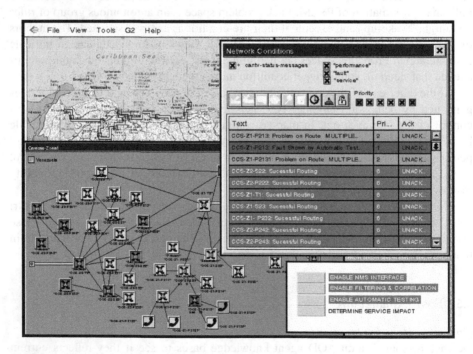

Fig. 3. Sample screensap from a G2 application. From http://www.gensym.com/products/operationsexpert.htm.

3.6 Tractability/Speed Results Known

Opposite= Tractability/ Speed Is an Open Issue
Repeating the above point on reliability, if a research prototype is to be deployed into the field, we need some assurance that it will execute at least as fast as events in the field.

Behavioral cloning builds decisions trees and such trees execute very quickly at run-time. While this is a significant advantage of behavioral cloning, we note that this comes at the cost of all the disadvantages mentioned above; e.g. poor explanatory capacity.

In terms of reasoning efficiency, an interesting middle ground between decision trees and BDI is the agent technology used by NASA in its remote agent experiment (RAX). NASA deployed RAX in the asteroid belt in May 1999. RAX built its own autonomous plans to react to flight events [12]. The representations within RAX were much simpler than (e.g.) the AOD BDI plans. The RAX development team claim that, after several years with exploring model-based diagnosis (MBD), that very simple representations can model even complex domains. Further, given regular propositional encodings of that domain knowledge, an incremental truth maintenance system (iTMS) [13] can build satisfactory plans very quickly.

4 Conclusion

The goal of this paper was to assess agent-oriented systems via two kinds of user-oriented queries. Firstly, our users were worried about the (non)-distinction between agents and objects. As seen above, the "OO mindset" contains about half a dozen key concepts: class, instance, encapsulation, inheritance, polymorphism, and so on. However, the key concepts of the AOD "agent-oriented" mindset make little reference to the key OO concepts. For example, OO makes no reference to the concept that AOD regards as central to agency: intentionality. Nor do the core OO concepts refer to explicit knowledge representation of domain and control knowledge, teaming, plans, communication, perception, beliefs, and desires. Further, the assessment criteria we would apply to agent systems are orthogonal to the key OO concepts and include ease of construction and maintenance, ability to explain agent knowledge, and promises of runtime performance, reliability.

Secondly, our users were concerned about the range of issues and the range of technologies clustered in Figure 4. This figure is a 2-D display of a n-dimensional space and so cannot be a totally accurate representation. However, it does clearly show the distance of FORTRAN to AOD's ideal agent technology. Further, the low-level representations of petri nets and the MBD-based RAX system make them poles apart from AOD's ideal agent. Behavioral cloning is surprisingly close to AOD's ideal; perhaps only because of its ease of construction.

Apart from Figure 4, we have also seen that different design goals select different agent implementation technologies:

- If the goal is human cognitive modeling, then avoid low-level representations. High-level representation schemes mentioned here were SOAR and the BDI-based tools.
- If committed to intentionality, then use BDI-based tools such as dMARS or the command agents extension.

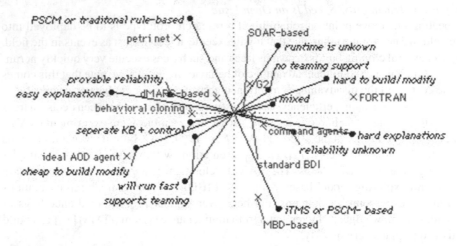

PrinCom, Domain: Agent implementation technologies, User: Tim Menzies
Context: Assessing agent approaches, 10 examples, 7 dimensions

This figure is generated from Figure 2 via a principle components analysis to grid the data. 2-D positions are generated via first isolating combination of factors that are strongly correlated. These factors define a transform space into which the various technologies described in this article can be mapped into a 2-D space. This diagram can be used to gain an intuitive view of what technologies are similar (they appear closer together on this diagram).

Fig. 4. Clusters of agent technologies. Generated from the web-based repertory grid server at `http://gigi.cpsc.ucalgary.ca/` using the dimensions of Figure 2.

– If the goal is raw execution speed, use low-level representations plus a fast theorem prover. Two such candidates are the decision trees from behavioral cloning or propositional encoding with the iTMS.
– If the goal is explanation/justification of system behaviour, use some technology that offers high level views of the system. Two such systems reviewed here are the graphical interfaces of G2 or systems that use high-level representations that match local domain knowledge (e.g. command agents).
– If the goal is highly-reliable systems, then use petri nets.
– If the goal is to model elaborate teaming interactions, then hire AI specialists and conduct a research program to extend the state-of-the-art in agent systems.
– If the goal is to reduce maintenance costs, then consider automatically generating the agent using behavioral cloning. Alternatively, if the goal is to increase revenue through maintenance requests, then use FORTRAN.

Acknowledgements. The contents of this paper were greatly enhanced by the lively discussion at the Australian workshop on agent-oriented systems organized by Leon

Sterling (Melbourne University) and Simon Goss (AOD). All views expressed here are the authors and may not reflect the consensus view of that workshop.

This research was partially conducted at West Virginia University under NASA contract NCC2-0979. The work was sponsored by the NASA Office of Safety and Mission Assurance under the Software Assurance Research Program led by the NASA IV&V Facility. Reference herein to any specific commercial product, process, or service by trade name, trademark, manufacturer, or otherwise, does not constitute or imply its endorsement by the United States Government.

References

1. G. Booch. *Object-Oriented Design with Applications (second edition)*. Benjamin/ Cummings, 1994.
2. I. Bratko, I. Mozetic, and N. Lavrac. *KARDIO: a Study in Deep and Qualitative Knowledge for Expert Systems*. MIT Press, 1989.
3. W. Clancey, P. Sachs, M. Sierhuis, and R. van Hoof. Brahms: Simulating practice for work systems design. In P. Compton, R. Mizoguchi, H. Motoda, and T. Menzies, editors, *Proceedings PKAW '96: Pacific Knowledge Acquisition Workshop*. Department of Artificial Intelligence, 1996.
4. M. d'Inverno, K. M., L. D., and M. Wooldridge. A formal specification of dmars. In A. Singh and M.Wooldridge, editors, *Intelligent Agents IV: Proc. of the Fourth International Workshop on Agent Theories. Architectures and Languages, Springer Verlag*, 1998.
5. B. Gaines and M. Shaw. Comparing the conceptual systems of experts. In *IJCAI '89*, pages 633–638, 1989.
6. K. Han and M. Veloso. Automated robot behaviour recognition applied to robot soccer. In *Proceedings of the Sixteenth Interntional Joint Conference on Artificial Intelligence. Workshop on Team Behaviour and Plan Recognition*, pages 47–52, 1999.
7. C. Heinze, S. Goss, T. Josefsson, K. Bennett, S. Waugh, I. Lloyd, G. Murray, and J. Oldfield. Interchanging agents and humans in military simulation. *AI Magazine*, 23(2), Summer 2002.
8. R. M. Jones, J. E. Laird, P. E. Nielsen, K. J. Coulter, P. G. Kenny, and F. V. Koss. Automated intelligent pilots for combat flight simulation. *AI Magazine*, 20(1):27–41, 1999.
9. O. Kummer. The petri nets bibliography; keyword: reliability. http://www.informatik. uni-hamburg.de/TGI/pnbib/keywords/r/reliability.html, 2000.
10. M. Lyu. *The Handbook of Software Reliability Engineering*. McGraw-Hill, 1996.
11. T. Menzies, E. Sinsel, and T. Kurtz. Learning to reduce risks with cocomo-ii. In *Workshop on Intelligent Software Engineering, an ICSE 2000 workshop, and NASA/WVU Software Research Lab, Fairmont, WV, Tech report # NASA-IVV-99-027, 1999*, 2000. Available from http://menzies.us/pdf/00wise.pdf.
12. N. Muscettola, P. P. Nayak, B. Pell, and B. Williams. Remote agent: To boldly go where no ai system has gone before. *Artificial Intelligence*, 103(1-2):5–48, August 1998.
13. P. P. Nayak and B. C. Williams. Fast context switching in real-time propositional reasoning. In *Proceedings of AAAI-97*, 1997. Available from http://ack.arc.nasa.gov:80/ic/projects/mba/papers/aaai97.ps.
14. A. Pearce, C. Heinz, and S. Goss. Meeting plan recognition requirements for real-time air-mission simulations, 2000.
15. D. Pearce. The induction of fault diagnosis systems from qualitative models. In *Proc. AAAI-88*, 1988.
16. W. Reisig. *Petri Nets*. Springer Verlag, 1982.

17. A. Roa and M. Georgeff. Bdi agents: From theory to practice. In *Proceedings of the First International Conference on Multi-Agent Systems, San Francisco, CA, June*, 1995.

18. C. Sammut, S. Hurst, D. Kedzier, and D. Michie. Learning to fly. In D. Sleeman, editor, *Ninth International Conference on Machine Learning*, pages 385–393. Morgan Kaufmann, 1992.

19. M. Shaw. *WebGrid: a WWW PCP Server*. Knowledge Systems Institute, University of Calgary, `http://Tiger.cpsc.ucalgary.ca/WebGrid/WebGrid.html`, 1997.

20. G. Tidar, C. Heinze, S. Goss, G. Murray, D. Appla, and I. Lloyd. Using intelligent agents in military simulations or 'using agents intelligently.'. In *Proc. of Eleventh Innovative Applications of Artificial Intelligence Conference, American Association of Artificial Intelligence*, 1999.

21. G. Tidhar, C. Heinze, and M. Selvestrel. Flying together: Modelling air mission teams. *Applied Intelligence*, 8(3):195–218, 1998.

22. M. Wooldridge and N. Jennings. Intelligent agents: Theory and practice. *The Knowledge Engineering Review*, 10(2):115–152, 1995. Available from `http://www.cs.umbc.edu/agents/introduction/ker.ps.Z`.

23. G. Yost and A. Newell. A Problem Space Approach to Expert System Specification. In *IJCAI '89*, pages 621–627, 1989.

Organising Logic-Based Agents

Michael Fisher, Chiara Ghidini, and Benjamin Hirsch

Logic and Computation Group
Department of Computer Science, University of Liverpool, UK
{M.Fisher,C.Ghidini,B.Hirsch}@csc.liv.ac.uk

Abstract. In this paper we address the task of organising multi-agent systems in order to collectively solve problems. We base our approach on a logical model of rational agency comprising a few simple, but powerful, concepts. While many other researchers have tackled this problem using formal logic, the important aspect of the work described here is that the logical descriptions of the agents are directly executable using the Concurrent METATEM framework, allowing the execution of agents described in a combination of temporal, belief and ability logics. Here, we are particularly concerned with exploring some of the possible logical constraints that may be imposed upon these agents, and how these constraints affect the ability of the agents to come together to collectively solve problems.

1 Introduction

In [8] we introduced a logical model of rational agency incorporating the key notions of *ability*, *belief*, and *confidence*, the last of these capturing a flexible motivational attitude. The novel aspect of this work is not just the model itself, but the fact that logical statements are directly executable and so agents are represented in a single language for purposes of both analysis and execution. In [8], we examine the use of this formal model in developing both individual agents and multi-agent systems. A key property, at least for individual agents, is[1]

$$(\mathsf{A}_i\varphi \wedge \mathsf{B}_i\Diamond\varphi) \Rightarrow \Diamond\varphi \tag{1}$$

This says that, if an agent i is able to perform φ, and also believes that φ will occur sometime in the future (i.e. is *confident* of φ), then it will actively make φ happen. For multi-agent systems, we must consider how an agent sends out messages trying to ascertain whether other agents are able to help it achieve its goals.

In this paper, we are concerned with two aspects:

---

[1] 'B' is the belief operator, 'A' is the ability operator and '$\Diamond$' is the temporal operator meaning "at some time in the future". Each can be subscripted by a specific agent identifier.

M.G. Hinchey et al. (Eds.): 'FAABS 2002, LNAI 2699, pp. 15–27, 2003.

1. the effect of modifying formulae such as (1) above to take account of individual agents behaviours, and,
2. the effect of constructing groups and teams using axioms/formulae of the above form.

Throughout, it is important to remember that all these formulae occur within a system that allows the direct execution of logical statements from an agent theory.

The structure of this paper is as follows. Section 2 presents the concurrent operational model in which logical statements are executed, and through which multi-agent systems are implemented. In Section 3, we focus on a variety of agent behaviours, and investigate how formulae such as (1) can be modified in order to represent the different agent behaviours. In the following section (Section 4) we extend our analysis of agent behaviours to group behaviours, and we make an attempt to modify formulae such as (1) in order to represent different kinds of group behaviours. Finally, in Section 5, we provide concluding remarks.

Finally, for the interested reader, the logical background concerning temporal logic, basic execution, belief and ability extensions is reviewed in Appendix A.

2   Concurrent METATEM

Concurrent METATEM [5] is an extension of METATEM which allows the specification and execution of multiple agents. It is a logic-based programming language comprising two elements: the representation of each individual agent's behaviour in the way described above; and an operational framework for agents that provides both asynchronous concurrency and broadcast message-passing. The basic tenets of this approach are that:

(i) all agents are concurrently active;
(ii) the basic mechanism for communication between agents is *broadcast* message-passing;
(iii) each agent defines how it will interact with its environment by using an "interface definition".

An exhaustive illustration of Concurrent METATEM is out of the scope of this paper, but the interested reader can refer to [5]. We are only interested here in highlighting that Concurrent METATEM provides a framework where agents can be grouped together, can communicate through identified messages (modelled as predicates), and in doing so can alter the internal state of the receiver(s). From the logical point of view, the only extension we need be concerned about, beyond the logic presented in Section A.1, is the subscripting of the '$\Diamond$' operator. Thus, $\Diamond_i \varphi$ is satisfied if, and only if, $\Diamond \varphi$ is satisfied in agent i's execution.

2.1   Agents and Groups

An important aspect of Concurrent METATEM is the notion of *grouping* [5]. A group is a organisational mechanism that collects and relates a set of individual agents within a multi-agent system. Messages are broadcast within groups.

Groups can be overlapping, contain sub-groups, and can even have different environmental conditions.

Fisher and Kakoudakis showed in [9] that groups should be treated similar to agents. Effectively, groups and agents are viewed as one and the same entity, avoiding the need to introduce separate mechanisms to deal with agent structuring and organisation. Thus, the structure of an agent in general is as follows:

$$Agent ::= \quad Control : Specification$$
$$Abilities : \mathcal{P}(Ability)$$
$$Content : \mathcal{P}(Agent)$$
$$Context : \mathcal{P}(Agent)$$

The *Control* describes the general behaviour of the agent. In particular it contains logical rules about how to deal with incoming and outgoing messages. The *Abilities* of an agent are the core of the agent — they specify the capabilities of the agent. The agent can choose to publicise some of these abilities to other agents. The *Content* resembles the group aspect of the agent. It contains the agents that are located *within* this agent. Groups an agent participates in are listed in the *Context* component. Provided that the agent environment is also represented as an agent, all agents in the system will be connected via these content/context sets.

Thus, all agents are groups and all groups are agents; 'standard' agents are just those with empty *Content*. In our framework, groups are dynamic, so agents can be added and removed from groups. Thus, an agent with empty *Content* (i.e. a 'standard', atomic agent) can evolve into one with non-empty *Content* (i.e. a group or team agent). How the group/team is organised is effectively controlled by the *Control* element of the group/team agent.

2.2 Communication

Given the view of agents $\equiv$ groups, we need to clearly define the way agents communicate. Generally, only predicates and formulae of the form $A\varphi$, $B\varphi$, $B\Diamond\varphi$, and $\Diamond\varphi$ are sent, where φ stands for a predicate.

Effectively, an agent has to deal with two distinct environments — its *Content*, that is the group the agent represents, and its *Context*, the group in which the agent participates. To cater for this, we need to introduce a little more notation: $\Uparrow\varphi$ denotes a message that is to be sent to the agent's *Context*, or received from the agent's *Content*. Similarly, $\Downarrow\varphi$ will be sent to the agent's *Content*, or received from its *Context*. If no direction is specified, the predicate is sent to (respectively, received from) all agents within the same *Context*. Thus, we can think of *send* as broadcasting messages to other agents on the same 'level', while $\Uparrow send$ sends a message 'up' through the hierarchy of agents, and $\Downarrow send$ sends a message 'down'.

We also introduce a special notation, $B_?\varphi, A_?\varphi$ to denote a simple request, rather than an informational message. These should be read as "Is there an agent that believes/is able to do φ?".

Agents have control over what kind of messages they want to listen to. This is accomplished by providing two lists of predicates, an IN list, and an OUT list. If a received message matches with a predicate in the IN list, the predicate is added to its knowledge base. Likewise, if an OUT predicate becomes true during execution, it will be broadcast. Agents can dynamically add and remove predicates from either list.

Additionally, agents can send messages explicitly using the special predicate $send(\varphi)$, as well as refer to receiving messages by using the predicate $receive(\varphi)$. The $send$ (or $receive$) predicate broadcasts (respectively, receives) messages. The annotation concerning ⇑and ⇓described above also applies to these $send$ and $receive$ predicates.

3   Varieties of Agent Behaviour

Given the motivation for φ to be achieved, i.e. $B_i\Diamond\varphi$, there are a number of ways in which this can actually be achieved. If agent i is itself able to carry out φ, then formula (1) above shows us how to do this:

$$(A_i\varphi \wedge B_i\Diamond\varphi) \Rightarrow \Diamond\varphi$$

If, however, $\neg A_i\varphi$, then the agent must find another way to achieve φ. Later in the paper we will examine ways in which the agent can utilise groups/teams of other agents in order to help it achieve φ. For the moment, however, we will consider just three of a large number of possibilities concerning how an agent might request external help in achieving φ. Likewise, we will only highlight three ways out of many concerning how agents can deal with incoming requests. While these examples only explore a few of the multitude of possible behaviours, we use them to show the power of the approach.

3.1   Initial Enquiry

Before agents can exhibit their different behaviour, they will need to establish that there are agents that actually can accomplish the requested task. Recall that $B\Diamond\varphi$ but $\neg A\varphi$, and so the initial message is:

$$B\Diamond\varphi \wedge \neg A\varphi \Rightarrow send(A_?\varphi)$$

All agents x that have the ability to bring about φ are required to answer truthfully, according to the following rule:

$$receive(A_?\varphi) \wedge A\varphi \Rightarrow send(A_x\varphi)$$

If an agent does not have the ability to do φ, it does not answer at all.

3.2   Behaviours of Requesting Agents

Assuming that at least one agent responded to the query about ability, we can now distinguish between different types of behaviours:

- A **trusting** agent, t, upon receiving the message that agent x has the ability to do φ, will trust that x will bring about φ without t's intervention, and therefore only asserts its confidence in x achieving φ within its own (local) knowledge base:

$$B_t \Diamond \varphi \wedge \neg A_\varphi \wedge receive(A_x\varphi) \ \Rightarrow \ B_t \Diamond_x \varphi$$

- A **cautious** agent, c, upon receiving the message that agent x has ability to do φ, will communicate that it believes that agent x will eventually make φ true:

$$B_c \Diamond \varphi \wedge \neg A_\varphi \wedge receive(A_x\varphi) \ \Rightarrow \ send(B_c \Diamond_x \varphi)$$

Note that this does not imply that agent x will be forced to actually execute φ.

- A **demanding** agent, d, upon receiving the message that agent x has the ability to do φ, will request that x actually executes φ:

$$B_t \Diamond \varphi \wedge \neg A_\varphi \wedge receive(A_x\varphi) \ \Rightarrow \ send(\Diamond_x \varphi)$$

Note that the *send*s by both the cautious and demanding agents broadcast the message to other agents, not just to x. As we will see later, this broadcast of information is particularly useful in developing team behaviour.

3.3   Behaviours of Responding Agents

The responding agents, upon receiving the above messages, can choose to either ignore or accept the requests. Again, we describe three distinct types out of a vast range of possible behaviours. As a basis we use the following formulae:

$$B_c \Diamond_x \varphi \wedge A_\varphi \Rightarrow \Diamond \varphi \tag{2}$$

$$\Diamond_x \varphi \wedge A_\varphi \Rightarrow \Diamond \varphi \tag{3}$$

$$B \Diamond \varphi \wedge A_\varphi \Rightarrow \Diamond \varphi \tag{4}$$

Rule (2) says that agent x will bring about φ if it gets to know that some other agent c believes that x will do φ. Rule (3) implies that x will honour demands to bring about φ. (Note that this is a much stronger request.) The last rule (4) is in fact formula (1), which deals with internal commitments.

- A **friendly** agent x will always try to help others, and will therefore not only honour direct requests, but will also execute tasks if other agents are confident that x is executing them. It therefore has rules (2), (3), and (4) in its rule set.

– A **neutral** agent x is less willing to help agents, and will therefore only have rules (3) and (4)

– Last but not least, the **unfriendly** agent never listens to requests or confidences of other agents, and only executes tasks it is confident of itself. Accordingly, it will only have rule (4).

4   Groups and Teams

The flexibility of the formal language, together with the fact that agents and groups are one and the same, allows us to utilise almost exactly the same formulae specified in Section 3 but now in a group context. Since communication is now from the group/team agent to its *Content* (i.e. the agents within its group) rather than to other external agents, we essentially just need to modify the formulae with a different 'direction' of communication. Thus, the initial enquiry becomes

$$B\Diamond\varphi \wedge \neg A\varphi \;\Rightarrow\; \Downarrow send(A_?\varphi)$$

asking about the (sub) agents' abilities. Similarly, the other formulae, as described in Section 3, are annotated as follows.

$$\Downarrow receive(A_?\varphi) \wedge A\varphi \;\Rightarrow\; \Uparrow send(A_x\varphi) \qquad \text{[Initial response]}$$
$$B_t\Diamond\varphi \wedge \neg A_\varphi \wedge \Uparrow receive(A_x\varphi) \Rightarrow\; B_t\Diamond_x\varphi \qquad \text{[Trusting agent]}$$
$$B_c\Diamond\varphi \wedge \neg A_\varphi \wedge \Uparrow receive(A_x\varphi) \Rightarrow\; \Downarrow send(B_c\Diamond_x\varphi) \qquad \text{[Cautious agent]}$$
$$B_t\Diamond\varphi \wedge \neg A_\varphi \wedge \Uparrow receive(A_x\varphi) \Rightarrow\; \Downarrow send(\Diamond_x\varphi) \qquad \text{[Demanding agent]}$$

We will now show how these formulae influence agents with non-empty *Content*, and indicate other logical rules that may be added in this context. Again, there are many different structures possible, but we will only highlight three here: *loose groups*, *tight groups*, and *teams*. For the sake of argument we assume all (sub) agents to be friendly.

4.1   Loose Groups

The *trusting* agent builds a very weak group. No information about the belief state of the group agent is passed among its *Contents*, and no direct requests are made. However, the trusting agent *does* change its own belief state — it asserts that agent x (in this case, one of its *Contents*) will be performing φ at some time in the future. It therefore can reason with this information.

In our framework, groups are fundamental. Because agents can participate in more than one group, we can introduce groups based on different principles. Loose groups are useful, for example in modelling agents that can 'see' each other, but have no further connection, agents that have limited abilities, or environments where communication is very expensive. Agents in loose groups are likely be members of stronger groups at the same time.

4.2   Teams

Cautious agents develop another group structure. Different to trusting agents, information about confidence is broadcast to the group. Therefore, all agents within the group can reason with this information. It also allows members to respond positively to queries if they have, for example, negotiated within another group in which they participate that some task is accomplished, even if they do not have the ability to do so themselves. Note, however, that the agent asking for confidence in φ again has no guarantee that φ will actually be accomplished.

This group structure is weaker than many definitions of teams (see, for example, [12]), yet the concept of cautious agents can easily be extended to share information necessary to model stronger team structures. For example, the cautious rule described above:

$$B_c \Diamond \varphi \wedge \neg A_\varphi \wedge \Uparrow receive(A_x \varphi) \Rightarrow \Downarrow send(B_c \Diamond_x \varphi)$$

ensures that all agents know that the group agent (i.e. c) is confident about φ (i.e. $B_c \Diamond_x \varphi$). An obvious rule to add, in all agents i, is

$$B_c \Diamond_x \varphi \wedge (c \in Context) \Rightarrow B_i \Diamond \varphi$$

ensuring that all members of the group/team have the same confidence (in such goals). Where $x \neq i$ then the agent i gains new, and potentially useful, information about the team activities.

4.3   Tight Groups

Demanding agents create by far the strongest type of group. Not only will the group as a whole get to know that the direct request to accomplish φ has been made, but they will be sure (rather than just believe) that φ will be executed. They therefore can reason with this information. Note that, in order for the team to function properly, all member agents should be friendly, and have no further restrictions on executing requested tasks. This means that the agent being asked to accomplish φ effectively loses some of its autonomy, in that it cannot decide any more on whether or not to actually pursue φ. While at first glance this seems to contradict the concept of an agent, it does make sense in many different team settings. For mission-critical goals, group/team agents might need influence/control over member's abilities.

We call this group structure a team, because the agents have very clear roles, and they are required to fulfil them when asked. This type comes the closest to traditional object-oriented programming, whereby participating agents lose (most of) their autonomy, and will execute the task that they are given.

4.4   Evolving Structures

One further aspect should be mentioned concerning these group or team agents. In the description above, we have not considered the question of how the different types of agent behaviours affect the construction and evolution of these structures, i.e. how groups or teams come into existence. While we will not give specific examples of this here, we note that, again, the cautious, trusting and demanding agents construct particular types of groups or teams. For example, while cautious (group) agents just collect agents together that have the required abilities, demanding (team) agents collect agents together that not only have the required abilities, but *will* apply them when requested.

A further aspect of the demanding agent is that we often require that agents that are added to the demanding agent's content must agree to shared/common goals, similar to the idea of joint intentions in teams [12].

5   Conclusion

In this paper, we have begun to use a high-level executable logic-based formalism in order to describe some of the ways in which multi-agent systems can be structured. While this work is still at an early stage, we believe that we have shown that the language is appropriate for specification, verification and implementation and provides a natural representation for quite complex multi-agent concepts. In particular, the combination of the logical specification of individual behaviour, together with the simple, yet powerful, concept of "agent ≡ group", provides an appropriate framework.

As mentioned above, this paper represents a starting point. There is much work to be investigated in the future. For example, we intend to carry out a more systematic study of a range of agents behaviours and communication rules, and will further investigate how agents can dynamically change their type, depending on their environment. Also, the interaction of agents participating in several (different) groups needs to be studied, as does the problems of nesting multiple contexts. Not least, we want to further refine the group structure, by giving agents the possibility to join groups only for a specific purpose, and to formalise the dynamics of groups by allowing agents to join groups for definite periods.

Finally, the implementation itself must be refined. Currently, there are versions incorporating grouping and versions incorporating the logical description of agents, but not both. A merging of these efforts must be carried out before the system can be tested on complex group/team organisational structures of the above form.

References

1. H. Barringer, M. Fisher, D. Gabbay, G. Gough, and R. Owens. METATEM: An Introduction. *Formal Aspects of Computing*, 7(5):533–549, 1995.
2. M. Benerecetti, F. Giunchiglia, and L. Serafini. Model Checking Multiagent Systems. *Journal of Logic and Computation, Special Issue on Computational & Logical Aspects of Multi-Agent Systems*, 8(3):401–423, 1998.
3. B. Chellas. *Modal Logic : An Introduction*. Cambridge University Press, 1980.
4. E. A. Emerson. Temporal and Modal Logic. In J. van Leeuwen, editor, *Handbook of Theoretical Computer Science*, pages 996–1072. Elsevier, 1990.

5. M. Fisher. Concurrent METATEM — A Language for Modeling Reactive Systems. In *Parallel Architectures and Languages, Europe (PARLE)*, Munich, Germany, June 1993. (Published in *Lecture Notes in Computer Science*, volume 694, Springer-Verlag).
6. M. Fisher. Implementing BDI-like Systems by Direct Execution. In *Proceedings of the Fifteenth International Joint Conference on Artificial Intelligence (IJCAI)*. Morgan-Kaufmann, 1997.
7. M. Fisher and C. Ghidini. Programming Resource-Bounded Deliberative Agents. In *Proceedings of International Joint Conference on Artificial Intelligence (IJCAI)*. Morgan Kaufmann, 1999.
8. M. Fisher and C. Ghidini. The ABC of Rational Agent Modelling. In *Proceedings of the First International Joint Conference on Autonomous Agents and Multiagent Systems (AAMAS)*, Bologna, Italy, July 2002.
9. M. Fisher and T. Kakoudakis. Flexible Agent Grouping in Executable Temporal Logic. In *Proceedings of the 12th International Symposium of Intensional Programming Languages*. World Scientific, 1999.
10. C. Ghidini and F. Giunchiglia. Local Models Semantics, or Contextual Reasoning = Locality + Compatibility. *Artificial Intelligence*, 127(2):221–259, April 2001.
11. A. Pnueli. The Temporal Logic of Programs. In *Proceedings of the Eighteenth Symposium on the Foundations of Computer Science*, Providence, USA, November 1977.
12. M. Tambe. Agent Architectures for Flexible, Practical Teamwork. In *National Conference on Artificial Intelligence (AAAI-97)*, 1997.

A   The Logical Background

The METATEM [1] language has been developed as a high-level mechanism for specifying and executing simple individual agents. It is based upon the principle of specifying an agent using temporal logic [11], and then *directly executing* this specification in order to provide the agent's behaviour. This approach provides a high-level programming notation, maintaining a close link between program and specification. Extensions of the METATEM language in order to incorporate (bounded) beliefs and a very simple notion of ability were described in [7] and [8], respectively.

A.1   Temporal Logic of Bounded Belief

The logic described here is called TLBB (Temporal Logic of Bounded Belief) and is essentially the one presented in [8]. The logic is essentially a standard propositional, discrete, linear temporal logic, extended with simplified operators characterising ability, and fused with a multi-context logic of belief. Thus, considering a set $I = \{1, \ldots, n\}$ of agents, the formulae of the logic are constructed using the following connectives and proposition symbols:

- a set, $\mathcal{P}$, of propositional symbols;
- propositional connectives, **true**, **false**, $\neg$, $\vee$, $\wedge$, and $\Rightarrow$;
- standard temporal connectives, $\bigcirc$, $\Diamond$, and $\square$;

- a set, $\{A_1, A_2, \ldots, A_n\}$, of ability operators; and
- a set, $\{B_1, B_2, \ldots, B_n\}$, of belief operators.

We restrict the definition of "ability formulae" in the following way: if φ is a well formed formula and it does not contain any occurrence of temporal connectives and belief operators, then $A_i\varphi$ is a well formed formula.

As described in the Introduction, confidence is expressed in terms of belief and temporal operators. An agent is confident in φ if, and only if, it believes that φ will eventually be true, i.e. $B\Diamond\varphi$. This rather unusual notion of confidence allows for a great deal of flexibility, while retaining the simplicity of the underlying logical model.

The semantics of the temporal part of the logic is defined in the standard way via the satisfiability relation on a discrete linear temporal model of time, m, with finite past and infinite future [4]. Thus, m is a sequence of states s_0, s_1, s_2, s_3, $\ldots$ which can be thought of as 'moments' in time. Associated with each of these moments in time, represented by a temporal index $u \in \mathbf{N}$, is a valuation π for the propositional part of the language. Intuitively, the temporal formula '$\bigcirc A$' is satisfied at a given moment in time if A is satisfied at the *next* moment in time, '$\Diamond A$' is satisfied if A is satisfied at *some* future moment in time, ' $\Box A$' is satisfied if A is satisfied at *all* future moments in time. The formal definition of the semantics of the temporal language used here is given below. Satisfiability and validity are defined in the usual way.

$$\langle m, 0 \rangle \models \mathbf{start}$$

$$\langle m, u \rangle \models \mathbf{true}$$

$$\langle m, u \rangle \models p \qquad \text{iff} \quad \pi(u, p) = T \quad (\text{where } p \in \mathcal{P})$$

$$\langle m, u \rangle \models \neg A \qquad \text{iff} \quad \langle m, u \rangle \not\models A$$

$$\langle m, u \rangle \models A \vee B \qquad \text{iff} \quad \langle m, u \rangle \models A \ \text{ or } \ \langle m, u \rangle \models B$$

$$\langle m, u \rangle \models \bigcirc A \qquad \text{iff} \quad \langle m, u + 1 \rangle \models A$$

$$\langle m, u \rangle \models \Box A \qquad \text{iff} \quad \forall u' \in \mathbf{N}. \text{ if } (u \leq u') \text{ then } \langle m, u' \rangle \models A$$

$$\langle m, u \rangle \models \Diamond A \qquad \text{iff} \quad \exists u' \in \mathbf{N}. (u < u') \text{ and } \langle m, u' \rangle \models A$$

In order to provide a semantics for the belief operators, the definition of a model is extended as follows. Let I^k be the set of (possibly empty) strings of the form $i_1 \ldots i_h$ with all the indexes $i_l, \ldots, i_h \in I$ and $|i_1 \ldots i_h| \leq k$. We call any $\alpha \in I^k$ a *belief context*. Belief contexts that agent ϵ can build can be organised in a structure such as that presented in Figure 1. Intuitively, each belief context in I^k represents a possible nesting of the belief operators. So, in Figure 1 the empty string ϵ represents the beliefs of the external agent ϵ, the string 1 represents the beliefs of agent 1 (from the point of view of ϵ), 21 represents the beliefs of agent 2 about the beliefs of agent 1 (from the point of view of ϵ), and so on.

We associate a logical language L_α as defined at the beginning of the section with each belief context. A *model M* for the logic is a set $M = \{m_\alpha\}_{\alpha \in I^k}$, where for each $\alpha \in I^k$ m_α is a discrete linear temporal model of time with finite past and infinite future as described above.

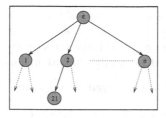

Fig. 1. The structure of belief contexts.

Let us assume at the moment that L_α does not contain ability operators. We have already seen how each m_α provides a semantics for the propositional and temporal part of L_α. In addition each m_α provides also a propositional valuation for the (atomic) formulae of the form $B_i\psi$. Finally, M satisfies a formula $\varphi \in L_\alpha$ if m_α satisfies it. The reader might now ask how we capture the intended relations between belief formulae in different belief contexts. For instance the fact that $B_i\psi$ in the belief context ϵ and ψ in the belief context i both mean that ϵ believes that i believes that ψ is true. In order to ensure that $B_i\psi$ is satisfied in the models for the belief context ϵ if, and only if, ψ is satisfied in the models for belief context i we impose additional constraints (5) and (6) in the definition of the model:

$$\text{if } m_\alpha \models B_i\varphi \text{ then } m_{\alpha i} \models \varphi \tag{5}$$

$$\text{if } m_{\alpha i} \models \varphi \text{ then } m_\alpha \models B_i\varphi \tag{6}$$

These constraints force the class of models we consider here to be contained in the class of models for a multi-context logic equivalent to modal K [10,2]. In addition, constraints (7) and (8)

$$\text{if } m_\alpha \models B_i\varphi \text{ and } B_i\varphi \in L_{\alpha i} \text{ then } m_{\alpha i} \models B_i\varphi \tag{7}$$

$$\text{if } m_\alpha \models \neg B_i\varphi \text{ and } B_i\varphi \in L_{\alpha i} \text{ then } m_{\alpha i} \models \neg B_i\varphi \tag{8}$$

force M to satisfy a multi-context version of modal axioms **4** and **5** respectively [3]. The fact that each belief context α is associated with exactly one discrete linear temporal model of time m_α forces M to satisfy a multi-context version of modal axioms **D** and **Fun**[2].

Let us now focus on ability. In order to maintain the simplicity of the formalism we define the semantics of A_i (for all $1 \le i \le n$) using a function $r_i : I^k \longrightarrow 2^{\text{wff}_{\text{TLBB}}}$ which associates a belief context α with the set of formulae $\varphi_1, \dots,$ $\varphi_n, \dots$ that agent i is able to achieve or believed to be able to achieve. The only properties that ability must satisfy are:

– agent i is able to achieve the conjunction of two facts (formulae) $\varphi \wedge \psi$ if, and only if, it is able to achieve both φ and ψ;

---

[2] The reader interested in a more detailed description of the logic may refer to [7] and [10].

- agent i is not able to achieve a contradiction;
- if an agent is able to achieve φ or is able to achieve ψ, then it must be able to achieve the disjunction $\varphi \vee \psi$ (but not vice-versa);
- ability is consistent w.r.t. logically equivalent formulae;

Formally, these properties are captured by imposing that r_i must satisfy:

$$\varphi \wedge \psi \in r_i(\alpha) \text{ iff } \varphi \in r_i(\alpha) \text{ and } \psi \in r_i(\alpha) \tag{9}$$

$$\varphi \wedge \neg\varphi \notin r_i(\alpha) \tag{10}$$

$$\text{if } \varphi \in r_i(\alpha) \text{ or } \psi \in r_i(\alpha) \text{ then } \varphi \vee \psi \in r_i(\alpha) \tag{11}$$

$$\text{if } \varphi \equiv \psi, \text{ then } \varphi \in r_i(\alpha) \text{ iff } \psi \in r_i(\alpha) \tag{12}$$

Then we say that a formula $A_i\varphi \in L_\alpha$ is satisfied at a certain moment in time u in m_α if, and only if, $\varphi \in r_i(\alpha)$.

A.2 Executing the Temporal Logic of Bounded Belief

We choose to retain a close link between theory and implementation by directly executing each agent specification. The mechanism used to carry out this execution is based upon the work in [6] which is, in turn, a modification of the METATEM approach [1]. Rather than going into detail concerning this approach, we simply outline the key elements below. A detailed description of the execution process, extended to handle formulae in TLBB, can be found in [7].

- Specifications of agent behaviour in TLBB are first translated to a specific normal form, SNF_{BB}, of the form

$$\textbf{start} \Rightarrow \bigvee_{b=1}^{r} l_b \qquad \text{(an } \textit{initial} \text{ rule)}$$

$$\bigwedge_{a=1}^{g} k_a \Rightarrow \bigcirc \left[\bigvee_{b=1}^{r} l_b \right] \qquad \text{(a } \textit{step} \text{ rule)}$$

$$\bigwedge_{a=1}^{g} k_a \Rightarrow \Diamond l \qquad \text{(a } \textit{sometime} \text{ rule)}$$

$$\bigwedge_{a=1}^{g} k_a \Rightarrow B_i \left[\bigvee_{b=1}^{r} l_b \right] \qquad \text{(a } \textit{belief} \text{ rule)}$$

Using SNF_{BB} the behaviour of an agent now (initial rule), in transition to the next moment in time (step rule), at some time in the future (sometime rule), and its beliefs (belief rule) can be represented. As an example of a simple set of rules which might be part of an agent description, consider the following

$$\textbf{start} \rightarrow sad$$

$$(sad \wedge \neg rich) \rightarrow \bigcirc sad$$

$$sad \rightarrow \mathbf{B}_{me} \bigcirc buy\_lottery\_ticket$$
$$lottery\_winner \rightarrow \Diamond rich$$

Here, agent *me* is sad at the beginning of time, and will continue to stay sad as long as it is poor. However, once it wins in the lottery, it will eventually be rich (and accordingly won't be sad any more). Also whenever the agent is *sad*, then it believes it will buy a lottery ticket at the next moment in time.
- The execution essentially forward chains through a set of such rules, gradually constructing a model for the specification.
- If a contradiction is generated, backtracking occurs.
- Eventualities, such as '$\Diamond rich$' are satisfied as soon as possible; in the case of conflicting eventualities, the oldest outstanding ones are attempted first. The choice mechanism takes into account a combination of the outstanding eventualities, and the deliberation ordering functions [6].
- As each $\mathbf{B}_i$ operator is expanded, a record of the depth of nesting of such operators is kept. Once the current bound is reached, exploration of the current belief context ceases.
- As in [7], the idea is that, if the original specification is satisfiable, then the execution algorithm will eventually build a model for the specification. Note that, as execution is not the focus of this paper, we will not consider such correctness here.

A Statechart Framework for Agent Roles that Captures Expertise and Learns Improved Behavior

Bahram Kimiaghalam[1], Abdollah Homaifar[1], and Albert C. Esterline[2]

[1]Dept. of Electrical Engineering and NASA ACIT Center, North Carolina A&T State University, Greensboro, NC 27411, USA
{bahram,homaifar}@ncat.edu
[2]Dept. of Computer Science and NASA ACIT Center, North Carolina A&T State University, Greensboro, NC 27411, USA
esterlin@ncat.edu

Abstract. We present work in progress that addresses a formalism and a system for computationally modeling human behavior where humans collaborate and communicate with other humans or automated systems with significant problem-solving ability. We conceptualize the simulated participants as agents. The fundamental notion is that of a role. An agent may assume one or more roles, and optimization measures are associated with roles. To represent coordination explicitly, we use an adaptation of Pazzi's Part-Whole Statecharts, which encapsulate coordination behavior. We include violation transitions to capture non-ideal behavior and violation states for repair. Fuzzy logic control is added to handle large domains and to resolve nondeterminism. A Statechart is represented internally with weighted rules, and an XCS classifier system is used to update the rule base in light of the outcomes of simulations; this provides a form of machine learning.

1 Introduction

We are developing a formalism and a system for computationally modeling human behavior where humans collaborate and communicate with other humans or automated systems with significant problem-solving ability. This system will be used for simulation-based training and mission rehearsal, intelligent tutoring, and deriving specifications for agents with human-like intelligence capabilities. Our framework will allow affordable knowledge acquisition since it would elicit knowledge directly from experts and refine and extend models automatically. It will be robust in the sense that components could be combined in ways not anticipated by the experts whose knowledge is modeled by the components, and this robustness will be affordable since adding a component would require only modification to the allowed communication patterns.

We conceptualize the simulated participants as agents, where an agent is an entity capable of autonomous action, that is, the agent, not the requester, decides whether to execute an action. We have successfully modeled (artificial) agents and human collaborators using several formalisms (cf., e.g., [1]), so the agent abstraction allows interoperability between human and sophisticated computational entities. The

M.G. Hinchey et al. (Eds.): FAABS 2002, LNAI 2699, pp. 28–36, 2003.

fundamental notion is that of a role; an agent may assume one or more roles. We explicitly represent coordination in the form of patterns of communication actions. Goals are implicit, and we do not address general problem-space search. This avoids heavy investment in knowledge acquisition and engineering (KA/E).

Case-based reasoning (CBR) for plans also avoids extensive KA/E and allows patterns of behavior to be refined and extended. CBR, however, still requires considerable engineering to enable indexing, causal analysis to diagnose failures, and plan repair, and it also relies on a good set of cases. In addition, CBR uses an informal representation for plans and a complex representation may be needed for an acceptable indexing function. Schema-based reasoning [2] roughly generalizes CBR where generalized knowledge in schemas largely replaces the records of individual cases of problem solving. Although our roles are similar to schemas, schemas are informal and require considerable complexity in practice hence involve expensive KA/E.

We advocate a formal representation of coordinated roles that facilitates execution (simulation). There are formal, executable languages for specifying a knowledge-based systems that use models of expertise. Using them, therefore, commits one to significant KA/E. Since we emphasize coordination, concurrency formalisms are obvious candidates for our framework. Modal logics (such as temporal logics) are the most abstract such formalisms and are appropriate for specifying required properties (e.g., safety and liveness properties). Process algebras are more concrete. A process algebra is a term algebra (whose terms are abstract programs) that emphasizes composition. The most concrete concurrency formalisms are automata, which represent system behavior directly. These automata include Petri nets, which give the precondition relations among events. They also include generalizations of finite-state automata that capture concurrency by allowing several states to be active simultaneously. The latter are attractive for our purposes since people naturally think of collaborative activity as progress through a sequence of states. A Statechart [3] is a generalization of a finite-state automaton that represents hierarchies of states and concurrent activity. Statecharts are used extensively by people without a great deal of training and without significant background in formal methods. In fact, they are included in the UML notation, the state-of-the-art notation for object-oriented software engineering. Unlike many notations popularly used in software engineering, however, Statecharts have a well-defined semantics; in fact, they can be translated into a process-algebraic notation. And model-checking techniques can be applied to Statecharts. Given a system described by an automaton with states and a property expressed in a temporal logic, model checking automates the verification that the property holds of the automaton.

In Statecharts, however, concurrent components communicate by broadcasting, which destroys encapsulation, making composition and reuse difficult. Pazzi [4] has introduced a specialization of Statecharts, Part-Whole Statecharts, that handles this problem by including a *whole*. Concurrent components communicate only with the whole, so all that need change when a concurrent part is added, removed, or changed is that segment of the whole directly relating to the communication behavior of that part. We adapt Part-Whole Statecharts for our purpose, with roles or agents as parts, giving RW-Statecharts ("Role-Whole Statecharts"). Firstly, we use fuzzy logic to mitigate the effects of a discrete, finite representation when the underlying domains are large, even uncountable, sets and when several candidate actions are combined. We also associate optimization measures with roles and systems. And we include violations to capture non-ideal behavior and violation states for repairs. This gives a form of fault tolerance and, with appropriate structuring, something similar to a transaction abstraction for coordinated activity.

For knowledge acquisition, we are developing an initial phase where an expert, with coaching as necessary from a knowledge engineer, uses a graphical interface to construct a RW-Statechart for a role. A team of experts similarly constructs a whole for the coordination of the roles in the entire RW-Statechart. Experts, however, typically are not good at expressing their know-how. Initial knowledge acquisition typically fails to capture "hidden knowledge" not readily expressed, and an expert may simply not recall certain possibilities. So we compile the RW-Statechart into a set of weighted rules, and such weights become part of our notion of a RW-Statechart. The experts can "play" the RW-Statechart by stepping through the roles. They make choices where the model is nondeterministic and update the model where it does not offer a preferred choice or is structurally deficient. Using fuzzy logic to resolve nondeterminism, a RW-Statechart can also be executed. The result of a play or an execution is summarized in a reward (or penalty) that takes into account the success or failure of the activity, the values for the optimization measures, and the severity of the violations. The weighted rule representation is part of an XCS classifier system that captures hidden knowledge by distributing the reward to rules according to their degree of involvement in reaching the final state. The use of fuzzy logic and an XCS classifier system in this context builds on our use of these features in adaptive path planning [5]. The rule base in the path-planning application was significantly simpler since the repertoire of events and actions was much smaller.

2   The Statechart Formalism

As mentioned, a Statechart is a generalization of a finite-state automaton that allows one to represent hierarchies of states and states that are concurrently active. A superstate that contains substates and transitions that elaborate its sequential behavior is called an XOR state since, when it is active, exactly one of its substates is active. A superstate that contains concurrent substates – "orthogonal components" – is called an AND state. A basic state has no substates so is neither an XOR nor an AND state. A transition has a label e/a indicating that, when the system is in the source state and event e happens, it can move to the target state on performing action a; the action part is optional. A transition may have a non-basic state as either its source or target. In fact, it may have several source states (in different orthogonal components) or several target states (again in different orthogonal components).

For example, consider the Statechart in Figure 1. The overall state, s, is an AND state: the system must be in both its ("orthogonal") substates, u and v. States u and v are XOR states. In state u, the system must be in either m or k (but not both). Similarly for states m (substates n1-2) and v (substates p1-4). An arrow starting from a darkened circle points to the default initial substate of an XOR state. The label on the transition from k to m indicates that, in state k, if event a1 happens, the system can move to state m on performing action b1. Likewise for the other transitions. An action done by one orthogonal component can be a triggering event for another. E.g., when component u transitions from k to m, it performs action b1, which is the triggering event for component v when in state p1 (which may then transition to state p2). This chart is *zoomed in* on all components. If, for example, we *zoom out* on component u, the substates of m and the transitions among them are suppressed.

A transition label more generally may be of the form e[c]/a (a again being optional), where c is a condition that must be true for the transition to fire. Finally, a history mechanism (denoted by H) may be included in a state. This indicates that, when the state is re-entered, the substate that was last active should again become active. This is useful for us for returning from the repair done in a violation state.

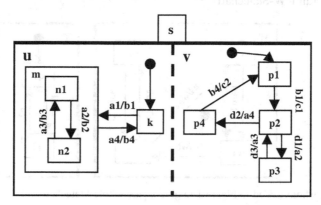

Fig. 1. An XOR state with two communicating substates

The Statechart formalism is characterized not only by hierarchy (XOR states) and orthogonality (AND states) but also by broadcast communication: an action in one orthogonal component can serve as a triggering event in any other orthogonal component. This implicit coordination, however, eliminates encapsulation. As mentioned, we thus adopt Pazzi's Part-Whole Statecharts. As an example, the Statechart in Figure 1 can be converted to a Part-Whole Statechart by adding (to the AND state s) the whole shown in Figure 2(a) and relabeling events a2, a3, and a4 in u as wa2, wa3, and wa4 and events b1 and b4 in v as wb1 and wb4. Now, suppose we want to add a new part, an XOR state r shown in Figure 2(b). Then the whole is updated as follows. Two new states, w11 and w41, say, are added. The transition labeled b1/wb1 now has w11 as its source (and w2 still as its target), and the transition labeled b4/wb4 now has w41 as its target (and w4 still as its source). We add a transition labeled c2/wc2 from w41 to w1 and one labeled a1/wa1 from w1 to w11. Also, the event a1 in u is changed to wa1 and the event c2 in r is changed to wc2.

In our RW-Statecharts, the parts represent roles or, recursively, agents whose parts are roles. When a role is defined, certain events and actions are clearly communications with other roles even if that role is not included in a RW-Statechart where these events and actions actually do communicate with another role. We call these *coordinating* events and actions. Other events and actions are *environmental*.

RW-Statecharts include a few enhancements. Time intervals, giving minimum and maximum times, can be assigned for the time a component spends in a given state and for the time it takes to do an action. We need these since timing is frequently critical to coordinated behavior. Violation states (as mentioned) are included; this allows valuable knowledge about local failures and recovery from them to be captured. For each action, we include a set of propositions that are assertions that should be true at that state. These allow us to characterize each state independently of its position in the RW-Statechart. For each action, we give two sets of propositions: the preconditions, which must be true for the action to be done, and its postconditions, which become true when it finishes. Given the assertions in states and triggering events, the pre- and postconditions are actually redundant, but they allow actions to be independently characterized. Optimization measures are associated with each role and with the overall RW-Statechart.

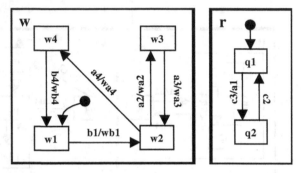

Fig. 2. (a) A whole, added to Figure 1 to give a part-whole Statechart and (b) a new part to be added to the part-whole Statechart

Since it is unreasonable to try to model many situations with relatively small sets of events, actions and states, we allow all aspects of a RW-Statechart to be parameterized. As long as the parameter values are drawn from finite sets, the parameterized version of Statecharts is a conservative extension of the non-parameterized version: one can replace each parameterized state with a set of states with one state for each combination of parameter values. In many cases, however, parameters have infinitely-valued types. We use fuzzy logic to discretize infinitely-valued domains. Each parameter, then, becomes a linguistic variable with a finite (usually small) number of attributes. For environmental events, this requires a classifier that, given real-valued sensor data, extracts the appropriate attribute. For actions on the environment, imagine several transitions from a given state that at a particular time have some claim to be triggered. Such a situation can be handled by a fuzzy logic controller (FLC) as long as the same action (with different parameter values) is involved. If different actions are involved, deciding which action to take becomes more difficult and requires the candidate actions to be comparable on some dimension.

3 Initial Knowledge Acquisition

We are developing a knowledge acquisition tool that can be used by experts with some coaching. For each role, an expert is expected to identify the environmental events and actions and the coordinating events and actions. We assume that the types of sensor data and effector actions are given and that the nature of inter-agent communication is sufficiently characterized so that communication actions can be identified along with the information they convey. At this point some environmental events will be operationalized in terms of the attributes of linguistic variables that discretize sensor data. Environmental actions are handled similarly except that the linguistic variables discretize effector actions. Each action is assigned its preconditions and postconditions; these can be refined and operationalized later. Time bounds on actions and states are optional at this point. The optimization measures are initially specified for each role; these can be refined and operationalized later.

Refinement directly by the experts involves zooming in on states to elaborate their structure and operationalizing events and actions. The experts should run through various scenarios, including those involving violations. Initial knowledge acquisition is complete when

- time bounds have been specified for actions and basic states,
- events and actions have been operationalized,
- the pre- and postconditions of actions and assertions in basic states have been operationalized, and
- repairs have been specified for all violations.

4   The Rule Representation of a RW-Statechart and Its Execution

We encode a RW-Statechart with rules of the form

    If (state, event) then (action, new state) with weight

where `weight` is a real number in some closed interval, say [0.0, 1.0], giving the extent to which the rule is actually used in executing the Statechart. (Weights are used by the FLC in determining actions.) Initially, the rules that represent the Statechart constructed by the experts all have weight 1.0 and all other rules (if any) have weight 0.0. We assume that parameters (assumed to be linguistic variables) have been eliminated by replacing each parameterized rule with a set of rules, one for each combination of parameter values.

The RW-Statechart, now compiled as a rule set, can be executed by starting at the initial state with a collection of the initially active basic states. Such a collection (a maximal state configuration in the terminology of [6]) is maintained throughout. Note that one can recover from this the collection of all active states by ascending state hierarchies. Space restrictions preclude further details of RW-Statechart execution. Generally, it should follow the operational semantics given in [6]. The FLC makes use of the weights on the rules to determine the action and next state from among the candidate transitions that may fire at a given point. Note that the presence of several candidate transitions can be interpreted as the presence of nondeterminism. So the FLC, rather than determining a unique action and next state, could randomly select one of the candidate transitions. This would be part of exploration, where we try actions independently of what we have learned (the weights on the rules) in the hope of coming across a better move. Another possibility is that the FLC simply presents the choices to the users. This is where the users play the Statechart: they try to cooperate so that required conditions are maintained and goals are satisfied while optimizing whatever optimization measures there are. This again is exploration.

5 XCS Classifiers

Removing rules or adding new rules to the rule base and/or changing the weights of the existing rules will change the system that is represented by the rule set. The flexibility of changing the system by changing the rules or their corresponding weights allows the utilization of evolutionary algorithms for finding the most suitable or appropriate rule set. Classifiers or their successors XCS classifiers [7] are a form of machine learning that are significant since they work as the heart of the rule-base used in training the system. With classifier systems, reshaping the whole knowledge base to reflect the new information gathered from executing or playing the system is fairly simple to carry out. In general, under the framework of reinforcement learning (reward/penalty feedback), the classifier system creates a flexible machine-learning scheme. When the system achieves a desired or goal state, the reward mechanism will distribute the rewards proportional to the degree of involvement of the rules in leading the system to this state. The rules that collect more rewards end up with higher weights. Occasionally new rules are created and/or some old rules are deleted from the rule set based on genetic algorithms process. Thus, a dynamic rule base representing the system will always be maintained. At any step, there may be several rules with different weights that fire yet suggest contradicting actions and/or new states. Despite the fact that merging techniques will be used to merge the fired rules, ultimately an FLC will determine the outcome.

In exploration, when a RW-Statechart is executed or played, the success of each role (and sometimes even a phase of a role) is evaluated on its own, and the success of the overall endeavor is also evaluated. The degree of success of a given unit involves how well it optimizes the optimization measures; a unit is penalized for any violations. A role with a goal is additionally heavily rewarded for achieving its goal. The reward assigned to a superstate is used to augment the reward assigned to the substates of that superstate from the evaluation of their isolated performances.

6 Training and Tutoring

The straightforward way this system would be used for training would be to have the novice play one or more roles. The roles of a RW-Statechart supply, in the terminology of model-tracing tutors (MTTs), an expert module. The other component of an MTT is a pedagogical model, which gives feedback whenever the student's actions fail to match the expert module's behavior. We could provide a pedagogical module by having the system execute in a parallel process the roles the student plays. When the student's actions diverge from the execution, play would be interrupted to coach the student and to use information entered by the expert when the role was defined to explain why the system made the choices it did. This would give an occasion for deep learning (such as learning principles and domain knowledge). Violation states within a role provide similar opportunities. The hierarchy in a RW-

Statechart facilitates what the literature on intelligent tutoring systems (ITS) calls *fading the scaffolding*: the tutorial activity is reduced as the student gains confidence [8]. This can be done by zooming out from the detail of a role. As the scaffold is faded, the student would be helped in going from one phase to another and in phases where he is unsure but would assume the initiative in phases where he is competent. To compare the student's behavior with the expert behavior, we need a way to construct the RW-Statechart detail from scenarios supplied by student behavior. On a grander scale, this would allow us to construct student models, used by ITSs to reconstruct the knowledge giving rise to student behavior.

7 Genetic Programming to Improve the Structure of a RW-Statechart

We are also exploring the possibility of utilizing the search process of genetic programming (GP) [9] to improve the hierarchical state structure of a RW-Statechart. This would require a hierarchical representation of the RW-Statechart in the chromosomes forming the population involved in the search. This, like the use of XCS classifiers, requires that a dynamic rule base representing the system always be maintained.

8 Theoretical Context

We have used XCS classifiers and FLCs to implement biofunctional learning and remembering [10]. Biofunctional theory views human learning as both holistic and piecemeal, and it accounts for a wide range of learning phenomena. There are two types of knowledge: ongoing brain activity (OBA) and momentary constellation firings (MCFs). In the current context, the roles assumed by an agent, compiled into a rule base, supply the OBA, and the action of the FLC provides the MCFs. The whole in a RW-Statechart represents situated joint activity whose patterns are internalized in the participating agents.

States in a RW-Statechart provide a sense of situation, which is a critical topic in several disciplines, such as the semantics of natural language. To conceptualize how constellations of events in a given situation carry information for various parts of the system, we are looking at the work of Barwise *et al.* on the flow of information.

9 Conclusion

We are developing a way of computationally modeling collaborating human behavior. We use an adaptation of a modular form of Statecharts that explicitly represents coordination in the form of patterns of communication actions. Our agent models have clear communication protocols for interfacing with any other modules with compatible protocols. Annotations can be added to Statechart structure to allow models to explain their behavior. Since Statecharts are largely graph-theoretical duals of hierarchical task networks, task planning techniques may be available to extend Statechart structure. XCS classifiers, working on a Statechart compiled into a rule base, allow a model to be refined and extended without additional knowledge engineering. This realistically reflects human learning as it is based on biofunctional learning theory. Our approach offers affordable knowledge acquisition, affordable robustness, and formal analysis of models of human behavior.

References

1. Mosley, K. and Esterline, A.: Modeling Societies of Agents and Users Using CSP. Proc. 5th World Multi-Conference on Systems, Cybernetics and Informatics (SCI-01), Orlando, Fl (2001)
2. Turner, Roy: Adaptive Reasoning for Real-World Problems: A Schema-Based Approach.. Lawrence Erlbaum Associates, Inc., Hillsdale, NJ (1994)
3. Harel, David.: Statecharts: A Visual Formalism for Complex Systems. Science of Computer Programming 8 (1987), pp. 231–274
4. Pazzi, L.: Extending statecharts for representing parts and wholes. Proceedings of the 23rd EUROMICRO Conference (1997)
5. Homaifar A., , Hawari, H., and Esterline, A.: Application of Biofunctional Learning and Remembering for Multi-Agent Goal Tracking. Proc. of SMC 2001 (2001)
6. Harel D., Pnueli A., Schmidt J.P., and Sherman R.: On the Formal Semantics of Statecharts. Proc. 2nd IEEE Symposium on Logic in Computer Science (1987), pp 54–64
7. Wilson, S. W.: State of XCS Classifier System Research. Technical Report No. 99.1.1, Prediction Dynamics, Concord MA (1999)
8. VanLehn, K. et al.: Fading and Deepening: The Next Steps for Andes and Other Model-Tracing Tutors. Proc. 5th Int. Conf. On Intelligent Tutoring Systems, ITS'00, Montréal (2000)
9. Koza, J. R.: Genetic Programming II: Automatic Discovery of Reusable Programs. MIT Press, Cambridge, MA (1994)
10. Iran-Nejad, A. and Marsh, E. G.: The figure and the ground of constructive brain functioning: beyond explicit memory processes. Educational Psychologist, vol. 7, no. 4 (1992) pp. 473–492.

Formal Specification of Interaction in Agent Societies

Virginia Dignum[1,2], John-Jules C. Meyer[2], Frank Dignum[2], and Hans Weigand[3]

[1]Achmea, The Netherlands,
email: virginia.dignum@achmea.nl
[2]University Utrecht, The Netherlands,
email: {virginia, jj, dignum}@cs.uu.nl
[3]Infolab, Tilburg University, The Netherlands,
email: weigand@uvt.nl

Abstract. The Agent Society framework that we have developed distinguishes between the mechanisms though which the structure and global behavior of the model is described and coordinated, and the aims and behavior of the service-providers (agents) that populate the model. In this framework contracts are used to integrate the top-down specification of organizational structures with the autonomy of participating agents. In this paper we introduce LCR, a very expressive logic for describing interaction in multi-agent systems. We also show how LCR behaves in contrary-to-duty situations common to deontic logic frameworks. LCR makes it possible to check whether agents in an agent society follow some desired interaction patterns and whether desired social states are preserved by agent activity. LCR is used as a formal basis for the framework for agents societies that we are developing.

1   Introduction

Agent-based computing has been an active research topic for many years. Agent concepts gained relevance in industry as adequate means to describe and build large and complex systems. Due to their autonomous, pro-active and social behavior, agents can better adapt to changes in their environment and solve problems they encounter during operation with limited intervention from the user. This has a large advantage over traditional systems for which the environment of the system had to be completely predictable or otherwise the system would not function correctly. However, if one creates a system with a number of autonomous agents it becomes unpredictable what the outcome of their interactions will be. In settings where the multi-agent system is used to implement a system with specific goals, this so-called emerging behavior can be perceived as a problem, because one does not want this emergent behavior to diverge from the overall goal of the system. Furthermore, it is unrealistic to think that any directed behavior will happen from the fact that agents happen to share some environment. Like humans, software agents will not work together just because they happen to be together, but require some external incentives for collaboration. We call such systems with specific goals, organizational systems.

We have developed an agent-oriented model for organizational systems, the **Agent Society Model** that emerges from the idea that in an organizational system, as in any organized society, interactions between members occur not just by accident but aim at achieving some desired global goals. That is, there are goals external to each

M.G. Hinchey et al. (Eds.): FAABS 2002, LNAI 2699, pp. 37–52, 2003.

individual agents that must be reached by the interaction of those agents. The desired global behavior of an organization is therefore external to the participating agents. Although agents will contribute to achievement of society goals, this happens only when such goals fit with the agents' own goals, or because of the agents' own motivation. Conceptually global organizational goals and rules cannot be attributed or modeled as part of the agents. Furthermore, we start from the fact that social structure is determined by organizational design and not dependent on the agents themselves.

The Agent Society Model distinguishes between the mechanisms though which the structure and global behavior of the model is described and coordinated, and the aims and behavior of the service-providers (agents) that populate the model [6, 16].

In order to represent interactions between agents in an open context, a framework is needed that is able to specify sequences of interaction scenes
- independently from the agent's internal design (**internal autonomy requirement**)
- without fixing the interaction structures completely in advance (**collaboration autonomy requirement**).

The framework consists of three interrelated models. The structure and coordination norms as intended by the organizational stakeholders are described in the **Organizational Model** (OM). Components of this model are roles, constraints, interaction rules, and communicative and ontology framework. Based on their own goals, individual agents join the society as enactors of roles. Possible agent populations of the organizational model are specified in the **Social Model** (SM) in terms of contracts that make explicit the commitments regulating the enactment of roles by individual agents. Finally, given an agent population, the **Interaction Model** (IM) describes possible interaction between agents. Depending on the aims and characteristics of the application, the OM will allow for more or less freedom for its agent population to decide and negotiate on how to interact with each other. In order to limit the unpredictability of the system that may arise due to the autonomous behavior of agents, agreements concerning role enacting and interaction are fixed in contracts. **Contracts** allow to integrate the top-down specification of organizational structures with the autonomy of participating agents. The use of contracts to describe activity of the system allows in one hand for flexibility in the balance between organizational aims and agent desires and on the other hand for verification of the outcome of the system.

In this paper we present a logical formalism for describing interaction in a agent society. The formalism enables the specification of social norms and interaction contracts. The logical formalism combines elements from deontic and branching time logic. In the remainder of this paper we will introduce the main features of this logic. The paper is organized as follows. In section 2 we give some rationale for the formalization of agent societies. Section 3 introduces LCR, the logic for contract representation that we have developed. In section 4 we show how several contrary-to-duty situations are handled in LCR. Section 5 described how LCR can be used to represent interaction contracts between agents. In section 6 we discuss related work on the formalization of organizational behavior on multi-agents systems. Finally, in section 7 we present our conclusions and indicate directions for further research.

2   Formal Specification of Agent Societies

Norms have been identified in social sciences as crucial tools for important (agent) societies issues such as coordination, cooperation, trust and reputation. A formalism for agent societies must be able to uniformly describe and reason about social structure (landmarks and roles) and interaction (social and interaction contracts). Such formalism facilitates the analysis of societies and verification through logical reasoning, that is, verification of society design gets down to prove inconsistencies in the logical description.

In systems where agents are assumed to be autonomous and intelligent, agents can, involuntarily or by deliberate choice, violate social norms and regulations and therefore one must be able to deal and reason about violations. The use of deontic logic as a formalism for multi-agent systems has been advocated by several researchers (cf. [15]). Deontic logic provides mechanisms to reason about violability of norms, that is, about how to proceed when norms are violated. In practice, logical formalisms for agents have been used to (1) specify agents in an abstract manner and to (2) verify and reason about agent behavior, independently of the implementation language used to represent the agent.

A more advanced form of agenthood, normative agents (that is, agents that can reason about norms and obligations) can bridge the gap between individual autonomous agents and the agent society, in the sense that the cognitive concept of obligation is the building block of complex social notions like coordination, cooperation, trust and reputation.

Furthermore, verification of the behavior of an open society, where the design of participating agents cannot be controllable, must be based on the externally observable effects of agent actions. That is, from the society perspective, different actions that bring about the same state of affairs in the world cannot be distinguished. From the above considerations, it follows that a logical formalism for the Agent Society Model must be able to represent:
- Deontic relations (obligations, prohibitions, permissions)
- Externally observable results of agent actions (changes in state caused through influence of agents)
- Temporal relationships (effect of actions and agreements is not instantaneous and not deterministic, several futures are possible at each moment depending on agent decisions and environment changes)
- Violations and reasoning about effects and recovery from violated states

3   Logic for Contract Representation

The Logic for Contract Representation (LCR) that we propose is based on a branching-time logic. This means that formulae are interpreted over tree-type branching structures that represent all conceivable ways the system can evolve. Nodes represent *states* and arcs correspond to the occurrence of *events*. A *path* represents a course of events and links states in the time structure according to the choices and possibilities available to agents at each moment. Our proposal extends the formalism based on Temporal and Deontic Logic, BTLcont, proposed by Dignum and Kuiper

[4]. BTLcont is in itself an extension to the well known branching-time temporal logic (CTL*) proposed by Emerson and Halpern [8, 10]. While Emerson and Halpern provide a sound and complete axiomatization for CTL*, we do not address the issue of completeness in this paper. Our main aim is to present an expressive semantics for contracts, that represent interaction between agents in an abstract way, that is, independent from the internal architecture of the agents.

We further extend branching time logic with a *stit* operator, E_a ('agent a sees to it that') based on Pörn [14]. This allows us to refer to the externally 'observable' consequences of an action instead of the action itself. Remember that agent internals are not visible from the organizational perspective, and therefore it is not possible to refer to specific actions of an agent. In our use of E_a we draw from the logic proposed by Wooldridge for the combination of a *stit* operator with a temporal logic [17].

Moreover, clauses in a contract (deontic expressions in LCR) indicate that something must happen (ideally something happens) but in fact it may never happen at all! A logic for contract representation must therefore be able to reason about states in which an obligation has been violated. Obligations have to do with the preference of individuals (or societies) to be in a certain state. $O_a\varphi$ (the obligation for agent a to see to it that φ holds) indicates that, in the society, it is preferable for a to be in a state where φ holds rather than in any other state. This does not mean that agent a cannot be in other states either by choice or necessity. A violation, viol(a,φ,δ), is interpreted as 'agent a is in a violation situation concerning the obligation to do φ before deadline δ'[1]. The basic idea is that worlds in which a violation proposition holds are less preferred by the agent concerned. Sanctions are defined in order to make it possible for violations to be redeemed.

3.1   Syntax of LCR

LCR is an extension of CTL*, which in turn is an extension of classical propositional logic[2]. Well-formed formulae of LCR are built of a set Φ of atomic propositions that may be combined using the classical proposition connectives $\vee$ ('or') and $\neg$ ('not'). Other propositional connectives such as $\wedge$ ('and'), $\rightarrow$ (logical implication) and $\leftrightarrow$ (logical equivalence) can be introduced as abbreviations. The language also contains the constants *true*, *false*, the CTL* operators A (always in the future), S (since), X (in the next state), Y (yesterday, or in the previous state), U (until), $\leq$ (before) and the *stit* operator E. Furthermore, we introduce a predicate viol(a, φ, δ) that holds in states where $O_a(\varphi \leq \delta)$ has been violated by agent a. The E operator is labeled with agents and/or group identifiers. Elements a, b, …, of a set Ags of agent identifiers are used as labels for E. For example E_a is read as 'agent *a* sees to it that'.

---

[1] When no deadline is specified for an obligation, the violation is simplified to viol(a, φ).

[2] In finite domains, the existential quantifier can be introduced as a finite disjunction and the universal quantifier as finite conjunction.

Definition 1   Syntax of LCR

The set of well-formed formulae of LCR is introduced inductively, given a set Φ of atomic propositions (including *true*, *false*). As in CTL*, LCR distinguishes between state formulas (evaluated in a state) and path formulas (evaluated in a path).

1. Every member of Φ is a state formula
2. If φ, φ_1 and φ_2 are state formulas, then so are $\neg\varphi$, $\varphi_1 \vee \varphi_2$, $Y\varphi$ and $\varphi_1 S \varphi_2$
3. If φ is a state formula, then so is $E_a\varphi$, for all $a \in$ Ags
4. If φ_1 and φ_2 are state formulas, then so is viol(a, φ_1, φ_2), for all $a \in$ Ags
5. Each state formula is also a path formula
6. If ψ is a path formula, then $A\psi$ is a state formula
7. If ψ, ψ_1, ψ_2 are path formulas, then so are $\neg\psi$, $\psi_1 \vee \psi_2$, $\psi_1 U \psi_2$, $\psi_1 \leq \psi_2$ and $X\psi$

3.2   Semantics of LCR

Usually different events are possible at any moment. That is, at each moment different futures are possible depending on the events in the world. We therefore have defined the semantics for LCR using branching time structures.

Definition 2   Branching Time Structure

A branching time structure is a tuple (W, R) where:

-    W is a set of worlds (**states**) and
-    $R \subseteq W \times W$ is the successor relation on states, such that the reflexive, transitive closure of R, R*, is a total tree relation.

R* represents all possible courses of system history. A **path** (or trace) through R is a sequence ($s_i \mid i \in \mathbb{N}$) such that $\forall i \in \mathbb{N}$ we have (s_i, s_{i+1}) $\in$ R. If t is a path then state t(i) is the i-th element of p. We assume that there is a state s_0, which is the root of (W, R). Furthermore, we represent the tail of the path starting with state t(i) by t[i].

Definition 3   Semantic Model

A semantic model M for LCR is a structure M = (W, R, π) where (W, R) is a branching time structure and π is a valuation function, which associates each $s \in$ W with the set of atomic propositions from Φ that are true in that world.

A path is a full and infinite sequence of states. Paths do not have to start from the root, but once started, there is always a following state in the path.. By acting, agents can influence the next state in a path. The actions of agents are some of the possible events in the graph. In order to be able to represent the influence of an agent on changes in the world, we introduce the notion of controllable and uncontrollable expressions.

3.2.1   Controllable and Non Controllable Propositions

Intuitively it only makes sense to specify $E_a\varphi$ for a formula φ if agent a can indeed 'see to it' that φ holds, that is if the agent can control or influence the truth value of φ. For instance, it does not make sense to express $E_a rains$ because the fact whether it rains or not is not something that an agent can control. Inspired by the work of Boutelier [2] and Cholvy and Garion [4], we partition for each agent a the set of atomic propositions Φ in any world w of M in two classes: C_a and $\bar{C}_a$ in which C_a is the set of atomic propositions that agent a can control and $\bar{C}_a$ the set of atomic propositions that a cannot control.

Definition 4   Valuation Function

1) Let π be the valuation function of a semantic model M = (W, R, π), which associates each s $\in$ W with the set of atomic propositions from Φ that are true in that world. For a set P of atomic propositions, $\pi(\mathbf{P})$ indicates the restriction of π to the propositions in P (that is, the subset of true propositions of P). For every agent a, π can thus be written as $<\pi(\,C_a\,),\ \pi(\,\bar{C}_a\,)>$, the composition of the restriction of π to the controllable atomic propositions of a and the non-controllable atomic propositions of a.

2) For a set P of atomic propositions, $\Pi(\mathbf{P})$ is the set of all valuations of atoms of P.

3) We need furthermore to define the concatenation of two valuation functions. Given two valuation functions u and v such that dom(u) $\cap$ dom(v) = $\emptyset$, $\mathbf{u.v(p)}$ is defined as:

$$u.v(p) = \begin{cases} u(p), p \in dom(u) \\ v(p), p \in dom(v) \end{cases}$$

Definition 5   Controllable and Uncontrollable Propositions

Given classes C_a and $\bar{C}_a$ defined as above,

1) a proposition φ is a-controllable in a state s $\in$ W, where M = (W, R, π) is a semantic model, iff $\forall u \in \Pi(\,\bar{C}_a\,)$, $\exists v_1, v_2 \in \Pi(\,C_a\,)$ and $\exists s_1 \in W$, $\pi(s_1) = u.v_1$, $\exists s_2 \in W$, $\pi(s_2) = u.v_2$, such that (M, s_1) $\models \varphi$ and (M, s_2) $\not\models \varphi$.

2) An expression is a-uncontrollable iff it is not a-controllable.

For example consider model M = (W, R, π) and the propositions p and q, such that p $\in$ C_a and q $\in$ $\bar{C}_a$. In this case, proposition p $\wedge$ q is not a-controllable, because q is not a-controllable, and if q is false, agent a cannot make p $\wedge$ q to be true. Tautologies are never a-controllable, that is, if something is always true, no agent can claim to see to it that it will become true.

Theorem

$\forall \varphi$, if $\models \varphi$ then φ is a-uncontrollable for agent a. That is, agent a cannot control tautologies.

Proof. Suppose φ such that $\exists \varphi$, $\models \varphi$ and φ is a-controllable. $\models \varphi$ implies $\forall s$, (M,s)$\models$ φ.. However from the definition of a-controllable there must be a s $\in$ W such that (M, s) $\models \neg \varphi$. Therefore φ cannot be a tautology.

3.2.2   Path and State Semantics

As in CTL*, we define the semantics for state and path formulae separately. A path formula is a formula that is interpreted with respect to a path through a branching time structure. Paths correspond to histories of the system. In contrast, a state formula is interpreted with respect to a system state. The semantics of path formulae are given via the path formula satisfaction relation represented by '$\models$' that relates tuples of the form (M, p), where M is a LCR-model, $M = (W, R, \pi)$, and t a path (or trace) in M, to path formulae of LCR. This relation is defined by the following rules:

(P1) $(M, t) \models \varphi$ iff $(M, t(0)) \models \varphi$, where φ is a state formula
(P2) $(M, t) \models \neg\psi$ iff   not $(M, t) \models \psi$
(P3) $(M, t) \models \psi_1\vee\psi_2$ iff $(M,t) \models \psi_1$ or $(M, t) \models \psi_2$
(P4) $(M, t) \models X\psi$ iff $\forall t': (t, t') \in R, (M, t') \models \psi$
(P5) $(M, t) \models \psi_1 U\psi_2$ iff $\exists i \in \mathbb{N}$ such that $(M, t[i]) \models \psi_2$ and
                                     $\forall k \leq i, (M, t[k]) \models \psi_1$
(P6) $(M, t) \models \psi_1 \leq \psi_2$ iff $\forall i \in \mathbb{N}$ such that $(M, t[i]) \models \psi_2$ and
                                     $\exists j \leq i, (M, t(j)) \models \psi_1$

The semantics of state formulae are given via the state formula satisfaction relation, also represented by '$\models$' that relates tuples of the form (M, s), where M is a LCR-model, $M = (W, R, \pi)$, and s a world in W, to state formulae of LCR. This relation is defined by the following rules:

(S1) $(M, s) \models p$ iff $p \in \pi(s)$, where $p \in \Phi$
(S2) $(M, s) \models \neg\varphi$ iff   not $(M, s) \models \varphi$
(S3) $(M, s) \models \varphi_1\vee\varphi_2$ iff $(M, s) \models \varphi_1$ or $(M, s) \models \varphi_2$
(S4) $(M, s) \models A\psi$ iff $\forall t \in paths(W, R)$, if $t(0) = s$ then $(M, t) \models \psi$
(S5) $(M, t(i)) \models Y\varphi$ iff $(M, t(i-1)) \models \varphi$
(S6) $(M, t(i)) \models \varphi_1 S\varphi_2$ iff $\exists k \leq i$ such that $(M, t(k)) \models \varphi_2$ and
                                     $\forall j, k < j \leq i, (M, t(j)) \models \varphi_1$
(S7) $(M, s) \models E_a\varphi$ iff   1) φ is *a-controllable*: $\forall s' \in W$, if $(s, s') \in R, (M, s') \models \varphi$
                                     2) φ is *a-uncontrollable: false*

The semantics of LCR are standard branching time semantics with the exception of $E_a\varphi$. $E_a\varphi$ is intended to represent the fact that agent a sees to it that φ is satisfied. The semantic rule for $E_a\varphi$ can be described informally as: agent a acts in world w in such a way that the truth of the a-controllable expression φ is guaranteed. The *stit* operator E_a ignores the means by which agent a will bring about a state of affairs. We furthermore introduce the operator $D_a\varphi$ that represents the fact that a specific state of affairs has indeed been brought about by an agent in the previous world. $D_a\varphi$, meaning 'φ has been done by a' is defined as:

$$(M, t(i)) \models D_a\varphi \text{ iff } \qquad (M, t(i-1)) \models \neg\varphi \wedge E_a\varphi$$

The following property holds for D_a:

$$\models D_a\varphi \rightarrow \varphi \qquad\qquad\qquad (1)$$

3.3   Representing Deontic Modalities in LCR

In a logic for the representation of contracts it must be possible to specify a time limit for realizing a certain state of affairs. Contracts express commitments that agents make to each other, that is an obligation for an agent to bring about a certain state of affairs (that is of interest to another agent). A deadline for the fulfillment of such obligations is usually indicated by the contract. A possible way to express deadlines is to indicate that an event should take place before a certain condition becomes true.

Moreover, clauses in a contract indicate that something must happen (it is desirable that something happens) but in fact if may never happen at all! A logic for contract representation must therefore be able to reason about situations (worlds in the semantics above) in which an obligation has been violated. Obligations have to do with the preference of individuals (or societies) to be in a certain state. $O_a\varphi$ indicates that, in the holding society, it is preferable for a to be in a state where φ holds than in any other state. This does not mean that agent a cannot be in other states either by choice or necessity. Worlds where a violation proposition holds are less preferred by the agent concerned.

We introduce obligation as a derived operator in LCR. Obligations in LCR express the fact that agent a is expected to bring about a certain state of a affairs (result) r before a certain condition (deadline) d has become valid.

Definition 6   Obligation with Deadline

The obligation of agent a to see to it that result ρ is achieve before an event δ happens, is defined in LCR as:

$$O_a(\rho \leq \delta) =_{def} A(\neg\delta U ((E_a\rho \wedge X(A\square\neg viol(a,\rho,\delta))) \vee X(\delta \wedge viol(a,\rho,\delta))))$$

Where $X(A\square \neg viol(a,\rho,\delta))$ indicates that this violation will not occur anymore in the future[3]. The obligation without deadline is a special case of the definition above:

$$O_a\rho =_{def} O_a(\rho \leq true)$$

It is interesting to note that in LCR the proposition $O_a(\rho \leq \delta) \wedge O_a(\neg\rho \leq \delta)$ is consistent. As actually is $O_a\rho \wedge O_a\neg\rho$. One or both of the obligations can be true due to the fact that the violation for that obligation is true.

The definition of obligation expresses the fact that in all worlds reachable from a world where $O_a(\rho \leq \delta)$ holds either the agent has seen to it that result ρ has been achieved or a violation of the obligation holds in those worlds. Intuitively, the idea is that an obligation will 'disappear' once the result is achieved within the deadline. However, this is not the case. Fulfilling an obligation does not mean that the obligation disappears but, once the result is achieved within the deadline, the obligation can never result in a violation anymore. Formally this is represented as:

$$\models O_a(\rho \leq \delta) \rightarrow \neg viol(a, \rho,\delta) S D_a(\rho \leq \delta) \tag{2}$$

---

[3] $\square\varphi$ is defined as: $\square\varphi =_{def} \neg(true U \neg\varphi)$.

Conditional obligations are obligations that only become active if the precondition becomes valid. Unlike regular obligations, that only hold once, a conditional obligation will come in force every time the condition holds.

Definition 7   Conditional Obligation with Deadline

The obligation of agent a to see to it that result ρ is achieved before an event ρ happens given that precondition π holds, is defined in LCR as:

$$O_a(\rho \leq \delta \mid \pi) \quad =_{\text{def}} \quad A((\pi \rightarrow O_a(\rho \leq \delta)) \, U(D_a\rho \vee \delta))$$

In this definition, the expression $U(D_a\rho \vee \delta)$ is necessary in order for the conditional obligation to be removed once it has been realized (or it cannot be done anymore because the deadline has passed). Otherwise, whenever π becomes true the obligation will arise. Because π can still be true after the obligation is fulfilled, the obligation will arise again and again.

Note that the special case of a conditional obligation, $O_a(\rho \leq \delta \mid true)$ is not the same as the regular obligation $O_a(\rho \leq \delta)$, but expresses an obligation that always holds. Another property of conditional obligations, is that they became 'normal' obligations whenever the precondition holds. Formally, this is expressed as:

$$\models O_a(\rho \leq \delta \mid \pi) \wedge \pi \wedge \neg\rho \wedge \neg Y\delta \rightarrow O_a(\rho \leq \delta) \tag{3}$$

Intuitively, one expects that once a deadline has passed, its violation will always hold, or at least until a sanction is performed. However this is not yet the case, if we consider the definitions above. We need thus to introduce the following axiom:

Axiom $\models viol(a, \rho, \delta) \rightarrow A(\, viol(a, \rho, \delta) \, U \, D_a\sigma)$

where σ is the sanction that will remove $viol(a, \rho, \delta)$, which can also be represented by $sanction(\sigma, a, \rho, \delta)$.

Sanctions themselves can be seen as obligations conditional on the occurrence of a violation. This leads to the following observation concerning the sanctions. If $sanction(\sigma, a, \rho, \delta)$, that is, σ is the sanction that will remove $viol(a, \rho, \delta)$, then:

$$O_a(\sigma \leq \delta' \mid viol(a, \rho, \delta)) \wedge viol(a, \rho, \delta) \rightarrow \tag{4}$$
$$((\neg viol(a, \rho, \delta) \wedge \neg viol(a, \sigma, \delta')) \vee ((viol(a, \rho, \delta) \wedge viol(a, \sigma, \delta'))S\delta'$$

So, either all the related violations disappear through performing the sanction or additional violations arise when it is not performed.

Obligations that hold in cases of violation of another obligation, such as sanctions, are known as contrary-to-duty obligations. Contrary-to-duty situations lead to some well-known paradoxes in standard deontic logic (SDL). In the next section we discuss some of these and describe how our formalism behaves in contrary-to-duty situations.

4   Contrary-to-Duty Imperatives

A contrary-to-duty obligation is an obligation that is only in force in a sub-ideal situation. This is often necessary to represent some aspects of legal systems.

Unfortunately, contrary-to-duty reasoning leads to notorious paradoxes of deontic logic. Paradoxes of deontic logic are logical expressions (in some logical language) that are valid in (many) well-known logical systems for deontic reasoning, but which are counterintuitive in a common sense reading [11]. The problem with most contrary-to-duty situations is that obligations referring to the most ideal situation conflict with obligations referring to less ideal cases. In contrast to many deontic logics, LCR explicitly represents the notion of violation. Intuitively, violation changes the context of (normative) reasoning. Violation contexts distinguish between ideal and sub-ideal contexts, varying in degree of 'ideality'.. Therefore, the representation of contrary-to-duty imperatives in LCR is in most cases straightforward.

It is not our intention to show here how LCR behaves for all the many contrary-to-duty situations that have been described for deontic logic, but we will take three versions of the Chisholm paradox [3], the forward, the parallel and the backward versions, as representative. Moreover, because our research is applied in the area of Knowledge Management and the support of Communities of Practice, we have taken examples from this areas for the informal description of the paradoxes.

Note that, from the definitions of obligation and conditional obligation in LCR, it can be proven that $O_a(\phi) \wedge O_a(\psi|\phi)$ does not imply $O_a(\psi)$. This is essential for the faithful representation of contrary-to-duty situations.

4.1   The Forward Version of the Chisholm Paradox

In this contrary-to-duty situation extra activities are obliged after a certain obligation holds, which do not hold otherwise. In our example, the rules of a knowledge sharing community are as follows: Meeting chairs must publish notes of the meeting (F1). When meeting notes are published, this must be announced to group members (after publishing) (F2). If not published, then it must not be announced (F3).

In SDL, a paradox follows from the case that notes are not published (F4). The formal specification of the above rules, in the generic case is:

(F1) $O_a(\phi)$ (a is obliged to publish meeting notes)
(F2) $O_a(\psi \mid \phi)$ (given that notes are published, a is obliged to announce it)
(F3) $O_a(\neg\psi \mid \neg\phi)$ (if not publish, a is obliged not to announce publication)
(F4) $\neg\phi$

From the way obligations are defined in LCR, F1 expresses that ϕ still has to be made true by a, that is $Ea(\phi)$, and in F2 the obligation $O_a\psi$ only holds in states where ϕ already holds. This implies a time difference between when ϕ should be true and ψ should be true. This is why this represents the forward version of the Chisholm paradox. Because, in our formalism, violation of norms is explicitly represented, this paradox does not result in states where a contradiction holds. Originating states can, however, be associated with a preference. The following table portrays the different states originating in this situation, where state S0 represents a state where the obligations hold and no action has been done and in each state only the relevant propositions are specified.

4.2   The Parallel Version of the Chisholm Paradox

This version of the Chisholm paradox is better known as the Forrester, or 'gentle murder' paradox. An example of this contrary-to-duty situation, that results in a paradox in SDL, is when the following. agreements hold in a community: Members of

Table 1. Forward version of Chisholm paradox in LCR

S_0	S_1	Possible next states	
$O_a(\varphi)$ (F1) $O_a(\psi \mid \varphi)$ (F2) $O_a(\neg\psi \mid \neg\varphi)$ (F3)	$\neg\varphi$ (F4) viol(a, φ) (from F1) $O_a(\neg\psi)$ (from F3)	$\neg\varphi$ (F4) ψ viol(a, φ) (from F1) viol(a,ψ) (from F3)	
		$\neg\varphi$ (F4) $\neg\psi$ viol(a, φ) (from F1)	

the community are not allowed to publish internal department reports (P1). But, if a member does publish an internal report, then it must be published in the discussion area (P2). Because publishing in the discussion area is a special case of publishing, this means that both activities are simultaneous (P3). The paradox arises when a report is published (P4). The generic formal specification of this situation is:

- (P1) $O_a(\neg\varphi)$ (a is obliged not to publish internal reports)
- (P2) $O_a(\varphi \rightarrow \psi)$ (if published, a must publish it in the discussion area)
- (P3) $\psi \rightarrow \varphi$ (publishing follows from publishing in discussion area)
- (P4) φ (a report is published)

Because, in our formalism, violation of norms is explicitly represented, this situation does not result in states where a contradiction holds. From P1 to P3, it is not possible in LCR to derive $O_a(\psi)$, which is usually the cause of the 'gentle murder' paradox in SDL. The following table portrays the different states originating in this situation, where state S0 represents a state where the obligations hold and no action has been done and in each state only the relevant propositions are specified. Because ψ can only be done at the same moment as φ, in states where φ holds either ψ or $\neg\psi$ must hold (ψ cannot happen at a latter state).

Table 2. Parallel version of Chisholm paradox in LCR

S_0	Possible next states	
$O_a(\neg\varphi)$ (P1) $O_a(\varphi \rightarrow \psi)$ (P2) $\psi \rightarrow \varphi$ (P3)	φ (P4) ψ viol(a, ¬φ) (from P1)	
	φ (P4) $\neg\psi$ viol(a, ¬φ) (from P1) viol(a, φ→ψ) (from P2)	

4.3   The Backward Version of the Chisholm Paradox

In this contrary-to-duty situation extra activities are obliged before a certain obligation holds, which are not obliged. In our example, this can be described by the situation in which the following community rules hold: Members must attend group meetings (B1). If one attends a meeting, then one must tell that one is coming (before) (B2). If one does not attend a meeting, then one must not tell that one is coming (B3). In SDL a paradox will occur when one does not attend a meeting (B4). The generic formal specification of this situation is:

(B1)	$O_a(\phi)$	(a is obliged to attend group meetings)
(B2)	$O_a(\psi \leq \phi)$	(If a attends, a must tell a is coming, before the meeting)
(B3)	$O_a(\neg\psi \leq \neg\phi)$	(If a doesn't attend, a must not tell a is coming)
(B4)	$\neg\phi$	

From this specification, one can see that LCR is utmost suitable to represent backward contrary-to-duty obligations due to the fact that in LCR deadlines are used explicitly. Because, in LCR, violation of norms is explicitly represented and there is a clear notion of time, the above situation does not result in states where a contradiction holds. The following table portrays the different states originating in this situation, where state S0 represents a state where the obligations hold and no action has been done and in each state only the relevant propositions are specified. Because ψ must be done before ϕ, in states where ϕ holds (B4) either ψ or $\neg\psi$ must already hold.

Table 3. Backward version of Chisholm paradox in LCR

S_0		Possible next states	
		$\neg\phi$	(B4)
		$\neg\psi$	
$O_a(\phi)$	(B1)	viol(a, ϕ)	(from B1)
$O_a(\psi \leq \phi)$	(B2)	$\neg\phi$	(B4)
$O_a(\neg\psi \leq \neg\phi)$	(B3)	ψ	
		viol(a, ϕ)	(from B1)
		viol(a, $\neg\psi$, $\neg\phi$)	(from B3)

5   Using Contracts to Model Interaction

The interaction structure as specified in the OM, gives a partial ordering of interaction scenes and the consequences of transitions from one to the other scene to the roles (creation, destruction, etc). That is, the interaction structure indicates the possibilities of an agent at each stage and the consequences of its choices. Explicit representation of commitments is necessary in order to know how to proceed if the norm is violated but first of all to inform the agents about the behavior they can expect from the other agents. In this way, coordination can become possible. A contract is a statement of intent that regulates behavior among organizations and individuals. A formal language for contract specification, such as LCR, allows the evaluation and verification of agent interaction..

Definition 8   Contract

We define a **contract, C**, as a tuple $C = (A, CC, S, T)$ where A is a set of agents, CC is a set of contract clauses (expressed as LCR formulae), S is the possible **stages** of the contract, and T gives the **transition rules** between states.

Transition rules are events in the domain that alter the status of the contract. Alternatively, a **stage graph** can be used to describe allowed states of the contract and the transition rules between states. The state graph represents the possible evolution(s) of the contract and the consequences of the changes in state to the different parties. Contract clauses are deontic expressions of LCR, that is, obligations, permissions or prohibitions, and as such may indicate deadlines and/or conditions.

Example

The following example is intended to illustrate the use of LCR to represent the interactions between two agent in a gent society. This contract expresses an exchange commitment agreed between agents S (a seller) and B (a buyer): S has agreed to sell B a bicycle for €500. S has 2 days to give the bicycle to B after which B must pay S within 1 day. If S does not provide the bicycle on time, then the exchange will not go through. If B does not pay on time then an extra €10 is due within 2 days. Formally, the clauses of this contract can be specified in LCR as[4]:

1. O_S(get-goods(B, bicycle) ≤ 2 days)
2. O_B(get-money(S, €500) ≤ 1 day | D_S(get-goods(B, bicycle) ≤ 2 days))
3. O_B(cancel-deal(S,B, bicycle, €500) ≤ 1 day | viol(S,get-goods(B,bicycle),2 days))
4. O_B(get-money(S, €510) ≤ 2 days | viol(B, get-money(S, €500),1 day))

The contract transition graph depicted in Fig. 1, represents the possible evolution of the contract and the consequences of the changes to the different parties. Transitions between contract stages are expressions representing events in the agent society. In the figure, arrows labeled r represent the achievement of the result and arrows labeled d represent that the deadline has passed without result. In each box only the relevant propositions are displayed. A bold box is the initial stage and double lined boxes are final stages. Stages S6 and S8 are not specified in the contract. Since most contracts are not exhaustive, such stages will probably appear in every contract graph. Consequences of reaching such stage can be determined by society norms (for example, guilty agent is expelled from society).

---

[4] Note that, for example, '2 days' abbreviates the expression that denotes a time 2 days from now (the evaluation moment), and is true only at that point in time.

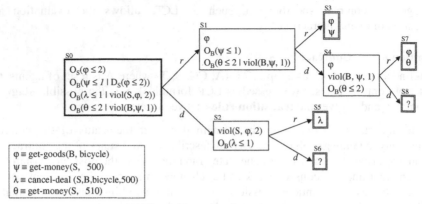

Fig. 1. Example of a contract

6   Related Work

A main question to which this paper contributes is how formalize the behavior of multi-agent systems, and how to relate this behavior to the global objectives of the system. Commitments play an important part in agent interactions. In situations where several agents cooperate within an organizational framework, designed to realize global society objectives, commitments are a means to specify expectations on the behavior of other participants. Several approaches to the formalization of interaction have been presented that are based purely in terms of organization concepts (and thus not referring to specific agents).

Behavioral approaches to the design of multi-agent systems are gaining terrain in agent research and several research groups have presented models similar to our proposal. Recent developments recognize that the modeling of interaction in MAS cannot simply rely on the agent's own (communicative) capabilities. Furthermore, organizational engineering of MAS cannot assume that participating agents will act according to the needs and expectations of the system design. Concepts as organizational rules [18], norms and institutions [7] and social structures [13] all start from the idea that the effective engineering of MAS needs high-level, agent-independent concepts and abstractions that explicitly define the organization in which agents live [19].

One of the first works in this area is that of Ferber and Gutknecht [9]. The organisation model structure they use includes high level concepts such as groups and roles within groups, and (intragroup and intergroup) role interaction. However expressive, AALAADIN does not offer primitives to describe interaction and coordination within and between groups and agents and the environment. This model was used as basis for a proposal for representation of social structures in AUML that does describe interaction between roles [13].

The model developed by the Alfebiite consortium is meant for the design of open agent societies and considers aspects of security and legal consequences of agent action in agent societies [1]. The model includes representation primitives for agents, constraints, communication language, roles, social states and agent owners. In our opinion, this model lacks primitives for the representation of groups and complex interaction and coordination in a society.

Esteva et al. [7] devise a formal specification language to design open agent systems as *electronic institutions* with focus on the normative aspects of societies. This proposal aims at the modeling of institutionalized electronic organizations (institutions). In this approach, roles are defined as patterns of behavior, normative rules are specified to limit or enlarge the space of agent actions and scenes are defined in order to represent the different contexts within an organization in which agents can interact. However, this framework takes a very low level approach to abstract interaction, by demanding that all interaction be expressed in terms of fully specified protocols.

A recent approach, based on deontic logic, is that of Pacheco and Carmo [12]. They propose a role based model for *organized collective agency*, based on the legal concept of *artificial person* and on a normative perspective on organizations. Their logic attempts to capture the concept of taking up a role. However, the logic does not include any temporal concepts, which makes it not suitable to represent real life organizations. Moreover, they lack a formal definition of roles (viewed as identifiers) and assume that roles are generated from the contracts between agents.

7   Conclusions

Contracts are used in an agent society to indicate agent conformance to some desired interaction patterns and to verify whether desired social states are preserved by agent activity. In this paper we have introduced LCR, a very expressive logic for describing interaction in multi-agent systems. This logic makes it possible to describe and verify contracts that specify interaction between agents. LCR is used as a formal basis for the framework for agents societies that we are developing. So far, we have concentrated on the logical representation of contracts. Future work needs to investigate how to reason formally about the interaction structure as a whole.

Acknowledgement. The authors wish to thank Andrew Jones for his valuable comments on a previous version of this paper presented at the 2nd FAABS workshop.

References

1.   Artikis, A., Pitt, J.: A Formal Model of Open Agent Societies. Proc. Autonomous Agents 2001, (2001) 192–193
2.   Boutelier, C.: Toward a Logic for Qualitative Decision Theory. In: Doyle, J., Sandewall, E., Torasso, P. (Eds.): Principles of Knowledge Representation and Reasoning, (1994).
3.   Chisholm, R.:Contrary-to-Duty Imperatives and Deontic Logic.Analysis 24,(1963), 33-36.
4.   Cholvy L., Garion C.: An Attempt to Adapt a Logic of Conditional Preferences for Reasoning with Contrary-To-Duties. In: Fundamenta Informaticae, 47 (2001).
5.   Dignum,F., Kuiper, R.: Specifying Deadlines with Dense Time using Deontic and Temporal Logic. In: International Journal of Electronic Commerce, 3(2), (1999), 67–86.

6. Dignum, V., Meyer, J.-J., Weigand, H., Dignum, F.: An Organizational-oriented Model for Agent Societies. In: Proc. Int. Workshop on Regulated Agent-Based Social Systems: Theories and Applications (RASTA'02), at AAMAS, Bologna, Italy, July, (2002).
7. Esteva, M., Rodriguez, J., Sierra, C., Garcia, P., Arcos J.: On the formal specifications of electronic institutions, In Dignum F., Sierra C. (Eds.): Agent-mediated Electronic commerce (The European AgentLink Perspective), LNAI 1991, (2001), 126–147.
8. Emerson, E.: Temporal and Modal Logic. In: J. van Leeuwen (Ed.): Handbook of Theoretical Computer Science, Elsevier Science Publishers (1990).
9. Ferber, J., Gutknecht, O.: A meta-model for the analysis and design of organizations in multi-agent systems. Proc. of ICMAS'98, IEEE Press, 1998.
10. Halpern J., Moses, Y.: A guide to the completeness and complexity of modal logic of knowledge and belief. Artificial Intelligence 54(3), (1992), 319–379.
11. Meyer, J.-J., Wieringa, R., Dignum, F.: The Role of Deontic Logic in the Specification of Information Systems. In Chomicki J., Saake, G. (eds.): Logics for Databases and Information Systems, pages 71–115, Kluwer Academics Publishers, (1998).
12. Pacheco O., Carmo, J.: A Role Based Model for the Normative Specification of Organized Collective Agency and Agents Interaction. Journal of Autonomous Agents and Multi-Agent Systems, to be published (2003).
13. Parunak, H. V. D. and Odell, J.: Representing Social Structures in UML. In: Wooldridge, M., Weiss, G., Ciancarini P. (Eds.): Agent-Oriented Software Engineering II, LNCS 2222, Springer-Verlag, (2002) 1–16.
14. Pörn, I.: Some Basic Concepts of Action. In: Stenlund, S. (Ed.): Logical Theory and Semantic Analysis. Reidel, Dordrecht (1974).
15. Van der Torre, L.: Contextual Deontic Logic: Normative Agents, Violations and Independence. In: Annals of Mathematics and Artificial Intelligence, Special Issue on Computational Logic in Multi-Agent Systems, 37(1-2): 33–63, January 2003.
16. Weigand, H., Dignum, V., Meyer, J.-J.: Specification by refinement and agreement: designing agent interaction using landmarks and contracts. In: Proceedings ESAW'02, Madrid, Spain, (2002).
17. Wooldridge, M.: Time, Knowledge, and Choice . In: M. Wooldridge, J. P. Mueller, M. Tambe, (Eds.): Intelligent Agents II, Springer-Verlag, (1996).
18. Zambonelli, F.: Abstractions and Infrastructures for the Design and Development of Mobile Agent Organizations. In: Wooldridge, M., Weiss, G., Ciancarini P. (Eds.): Agent-Oriented Software Engineering II, LNCS 2222, Springer-Verlag, (2002), 245–262.
19. Zambonelli, F., Jennings, N., Wooldridge, M.: Organizational Abstractions for the Analysis and Design of Multi-agent Systems. In: Ciancarini, P., Wooldridge, M. (Eds.): Agent-Oriented Software Engineering, LNCS 1957, Springer, (2000), 235–251.

Formal Verification for a Next-Generation Space Shuttle

Stacy D. Nelson[1] and Charles Pecheur[2]

[1] Nelson Consulting, NASA Ames Research Center, M/S 269-2, Moffett Field, CA 94035,
USA
nelsonconsult@aol.com
[2] RIACS, NASA Ames Research Center, M/S 269-2, Moffett Field, CA 94035, USA
pecheur@ptolemy.arc.nasa.gov

Abstract. This paper discusses the verification and validation (V&V) of advanced software used for integrated vehicle health monitoring (IVHM), in the context of NASA's next-generation space shuttle. We survey the current V&V practice and standards used in selected NASA projects, review applicable formal verification techniques, and discuss their integration into existing development practice and standards. We also describe two verification tools, JMPL2SMV and Livingstone PathFinder, that can be used to thoroughly verify diagnosis applications that use model-based reasoning, such as the Livingstone system.

1 Introduction

NASA is investing in the future of space transportation by investigating automated and integrated technologies for monitoring the health of future space shuttles and their ground support equipment. This application field, known as Integrated Vehicle Health Management (IVHM), is being developed in by the aerospace industry under the auspices of NASA's Space Launch Initiative (SLI) program.

The proposed IVHM system includes advanced software technologies such as model-based diagnosis using NASA's Livingstone system. This holds the promise of automating the diagnosis across a number of subsystem components and possible scenarios that is not tractable for more conventional diagnosis techniques. On the flip side, however, it also carries the burden of verifying that this very complex system will perform as expected in all those situations.

This paper is based on a survey of V&V techniques for IVHM, carried at NASA Ames in support of Northrop Grumman's IVHM project [16,17,18]. Section 2 gives an overview of IVHM for space vehicles, Section 3 surveys software verification and validation practices at NASA, Section 4 discusses applicable formal methods and ways to incorporate them into the software process in accordance with standards, Section 5 presents our tools for V&V of model-based diagnosis, and Section 6 discusses ongoing work on maturing these tools and infusing them in the IVHM design process.

M.G. Hinchey et al. (Eds.): FAABS 2002, LNAI 2699, pp. 53–67, 2003.

2 Advanced Health Management for Space Vehicles

Advanced health management for space vehicles makes it possible to detect, diagnose, and in some cases, remediate faults and failures without human intervention. This is critical to future space exploration because longer missions into deep space cannot be effectively managed from earth due to the length of time for a telemetry stream to reach earth from the space vehicle. It is also important to NASA's Space Launch Initiative focusing on affordable low earth orbit space vehicle, like the U.S. Space Shuttle, in order to improve crew safety and reduce costs.

NASA's Space Launch Initiative 2nd Generation Reusable Launch Vehicle (2nd Gen RLV) program is investing into future space transportation technologies, towards a flexible, commercially-produced fleet of reusable launch vehicles. The objective of the current Risk Reduction Phase is to enable a mid-decade competition such that critical technology demonstrations for each proposed architecture are adequately integrated, funded, and scheduled.

Integrated Vehicle Health Management, or IVHM, is one of the technology areas supported as part of 2nd Gen RLV. Simply stated, IVHM exists to diagnose/prognose, evaluate and remediate failure modes. The system is composed of a generic (in-flight & maintenance) architecture suitable for building an IVHM system from health management subsystems developed by different vendors [19].IVHM consists of both flight vehicle (FV-IVHM) and ground (GIVHM) components. FV-IVHM is primarily concerned with diagnosing and prognosing failures that have or might occur during the current flight. Any response to or remediation of these failures would occur during the current flight. GIVHM is primarily concerned with diagnosing/prognosing failures that may occur on the ground prior to take off or on a subsequent flight. This includes any pre-existing failure states. Both FV-IVHM and GIVHM contain model-based reasoning software.

Model-Based diagnosis is one of the key technologies currently adopted for next-generation shuttle IVHM. Model-Based Reasoning consists of applying a general-purpose *reasoning engine* to a declarative *model* of the application's artifacts. Specifically, model-based diagnosis uses a description the different components in the system and their interactions, including the failure modes of each component. These models capture all the application-relevant information in an abstract, concise, declarative representation. The diagnosis program itself is re-usable across different diagnosis applications.

Livingstone is a model-based diagnosis system developed at NASA Ames [26]. Livingstone models describe the normal and abnormal functional modes of each component in the system. Livingstone observes the commands issued to the plant and uses the model to predict the plant state. It then compares the predicted state against observations received from the actual sensors. If a discrepancy is found, Livingstone performs a diagnosis by searching for the most likely configuration of component modes that are consistent with the observations.

3   Software V&V at NASA

Software V&V is defined as the process of ensuring that software being developed or changed will satisfy functional and other requirements (verification) and each step in the process of building the software yields the right products (validation). A survey of current practice in Verification & Validation (V&V) of safety-critical software across NASA was conducted to support initial planning and analysis for V&V of the 2nd Generation Re-usable Launch Vehicle IVHM.

Three missions were selected as being representative of current software V&V practices: Checkout & Launch Control System (CLCS); X-37 IVHM Experiment; and Deep Space One (DS1) – Remote Agent (RA) including review of the Formal Verification conducted on RA. The following sections summarize survey results for CLCS, DS1 and the Formal V&V conducted on RA. X-37 is not included because, while the V&V effort was excellent, the experiment was at an early stage and less useful information could be collected.

3.1   Check-out and Launch Control (CLCS) System

The objective of the CLCS Project was to provide a real-time computerized Space Shuttle checkout system used to control and monitor test operations and launch. The CLCS project had comprehensive V&V plans based on NASA standards and contained in an online repository (http://clcs.ksc.nasa.gov/docs/test-specs.html). CLCS was canceled in August 2002; however, review of this project revealed two important lessons:

1. using the spiral or evolutionary strategy described in IEEE 12207.2 Annex I is more cost effective than the waterfall strategy; and
2. it is important to evaluate IV&V budget requirements early in the project. For example, a manned mission or program costing more than $100M requires review by the NASA Independent Verification and Validation (IV&V) team.

3.2   Remote Agent

The objective of the Deep Space One (DS1) mission was to test 12 advanced technologies in deep space so these technologies could be used to reduce the cost and risk of future missions. One of the 12 technologies on DS1 was Remote Agent, a software product designed to operate a spacecraft with minimal human assistance. The successful demonstration of Remote Agent on DS1 lead its team to become co-winners of the NASA 1999 Software of the Year Award.

The V&V of DS1 used a number of testbeds, as detailed in Table 1. V&V was conducted via carefully planned operations scenarios and tests were distributed among low, medium and high-fidelity testbeds, which improved project team agility and reduced testing costs. Operations scenarios were used effectively to test nominal and off-nominal events. Operational Readiness Tests identified procedural problems during "dress rehearsal" so they could be corrected before the actual mission.

Table 1. Deep Space One – Remote Agent Testbeds

Testbed	Fidelity	CPU	Hardware	Availability	Speed	Readiness Dates
Spacecraft	Highest	Rad6000	Flight	1 for DS1	1:1	05/99
DS1 Testbed	High	Rad6000	Flight spares + DS1 sims	1 for DS1	1:1	04/99
Hotbench	High	Rad6000	Flight spares + DS1 sims	1 for DS1	1:1	03/99
Papabed	Medium	Rad6000	Flight spares + DS1 sims	1 for DS1	1:1	11/98
Radbed	Low	Rad6000	RAX Simulators	1 for RAX	1:1	04/98
Babybed	Lowest	PowerPC	RAX Simulators	2 for RAX	7:1	02/98
Unix	Lowest	SPARC UNIX	RAX Simulators	Unlimited	35:1	08/97

Throughout initial stages of the project, the goal of testing was to discover bugs so they could be repaired. As it grew closer to take off; however, the discovery of a bug did not automatically imply it would be fixed. Instead, a Change Control Board (CCB) composed of senior RA project members reviewed the details of each bug and proposed fix to assess the risk of repair. The CCB became increasingly conservative near mission launch date preferring to work around bugs rather than risk inadvertently breaking more code during while repairing a bug.

3.3 Formal V&V of Remote Agent's Executive

Incidentally, the executive part of the Remote Agent has been the target of a very illustrative formal verification experiment [6]. The results came in two phases.

In 1997, a team from the ASE group at Ames used the Spin model checker [9] to verify the core services of Remote Agent's Executive (EXEC) and found five concurrency bugs. Four of these bugs were deemed important by the executive software development team, which considered that these errors would not have been found through traditional testing. Once a tractable Spin model was obtained, it took less than a week to carry out the verification activities. However, it took about 1.5 work-months to manually construct a model that could be run by Spin in a reasonable length of time, starting from the Lisp code of the executive.

In May 1999, as the Remote Agent was run in space Deep Space One, an anomaly was discovered in the EXEC. Shortly after, the ASE team took the challenge of performing a "clean room" experiment to determine whether the bug could have been found using verification and within a short turnaround time. Over the following weekend, they successfully revealed and demonstrated the bug using the group's Java PathFinder tool [7]. As it turns out, the bug was a deadlock due to improper use of synchronization events, and was isomorphic to one of the five bugs detected in another part of EXEC with Spin two years before. This verification effort clearly demonstrated that advanced V&V techniques can catch the kind of concurrency bugs that typically pass through heavy test screens and compromise a mission.

3.4 Software Process Standards

In order for advanced software to fly on spacecraft or aircraft, it must be approved by relevant authorities—NASA for space, the Federal Aviation Authority (FAA) for civil aviation. This approval generally involves conformance with some established software process and V&V standards. The following NASA Standards are relied upon for guidance:

- *NASA* NPG 2820 *"Software Guidelines and Requirements"* [14]. This document references IEEE/EIA Standards 12207.0, 12207.1 and 12207.2 [10,11,12], which are themselves based on ISO/IEC 12207. This series is in widespread use in the industry.
- *NASA* NPG 8730 *"Software Independent Verification and Validation (IV&V) Management"* [15] discusses the requirements for independent verification and validation. In a nutshell, a manned mission and any mission or program costing more than $100M will require IV&V.

In addition to the NASA standards, RTCA DO-178B, "Software Considerations in Airborne Systems and Equipment Certification" [24] contains guidance for determining that software aspects of airborne systems and equipment comply with airworthiness certification requirements.

In summary, to comply with the above described standards, each project must have a well-defined process with discrete phases and thoroughly documented work products for each phase.

4   Formal Methods for IVHM V&V

IVHM considerably increases the complexity of the software V&V task, in two different ways:

- The software components are more complex and may involve non-conventional programming paradigms. For example, model-based reasoning uses a logic reasoning component issued from artificial intelligence research; furthermore, a lot of the application-specific complexity lies in the model rather than in the diagnosis program itself.
- The state space to be covered is incomparably larger, as the IVHM system aims at properly handling, at least partly autonomously, a large set of possible faults under a broad range of unforeseen circumstances. This contrasts with the current largely human-based approach to diagnosis, with a number of mission controllers monitoring the vehicle's telemetry.

These two aspects pose a serious challenge to conventional V&V approaches based on testing. To achieve the required level of confidence in IVHM software, more advanced methods need to be applied. This section surveys the main formal analysis techniques issued from the research community and discusses their applicability to IVHM systems. It summarizes the results from the second report of the survey [17].

4.1   The Verification Spectrum

The term "Formal Methods" refers to various rigorous analysis and verification techniques based on strong mathematical and logic foundations. In principle, formal verification will guarantee that a system meets the specifications being verified, whereas informal techniques can only detect errors or increase confidence. In practice though, the limit is blurred by the abstractions, restrictions and simplifications needed to express the system into a formal representation amenable to formal analysis. One should rather think of a spectrum of techniques, with various degrees of formality.

Below is an overview the broad categories of verification methods. The methods are ordered in increasing level of formality. Generally, more formal methods provide greater assurance, at the cost of greater required expertise—from testing methods used throughout the software industry, up to theorem proving techniques mastered only by a few experts. Nevertheless, there can be wide variations between tools and applications within a category, and many approaches blend aspects of different categories.

- **Testing** consists in executing the system through a pre-established collection of sequences of inputs (*test cases*), while checking that the outputs and the system state meet the specification. This is the most common, and often the unique, mechanized verification technique used in most projects. It defines the baseline against which other techniques should be compared. The test cases are commonly developed and tuned manually by application experts, a cumbersome, error-prone and very time-consuming task. A *test harness* also has to be developed, to simulate the operational environment of the tested system. As a result, testing is often the most costly part of the whole development phase, especially in safety-critical applications such as space transportation.
- **Runtime Monitoring** consists in monitoring a system while it is executing, or scrutinizing the artifacts (event logs, etc) obtained from that execution. It can be used to control complex specifications that involve several successive events. In some cases, it can even flag suspicious code even if no error actually occurs. Runtime monitoring typically requires little computing resources and therefore scales up well to very large systems. On the other hand, it will only observe a limited number of executions and thus gives only uncertain results. In the case of error predictions, it can also give false negatives, i.e. flag potential errors that cannot actually occur. Applications of runtime monitoring at NASA include the analysis of generated plans using database queries at Jet Propulsion Labs [5] and NASA Ames' JPaX tool for monitoring Java programs [8].
- **Static Analysis** consists in exploring the structure of the source code of a program to extract information or verify properties, such as absence of array bound violations or non-initialized pointer accesses [20]. In principle, static analysis can be applied to source code early in the development and is totally automatic. There is, however, a trade-off between the cost and the precision of the analysis, as the most precise algorithms have a prohibitive complexity. More efficient algorithms make approximations that can result in a large number of *false positives*, i.e. spurious error or warning messages. NASA has performed several experiments using PolySpace, a static analyzer for C programs [23].
- **Model Checking** consists in verifying that a system satisfies a property by exhaustively exploring all its reachable states [3,1]. This requires that this state space be finite—and tractable: model checking is limited by the *state space explosion* problem, where the number of states can grow exponentially with the size of the system. Tractability is generally achieved by abstracting away from irrelevant details of the system. When the state space is still to big or even infinite, model checking can still be applied: it will not be able to prove that a property is satisfied,

but can still be a very powerful error-finding tool. Model checking in itself is automatic, but the modeling phase can be a very arduous and error-prone effort. Model checkers often impose their own modeling language, though more and more tools now apply directly to common design and programming languages (UML, Java), either natively or through translation. **Symbolic model checking** is an advanced form of model checking that considers whole sets of states at each step, implicitly and efficiently encoded into data structures called Binary Decision Diagrams (BDDs). Symbolic model checking can address much larger systems than explicit state model checkers, though the complexity of the BDDs can outweigh the benefits of symbolic computations. One of the major symbolic model checkers is SMV from Carnegie-Mellon University (CMU) [2], which has been used in this project, as detailed in Section 5.1.

- **Theorem Proving** consists in building a computer-assisted logic proof that the system satisfies the specifications, where both are suitably represented in the mathematical framework of the proof system being used. When applicable, theorem proving provides the "Holy Grail" of V&V, as it has the potential to provide a mathematically correct, computer-verified proof of compliance. However, the proof systems needed for this kind of endeavor demand a lot of user guidance; proving the final specification will typically require providing and proving a number of intermediate properties (e.g. loop invariants). Although modern proof systems provide ever more elaborate *tactics* that automatically chain more elementary proof steps, this kind of verification still requires a lot of expertise and work, and is most often performed on small-scale designs by specialized researchers.

No matter how effective more formal methods can be, *testing* remains an essential element of the V&V process. In addition, our findings recommended that *model checking*, *static analysis* and *runtime verification* be added to the set of methods applicable to V&V of IVHM. *Theorem proving* was not recommended, due to the excessive effort and expertise it requires, and because it was not considered appropriate for the large, complex IVHM systems under consideration. The next section discusses where these different techniques fit into the software development process.

4.2 Formal Methods in the Software Process

In order to ensure that formal verification techniques meet the V&V standards, the following guidance is provided for integrating formal methods into the Software Life Cycle.

Effective software development requires a well-defined process with discrete Software Life Cycle phases including documented work products (called deliverables) for each phase; analysis procedures established to ensure correctness of deliverables; and scheduled reviews of major product releases. These items have to be defined in order for formal methods to be integrated in the software V&V process.

Formal methods can be applied to any or all phases of the Software Life Cycle. They may be used to enhance rather than replace traditional testing; although traditional testing efforts may be significantly reduced when formal methods are used effectively. Different types of formal methods can be used at different stages in the life cycle: model checking may be applied at the different levels of the design phase, down to program code; static analysis is typically geared towards executable code;

runtime monitoring is applicable at different stages in the integration and testing phase, every time real code is being executed.

Table 2. Recommendations for Formal Methods in the V&V Process (SW = Software, SRA = System Requirements Analysis, SWRA = Software Requirements Analysis)

Formal Methods	Applicable SW Life Cycle Phase	Formal Verification Activities
Any Formal Methods Technique	SRA/SWRA	Perform a new development activity called "formalization" to create a new work product called a "formal specification". Enhance traceability tools and techniques to track new products such as formal specifications and proofs, and their relationships to existing products
Model Checking (Theorem Proving)	SRA/SWRA	Perform a new analysis activity called "proving assertions" to enhance the correctness of the formal specification and to understand the implications of the design captured in the requirements and specification. Perform an Official Review of the formal specification to check the coverage, correctness, and comprehensibility of the formal specification.
Model Checking	SWRA and SW & Model Detailed Design	Perform a new analysis activity called "modeling", producing a new work product called a "formal model". Perform a new activity called "formal analysis" where model checking is applied to the formal models. Model checking enables all execution traces to be verified. This improves the accuracy and reliability of the product and allows early error detection and correction. It may also reduce the amount of traditional testing required.
Model Checking	SWRA and SW & Model Detailed Design	Perform an Official Review of the model to check for correctness
Static Analysis	SW & Model Detailed Design and SW Coding	Use Static Analysis tools in addition to a compiler during code development. This can reduce the amount of traditional unit testing required while increasing the accuracy of the program.
Model Checking	SW Coding and SW & Model Unit Testing	If available for the programming language and platform used, use model checkers in addition to standard debugging and test control tools. This can greatly improve the odds of detecting some errors, such as race conditions in concurrent programs.
Runtime Monitoring	SW Coding, SW & Model Unit Testing, SW Qualification Testing, System Qualification Testing	Use Runtime Monitoring during simulation testing at each phase where program code gets executed. This can provide more information about potential errors.

Planning for formal methods includes activities at each level in the life cycle. At the beginning of the program, staffing requirements for formal methods and enhanced project guidelines must be considered: The software development team must include at least one team member knowledgeable in formal methods. Formal V&V guidelines, standards, and conventions should be developed early and followed carefully. The V&V team must plan how and when to use formal methods; therefore, these new planning steps are recommended: 1) determine which software or software components will benefit from use of formal methods, 2) select the appropriate type of formal methods, 3) choose the formal methods toolkit and 4) enhance life cycle activities for activities associated with formal methods. Table 2 summarizes recommendations for enhancing the life cycle.

Metrics are important to track effectiveness of formal verification activities. Potentially useful metrics for formal verification include:

- Number of issues found in the original requirements (i.e., the requirements in their English description form, before being formalized), along with a subjective ranking of importance (e.g., major, minor)
- Amount of time spent in reviewing and in inspection meetings, along with a number and type of issues found during this activity
- Number of issues found after requirements analysis, along with a description of why the issue was not found (e.g., inadequate analysis, outside the scope of the analysis, etc.)

Metrics specific to model checking include: amount of time spent in model development (both human and CPU time) and amount of coverage.

5 V&V of Model-Based Diagnosis

A model-based diagnosis system such as Livingstone involves the interaction between various components: the reasoning engine that performs the diagnosis, the model that provides application-specific knowledge to it, the physical system being diagnosed, the executive that drives it and acts upon diagnosis results. There are multiple facets of such a system that need to be verified, and different verification techniques that can be applied to that objective. In this section, based on our third report [18], we present two tools developed at NASA Ames for verifying Livingstone-based applications, and discuss their applicability as part of the larger V&V process.

5.1 Symbolic Model Checking of Livingstone Models

By their abstract, declarative nature, the models used for diagnosis lend themselves well to formal analysis. In particular, Livingstone models are semantically very close to those used by symbolic model checkers such as SMV. The languages are different, though, so a translation is necessary.

In many previous experiences in model checking of software, this translation had to be done by hand, and was by far the most complex and time-consuming part, that has hindered adoption of formal verification by the software industry. Instead, the goal is for Livingstone application developers to use model checking to assist them in designing and correcting their models, as part of their usual development environment. To achieve that, we have developed, in collaboration with Reid Simmons at CMU, a translator to automate the conversion between Livingstone and SMV [22]. The translator supports three kinds of translation, as shown in Figure 1:

- The Livingstone *model* is translated into an SMV model amenable to model checking.

- The *specifications* to be verified against this model are expressed in terms of the Livingstone model and similarly translated.
- Finally, the *diagnostic traces* produced by SMV are converted back in terms of the Livingstone model.[1]

The translation of Livingstone models to SMV is facilitated by the strong similarities between the underlying semantic frameworks of Livingstone and SMV: both boil down to a synchronous transition system, defined through propositional logic constraints on states and transitions. Based on this, the translation is mostly a straightforward mapping from JMPL to SMV language elements. The specifications to be verified with SMV are provided in a separate file, expressed in a syntax that extends the existing JMPL syntax for logic expressions. They are translated into the CTL temporal logic used by SMV and appended to the SMV model file. CTL is very expressive but requires a lot of caution and expertise to be used correctly. To alleviate this problem, the translator also supports a number of pre-defined templates and auxiliary operators corresponding to Livingstone-relevant properties and features, such as consistency of the model or the number of failed components. Finally, any error traces reported by SMV are translated back to their Livingstone counterpart—this recent addition is further discussed in section 6.

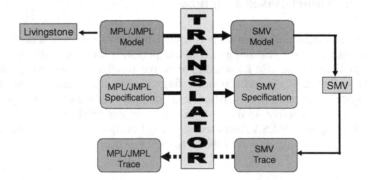

Fig. 1. Translation from Livingstone to SMV.[2]

The translator has been successfully applied to several Livingstone models, such as the Deep-Space One spacecraft, the Xavier mobile robot from CMU and the In-Situ Propellant Production system (ISPP) developed at NASA Kennedy Space Center for Mars missions. The ISPP experience was the most extensive; it did produce useful feedback to the Livingstone model developers, but also experimented with the potentials and challenges of putting such a tool in the hands of application practitioners. Models of up to 10^{55} states could still be processed in a matter of minutes with an enhanced version of SMV. Experience shows that Livingstone models tend to feature a

---

[1] The reverse translation of traces, shown as a dotted arrow, was not available when the survey was made but has since then been implemented.

[2] The original translator applied to an earlier, Lisp-style syntax for Livingstone models (Model Programming Language, or MPL). The translator has later been upgraded to the current Java-like syntax (called JMPL).

huge state space but little depth, for which the symbolic processing of SMV is very appropriate.

5.2 Extended Simulation with Livingstone PathFinder

Although model-based verification using SMV allows a thorough analysis of Livingstone models, it does not check whether the actual diagnosis engine performs that diagnosis as required. In a complementary approach, we have developed a tool called **Livingstone PathFinder** (**LPF**) that automates the execution of Livingstone, coupled to a simulated environment, across a large range of scenarios. The system under analysis consists of three parts, as illustrated on figure 2:

- The Livingstone *engine* performing the diagnosis, using the user-provided Livingstone model.
- A *simulator* for the device on which diagnosis is performed.
- A *driver* that generates the commands and faults according to a script provided by the user.

Currently, a second Livingstone engine is used for the simulator. The tool architecture is modular, however, and the different components are accessed through generic programming interfaces (APIs) so that their content can be easily changed.

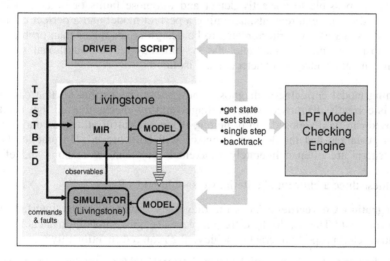

Fig. 2. Architecture of the Livingstone PathFinder tool, showing the diagnosis engine (MIR), the simulator and the driver.

Both Livingstone and its environment are instrumented to allow a closer and more efficient control of the execution, using backtracking to explore alternate paths and observing states to prune redundant executions. This amounts to applying the same state space search as used for model checking. Each forward step consists of a whole diagnosis cycle, where the next event is produced by the driver, applied to the simulator and observed by the diagnosis system. When the current execution terminates (at the end of the scenario or because no consistent next state could be found), LPF backtracks step by step, looking for further alternate executions in previous states. Typically, these alternate paths will explore different failure scenarios. The exploration proceeds along the next alternate path, in a depth-first manner, until the entire tree of possible executions has been covered. [3]

5.3 Correctness and Reliability Criteria

The two tools presented in the previous section only partially address the verification needs of a Livingstone-based application. To put this in perspective, we introduce the following classification of correctness and reliability criteria for model-based diagnosis:

- **Model Correctness:** Is the model a valid abstraction of the actual physical plant? In particular, the model should also be internally well-formed, that is, fulfill generic sanity criteria, such as consistency and completeness.
- **Diagnosis Correctness:** Does the diagnosis engine perform correctly? Note that this verification needs to be addressed once, typically by the engine developers. Once the engine has been verified, it can be viewed as a stable, trusted part, much in the same way as programmers view their programming language compiler.
- **Diagnosability:** Is it possible to perform the required diagnosis? More precisely, is it always possible to correctly detect and diagnose faults or other conditions as specified in the requirements, assuming a perfect model and a perfect engine? Deficiencies against this criterion tend to be design issues rather than problems in the diagnosis system. For example, the system may require additional sensors if a fault can not be adequately detected and isolated.

Assuming model correctness, diagnosis correctness checks that all that can be diagnosed is correctly diagnosed, whereas diagnosability checks that all that needs to be diagnosed can be diagnosed. In principle, if we can fulfill all three conditions, then we can guarantee that the desired diagnosis will be achieved. In practice however, these criteria are often deliberately weakened for technical reasons and efficiency purposes.

To these three architectural criteria, we should add a fourth:

- **Integration Correctness:** Does the diagnosis system correctly interface with its environment? That is, do the different pieces (engine, model, physical system, executive, etc.) properly interact to achieve the required functionality?

Model checking of diagnosis models can definitely address model correctness issues. The translator directly provides specification templates for generic sanity criteria. It can also be used to verify that the model satisfies documented properties of the system, provided those properties can be expressed at the level of abstraction of the model. For example, flow conservation properties have been verified this way. More thorough verification may require case-specific technology, e.g. for comparing models of different nature. Livingstone PathFinder could be modified to perform a comparative simulation for that purpose. We have recently successfully experimented

---

[3] The architecture supports other automated or interactive simulation algorithms. Indeed, an implementation of guided search has just been completed.

with using symbolic model checking to verify diagnosability, using a duplicated version of the Livingstone model [21]. Livingstone PathFinder can also detect diagnosability problems. Since it performs a focused verification based on running the real engine on real test cases, it provides better fidelity but less coverage. It also provides assurance into diagnosis correctness, though within the same focused scenario limits. Finally, LPF gives a limited assurance in integration correctness, by running the real engine into a simulated environment. This part could be strengthened by plugging higher-fidelity simulators in LPF, and encompassing more components within the LPF-controlled simulation.

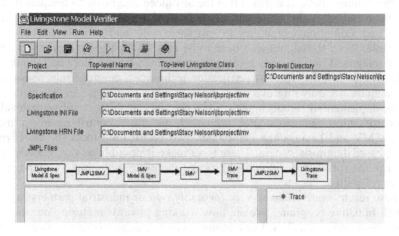

Fig. 3. The Livingstone Model Verifier graphical interface (detail).

6 Maturing V&V Technology

As a follow-up on the survey and recommendations presented in the previous sections, work is currently underway to extend formal verification of Livingstone models by enhancing the functionality of JMPL2SMV and Livingstone PathFinder (LPF) and making them easy for a typical engineer to use, without the high cost of hiring formal methods specialists to run them. Enhancements include the following list:

- The SMV Trace Translation tool completes the automated translation provided by JMPL2SMV between Livingstone models and SMV models by translating traces produced by SMV back in terms of Livingstone model elements.
- A number of new specification patterns have been added to the JMPL2SMV translator, to further simplify the task of specifying the properties to be verified by the model checker.
- A graphical front-end interface has been developed to simplify the use of JMPL2SMV, automate the interactions between SMV and the different translators, and provide better visualization capabilities (Figure 3). The resulting tool, called Livingstone Model Verifier (LMV), appears as an integrated model checker for

Livingstone models. A similar interface has also been developed for the Livingstone PathFinder tool.

7 Conclusions and Perspectives

What we have presented here is the result of a six-month, one-person investigation and was therefore necessarily focused on selected applications and tools. Nevertheless, our findings have confirmed that the advanced diagnosis techniques that are being considered for future space transportation vehicles also require advances in verification and validation techniques to guarantee safe and reliable operation. To be applicable, those techniques also need to be easy enough to be used by practitioners and be integrated into existing development frameworks, practices and standards.

We discussed how rigorous verification techniques, coming from research in formal methods, not only improve safety by improving confidence in the system, but can also be implemented and documented in accordance with strict software development and certification standards. We presented our own contributions to the field, JMPL2SMV and Livingstone PathFinder, two verification tools for the Livingstone model-based diagnosis system. These tools make it possible to verify model accuracy earlier in the software development process; therefore, reducing costs and improving system reliability.

These results were received very favorably by our industrial partners in the Space Launch Initiative program. We are now working towards maturing our tools and infusing them into a real IVHM development environment, to demonstrate and evaluate the impact formal methods can bring to the V&V of advanced, safety-critical software architectures.

References

[1]   Beatrice Bérard, Michel Bidoit, Alain Finkel, Francois Laroussinie, Antoine Petit, Laure Petrucci, Philippe Schnoebelen with Pierre McKenzie. Systems and Software Verification Model-Checking Techniques and Tools. Springer, 1998

[2]   J. R. Burch, E. M. Clarke, K. L. McMillan, D. L. Dill, and J. Hwang. Symbolic model checking: 10^{20} states and beyond. *Information and Computation*, 98(2):142–170, June 1992.

[3]   Edmund M. Clarke, Jr., Orna Grumberg, Doron A. Peled. Model Checking. The MIT Press, 2000.

[4]   Ken Costello. Private communication. NASA IV&V Facility, October 13, 2001.

[5]   Martin S. Feather. Rapid Application of Lightweight Formal Methods for Consistency Analyses. IEEE Transactions on Software Engineering, Vol. 24, No. 11, November 1998, pp. 949–959.

[6]   Klaus Havelund, Mike Lowry, SeungJoon Park, Charles Pecheur, John Penix, Willem Visser, Jon L. White. Formal Analysis of the Remote Agent Before and After Flight. Proceedings of 5th NASA Langley Formal Methods Workshop, Williamsburg, Virginia, 13-15 June 2000.

[7]   K. Havelund, T. Pressburger. Model Checking Java Programs Using Java PathFinder. International Journal on Software Tools for Technology Transfer (STTT) 2(4), April 2000.

[8]   Klaus Havelund, Grigore Rosu. Monitoring Java Programs with Java PathFinder. First Workshop on Runtime Verification (RV'01), Paris, France, 23 July 2001. Electronic Notes in Theoretical Computer Science, Volume 55, Number 2, 2001

[9]   G. J. Holzmann. The model checker SPIN. *IEEE Transactions on Software Engineering*, 23(5), May 1997.

[10]   IEEE/EIA. Industry Implementation of International Standard ISO/IEC: ISO/IEC12207 Standard for Information Technology—Software life cycle processes. IEEE/EIA 12207.0-1996.

[11]   IEEE/EIA. Industry Implementation of International Standard ISO/IEC: ISO/IEC12207 Standard for Information Technology—Software life cycle processes—Life cycle data. IEEE/EIA 12207.1-1997.

[12]   IEEE/EIA. Industry Implementation of International Standard ISO/IEC: ISO/IEC12207 Standard for Information Technology—Software life cycle processes—Implementation Considerations. IEEE/EIA 12207.2-1997.

[13]   N. Muscettola, P. P. Nayak, B. Pell, and B. Williams. Remote Agent: To boldly go where no AI system has gone before. Artificial Intelligence, 103(1-2):5–48, August 1998.

[14]   NASA. NASA Software Guidelines and Requirements. NASA NPG 2820.DRAFT, 3/19/01.

[15]   NASA. Software Independent Verification and Validation (IV&V) Management. NASA NPG 8730.DRAFT 2, 30 Nov 2001.

[16]   Stacy Nelson, Charles Pecheur. NASA processes/methods applicable to IVHM V&V. Project report, NASA/CR-2002-211401, April 2002.

[17]   Stacy Nelson, Charles Pecheur. Methods for V&V of IVHM intelligent systems. Project report, NASA/CR-2002-211402, April 2002.

[18]   Stacy Nelson, Charles Pecheur. Diagnostic Model V&V Plan/Methods for DME. Project report, NASA/CR-2002-211403, April 2002.

[19]   Northrop Grumman, NASA, DSI. *2nd Generation RLV Risk Reduction Program: TA-5 (IVHM) Project Notebook.* Edited by: Stephen A. Brown. Northrop Grumman, El Segundo, CA, 07/20/01.

[20]   F. Nielson, H. R. Nielson, C. Hankin. Principles of Program Analysis. Springer, 1999.

[21]   Charles Pecheur, Alessandro Cimatti. Formal Verification of Diagnosability via Symbolic Model Checking. Workshop on Model Checking and Artificial Intelligence (MoChArt-2002), Lyon, France, July 22/23, 2002.

[22]   Charles Pecheur and Reid Simmons. From Livingstone to SMV: Formal verification for autonomous spacecrafts. In Proceedings of First Goddard Workshop on Formal Approaches to Agent-Based Systems, April 2000. Lecture Notes in Computer Science 1871, Springer Verlag.

[23]   PolySpace Technologies. C Verifier. http://www.polyspace.com

[24]   RTCA. Software Considerations in Airborne Systems and Equipment Certification. RTCA (Requirements and Technical Concepts for Aviation) /DO-178B, December 1, 1992.

[25]   John Rushby. Assurance for Dependable Systems (Disappearing Formal Methods). Presentation at Safecomp, Budapest, September 2001, TU Vienna, March 2001 and NSA March 2001.

[26]   B. C. Williams and P. P. Nayak. A model-based approach to reactive self-configuring systems. In Proceedings of AAAI-96, 1996.

Automated Protocol Analysis in Maude

Jeffrey Van Baalen and Thomas Böhne

Department of Computer Science
University of Wyoming
Laramie WY 82071, USA
{jvb,tobox}@cs.uwyo.edu,
http://www.cs.uwyo.edu/~tobox/

Abstract. We present an approach to automated protocol analysis using the Maude rewrite system. We describe the process of translating high-level protocol specifications from the *Common Authentication Protocol Specification Language* (CAPSL) into an executable Maude specification. After this translation step, we dynamically extend the specification by adding an intruder agent. Based on this representation of a protocol environment, different model checkers can be applied to evaluate whether all protocol properties hold in the presence of the intruder.

1 Introduction

Due to the enormous growth of the Internet, there is a massive increase in the electronic flow of sensitive information. As a result, there is an increasing demand for secure and fault-tolerant agent-based communication protocols. However, in the past few years flaws have been discovered in many of the protocols in common use [1]. Hence, a significant amount of work is being conducted on formal techniques for analyzing communication protocols. Since manual protocol analysis turns out to be overwhelming and error prone, automated approaches based on theorem proving or model checking appear promising.

A number of protocols have been analyzed using various types of software tools, but most of those tools have been specifically implemented for a single protocol or small sets of protocols [2,3,4]. These designs often require changes in the source code to model different kinds of protocols, and—even worse—the protocol specifications need to be translated into a special input format. This process turns out to be error prone, so more general solutions are being pursued (e.g., [5]).

In FAABS-I [6], we reported on a system to verify fault-tolerance properties of agent-based systems. We described a framework in which a specification of an agent-based system was written as a module in the Maude executable specification language [7]. Also, specifications of different fault-models were written as separate Maude modules. Using the module composition facilities in Maude, the system specification was combined with a specification of a fault-mode and model-checked to verify that the system had desired properties in the presence of different types of faults.

M.G. Hinchey et al. (Eds.): 'FAABS 2002, LNAI 2699, pp. 68–78, 2003.

Since then we have expanded our goals and are pursuing a general approach to the analysis of security protocols for agent-based systems. This paper presents a fully automated approach to generating environments for security protocols and intruder models in Maude. This work extends the work reported in [6] in several ways. One way is that instead of specifying an agent-based communication protocol directly in Maude, the Common Authentication Protocol Specification Language [8] (CAPSL) is used. CAPSL specifications contain protocol descriptions as well as desired properties of those protocols all written in a high-level language specialized to protocols. Our tool automatically translates each such specification into a Maude module. Then a separate intruder module and desired properties of the protocol are automatically generated. The protocol module and intruder module are combined and the given properties are model checked using either a linear temporal logic (LTL) model checker built into Maude or a computation tree logic (CTL) model checker that we have developed in Maude. A detailed description (including the source code) of the whole system can be found in [9].

Several advantages of the Maude system simplified the design of our automated protocol analyzing tool. The concept of sending and receiving messages can be mapped to rewriting logic easily [10]; the support of mix-fix operators provides for a direct translation of specifications into program code. The generated modules are executable—meaning that a *specification* in Maude can already be tested and executed. The latest versions of Maude come with a built-in LTL model checker (written in C++) that is significantly faster than model checker modules written in Maude.

Section 1 gave a very brief introduction to the prior research on protocol analysis, and the tool that we have developed. Section 2 will describe this translator in detail, using a well known protocol as an example. Section 3 sums up advantages and disadvantages of our approach, shows current restrictions and ways to remove them in future work. Section 4 draws a conclusion.

2 The Translation Process

2.1 CAPSL

As mentioned, CAPSL is used to specify communication protocols and desired properties of those protocols. It was developed at Stanford Research Institute (SRI), and a library of more than fifty CAPSL protocol specifications has been built. The intention of the SRI research group is to translate CAPSL specifications into the CAPSL Intermediate Language [11] (CIL), also defined by the SRI group. The CIL translations can be used as input for many different analysis tools (i.e., Maude, PVS), but, as of this writing, translation software (called connectors) still needs to be written. For example, [12] shows an approach to designing a CIL connector to Maude.

Instead of following this route, we have defined the syntax of CAPSL directly in Maude and have written Maude code to translate CAPSL specifications into

Maude executable specifications. The following example is the CAPSL specification of the well-known Needham-Schroeder Public Key (NSPK) protocol [2] whose purpose is to enable two principals to exchange secrets in order to verify each other's identity.

```
PROTOCOL NSPK;
VARIABLES    A, B: PKUser;
             Na, Nb: Nonce, CRYPTO;
ASSUMPTIONS  HOLDS A: B;
MESSAGES     A -> B: {Na, A}pk(B);
             B -> A: {Na, Nb}pk(A);
             A -> B: {Nb}pk(B);
GOALS        SECRET Na;           SECRET Nb;
             PRECEDES B: A | Na;  PRECEDES A: B | Nb;
END;
```

This specification defines a protocol with two agents, A and B, and it is assumed that A knows about B. A public key encryption scheme is used. In this scheme, each agent is the only one that knows its secret key, but every agent knows every other agent's public key (e.g., A knows pk(B)). Finally, the only way to recover data encrypted with a public key is to use the corresponding secret key (i.e., $\{\{D\}\text{pk}(A)\}\text{sk}(A) = D$).

During each protocol run two nonces (unguessable numbers) are generated. First, A generates the nonce (Na) and sends it to B along with its own identity. These are encrypted with the public key of B (so only B can recover the data). Then B sends Na back to A along with a nonce it generates (Nb) encrypted with A's public key. Finally, A sends Nb back to B appropriately encrypted. The goals in the specification state that Na and Nb should remain secret (known only to A and B), that when A completes its run it agrees with B on the value of Na, and when B completes its run it agrees with A on the value of Nb.

Those familiar with the security protocol literature will note the similarity between specification of the messages above and the specifications that appear in the literature.

2.2   Protocol Environments

A CAPSL specification is directly input into our system. From such a specification, we generate a *protocol environment*. Such an environment is a Maude module that simulates the protocol. An environment contains an initial *configuration* of a protocol run and rewrite rules that manipulate configurations to simulate the behavior of protocol messages. A configuration contains data structures for messages and for *principals*. Principals are objects representing the agents that participate in a protocol. The principal for an agent is used to store information that it knows as a protocol run proceeds.

A configuration is defined more precisely as a four-tuple (Ms, Nc, Sc, Ps), where

- *Ms* is a set of messages that are currently traveling through the network. When principals receive messages, they remove them from the set, and sending messages inserts them into the set.
- *Nc* is a nonce counter. Each time a principal instantiates a nonce with a fresh value, it just takes the value of the nonce counter and increments it by one.[1]
- *Sc* is a session counter. Each time a new session is started, the counter is incremented by one. This is necessary to distinguish between separate runs of the protocol.[2]
- *Ps* is a set of principals.

Principals are three-tuples (N, Ks, Ss) for each regular protocol host, where

- *N* is the name of the principal.
- *Ks* is the initial knowledge of that principal.
- *Ss* is a set of sessions. Sessions are three-tuples $[Sid, Mid, AS]$ where *Sid* is an identifier unique to each separate run of the protocol, *Mid* is a message identifier that is initialized to zero and is incremented by one each time the principal processes a message, and *AS* is a set of assignments of values to protocol variables which is initially empty in a new session, with new assignments being added throughout the protocol run.

The initial configuration (*initConfig*) contains an empty message set and the nonce and the session counter are initialized to zero. The only element that has to be generated dynamically is the principal set. For example, an entry is created for each principal mentioned in the CAPSL specification (in the case of NSPK, *A* and *B*) and the appropriate knowledge is added to those entries. In the case of NSPK, add *B* to the knowledge of *A*, as specified in the HOLDS statement:

$$initConfig = (\emptyset, 0, 0, \{[A, \{B\}, \emptyset], [B, \emptyset, \emptyset]\}) \ .$$

The rewrite rules of a protocol environment simulate the behavior of each message by manipulating the environment. For example, the rule for the message $A \rightarrow B : \{Na, A\}\text{pk}(B)$, generates the nonce *Na*, records this in the principal for *A*, and places a message from *A* to *B* of the appropriate form in the configuration.

In general, for a protocol specification, our system generates one rewrite rule to initiate a run by sending the first message (see Fig. 1). Then for each message $i = 2, \ldots, n$, the system generates a rule to receive message $i - 1$, to update the receiver's knowledge, and to send message i. Also, the system generates a rule to receive message n and complete a protocol run. For example, the rule for the first message in NSPK looks like:

---

[1] The intruders do not exploit the fact that nonces are guessable. Hence, it has so far been unnecessary to generate random numbers for nonces.

[2] Some errors in protocols only come to light when more than one run occurs simultaneously.

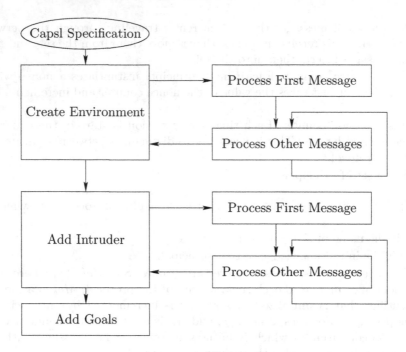

Fig. 1. Design overview

$$\big(Ms, Nc, Sc, \{[A, Ks, Ss], rest\}\big)$$
$$\Rightarrow \big(Ms \cup (A \to B : \{Na, A\}\mathrm{pk}(B)), Nc + 1, Sc + 1,$$
$$\{[A, Ks, Ss \cup \{(Sc, 1, \mathrm{Na} = Nc, \mathrm{A} = A, \mathrm{B} = B)\}], rest\}\big)$$
$$\text{if } B \in Ks .$$

Hence, if the initial configuration contains a principal A whose initial knowledge contains a principal B, add the message above to the message set, increment the nonce and session counters, and update A's knowledge of variable assignments. Note that the nonce counter has been used to create a new value for Na.

The protocol environment constructed from a CAPSL specification is executable, so a specification can be tested by running the Maude rewrite engine on the environment's initial configuration. For example, the configuration after one NSPK run looks like this:

$$\big(\emptyset, 2, 1, \{ \ [A, \{B\}, \{0, 2, \mathrm{A} = A, \mathrm{B} = B, \mathrm{Na} = 0, \mathrm{Nb} = 1\}],$$
$$[B, \emptyset, \{0, 2, \mathrm{A} = A, \mathrm{B} = B, \mathrm{Na} = 0, \mathrm{Nb} = 1\}]\}\big) \ .$$

More interestingly, we extend the environment by rewrite rules that represent an intruder and temporal formulas that represent the goals of a protocol. Our tool generates both the intruder and the formulas from an analysis of the CAPSL specification.

2.3 Extending the Protocol Environment by an Intruder

To simulate the presence of an intruder, we add a principal for the intruder to the initial configuration and generate rewrite rules enabling the intruder to send, receive, and intercept messages. All this is generated automatically based on the form of the messages in the CAPSL specification (again, see Fig. 1).

The intruder can be an honest participant in the protocol and/or it can send fake messages based on information it learns by intercepting (or overhearing) honest messages. Therefore we assume that the intruder knows the names of all other agents, and vice versa (all honest agents can initiate a protocol run with the intruder, other agents and themselves).[3] The intruder principal contains attributes for holding the content of intercepted messages. When the intruder intercepts a message containing tokens that it cannot decrypt, it stores those tokens for later decryption (in case it later intercepts the decryption key) or replay.[4] Data sent in the clear or contained in tokens that the intruder can decrypt are also stored. Hence, the intruder builds up sets of different kinds of data it has learned. It uses these data to construct and send fake messages to the honest hosts in a protocol. Obviously, the rewrite rules that model the intruder do not access or change the representation of the other agents. Like the other agents, the intruder implicitly knows its own secret key and all other public keys, so they do not have to be specified as initial knowledge. The initial configuration for the NSPK protocol including the intruder principal looks like this:

$$initConfig = (\emptyset, 0, 0, \{ [A, \{A, B, I\}, \emptyset], [B, \{A, B, I\}, \emptyset],$$
$$[I, \text{Keys} : \emptyset,$$
$$\text{Agents} : \{I, A, B\},$$
$$\text{Nonces} : \emptyset,$$
$$\text{encryptedTokens} : \emptyset]\}) \ .$$

Our tool uses the form of the messages in the CAPSL specification to generate the intruder so that it will only send messages that honest hosts will accept as being of the correct form. For example, for NSPK, one intruder rule generated

---

[3] This assumption seems reasonable; the intruder could as well learn about the other agents by first overhearing a regular protocol session. However, the search space for our brute-force protocol analysis grows exponentially with the number of parallel runs. Hence we try to minimize the number of runs that are necessary to find a flaw.

[4] One should note that finding out which terms can be decrypted or accessed is not trivial. Suppose the intruder overheard an encrypted message, and learns about the appropriate decryption key later on. Then the intruder has to apply the key to the encrypted term, and recursively apply it to any subterm. During this process, new keys might be learned, so all other encrypted terms need to be checked again.

sends a message of the form $\{Na, Nb\}\mathrm{pk}(A)$ to the honest host A if the intruder learns of two nonces (Na, Nb) used in the protocol run (or a separate run occurring simultaneously). The intruder can also send this message if it overheard a previous message containing the term $\{Na, Nb\}\mathrm{pk}(A)$. In this case the intruder would send a token without knowing its content.

Our implementation of intruders is greatly simplified by the fact that we can rely on the space of all possible rule sequences being searched. Hence, intruder rules are written to send messages nondeterministically, relying on the fact that different rule sequences will actually send those messages at all possible different points in a protocol run. So, for example, the model checker's search will guarantee that in every sequence in which the intruder learns Na and Nb, all following subsequences will be examined in which the fake message $\{Na, Nb\}\mathrm{pk}(A)$ is sent to all honest hosts at all different times.

The following list shows the names and brief explanations of all rewrite rules that our tool generates to model the NSPK protocol:

NSPK_init: allows a regular host to initiate a protocol run.

NSPK_step_2: receives message one, and sends message two for a regular host.

NSPK_step_3: receives message two, and sends message the final message for a regular host.

NSPK_cleanup: models receipt of the final message for a regular host.

Intruder_remember_content: allows the intruder to overhear an arbitrary message.

Intruder_start_session_content: allows the intruder to start a new session by assembling a valid first message (from elements that it learned in previous runs).

Intruder_start_session_token: allows the intruder to start a new session by replaying an encrypted token (that it learned in a previous run).

Intruder_fake_content_2: reply to a first protocol message by assembling a valid response from known protocol variables.

Intruder_fake_token_2: reply to a first protocol message by replaying an encrypted token (from another protocol run).

Intruder_fake_content_3: see **Intruder_fake_content_2**.

Intruder_fake_token_3: see **Intruder_fake_token_2**.

This relatively short list of rewrite rules shows a trade-off between a complete brute-force approach and a more directed search. The intruder rules could probably be reduced to two rules, namely **Intruder_remember_content** and new rule that tries to send all messages that can be assembled from the intruder's knowledge. However, that behavior would definitely lead to a search space explosion, especially for sophisticated protocols. On the other hand, too many restrictions on the intruder's abilities will prevent flaws from being found.

As mentioned above, our design assures that only messages of the correct format are being send. This keeps the search space at a reasonable size, without losing too much generality.[5] For a detailed description of the translation process, see [9].

2.4 Modeling Protocol Goals

To specify the goals appearing in a CAPSL specification, our tool generates an LTL or a CTL formula, so that either Maude's built-in LTL model checker can be used to check the goals or our CTL model checker can be applied. The LTL model checker is invoked on a formula of the form $initConfig \models \phi$, where ϕ is the LTL formula to check. When invoked, the model checker tries to verify the truth of ϕ, expanding the search space by applying rewrite rules of the protocol environment to configurations in all possible ways, beginning with $initConfig$.

The LTL formula generated from CAPSL goals contains references to functions defined equationally in the Maude module generated for an intruder. For example, for the goals of NSPK, our tool will generate

$$initConfig \models \Box \left(\neg \, secretExposed(Na) \wedge \neg \, secretExposed(Nb) \right.$$
$$\left. \wedge \neg \, disagreement(A, B, Na) \wedge \neg \, disagreement(B, A, Nb) \right) \, ,$$

where the functions $secretExposed$ and $disagreement$ are also dynamically generated based on the protocol specification. The formula reads "starting in configuration $initConfig$, it is always true that Na and Nb are not exposed, and A and B do not disagree upon the values of Na and Nb (depending on who has finished the protocol run)". For example, the CAPSL term PRECEDES B: A | Na; from the NSPK specification is translated to $disagreement(A, B, Na)$, which evaluates to $true$ if a configuration contains a protocol run between A and B, where A has finished the protocol run but A and B do not agree upon the value of Na.[6] The function $secretExposed$ is designed similarly: it evaluates to $true$ if a configuration contains a protocol run where the intruder finds out the value of a secret variable without acting as a legitimate host in the appropriate protocol run.

2.5 Applying a Model Checker

Finally, we can apply the LTL model checker to evaluate if the LTL formula holds, and either receive the result $true$ (no bug was found) or a sequence of environment states which show how the insecure state was reached.

Figure 2 shows the protocol flaw that our system discovered. It consists of two parallel sessions, where the intruder impersonates A while running the protocol with B. At the end, B thinks it ran the protocol with A, although A has never heard of B. This flaw was first reported in [2].

---

[5] Under these assumptions, our tool does not detect type-flaw attacks. Type-flaw attacks occur in protocols where agents might accept incorrectly typed messages (i.e., the name of an agent is interpreted as a nonce).

[6] We chose to use $\neg \, disagreement$ instead of $agreement$, because Maude's partial matching ability provides for a simple implementation of $disagreement$. The same argument counts for $\neg \, secretExposed$ and $secret$.

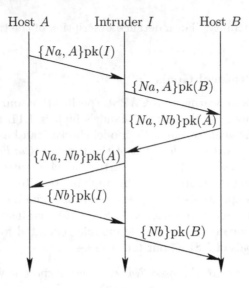

Host A Intruder I Host B

Fig. 2. Exploiting a bug in NSPK

3   Evaluation

Because the LTL model checker is built into Maude, it has the advantage of speed over our CTL model checker. However, with this speed comes two disadvantages. First, the LTL model checker can only be used on problems with finite state spaces. Some specifications of protocols have infinite state spaces. Second, for some finite state spaces, the LTL model checker consumes all of the memory on our systems.

In cases where these disadvantages surface, we use our CTL model checker instead. While this model checker is slower because it is implemented in Maude, it uses iterative deepening search and is three-valued (i.e., a CTL formula can be evaluated as unknown). As a result, it is much more memory efficient and can be used to check to a bounded depth in an infinite state space. The CTL model checker can often determine a definite truth value for a formula even for problems with infinite state spaces.

Once Maude Version 2 is released, an interesting project would be the connection to real networks and protocol implementations. Maude Version 2 will have TCP/IP networking capabilities, so it might be possible to execute the specifications in a real network.

CAPSL is a highly extensible language, and contains some constructs which are rarely used in protocol specifications. Therefore, we decided to implement only a subset of the CAPSL language to focus on the actual protocol analysis.

More research could be carried out on the design of the rewrite rules and equations. Different designs should be tested and evaluated (i.e., a rewrite rule that *sends* a message could check if that message can actually be received by another agent, or sending and receiving might be processed in one single rewrite rule). Testing different model checkers and search algorithms might also lead to better results. In this sense better could mean quicker, less memory consuming, or with fewer restrictions on the search space.

4 Conclusion

We provided a framework for completely automated protocol analysis, starting at a well defined input specification, and ending up with an executable specification of a protocol environment, an intruder, and a connection to an LTL or CTL model checker.

The ability to easily use two different model checkers illustrates an important advantage of Maude's meta-level architecture for our purposes. Our grand plan is to develop a tool suite for analyzing many different kinds of properties of agent-based systems. Such analyses could include different kinds of static analysis (e.g., type checking) of specifications, different kinds of dynamic analysis (e.g., model checking), and different types of theorem proving (e.g., inductive proofs used to justify simplifications of a state space to make model checking possible in that space). It has been our experience (as well as others [13]) that Maude's meta-level architecture greatly simplifies the development of such integrated architectures. For example, to use a different model checker, only the specification of the goals needs to be adapted; the usage of all other components is defined by Maude's module syntax and semantics.

Another advantage of our intruder based design is that once a protocol flaw is found, we can extract from the counterexample an intruder that exploits the weakness.

References

[1] Abadi, M., Needham, R.M.: Prudent engineering practice for cryptographic protocols. Software Engineering **22** (1996) 6–15
    http://citeseer.nj.nec.com/abadi96prudent.html.
[2] Lowe, G.: Breaking and fixing the Needham-Schroeder public-key protocol using FDR. In: Tools and Algorithms for Construction and Analysis of Systems. (1996) 147–166 http://citeseer.nj.nec.com/lowe96breaking.html.
[3] Lowe, G.: Some new attacks upon security protocols. In: PCSFW: Proceedings of The 9th Computer Security Foundations Workshop, IEEE Computer Society Press (1996) http://citeseer.nj.nec.com/article/lowe96some.html.
[4] Lowe, G.: A family of attacks upon authentication protocols. Technical report, Department of Mathematics and Computer Science, University of Leicester (1997) http://citeseer.nj.nec.com/lowe97family.html.
[5] Lowe, G.: Casper: A compiler for the analysis of security protocols. In: PCSFW: Proceedings of The 10th Computer Security Foundations Workshop, IEEE Computer Society Press (1997) http://citeseer.nj.nec.com/lowe98casper.html.
[6] Baalen, J.V., Caldwell, J.L., Mishra, S.: Specifying and checking fault-tolerant agent-based protocols using Maude. In: FAABS. (2000) 180–193 http://citeseer.nj.nec.com/vanbaalen00specifying.html.

[7] Clavel, M., Durán, F., Eker, S., Lincoln, P., Martí-Oliet, N., Meseguer, J., Quesada, J.F.: Maude: Specification and programming in rewriting logic (1999) Manual distributed as documentation of the Maude system, Computer Science Laboratory, SRI International. http://maude.csl.sri.com/manual.

[8] Denker, G., Millen, J., Rueß, H.: The CAPSL integrated protocol environment. Technical Report SRI-CSL-2000-02, Computer Science Laboratory, SRI International (2000) http://www.csl.sri.com/papers/sri-csl-2000-02/.

[9] Böhne, T.: A general intruder for security protocols in Maude. Master's thesis, University of Wyoming (2002)

[10] Denker, G., Meseguer, J., Talcott, C.: Protocol specification and analysis in Maude. In: In Proceedings of Workshop on Formal Methods and Security Protocols. (1998) http://maude.csl.sri.com/papers/abstract/DMTprotocol_1998.html.

[11] Denker, G., Millen, J.: CAPSL intermediate language. In: Formal Methods and Security Protocols (CAV Workshop). (1999) http://citeseer.nj.nec.com/denker99capsl.html.

[12] Denker, G.: Design of a CIL connector to Maude. In: 2000 Workshop on Formal Methods and Computer Security, Chicago, USA (2000) http://www.csl.sri.com/users/denker/publ/Den00.ps.gz.

[13] Clavel, M., Durán, F., Eker, S., Meseguer, J.: Building equational proving tools by reflection in rewriting logic. In: Proceedings of the CafeOBJ Symposium '98, Numazu, Japan, CafeOBJ Project (1998) http://maude.csl.sri.com/papers.

Towards Interaction Protocol Operations for Large Multi-agent Systems

Joaquín Peña, Rafael Corchuelo, and José Luis Arjona

Dpto. de Lenguajes y Sistemas Informáticos
Avda. de la Reina Mercedes, s/n. Sevilla 41.012 (Spain)
joaquinp@lsi.us.es, www.lsi.us.es/~tdg

Abstract. It is widely accepted that role-based modelling is quite adequate in the context of multi-agent systems (MAS) modelling techniques. Unfortunately, very little work has been reported on how to describe the relationships between several role models. Furthermore, many authors agree on that protocols need to be encapsulated into high-level abstractions. The synthesis of role models is an operation presented in the OORAM methodology that allows us to build new role models from others in order to represent the interrelations they have. To the best of our knowledge this operation has to be performed manually at protocol level and works with protocols expressed by means of messages. In this paper, we present two algorithms to extract the protocol of a role from the protocol of a role model and vice versa that automate the synthesis or role models at the protocol level. Furthermore, in order to deal with protocol descriptions in a top down approach both operations work with protocols expressed by means of an abstraction call multi-role interaction (mRI).

1 Introduction

When a large system is modelled, complexity becomes a critical factor that has to be dealt with properly. In order to tackle complexity G. Booch recommended several powerful tools such as: Decomposition, Abstraction, and Hierarchy [5]. In addition, these tools were also presented as appropriate for Agent-Oriented Software Engineering (AOSE) for complex MAS, and were adapted to this field in [18] as follows:

- Decomposition: It is based on the principle *divide and conquer*. Its main advantage is that it helps to limit the designers scope to a portion of the problem.
- Abstraction: It is based on defining simplified models of the system that emphasises some details and avoid others. It is interesting since it limits the designer scope of interest and the attention can be focused on the most important details.
- Organisation/Hierarchy: It relies on identifying and managing the relationships between the various subsystems in the problem. It makes it possible to

M.G. Hinchey et al. (Eds.): 'FAABS 2002, LNAI 2699, pp. 79–91, 2003.

group together various basic components and deal with them as higher-level units of analysis, and, provides means of describing the high-level relationships between several units.

Unfortunately, we think that these tools have not been carefully applied in the approaches that are appearing in this field. We have identified several problems in current methodologies that our approach tries to solve.

On the one hand, there exists a huge semantic gap in MAS protocol description methodologies because most of them first identify which tasks have to be performed, and then use low level descriptions such as sequences of messages to detail them. Although these messages may represent a high level view of a protocol, which shall be refined later, the tasks that are performed are formulated as a set of messages. This representation implies that the abstraction level falls dramatically since a task requires several messages to be represented. For instance, an information request between two agents must be represented with two messages at least (one to ask, and another to reply). This introduces a semantic gap between tasks and their internal design since it is difficult to identify the tasks represented in a sequence of messages. This representation becomes an important problem regarding readability and manageability of large MAS and can be palliated using the abstraction tool presented above.

On the other hand, in AOSE is widely accepted that describing the system as a set of role models that are mapped onto agents is quite adequate since it applies the *decomposition* tool [6,12,21,19,22,23,34]. Unfortunately, we have failed to find methodologies for MAS that use some interesting ideas about role modelling presented by Reenskaug and Andersen in the OORAM methodology [1,27]. Obviously, when we deal with a complex and large systems several role models may appear, and usually, they are interrelated. The role model synthesis operation [2], attempts to detail how role models are related, thus applying the *organisation tool*. This operation consists of describing new synthesised role models in terms of others. In a synthesised role model, new roles may appear and synthesised roles may also appear as aggregation of others. Unfortunately, OORAM also suffers from the first problem we have shown above since it deals with behaviour specification in terms of messages.

In this paper, we provide the first step towards the solution of these problems enumerated above using the tools proposed by Booch: i) In order to apply the *abstraction tool*, we have defined an abstraction called multi-role interaction (mRI) which encapsulates the interaction protocol (hereafter protocol) corresponding to a task that is performed by an arbitrary number of roles. mRIs are used as first modelling class elements to represent an abstract view of the protocol of a role model which can be refined with the techniques proposed in [25]. ii) In order to apply the *organisational tool*, we have also defined two operations on protocols (described in terms of mRIs) to automate and ease the synthesis operation since it operates on interaction protocols of a role instead of with the whole interaction protocol of a role model: the first one, called decomposition, infers a role protocol from a role model protocol automatically; and the second one, that we called composition, infers a role model protocol from a set of role protocols automatically.

This paper is organized as follows: in Section 2, we present the related work and the advantages of our approach over others; in Section 3, we present the example we use; in Section 4, we present the protocol abstraction we have defined; in Section 5, we show how to describe the protocol of a role model; in Section 6, we present the algorithms to compose and decompose protocols, and, in Section 7, we present our main conclusions.

2   Related Work

In the context of distributed systems many authors have identified the need for advanced interaction models and have proposed multi-object interactions that encapsulates a piece of protocol between several objetcs [24]. Furthermore, most object-oriented analysis and design methods also recognise the need for coordinating several objects and provide designers with tools to model such multi-object collaborations. Different terms are used to refer to them: object diagrams [4], process models [7], message connections [8], data-flow diagrams [28], collaboration graphs [32], scenario diagrams [27], collaborations [13,29]. In MAS methodologies many authors have also proposed abstraction to model co-ordinated actions such as nested protocols [3], interactions [6] or micro-protocols [22], and so on. Unfortunately, the abstractions presented above are usually used to hide unnecessary details at some level of abstraction, reuse the protocol descriptions in new systems, and improve modularity and readability; however, most designers use message–based descriptions.

We think that most AOSE approaches model protocols at low level of abstraction since they require the designer to model complex cooperations as message-based protocols from the beginning. This issue has been identified in the GAIA Methodology [33], and also in the work of Caire *et. al.* [6], where the protocol description process starts with a high level view based on describing tasks as complex communication primitives (hereafter interactions). We think that the ideas presented in both papers are adequate for this kind of systems where interactions are more important than in object-oriented programming. As the methodologies GAIA and Caire's Methodology, we also use interactions (mRIs) to deal with the first stage of protocol modelling.

In the GAIA methodology, protocols are modelled using abstract textual templates. Each template represents an interaction or task to be performed between an arbitrary number of participants. In [6], Caire *et al.* propose a methodology in which the first protocol view is a static view of the interactions in a system. Later, the internals of these interactions are described using AUML [3].

Unfortunately, the operations we propose are difficult to be integrated with these methodologies. The reason why this happens is that we have found neither an interaction model for MAS able to describe formally a sequence protocol abstractions, nor operations on these high level protocol definitions. GAIA protocol descriptions, for example, are based on textual description thus it is difficult to reason formally on them. In Caire's methodology, it is not shown how to sequence interactions. Although Koning *et al.* describe the sequence of execution of their abstraction using a logic-based formulae (*CPDL*), which consists of an extension of transition function of Finite State Automata (hereafter FSA), they do not define operations to operate with protocols. In our approach, we also define the sequence of mRI by means of Finite State Automaton (FSA) which has been also used by others authors at message level. We have chosen FSAs because this technique has been proved to be adequate for representing the behaviour of reactive agents [11,14,16,22].

Regarding the operations we present to the best of our knowledge the decomposition operation has not been defined before in this context. This operation can be useful for reuse, performing synthesis of role models since it operates with the protocol of a role instead of with the whole protocol and to map several protocol onto the same agent class. Unfortunately, in OORAM methodology such operation has to be applied manually to UML sequence diagrams.

The inverse operation, that we call composition, has been already defined by other authors, but, to the best of our knowledge, they do not use interaction with an arbitrary number of participants as we do [9,16,30,31]. This operation can be useful for building new role models reusing already defined role protocols stored in a behaviour repository, performing tests for adaptive behaviours [16], deadlock detection or to understand easily the protocol of a new role model [25]. Unfortunately, in OORAM this operation has to be also performed manually.

3   The Example

To illustrate our approach, we present an example in which a MAS delivers satellite images on a pay per use basis. We have divide the problem into two role models: one whose goal is obtaining the images (*images role model*) and the other for paying them (*purchase role model*). This decomposition of the problem allow us to deal with both cases separately.

In the *Images role model* the user (role *Client*) has to specify the images features that he or she needs (resolution, target, format, etcetera). Furthermore, we need a terrestrial centre (role *Buffer*) to store the images in a buffer because the throughput of a satellite (role *Satellite*) is higher than the average user can process and we need to analyse images features in order to determine their total price which is the goal of role *Counter*.

In the *Purchase role model* we need to contact the payment system to conclude the purchase. It involves three different roles: a customer role (Customer), a customer account manager role (*Customer's Bank*), and a terrestrial centre account manager role (*Buffer's Bank*). When a customer acquires a set of images he uses his or her debit–card to pay them, the agent playing role *Customer* agrees with a *Customer's Bank* agent and *Buffer's Bank* agent on performing a sequence of tasks to transfer the money from the customer account to the buffer account. If the *Customer's Bank* cannot afford the purchase because it has not enough money, the *Customer's Bank* agent then pays on hire–purchase.

4   Our Protocol Abstraction: Multi-role Interactions

The description of the protocol of a role model is made by means of mRIs. This provides an abstract view of the protocol that makes it easier to face the problem at the first stages of system modelling. Thus, we do not have to take into account all the messages that are exchanged in a role model in stages where these details have not been identified clearly.

A multi-role interaction (mRI) is an abstraction that we propose to encapsulate a set of messages for an arbitrary number of roles. At conceptual level, an mRI encapsulates each task that a role model should execute to perform its goal. These tasks can be inferred in a hierarchical diagram [20] where we can identify which tasks shall execute each role model.

mRIs are based on the ideas presented in two interaction models for distributed systems [15,10]. We have made that choice because both models have a set of formal tools that may be used for MAS systems improving the power of our approach, this allows, to perform deadlock testing and automatic interaction refinements [25] or efficient distributed implementations [26]. The definition of an mRI is:

$$\{(G(\beta))\} \ \& \ mRI\_name[r_1, r_2, \ldots, r_N]$$

Where mRI_name is an unified identifier of the interaction and $r_1, r_2, \ldots, r_N$ are the roles that execute the mRI mRI_name. β is the set of beliefs of agents playing the roles implied in the mRI and $G(\beta)$ is a boolean condition over β. This guard is partitioned in a set of subconditions, one for each role. $G(\beta)$ holds iff the conjunction of all subconditions of each role is *true*.

The idea behind guarded interactions has been adapted from the interaction model in which our proposal is based; furthermore, Koning *et al.* also adopt a similar idea. It promotes the proactivity of agents as we can see in [10,22] because agents are able to decide whether executing an mRI or not.

Thus, an mRI x shall be executed if the guard of the mRI holds and all roles that participate on it are in a state where the x is one of mRIs that can be executed. Furthermore, all of them must not be executing other mRIs since the interaction execution is made atomically and each role can execute only one mRI at the same time. For example, if we consider FSAs in Figure 3 after executing an mRI sequence that makes the the *Satellite* to be in state 1, the *Buffer* in state 4, the *Client* in state 8 and the *Counter* in state 11, if all the guards holds, we can execute *Receive*, *Send* or *LastSat*. In this case *LastBuffer* cannot be executed because it requires the *Buffer* to be in state 5.

Finally, for each interaction we should describe some details that we enumerate roughly below since it is not the purpose of this paper. To describe an mRI internally, we should include the sequence of messages using AUML. Furthermore, we may use coordination or negotiation patterns from a repository if its possible (FIPA has define a repository of interaction patterns [1]) and an objective

---

[1] http://www.fipa.org/specs/fipa00025/XC00025E.html

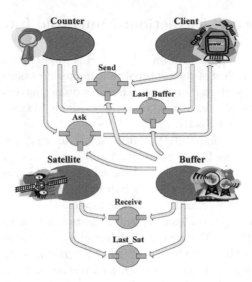

Fig. 1. Collaboration diagram of *Images role model*

function that determines which of available mRIs shall be better to execute if several of them can do so at the same moment.

Regarding the example, the description of one of the mRIs of the *Images role model* which it is used to ask for images (see Figure 3) is:

$$\{Counter.Connected(Buffer.ID())\&Counter.enable()\}\&$$
$$ask[Client, Buffer, Counter]$$

The rest of the mRIs in the *Images role model* are: *ask*, which is used to ask for images, *send*, which sends an image from the *Satellite* to the *Buffer*, *receive*, which sends an image from *Buffer* to *Client*, *LastSat*, which indicates the last image for transferring from *Satellite* to *Buffer* and stores information about images in a log file, and, *LastBuffer*, which indicates the last image for transferring from *Buffer* to *Client* and makes the *Counter* to calculate the bill. The static relation between these mRIs and the roles that perform them is represented in the collaboration diagram in Figure 1.

5   Modelling the Protocol of a Role Model

Once the roles and its mRIs have been identified we must describe how to sequence them. Thus, the protocol of a role model is defined as the set of sequences of mRIs execution it may performs. We can use two equivalent representations to describe the protocol of a role model (see Figure 2):

– Representing the protocol of the role model as a set of FSAs, one for each role (see Figure 3). Thus, in a role model with N roles we have N FSAs

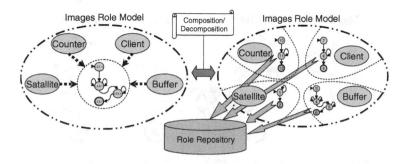

Fig. 2. Composition/Decomposition of protocol for the *Images role model*

A_i where each $A_i = (S_i, \Sigma_i, \delta_i, s_i^0, F_i)$, where S_i is a set of states, Σ_i is a vocabulary where each symbol $\sigma \in \Sigma_i$ represents an mRI, $\delta_i : S_i \times \Sigma_i \to S_i$ is the transition function that represents an mRI execution, $s_i^0 \in S_i$ is a initial state and $F_i \subseteq S_i$ is the set of final states. Thus, the set of words produced by this set of FSAs is set of possible traces of execution of mRIs. All this FSAs executes its transitions coordinately as it is shown in Section 4. Roughly speaking, when an mRI is executed by more than one role we must perform a transition in all of its participant roles. Each of these transitions represents the part of the mRIs that each of them performs. Whereby, to execute an mRI we must transit from one state to another in all the roles that participate in it.

– Representing the protocol of the role model as a whole using a single FSA for all the roles (see Figure 4). This FSAs is of the form $B = (S, \Sigma, \delta, s^0, F)$ where S is a set of states that represents one state for each FSA of roles, Σ is a vocabulary where each symbol $\sigma \in \Sigma$ represents an mRI, $\delta_i : S \times \Sigma \to S$ is the transition function that represents an mRI execution, $s_i^0 \in S_i$ is the initial state and $F \subseteq S$ is the set of final states. Thus, the set of words produced by this FSA is set of possible traces of execution of mRIs.

If we are dealing with a new role model, it may be more adequate to use a single FSA than one for each role since we see the problem in a centralised manner. The protocol for the *Images role model* by means of a single FSA is shown in Figure 4.

Once the protocol of all role models in our system have been described we can synthesise those role models that are interrelated. In our example, both role models are interrelated since the images obtained in the *Images role model* have to be paid using the *Purchase role model*.

In order to synthesise role models, we have to identify which roles are related and we have to merge their protocols to create the new synthesised role model. In our example, the synthesised role model *Purchase-Images role model* in Figure 5 is build by creating a new role where the protocol of the *Customer* and the *Client* is merged.

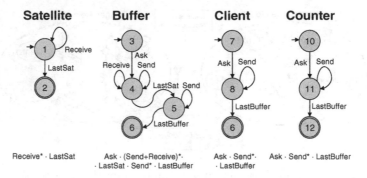

Fig. 3. FSAs of roles of *Images role model*

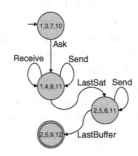

Fig. 4. FSA of *Images role model*

Thus, we have to know the protocol of both the *Customer* and the *Client* in order to build the new role model. This can be done using the decomposition operation.

Once we have built the protocol of the *Client/Customer* role, it is difficult to infer mentally which shall be the protocol of the new synthesised role model. Then, we can use the composition operation to infer it. In addition, we can perform deadlock testing in order to assure the correctness of the new protocol [25].

6   Composition and Decomposition of Interaction Protocols

These operations perform a transformation from one representation of protocol to another. As it is shown in the followings sections, these operations do not take guards into account. As we have shown above, a guard allows agents to decide if they want to execute an mRI or not. Thus, guards can make some execution traces of the protocol impossible. Unfortunately, we cannot determine this at design time. Even, if we are dealing with adaptive agents these decision can change at runtime. Thus, in both operations, we work with the set of all possible traces leaving proactivity as a runtime feature.

6.1 Composition

The composition operation is an algorithm that builds a role model FSA from a set of FSA of roles obtained from a behaviour repository or from synthesis of role models.

To represent the role protocol of each role in a role model we use the FSAs $A_i = (S_i, \Sigma_i, \delta_i, s_i^0, F_i)$ $(i = 1, 2, \ldots, N)$. Thus, the composition algorithm is defined as a new FSA of the form $B = (S, \Sigma, \delta, s^0, F)$, where:

- $S = S_1 \times \ldots \times S_N$,
- $\Sigma = \bigcup_{i=1}^{n} \Sigma_i$,
- $\delta(a, (s_1, \ldots, s_n)) = (s_1', \ldots, s_N')$ iff $\forall\ i \in [1..N] \cdot (a \notin \Sigma_i \wedge s_i = s_i') \vee$
  $\vee\ (a \in \Sigma_i \wedge \delta(a, s_i) = s_i')$,
- $s^0 = (s_1^0, \ldots, s_N^0)$, and
- $F = F_1 \times \ldots \times F_N$.

This algorithm builds the new FSA exploring all the feasible executions of mRIs. Their states are computed as the cartesian product of all states. Each state of this FSA is formed by a N-tuple that stores a state of each role. To execute an mRI, we have to preform it from a tuple-state where the mRI can be execute to change to a new tuple-state where the states of roles implied in the mRI shall only change. Thus, for each new tuple-state we check if an mRI may be executed (all their roles can do it from its corresponding state in the tuple-state); if so, we add it to the result. Finally, the final state of the role model FSA is formed of all possible combinations of final states of each A_i and the initial state is a tuple with the initial state of each A_i.

Intuitively, it is easier to comprehend a protocol if it is described by means of a single FSA than if we use a set of them. Furthermore, we can perform deadlock testing on it to assure that the synthesis we have made is deadlock free and results in what we have thought when we synthesised them. Furthermore, this representation is easier to understand than several separated FSAs. With this operation, we can obtain automatically the FSA in Figure 4 that represents the protocol executed by the FSAs in Figure 3 of *Images role model*.

6.2 Decomposition

To obtain the protocol of a role we must take into account the mRIs a role execute only. That is to say, we can take all the possible traces that the FSA of the role model produces and ignore the mRIs that the role does not execute. For instance, if we take the a trace *(Ask, Receive, Receive, Send, LastSat, Send, LastBuffer)* from the FSA of the *Images role model*, the trace that the role *Satellite* executes is *(Receive, Receive, LastSat)* since it participates only in mRIs *Receive* and

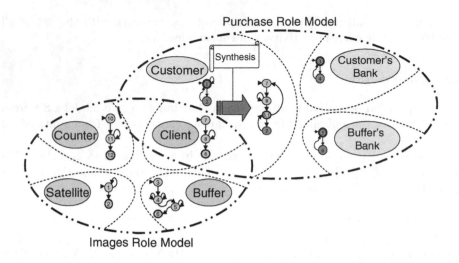

Fig. 5. Example of synthesis operation. Images and Purchase role models

LastSat. If we perform the same operation for all the traces produced by the FSA of a role model for each of its roles, we can obtain their protocol.

In [17, page 60] it is proved that if we take a regular expression r we can obtain a new regular expression $r' = h(r)$ where h is a function that replaces each occurrence of symbols a in r by another regular expression obtaining r'. If $L(r)$ is the language accepted by r, it is proved that $h(r) = h(L(r)) = r'$, that it is to say, the language accepted by r' is the same language accepted by applying h(r) to every word in $L(r)$.

Thus, we can perform the decomposition operation to obtain the FSAof each role from the FSA of a role model as follows:

- We obtain the regular expression of the FSA of the role model using one of the algorithms presented in [17]. In our example, it is: $Ask \cdot (Send + Receive)^* \cdot LastSat \cdot Send^* \cdot LastBuffer$.
- We take the regular expression of each role and we replace the mRISs where the role do not participate by ϵ (empty word). For example, the result for the *Client* role is: $Ask \cdot Send^* \cdot LastBuffer$.
- Finally, we build the FSA corresponding to each regular expression obtained in the previous step using the algorithms presented in [17].

As we illustrate in Figure 2, we can use this algorithm to obtain the FSAs showed in Figure 3 from the FSA in Figure 4. If we compose then again, we obtain the same result.

As we have sketched in Section 5, we can use one of the FSA obtained to build a new synthesised role where the *Customer* and the *Client* are merged generating the protocol represented in Figure 5. In this Figure the mRI *Approval* is used to check if the *Customer* has enough money to perform the purchase, *Transfer* is used to transferring the money from *Customer's Bank* to *Buffer's Bank*, and

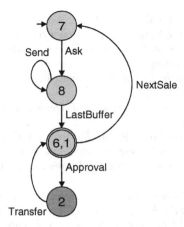

Fig. 6. FSAs of synthesised role: Customer and Client

NextSale prepares the *Customer* and *Client* for next purchase. Finally, we can compose the protocol of both role models in order to improve the readability of the description or to perform deadlock testing.

7   Conclusions

In this paper, we have presented an approach that puts together several ideas from different research contexts to ease protocol modelling of large MASs since our approach provides the tools to decompose, abstract and organise the descriptions.

With this purpose, we have presented two operations to automatically tackle with protocols. These operations are useful for large MASs since they allow us to define the interrelation of several role models as a new synthesised role model without dealing with protocols manually. Furthermore, they ease the reuse of protocol already defined for other systems.

In our approach, we also propose mRIs for avoiding to determine all the messages that agents have to interchange in early modelling stages. This allows us to describe protocols in a layered method since we can describe the tasks that a role model has to perform at a high level of abstraction to describe each mRI internally later.

References

1. E. Andersen. *Conceptual Modeling of Objects: A Role Modeling Approach*. PhD thesis, University of Oslo, 1997.
2. E. P. Andersen and T. Reenskaug. System design by composing structures of interacting objects. In Ole Lehrmann Madsen, editor, *ECOOP '92, European Conference on Object-Oriented Programming, Utrecht, The Netherlands*, volume 615 of *Lecture Notes in Computer Science*, pages 133–152. Springer-Verlag, New York, NY, 1992.

3. B. Bauer, J. Muller, and J. Odell. Agent uml: A formalism for specifying multiagent interaction. In M. Wooldridge and P. Ciancarini, editors, *Proceedings of 22nd International Conference on Software Engineering (ISCE)*, LNCS, pages 91–103, Berlin, 2001. Springer-Verlag.
4. G. Booch. *Object-Oriented Design with Applications*. Benjamin/Cummings, Redwood City, CA, 1990.
5. G. Booch. *Object–Oriented Analysis and Design with Applications*. Addison-Wesley, 2 edition, 1994.
6. G. Caire, F. Leal, P. Chainho, R. Evans, F. Garijo, J. Gomez, J. Pavon, P. Kearney, J. Stark, and P. Massonet. Agent oriented analysis using MESSAGE/UML. In *Proceedings of Agent-Oriented Software Engineering (AOSE'01)*, pages 101–108, Montreal, 2001.
7. D. de Champeaux. Object-oriented analysis and top-down software development. In *Proceedings of the European Conference on Object-Oriented Programming, ECOOP'91*, volume 512 of *Lecture Notes in Computer Science*, pages 360–375. Springer–Verlag, 1991.
8. P. Coad and E. Yourdon. *Object-Oriented Analysis*. Computing Series. Yourdon Press, Englewood Cliffs, NJ, 1990.
9. J. C. Corbett. Evaluating deadlock detection methods for concurrent software. *IEEE Transactions on Software Engineering*, 22(3):161–180, March 1996.
10. J. C. Cruz. OpenCoLaS a coordination framework for CoLaS dialects. In *Proceedings of COORDINATION 2002*, York, United Kingdom, 2002.
11. D. Denning. *Information warfare and security*. Addison-Wesley, Reading, MA, USA, 1999. ACM order number 704982.
12. R. Depke, R. Heckel, and J. M. Kuster. Improving the agent-oriented modeling process by roles. In Jörg P. Müller, Elisabeth Andre, Sandip Sen, and Claude Frasson, editors, *Proceedings of the Fifth International Conference on Autonomous Agents*, pages 640–647, Montreal, Canada, May 2001. ACM Press.
13. D.F. D'Souza and A.C. Wills. *Objects, Components, and Frameworks with UML: The Catalysis Approach*. Addison-Wesley, Reading, Mass., 1999.
14. L. J. Fogel, A. J. Owens, and M. J. Walsh. *Artificial Intelligence through Simulated Evolution*. John Wiley & Sons, New York, 1966.
15. N. Francez and I. Forman. *Interacting processes: A multiparty approach to coordinated distributed programming*. Addison-Wesley, 1996.
16. D. F. Gordon. APT agents: Agents that are adaptive, predictable, and timely. *Lecture Notes in Computer Science*, 1871:278–293, 2001.
17. J. E. Hopcroft and Jeffrey D. Ullman. *Introduction to Automata Theory, Languages, and Computation*. Addison-Wesley, Reading, Massachusetts, 1979.
18. N. R. Jennings. Agent-Oriented Software Engineering. In Francisco J. Garijo and Magnus Boman, editors, *Proceedings of the 9th European Workshop on Modelling Autonomous Agents in a Multi-Agent World : Multi-Agent System Engineering (MAAMAW-99)*, volume 1647, pages 1–7. Springer-Verlag: Heidelberg, Germany, 30– 2 1999.
19. E. Kendall. Agent software engineering with role modelling. In P. Ciancarini and M. Wooldridge, editors, *First International Workshop of Agent-Oriented Software Engineering, AOSE 2000*, number 1957 in LNCS, pages 163–170, Limerick, Ireland, June 2001. Springer-Verlag.
20. E. Kendall, U. Palanivelan, and S. Kalikivayi. Capturing and structuring goals: Analysis patterns. In *Proceedings of the 3rd European Conference on Pattern Languages of Programming and Computing*, Germany, July 1998.

21. E. A. Kendall. Role modeling for agent system analysis, design, and implementation. *IEEE Concurrency*, 8(2):34–41, April/June 2000.
22. J. Koning, M.Huget, J. Wei, and X. Wang. Extended modeling languages for interaction protocol design. In M. Wooldridge, P. Ciancarini, and G. Weiss, editors, *Proceedings of Second Internationa Workshop on Agent-Oriented Software Engineering (AOSE'02)*, LNCS, Montreal, Canada, May, 2001. Springer-Verlag.
23. J. Odell, H. V. D. Parunak, and B. Bauer. Representing agent interaction protocols in uml. In *Proceedings of the 1th Int. Workshop on Agent-Oriented Software Engeenering (AOSE'2000)*, number 1957 in LNCS, page Apendix, Limerick, Ireland, June 2000. Springer-Verlag.
24. G. Papadopoulos and F. Arbab. Coordination models and languages. In *Advances in Computers*, volume 46. Academic Press, 1998.
25. J. Peña, R. Corchuelo, and J. L. Arjona. A top down approach for mas protocol descriptions. In *ACM Symposium on Applied Computing SAC'03*, page to be published, Melbourne, Florida, USA, 2003. ACM Press.
26. J.A. Pérez, R. Corchuelo, D. Ruiz, and M. Toro. An order-based, distributed algorithm for implementing multiparty interactions. In *Fifth International Conference on Coordination Models and Languages COORDINATION 2002*, pages 250–257, York, UK, 2002. Springer-Verlag.
27. T. Reenskaug. *Working with Objects: The OOram Software Engineering Method.* Manning Publications, 1996.
28. J. Rumbaugh, M. Blaha, W. Premerlani, F. Eddy, and W. Lorensen. *Object-Oriented Modeling and Design.* Prentice Hall, Schenectady, New York, 1991.
29. J. Rumbaugh, I. Jacobson, and G. Booch. *The Unified Modeling Language Reference Manual.* Object Technology Series. Addison Wesley Longman, Reading, Massachussetts, 1999.
30. C. Shih and J. A. Stankovic. Survey of deadlock detection in distributed concurrent programming environments and its application to real-time systems. Technical Report UM-CS-1990-069, 1990.
31. M. Y. Vardi and Pierre Wolper. An automata-theoretic approach to automatic program verification (preliminary report). In *Proceedings 1st Annual IEEE Symp. on Logic in Computer Science, LICS'86, Cambridge, MA, USA, 16–18 June 1986*, pages 332–344. IEEE Computer Society Press, Washington, DC, 1986.
32. R. Wirfs-Brock and B. Wilkerson. *Designing Object-Oriented Software.* Prentice-Hall, August 1990.
33. M. Wooldridge, N. R. Jennings, and D. Kinny. The gaia methodology for agent-oriented analysis and design. *Autonomous Agents and Multi-Agent Systems*, 3(3):285–312, 2000.
34. F. Zamboneli, N. R. Jennings, and M. Wooldridge. Organizational abstraction for the analysis and design of multi-agent system. In *Proceedings of the 1th Int. Workshop on Agent-Oriented Software Engeenering (AOSE'2000)*, number 1957 in LNCS, pages 235–252, Limerick, Ireland, June 2000. Springer-Verlag.

Formal Modeling and Supervisory Control of Reconfigurable Robot Teams

Kiriakos Kiriakidis[1] and Diana F. Gordon-Spears[2]

[1] Department of Weapons and Systems Engineering
United States Naval Academy
105 Maryland Avenue
Annapolis, MD 21402
kiriakid@novell.nadn.navy.mil
[2] Computer Science Department
College of Engineering
University of Wyoming
Laramie, WY 82071
dspears@cs.uwyo.edu

Abstract. Teams of land-based, airborne, or submerged robots constitute a new breed of robotic systems for which the issue of controlled
behavior arises naturally. In this paper, we model the dynamics of a reconfigurable (adaptable) robot team within the formalism of the discrete
event system framework from control theory. The adaptation to be handled is one or more robots switching offline. This paper presents a novel
method for learning and verification following adaptation – to restore
supervision and assure the behavior of the team.

1   Introduction

Adaptability is key to survival in dynamic, real-world situations. Successful task
achievement must be accomplished by graceful recovery from unexpected circumstances, e.g., by "steering" a system back on course to achieve its mission
despite failures. The contribution of this paper is in presenting a novel, practical method for multi-robot systems to adapt "safely," i.e., to remain within
the bounds of specified properties that ensure successful task completion. We
assume that a Finite State Automaton (FSA) models the behavior of an individual robot. To capture the collective behavior of a robot team whose composition changes, we construct an *event-varying* Discrete Event System (DES) as
the team's model. To control the natural behavior of such DES, we follow the
approach of supervisory control theory [10,13,17]. Adaptation is achieved with
machine learning, behavioral assurance is tested with formal verification, in particular, automata-theoretic model checking [11], and recovery is ensured via a
novel pair of algorithms. The primary focus of this paper is on formalizing and
implementing an approach to successful recovery. In particular, we explore how
a reconfigurable robot team can recover effective supervisory control to ensure
task achievement when faced with unexpected robotic failures or re-grouping,

M.G. Hinchey et al. (Eds.): 'FAABS 2002, LNAI 2699, pp. 92–102, 2003.
© Springer-Verlag Berlin Heidelberg 2003

i.e., a shift in the team composition. This paper presents a substantial extension of the earlier research of Kiriakidis and Gordon reported at FAABS'00 [9].

Note that the method of supervisory control of DES addresses a number of related problems, albeit on the typical assumption that the system is fixed and known [3,15,16]. At present, the literature offers only a few works on adaptive or robust supervisory control to tackle the problem of uncertainty in the DES model [2,12,18]. Furthermore, although this prior work advances the development of a theory for uncertain DES, the literature lacks any design methods for emerging engineering applications. Here, we present a practical engineering method that has been tested on a team of robots.

There are numerous important potential applications of our approach. One example is teams of planetary rovers that adapt to unanticipated planetary conditions while remaining within critical mission parameters. Another example is automated factory robot teams that adapt to equipment failures but continue operation within essential tolerances and other specifications. As a third example, supportive groups of automated military equipment transport vehicles would require both flexibility and behavioral assurance. Finally, consider the application of groups of robots for hazardous waste cleanup. This is yet another example illustrating the need for both responsiveness to failures and behavioral predictability.

2   Problem Formulation

In this paper, we consider robots that, in addition to equipment (e.g., sensors) necessary to carry out tasks, comprise a receiver and transmitter device as a means of communication with a coordinator (supervisor). We shall refer to a collection of robots that are collaborating with a common coordinator as a *robotic group*. The coordinator shapes the group's collective behavior by imposing cooperation between individual robots. In turn, cooperation implies that the robotic group possesses a set of desired *properties*, characteristic of its functionality. For example, a desired property of a delivery system whose function is to transport an object from point A to point Z is that delivery at Z eventually follows delivery at A.

In general, the robotic group may be operating on its own or as part of a larger system of peer groups. To model a particular group, we recognize that its behavior is associated with two classes of *events*. First, there are events that describe, in a well-defined sense, the tasks that each robot executes. The coordinator can manipulate those events to ensure multi-robot coordination. Second, there are events unpreventable by the coordinator such as when individual units (robots) switch coordinators or fail during operation. To update the state of the robotic group, the supervisor needs to know the event that a robot has just executed in order to identify its current task or determine that it has gone offline. Moreover, the structure of the event-driven model needs to be able to capture the new situation when the coordinator loses (or gains) a robot. To provide for this, we shall assume a model that is also event-varying.

In this paper, we are going to focus our attention on the behavior of a robotic group and address the problem of maintaining the desired properties of the group in spite of unavoidable events. We shall employ the theory of automata, express each desired property as a sequence of events, and embed the resulting sequences in a desired language. To guarantee the desired language, we synthesize the group's coordinator, in the context of the supervisory control method [1,14], so that it adapts to changes that have occurred in the group.

3   Formally Modeling a Reconfigurable Robot Team as an Event-Varying DES

Each robot has autonomy to complete a task (e.g., to transport an object from point A to point B). A robot is in a certain *state*, s, while a task is occupying it or it is waiting to start a new task. An *event*, σ, occurs when a robot starts a new task; thus, events coincide with state transitions. Before it starts a task and after it has completed one, the robot normally notifies the supervisor. Upon the completion of its current task, a robot is ready to execute another event.

The supervisor/coordinator decides which events are enabled and accordingly notifies the robots. Clearly, these events constitute an observable and controllable model. There are also uncontrollable events. A robot may be unable to start or finish a task. For example, a unit may have broken down or started to collaborate with another supervisor. These uncontrollable events are not part of the model per se, but their occurrence necessitates changes in the model. These events, however, are observable. If a robot starts to cooperate with another group, it will notify its old supervisor. For a robot that has broken down but is unable to notify its supervisor, the supervisor will assume that the robot is offline after a certain amount of time has elapsed.

Let us formalize the modeling of a robot group using the DES framework. The basic DES framework was developed in Ramadge and Wonham [14] and is further explained in [10]. We extend the basic framework here to handle uncontrollable events where robots may go offline. Each unit (robot), i, has its own alphabet, Σ_i, which comprises controllable events (its actions) only, and each admits an FSA model, G_i, $i \in \mathcal{I}_M$, where $\mathcal{I}_M$ is an index set and M the number of units in the group initially. We also define the group alphabet, $\Sigma = \bigcup \Sigma_i$. Formally, an FSA is a quintuple $G = (X, \Sigma, \delta, s_0, X_m)$ where X is the set of states, δ the transition function, s_0 the initial state, X_m the set of marked (task completion) states. Strings in the the the language if G, $L(G)$, and strings in the marked language of G, $L_m(G)$ (i.e., strings terminating in a marked state), are sequences of events. Marked states signify task completion. To take into account that robots may go offline, we define the FSA Λ, that is based on the following alphabet of all the uncontrollable events:

$$\Sigma_\lambda = \{\lambda_{i_k} \mid i_k \in \mathcal{I}_M, \text{ where } k \in \mathcal{I}_N, \ i_k \neq i_{k'} \text{ for } k \neq k', \ k' \in \mathcal{I}_N\}$$

where $N \leq M$ is the maximum number of units that may go offline. The occurrence of the event λ_{i_k} coincides with the loss of the robot number i_k. In accordance with the FSA Λ, each uncontrollable event occurs only once. After the event λ_{i_k} the robotic group comprises only $M - k$ robots.

Before any uncontrollable event occurs, the natural language of the robotic group stems from the following parallel composition:[1]

$$G_\epsilon := G_1\|G_2\|\ldots\|G_M$$

where ϵ is the empty string. When an uncontrollable event occurs, the parallel composition changes. After the uncontrollable event λ_{i_1}, $i_1 \in \mathcal{I}_M$, occurs, the model becomes

$$G_{\lambda_{i_1}} := G_1\|\ldots\|G_{i_1-1}\|G_{i_1+1}\|\ldots\|G_M$$

Upon the occurrence of the uncontrollable events $\lambda_{i_2}, \ldots, \lambda_{i_k}$, where $k \leq N$, the respective models are as follows:

$$G_{\lambda_{i_1}\lambda_{i_2}} = (G_{\lambda_{i_1}})_{\lambda_{i_2}}, \quad \ldots, \quad G_{\lambda_{i_1}\cdots\lambda_{i_k}} = (G_{\lambda_{i_1}\cdots\lambda_{i_{k-1}}})_{\lambda_{i_k}} \tag{1}$$

Let r be a string of events in the language generated by Λ, i.e., $r \in L(\Lambda)$ identifies a sequence of units that goes offline. Then, the set of all possible models $\mathcal{G} = \{G_r \mid r \in L(\Lambda)\}$. Consider the FSA-valued function $G : (\Sigma \cup \Sigma_\lambda)^* \to \mathcal{G}$, where for the empty string, ϵ, the model of robotic group $G(\epsilon) = G_\epsilon$. Suppose a string of events $q_k \in (\Sigma \cup \Sigma_\lambda)^*$ includes the string of uncontrollable events $r_k = \lambda_{i_1}\ldots\lambda_{i_k}$. Then, the occurrence of an event σ affects the group's model as follows:

$$G(q_k\sigma) = \begin{cases} G(q_k), & \sigma \notin \Sigma_\lambda \\ G_{r_k\sigma}, & \sigma \in \Sigma_\lambda \end{cases}$$

for $k = 1, \ldots, N-1$. This event-varying DES captures the changes in the behavior of the robotic group as individual robots go offline.

4 Adaptive Supervisory Control

As mentioned earlier, the coordinator of a robotic group restricts the group's natural behavior in order to ensure that the group possesses certain desired properties. In the context of supervisory control, the coordinator accomplishes this by specifying and executing the desired language. In Section 2, we introduced the notion of the desired language as one that guarantees a set of desired properties. Let $P_1, \ldots, P_L$ and D denote the FSAs of desired properties and the current desired language, respectively. The current desired language, $L(D)$, satisfies the set of desired properties, $\mathcal{P} = \{P_1, \ldots, P_L\}$, iff $L(D) \subseteq L(P_i)$, for each $i \in \mathcal{I}_L$ or, for brevity, $L(D) \subseteq L(\mathcal{P})$. The languages $L(D)$ and $L(\mathcal{P})$ consist of strings with events in the alphabets $\Sigma^D \subseteq \Sigma$ and $\Sigma^{\mathcal{P}} \subset \Sigma$, respectively.

Before any uncontrollable event occurs, $L(D_\epsilon)$ is the set of all allowable action sequences for the robotic group G_ϵ. In general, the initial desired language FSA,

---

[1] Because the alphabet Σ_i may be different for each robot i, this parallel composition is a shuffle product [14].

D_ϵ, is constructed by an expert engineer. First, the desired language must be such that $L(D_\epsilon) \subseteq L(G_\epsilon)$. Second, it ought to satisfy each desired property, P_i, $i \in \mathcal{I}_L$. For example, P_i might state that an object that has been picked up must eventually be delivered. Third, the expert engineer may require that the initial desired language meet performance criteria more specific but less essential than the desired properties. Without supervision the robotic system may be unable to satisfy the desired properties, for, in general, $L(\mathcal{P}) \subseteq L(G_\epsilon)$.

Based on the event-varying DES that models the robotic group, we propose a learning algorithm to modify the desired language specified to the supervisor after each occurrence of an uncontrollable event. Upon execution of the uncontrollable event λ_{i_1}, the learning algorithm removes the events that pertain to the i_1-th robot from the desired language FSA, D_ϵ. In turn, the algorithm repairs the resulting (possibly fractured or disconnected) FSA and yields a candidate desired language. A verification algorithm checks the candidate in order to ensure that the desired properties, $\mathcal{P}$, are still valid. For verification, we use the method of Automata-Theoretic (AT) model checking [11]. In brief, AT model checking assumes D and P are expressed as FSAs, and it checks whether $L(D) \subseteq L(P)$.

If the verification is successful, then the candidate is indeed a desired language, whose FSA we denote as $D_{\lambda_{i_1}}$. Clearly, it holds that $L(D_{\lambda_{i_1}}) \subset L(G_{\lambda_{i_1}})$. If the verification fails, we resort to an alternate learning algorithm that results in a smaller language, which, however, guarantees the desired properties. The procedure above repeats itself during a string of uncontrollable events r and, thus, generates a succession of desired language FSAs $\mathcal{D} = \{D_r \mid r \in L(\Lambda), \emptyset \neq L(D_r) \subseteq L(\mathcal{P}) \text{ and } L(D_r) \subseteq L(G_r)\}$. The supervisor synthesis step derives from the following result.

Proposition 1. Consider the event-varying DES (1) presented in Section 3, and the succession of desired languages $\mathcal{D}$. Suppose that the supervisor for (1) is the FSA-valued function $S : (\Sigma \cup \Sigma_\lambda)^* \to \mathcal{D}$ where $S(\epsilon) = D_\epsilon$ and

$$S(q_k \sigma) = \begin{cases} S(q_k), & \sigma \notin \Sigma_\lambda \\ D_{r_k \sigma}, & \sigma \in \Sigma_\lambda \end{cases} \tag{2}$$

Then for $k = 1, \ldots, N - 1$, the supervised language $L[G(q_k \sigma) \| S(q_k \sigma)] \subseteq L(\mathcal{P})$.

Proof: Consider the desired language $L(D_r)$ for each $r \in L(\Lambda)$. First, from the hypothesis, $L(D_r)$ is non-empty and $L(D_r) \subseteq L(G_r)$. Second, $L(D_r)$ is prefix closed, i.e., $pr[L(D_r)] = L(D_r)$, for it is a generated language [1]. Third, $L(D_r)$ is controllable with respect to $L(G_r)$, for there are no uncontrollable events in $L(G_r)$. Then, for $\sigma \in \Sigma_\lambda$, the supervisor in (2) yields $L[G(q_k \sigma) \| S(q_k \sigma)] = L(D_{r_k \sigma})$; see [10]. Similarly, for $\sigma \notin \Sigma_\lambda$, $L[G(q_k \sigma) \| S(q_k \sigma)] = L(D_{r_k})$. ∎

5   Adaptive Supervisory Control

This section addresses the situation wherein the robots must adapt. As mentioned earlier, the coordinator of a robotic group restricts the group's natural behavior in order to ensure that the group possesses certain desired properties.

In the context of supervisory control, the coordinator accomplishes this by specifying and executing a desired language, i.e., one that guarantees a set of desired properties. Let P and D denote the FSAs of a desired property and language, respectively. Then, a desired language, $L(D)$, satisfies a set of desired properties, $\mathcal{P} = \{P_1, \ldots, P_L\}$, iff $L(D) \subseteq L(P_i)$, for each $i \in \mathcal{I}_L$. This is ensured initially by formal verification.

Based on the event-varying DES that models the robotic group, we propose a learning algorithm to modify the desired language (which is used to generate the supervisor) after each occurrence of an uncontrollable event. At first, the desired language satisfies: $L(D_\epsilon) \subseteq L(G_\epsilon)$. Upon execution of the uncontrollable event λ_{i_1}, the learning algorithm removes the events that pertain to the i_1-th robot from the desired language FSA, D_ϵ. In turn, an algorithm called Maxmend repairs the resulting (probably fractured) FSA to yield a candidate desired language that is a subset of $L(G_{\lambda_{i_1}})$. A verification algorithm (model checking) checks the candidate in order to verify that the desired properties, $\mathcal{P}$, are still valid. If the verification is successful, then the candidate is indeed a desired language, whose FSA we denote as $D_{\lambda_{i_1}}$. If the verification fails, we resort to an alternate learning algorithm, called Quickmend, that results in a smaller language, which, however, guarantees that the desired properties hold, without the need for verification again [4]. The procedure above repeats itself during a string of uncontrollable events r and, thus, generates a succession of desired languages $\mathcal{D} = \{D_r \mid r \in L(\Lambda), \emptyset \neq L(D_r) \subseteq L(\mathcal{P}) \text{ and } L(D_r) \subseteq L(G_r)\}$.

Figures 1 and 2 show our algorithm Maxmend for repairing the FSA D following learning. Our motivation in designing this algorithm was a desire to preserve as much of the original FSA as possible, including preserving the order of transitions. In these figures, $\Psi_{pre}^D(s)$ is the set of all pre-learning successor states of state s in FSA D, $\Psi_{post}^D(s)$ is the set of all post-learning successors of s, $\delta_{pre}^D(s, \sigma)$ is the particular pre-learning successor of state s for event σ, and $\delta_{post}^D(s, \sigma)$ is the post-learning successor of s for event σ. Also, Σ_{pre}^D is the set of all pre-learning events, Σ_{post}^D is the set of all post-learning events, and Σ_Δ^D is the set of events deleted by learning. In other words, $\Sigma_{post}^D = \Sigma_{pre}^D \setminus \Sigma_\Delta^D$. Finally, X^D is the set of all states in the FSA D.

Let us now proceed to describe procedure Maxmend in words. Prior to calling procedure "repair-method" (Figure 1), variable "visited" is initialized to false for every state in the FSA. Procedure repair-method is then called with the initial FSA state as parameter s. Procedure repair-method does a depth-first search through the set of all states that are accessible from the initial state after learning. For each state visited on the depth-first search, "visited" is set to true so that it is not re-visited. Each state s that is visited which has no post-learning successors is considered an "unlinked-vertex." In this case, procedure "find-linked-vertex" (Figure 2) is called to find the first pre-learning descendant of the unlinked-vertex that has a post-learning successor. This descendant is considered to be the "linked-vertex." Procedure "copy-connections" (Figure 2) sets the successors of the unlinked-vertex equal to the successors of the linked-vertex for all post-learning events. If time permits, following this repair method

```
procedure repair-method (s)
visited(s) = true;
if (( Ψ_{post}^{D}(s) == ∅) and
(Ψ_{pre}^{D}(s) ≠ ∅)) then {
    unlinked-vertex = s;
    linked-vertex = 0;
    for each τ ∈ Σ_{Δ}^{D} do {
        if ((δ_{pre}^{D}(s,τ) ≠ 0) and
        (δ_{pre}^{D}(s,τ) ≠ s)) then {
            for each s' ∈ X^{D} do
                visited2(s') = 0;
            od
            find-linked-vertex(δ_{pre}^{D}(s,τ));
            exit for-loop; } }
        fi
    od
    if ((linked-vertex ≠ 0) and
    (linked-vertex ≠ unlinked-vertex)) then
        copy-connections(unlinked-vertex, linked-vertex); }
    fi
fi
for each σ ∈ Σ_{post}^{D} do
    if ((visited(δ_{post}^{D}(s,σ)) == false) and
    (δ_{post}^{D}(s,σ) ≠ 0)) then
        repair-method(δ_{post}^{D}(s,σ));
    fi
od
end
```

Fig. 1. The algorithm Maxmend for FSA repair with verification.

the FSA may be simplified by removing unused (i.e., inaccessible) states and grouping states into equivalence classes using a state minimization algorithm [8].

The disadvantage of this repair algorithm is that it requires re-verification to be sure the resulting FSA still satisfies the property after the repair has been done. The reason that re-verification is required is that the process of mending (repair) adds new FSA transitions, which results in new strings of events. There is no guarantee that these new strings will satisfy the desired properties. In the event that re-verification fails, i.e., it indicates that the property has been violated, we propose the following alternative.

Figure 3 shows the Quickmend algorithm for repairing the desired language FSA after learning occurs. Prior to calling the algorithm of Figure 3, "visited" is initialized to false for every state in the FSA. Procedure "repair-method" is then called with the initial FSA state as parameter s. Procedure repair-method does a depth-first search through the set of all pre-learning states that are ac-

```
procedure find-linked-vertex (s)
visited2(s) = true;
for each σ ∈ Σ_pre^D do
    if (δ_post^D(s, σ) ≠ 0) then {
        linked-vertex = s;
        exit-for-loop; }
    else if ((δ_pre^D(s, σ) ≠ 0) and
    (visited2(δ_pre^D(s, σ)) == false)) then
        find-linked-vertex(δ_pre^D(s, σ));
    fi
od
end


procedure copy-connections (s1, s2)
for each σ ∈ Σ_post^D do {
    δ_post^D(s1, σ) = δ_post^D(s2, σ);
    if (δ_post^D(s2, σ) == s2) then
        δ_post^D(s1, σ) = s1; }
    fi
od
end
```

Fig. 2. The subroutines of the Maxmend algorithm for FSA repair.

cessible from the initial state, and "visited" is set to avoid re-visitation. When the algorithm has visited all states, it pops the recursion stack to re-visit the states beginning with the last (i.e., it then visits the states in reverse order). For each state s visited in reverse order, the algorithm tests whether s has any post-learning successors. If not, it deletes all post-learning pointers to that state. Optionally, the FSA may be further simplified, e.g., by removing unused states.

Time complexity analyses of these two novel algorithms Maxmend and Quickmend may be found in [5,6,7]. Once a satisfactory desired language is found, automatic generation of a new supervisor follows the method of [10,14]. This results in effective recovery of supervisory control, as well as preservation of properties that ensure task achievement.

6   Application to a Delivery System

In the laboratory, we tested the adaptive supervisory control approach on a delivery system that comprises a group of three mobile robots (G_1, G_2, and G_3), as well as a coordinator (supervisor). The coordinator consists of a field computer, which stays near the group and executes the supervisor's automaton, and a main computer that devises the automaton and uploads it to the field computer. The goal of the robotic group is to deliver a number of objects from location A to location D. A set of sensors allows each mobile robot to detect

```
procedure repair-method (s)
visited(s) = true;
for each σ ∈ Σ^D_pre do
    if ((δ^D_pre(s,σ) ≠ 0) and (visited(δ^D_pre(s,σ)) == false)) then
        repair-method(δ^D_pre(s,σ));
    fi
od
if (Ψ^D_post(s) == ∅) then
    for each s' ∈ X^D do
        for each σ ∈ Σ^D_post do
            if (δ^D_post(s',σ) == s) then
                δ^D_post(s',σ) = 0;
            fi
        od
    od
fi
end
```

Fig. 3. The algorithm Quickmend for FSA repair without verification.

the object (e.g., a puck) and find the location to deliver it. The communication between the main and field computers, as well as the field computer and each robot, is based on infrared transceivers.

Each robot has autonomy to complete a task, but it needs the coordinator's authorization before it starts a new task. The job of the coordinator's field computer is to disable certain state transitions (events) and enable other events in order to constrain the group's natural language so that it satisfies the following desired property:

P: *If G_1 picks-up, then G_3 will eventually deliver.*

Completion of the task originally involves coordination of all three of the robots. We then simulate the failure of robot G_2. Despite this failure, the adaptive supervision method described in this paper guarantees that the above desired property is preserved, i.e., the task is successfully completed. In summary, using the method described in this paper, the robotic group adapts and also meets its objective.

7   Conclusions and Future Work

This paper describes a practical method for the modeling and control of teams of robots, despite dynamically changing team composition. The method consists of applying learning to adapt to the situation of units going offline, followed by algorithmic revisions and verification of the desired language FSA, which is used for supervisory control. The practicality of our method has been demonstrated on a team of actual robots under supervision.

Future work will extend the current approach to handle the case of new units dynamically joining a team (i.e., added units). In parallel, we will continue to validate our approach on a variety of real-world applications.

Acknowledgements. This work was supported by the Naval Academy Research Council and the Office of Naval Research Grants N0001499WR20020 and N0001499WR20010.

References

1. C. G. Cassandras and S. Lafortune, *Introduction to Discrete Event Systems*. Boston, Massachusetts: Kluwer Academic Publishers, 2001.
2. Y.-L. Chen, S. Lafortune, and F. Lin, "How to reuse supervisors when discrete event systems evolve," in *Proceedings of the IEEE Conference on Decision and Control*, (San Diego, CA), pp. 1442–1448, 1997.
3. Y. Du and S. H. Wang, "Control of discrete-event systems with minimal switching," *International Journal of Control*, vol. 48, no. 3, pp. 981–991, 1988.
4. D. Gordon, "Asimovian adaptive agents," *Journal of Artificial Intelligence Research*, vol. 13, pp. 95–153, 2000.
5. K. Kiriakidis and D. Gordon, "Supervision of multiple-robot systems," in *Proceedings of the American Control Conference*, (Arlington, VA), June 2001, pp. 2117–2118.
6. D. Gordon and K. Kiriakidis, "Adaptive supervisory control of interconnected discrete event systems," in *Proceedings of the 2000 IEEE Conference on Control Applications*, (Anchorage, AK), Sept. 2000, pp. 935–940.
7. D. Gordon and K. Kiriakidis, "Design of adaptive supervisors for discrete event systems via learning," in *Proceedings of the ASME Dynamic Systems and Control Division, International Mechanical Engineering Congress and Exposition*, (Orlando, FL), Nov. 2000, pp. 365–370.
8. J. Hopcroft and J. Ullman, *Introduction to Automata Theory, Languages, and Computation*. Menlo Park, California: Addison-Wesley, 1979.
9. K. Kiriakidis and D. Gordon, "Supervision of multiple-robot systems," abstract in *Lecture Notes in Artificial Intelligence, Volume 1871* (Proceedings of FAABS'00), Springer-Verlag, 2001.
10. R. Kumar and V. K. Garg, *Modeling and Control of Logical Discrete Event Systems*. Boston, Massachusets: Kluwer Academic Publishers, 1995.
11. P. Kurshan, *Computer Aided Verification of Coordinating Processes*. Princeton, New Jersey: Princeton University Press, 1994.
12. F. Lin, "Robust and adaptive supervisory control of discrete event systems," *IEEE Transactions on Automatic Control*, vol. 38, no. 12, pp. 1842–1852, 1993.
13. P. J. Ramadge and W. M. Wonham, "Supervisory control of a class of discrete event processes," *SIAM J. Control and Optimization*, vol. 25, no. 1, pp. 206–230, 1987.
14. P. J. Ramadge and W. M. Wonham, "The control of discrete event systems," *Proceedings of the IEEE*, vol. 77, no. 1, pp. 81–98, 1989.
15. J. G. Thistle, "Supervisory control of discrete event systems," *Mathematical and Computer Modelling*, vol. 23, no. 11, pp. 25–53, 1996.

16. W. M. Wonham and P. J. Ramadge, "Modular supervisory control of discrete-event systems," *Mathematics of Control, Signals, and Systems*, vol. 1, no. 1, pp. 13–30, 1988.
17. W. M. Wonham and P. J. Ramadge, "On the supremal controllable sublanguage of a given language," *SIAM J. Control and Optimization*, vol. 25, no. 3, pp. 637–659, 1987.
18. S. Young and V. K. Garg, "Model uncertainty in discrete event systems," *SIAM J. Control and Optimization*, vol. 33, no. 1, pp. 208–226, 1995.

Computational Models for Multiagent Coordination Analysis: Extending Distributed POMDP Models

Hyuckchul Jung, Ranjit Nair, Milind Tambe, and Stacy Marsella

Computer Science Department and Information Sciences Institute
University of Southern California, Los Angeles, USA
{jungh,nair,tambe}@usc.edu,marsella@isi.edu

Abstract. Recently researchers in multiagent systems have begun to focus on formal POMDP (Partially Observable Markov Decision Process) models for analysis of multiagent coordination. However, prior work has mostly focused on analysis of communication, such as via the COM-MTDP (Communicative Markov Team Decision Problem) model. This paper provides two extensions to this prior work that goes beyond communication and analyzes other aspects of multiagent coordination. In particular, we first present a formal model called R-COM-MTDP that extends COM-MTDP to analyze team formation and reorganization algorithms. R-COM-MTDP enables a rigorous and systematic analysis of complexity-optimality tradeoffs in team (re)formation approaches in different domain types. It provides the worst-case complexity analysis of the team (re)formation under varying conditions, and illustrates under which conditions role decomposition can provide significant reductions in computational complexity. Next, we propose COM-MTDP as a formal framework to analyze DCSP (Distributed Constraint Satisfaction Problem) strategies for conflict resolution. Different DCSP strategies are mapped onto policies in the COM-MTDP model, and agents compare strategies by evaluating their mapped policies. Thus, the two COM-MTDP based methods could open the door to a range of novel analyses of multiagent team (re)formation, and facilitate automated selection of the most efficient strategy for a given situation.

1 Introduction

Research in multiagent teamwork and cooperative multiagent systems has led researchers to develop successful practical multiagent applications. As the systems have matured, new competitive evaluation techniques are becoming increasingly popular (e.g., Robocup[2], RoboCup Rescue[3], TAC[11], Planning[6]). However, systematic techniques for performance analysis of these systems are still lacking. Thus, it is difficult to quantitatively compare the coordination approaches or behaviors employed in these systems, and understand which approach will dominate in particular circumstances.

Recently developed approaches[8,9,15] based on Distributed POMDPs and MDPs are beginning to remedy this problem, by providing tools for analysis

M.G. Hinchey et al. (Eds.): 'FAABS 2002, LNAI 2699, pp. 103–114, 2003.

as well as synthesis of multiagent coordination algorithms such as STEAM[10]. For instance, Pynadath and Tambe introduced COM-MTDP[9] (COMmunicative Multiagent Team Decision Problem) for analysis of communication actions in teams. While this work is promising, it has mostly focused on analysis of communication actions in multiagent systems. We extend this prior work to analyze other types of coordination beyond communication. We present two key extensions. The first extension focuses on taking and changing of roles in a team. The second extension illustrates analysis of value selection strategies in DCSP (Distributed Constraint Satisfaction Problem)[13].

Based on COM-MTDP, we build R-COM-MTDP, a model for analysis of team formation and reformation. The point here is not just that we can build R-COM-MTDP, but that we establish a methodology via which further such analyses could be performed. Using R-COM-MTDP, we specifically provide the worst case complexity analysis of the team (re)formulation under varying communication and observability conditions, and illustrate under which conditions role decomposition can provide significant reductions in computational complexity.

In addition to the extension of COM-MTDP model for team (re)formation, we propose COM-MTDP as a formal framework to analyze different value selection strategies of DCSP (Distributed Constraint Satisfaction Problems). DCSP value selection strategies are mapped onto policies in COM-MTDP, and compared by evaluating the policies. DCSP is a key method for conflict resolution in multiagent systems, and this COM-MTDP based approach will enable agents to predict the performance of their strategies and select the best one for fast conflict resolution convergence.

2   COM-MTDP: Communicative Markov Team Decision Problem

Given a team of agents, α, COM-MTDP model[9] is a tuple, $\langle S, A_\alpha, \Sigma_\alpha, P, \Omega_\alpha, O_\alpha, B_\alpha, R_\alpha \rangle$. S is a set of world states. $A_\alpha = \prod_{i \in \alpha} A_i$ is a set of combined actions where A_i is the set of actions for agent i. $\Sigma_\alpha = \prod_{i \in \alpha} \Sigma_i$ is a set of combined messages, where Σ_i is the set of messages for agent i. P controls the effect of agents' actions in a dynamic environment: $P(s, \mathbf{a}, s') = Pr(S^{t+1} = s | S^t = s', A_\alpha^t = \mathbf{a})$ where S^t denotes the world state at time t. $\Omega_\alpha = \prod_{i \in \alpha}$ is a set of observations where Ω_i is the set of observation of an agent i. Observation function, $O_\alpha(s, \mathbf{a}, \omega) = Pr(\Omega_\alpha^t = \omega | S^t = s, A_\alpha^{t-1} = \mathbf{a})$, specifies the probability distribution of joint observations of the agent team α, and can be classified as follows:

- **Collective Partial Observability**: no assumption on the observations.
- **Collective Observability**: unique world state for the combined observation of the team $\alpha : \forall \omega \in \Omega_\alpha, \exists s \in S$ such that $\forall s' \neq s, Pr(\Omega_\alpha^t = \omega | S^t = s') = 0$.
- **Individual Observability**: unique world state for each individual agent's observation: $\forall \omega \in \Omega_i, \exists s \in S$ such that $\forall s' \neq s, Pr(\Omega_i^t = \omega | S^t = s') = 0$.

$B_\alpha = \prod_{i \in \alpha} B_i$ is the set of combined belief states, where B_i circumscribes the set of possible belief states for an agent i. Agent i makes decisions of which action to take and which message to communicate based on its belief state $b_i^t \in B_i$ derived by its observations and communicated messages through time t. With communication, belief state is divided into *pre-communication* belief state and *post-communication* belief state denoted by $b_{\bullet\Sigma}^t$ and $b_{\Sigma\bullet}^t$, respectively. π_{iA} is a domain-level *policy* defined as a mapping from belief states to actions, π_{iA} : $B_i \to A$.

COM-MTDP reward function represents a team's joint preference over states and the cost of actions and communication, $R : S \times \Sigma_\alpha \times A \to \Re$. Here, R is the sum of two rewards: (i) domain-action-level-reward, $R_{\alpha A} : S \times A_\alpha \to \Re$, and (ii) communication-level-reward, $R_{\alpha\Sigma} : S \times \Sigma_\alpha \to \Re$. COM-MTDP domains can be classified based on communication availability and its cost: (i) **General communication**: no assumption on Σ_α or $R_{\alpha\Sigma}$, (ii) **No communication**: $\Sigma_\alpha = 0$, and (iii) **Free communication**: $\forall \sigma \in \Sigma_\alpha, R_{\alpha\Sigma}(\sigma) = 0$.

3   R-COM-MTDP Model

Roles reduce the complexity of action selection and also enable better modeling of real systems since each agent's role restricts its domain-level actions. Hence, we build on existing multiagent coordination models, especially COM-MTDP, to include roles, and add "local state" which is another key multiagent concept but is missing in current models. In this section, we define a R-COM-MTDP as an extended tuple, $\langle S, A_\alpha, \Sigma_\alpha, P, \Omega_\alpha, O_\alpha, B_\alpha, R_\alpha, \mathcal{RL} \rangle$.

$\mathcal{RL} = \{r_1, \ldots, r_s\}$ is a set of all roles that α can undertake. Each instance of role r_j requires some agent $i \in \alpha$ to fulfill it. Agents' domain-level actions are now divided into two types:

Role-Taking Actions: $\Upsilon_\alpha = \prod_{i \in \alpha} \Upsilon_i$ is a set of combined role taking actions, where $\Upsilon_i = \{\upsilon_{ir_j}\}$ contains the role-taking actions for agent i. $\upsilon_{ir_j} \in \Upsilon_i$ means that agent i takes on the role $r_j \in \mathcal{RL}$. An agent's role can be uniquely determined from its belief state and policy.

Role-Execution Actions: $\Phi_\alpha = \prod_{i \in \alpha} \Phi_i$ is a set of combined execution actions, where $\Phi_i = \bigcup_{\forall r_j \in \mathcal{RL}} \Phi_{ir_j}$. Φ_{ir_j} is the set of agent i's actions for executing role $r_j \in \mathcal{RL}$, thus restricting the actions that an agent can perform in a role.

The distinction between role-taking and -execution actions ($A_\alpha = \Upsilon_\alpha \cup \Phi_\alpha$) enables us to separate their costs. We can then compare costs of different role-taking policies analytically and empirically. Within this model, we can represent the specialized behaviors associated with each role, and also any possible differences among the agents' capabilities for these roles. The domain-action-level-reward of R-COM-MTDP is further separated into reward for role-taking and role-execution actions. Here, we view the role taking reward as the cost for taking up different roles in different teams: e.g., if a satellite agent changes its role to join a new sub-team tracking a new star, there can be a delay in tracking. However, change of roles may potentially provide significant future rewards.

Furthermore, we can define a role-taking policy, $\pi_{i\Upsilon} : B_i \to \Upsilon_i$ for each agent's role-taking action, a role-execution policy, $\pi_{i\Phi} : B_i \to \Phi_i$ for each agent's role-execution action, and a communication policy $\pi_{i\Sigma} : B_i \to \Sigma_i$ for each agent's communication action. The goal is to come up with joint policies for an agent team α, $\pi_{\alpha\Upsilon}$, $\pi_{\alpha\Phi}$ and $\pi_{\alpha\Sigma}$ that will maximize the total reward over a finite horizon T.

Extension for Explicit Local States (S_i): we often find that only a distinct part of the state space S is relevant for each individual agent that performs distinct roles within a team. Representing the world state as orthogonal features (i.e., $S = \Xi_1 \times \Xi_2 \times \cdots \times \Xi_n$), we can identify the subset of features of the world state that affect the observation of agent i. For each agent i, this subset of features is referred as its *local state*, $S_i = \Xi_{i1} \times \Xi_{i2} \times \cdots \times \Xi_{im_i}$. The local state is dynamic and could vary with the change of agents' roles, world states, etc. By definition, the observation that agent i receives at time t is independent of any features not covered by S_i^t: $\Pr(\Omega_i^t = \omega | S^t = \langle \xi_1, \xi_2, \ldots, \xi_n \rangle, A_\alpha^{t-1} = \mathbf{a}, \Omega_{\alpha \backslash \{i\}}^t = \omega_{\alpha \backslash \{i\}}) = \Pr(\Omega_i^t = \omega | S_i^t = \langle \xi_{i1}, \ldots, \xi_{im_i} \rangle, A_\alpha^{t-1} = \mathbf{a}, \Omega_{\alpha \backslash \{i\}}^t = \omega_{\alpha \backslash \{i\}})$, where $\Omega_{\alpha-i}^t = \prod_{j \in \alpha \backslash \{i\}} \Omega_j^t$. Here, another class of observation function is defined:

- **Local Observability**: Each individual's observation uniquely determines its local state: $\forall \omega \in \Omega_i, \exists s \in S_i$ such that $\forall s' \neq s, \Pr(\Omega_i^t = \omega | S_i^t = s') = 0$.

4   Complexity of R-COM-MTDPs

R-COM-MTDP enables a critically needed systematic investigation of the complexity for generating optimal policies under different communication and observability conditions. Refer to [5] for detailed theorem proofs.

Theorem 1. *R-COM-MTDP is reducible to an equivalent COM-MTDP and vice versa.*

Thus, the problem of finding optimal policies for R-COM-MTDPs has the same complexity as the problem of finding optimal policies for COM-MTDPs[9]. Table 1 shows the computational complexity for various classes of R-COM-MTDP domains, where the results for individual, collective, and collective partial observability follow from COM-MTDPs. New results in Table 1 come from analyzing the key addition in R-COM-MTDP, that of local states and local observability.

Theorem 2. *A collectively observable R-COM-MTDP is reducible to an equivalent locally observable R-COM-MTDP.*

While collective observability is a team's global property, we can still generate from it a locally observable R-COM-MTDP. A locally observable R-COM-MTDP is not collectively observable however. By definition, a locally observable

Table 1. Computational Complexity

	Ind. Obs.	**Coll. Obs.**	**Coll. Part. Obs.**	**Loc. Obs.**
No Comm.	P-Comp.	NEXP-Comp.	NEXP-Comp.	NEXP-Comp.
Gen. Comm.	P-Comp.	NEXP-Comp.	NEXP-Comp.	NEXP-Comp.
Free Comm.	P-Comp.	P-Comp.	PSPACE-Comp.	PSPACE-Comp.

R-COM-MTDP is collectively partially observable (the most general observability class). Since under no communication, the complexity of both collectively
observable R-COM-MTDP and collectively partially observable R-COM-MTDP
is NEXP-complete, Theorem 2 implies that the complexity of locally observable
R-COM-MTDP under no communication is also NEXP-complete. This explains
the NEXP-complete entries for local observability in Table 1. We can also show:

Theorem 3. *The decision problem of determining if there exist policies, $\pi_{\alpha\Sigma}$
and $\pi_{\alpha A}$, for a given R-COM-MTDP with free communication and local observability, that yield a total reward at least K over finite horizon T is PSPACE-
complete.*

Role Decomposition: while roles are seen to be central in designing multiagent systems, some designers exploit roles further by decomposition of the
multiagent coordination problem into smaller subproblems, isolating the specific
factors relevant to each of the separate roles[14]. The qualitative intuition behind this *role decomposition* is that this separation simplifies the overall problem
facing the agent team.

For role decomposition, the following three constraints must hold. First, the
dynamics of the local state must depend on only the current local state and
the agent's domain-level action: $\Pr(S_i^{t+1}|S^t = \langle \xi_1, \ldots, \xi_n \rangle, A_\alpha^t = \Pi_{j \in \alpha} a_j) =
\Pr(S_i^{t+1}|S_i^t = \langle \xi_{i1}, \ldots, \xi_{im_i} \rangle, A_i^t = a_i)$. Second, agent's observations are indepen-
dent and governed by the following observation functions, $O_i(s, a, \omega) = Pr(\Omega_i^t =
\omega|S_i^{t-1} = s, A_i^{t-1} = a)$ which implies that the observations of agent i at time
t are unaffected by the observations and actions of other agents. Finally, we
also structure the reward function so that the agents' actions earn independent
rewards: $R_\alpha(s, \prod_{i \in \alpha} a_i) = \sum_{i \in \alpha} R_i(s_i, a_i)$, where R_i is the local reward function
for agent i and s_i is its local state. We now examine the computational savings
given role decomposition.

Theorem 4. *The decision problem of determining if there exist policies, $\pi_{\alpha\Upsilon}$,
$\pi_{\alpha\Phi}$ and $\pi_{\alpha\Sigma}$, for a R-COM-MTDP with role decomposition, that yield a total
reward at least K over some finite horizon T is PSPACE-complete.*

Theorem 5. *The decision problem of determining whether there exist policies,
$\pi_{\alpha\Upsilon}$, $\pi_{\alpha\Phi}$ and $\pi_{\alpha\Sigma}$, for a R-COM-MTDP with role decomposition in a locally
observable domain, that yield a total reward at least K over some finite horizon
T is P-complete.*

Table 2. Computational Complexity after Role Decomposition

	Ind. Obs.	Coll. Obs.	Coll. Part. Obs.	Loc. Obs.
No Comm.	P-Comp.	PSPACE-Comp.	PSPACE-Comp.	P-Comp.
Gen. Comm.	P-Comp.	PSPACE-Comp.	PSPACE-Comp.	P-Comp.
Free Comm.	P-Comp.	P-Comp.	PSPACE-Comp.	P-Comp.

Table 2 demonstrates that role decomposition can significantly lower computational complexity and together with Table 1, it allows us to compare the relative value of communication and role decomposition in simplifying the decision problem. Examining the bottom two rows of Table 1, we see that, under collective observability, having the agents communicate all of their observations all of the time reduces the problem from NEXP to P. Examining the difference between Tables 1 and 2, we see that role decomposition, in contrast, reduces the problem to only PSPACE under collective observability (top row, Table 2). However, under *local* observability, full communication reduces the problem from NEXP to PSPACE, while role decomposition produces a decision problem that is only P.

5   DCSP Strategy Analysis with COM-MTDP

Distributed Constraint Satisfaction Problem (DCSP) techniques have been applied to various application problems such as distributed sensor network [4]. In this section, we introduce DCSP and a COM-MTDP-based model to analyze the performance of different DCSP value selection strategies.

5.1   Distributed Constraint Satisfaction Problem (DCSP)

A Constraint Satisfaction Problem (CSP) is commonly defined by a set of n variables, $X = \{x_1, ..., x_n\}$, each element associated with value domains $D_1, ..., D_n$ respectively, and a set of k constraints, $\Gamma = \{C_1, ..., C_k\}$. A solution in CSP is the value assignment for the variables which satisfies all the constraints in Γ. A distributed CSP is a CSP in which variables and constraints are distributed among multiple agents[13]. Formally, there is a set of m agents, $Ag = \{A_1, ..., A_m\}$. Each variable (x_i) belongs to an agent A_j. There are two types of constraints based on whether variables in the constraint belong to a single agent or not:

- For a constraint $C_r \in \Gamma$, if all the variables in C_r belong to a single agent $A_j \in Ag$, it is called a *local constraint*.
- For a constraint $C_r \in \Gamma$, if variables in C_r belong to different agents in Ag, it is called an *external constraint*.

Figure 1-a illustrates an example of DCSP: each agent A_i (denoted by a big circle) has a local constraint LC_i and there is an external constraint C_{ij} between

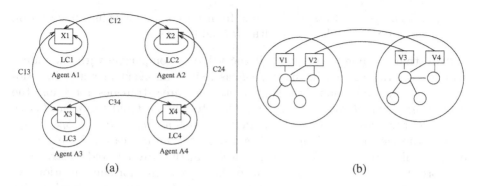

Fig. 1. Model of agents in DCSP

A_i and A_j. As illustrated in Figure 1-b, each agent can have multiple variables. There is no limitation on the number of local/external constraints for each agent. Solving a DCSP requires that agents not only satisfy their local constraints, but also communicate with other agents to satisfy external constraints.

Asynchronous Weak Commitment Search Algorithm (AWC): AWC is a sound and complete algorithm which shows the best performance among the published DSCP algorithms[12,13]. In the AWC approach, agents asynchronously assign values to their variables from available domains, and communicating the values to neighboring agents. Each variable has a non-negative integer priority that changes dynamically during search. A variable is consistent if its value does not violate any constraints with higher priority variables. A solution is a value assignment in which every variable is consistent.

For simplification, suppose that each agent has exactly one variable and constraints between variables are binary. When the value of a variable is not consistent with the values of neighboring agents' variables, there can be two cases: (i) *good* case where there exists a consistent value in the variable's domain; (ii) *nogood* case that lacks a consistent value. In the nogood case, an agent increases its priority to *max+1*, where *max* is the highest priority of neighboring agents' variables. This priority increase makes previously higher agents select new values to satisfy the constraint with the new higher agent.

DCSP Value Selection Strategies in AWC Framework: While AWC relies on the *min-conflict* value selection strategy[7] that minimizes conflicts with other agents, new novel value selection strategies were introduced based on *local cooperativeness* (*local cooperativeness* measures how many compatible values are available in neighboring agents' domains)[1]:

- S_{low}: Each agent selects a new value from its consistent values maximizing the sum of compatible values with its *lower* priority neighbor agents.
- S_{high}: Each agent selects a new value from its consistent values maximizing the sum of compatible values with its *higher* priority neighbor agents.

– S_{all}: Each agent selects a new value from its consistent values maximizing the sum of compatible values with *all* neighbor agents.

Note that a value is consistent if the value is compatible with the values of higher priority agents. In the *nogood* case, since an agent increases its priority, every value in its domain is consistent. The three strategies above and the original *min-conflict* strategy can be applied to the *good* and the *nogood* case. Therefore, there are 16 strategy combinations such as $S_{low} - S_{high}$ (S_{low} is applied in the *good* case and S_{high} is applied to the *nogood* case). Since we will consider only strategy combinations, henceforth, they are referred as strategies for short. While agents' strategies can be heterogeneous, for simplification, we assume that every agent applies the same strategy. Performance evaluation with heterogeneous strategies will be considered in our future work.

It was shown that the value selection strategies described above have a great impact on conflict resolution convergence in solving DCSPs[1]. However, there was no universal best strategy for different problem domains. To gain maximum efficiency, it would be essential to predict the right strategy to use in a given domain. In the next section, we propose COM-MTDP as a formal framework for such strategy performance analysis. The DCSP strategies defined in [1] are used as exemplar strategies for the analysis. However, note that the approach described in the next section can be applied to other types of DCSP strategies.

5.2   Mapping DCSP onto COM-MTDP

In this section, we provide an initial mapping of DCSP onto COM-MTDP. While communication, observation, observation function, and belief state are key parts of COM-MTDP, they are not as relevant here and will not be discussed in this initial mapping. For instance, in AWC, each agent always communicates its changed value to neighboring agents without reasoning for communication. Future work will take them into account for strategy analysis: e.g., an agent may consider communication cost before communicating its local solution.

In a general mapping, the first question to address is the issue of state representation. One typical representation could be a vector of values of all variables in a given DCSP. However, this representation leads to a huge problem space. To avoid combinatorial space explosion in problem space, abstract state representation is used in the initial mapping. In particular, a COM-MTDP state s is represented by the combination of agents' local states (s_i) that specify the status of constraint violation. A status indicates whether an agent is in the *good* case or in the *nogood* case.

To further reduce the problem space with a large number of agents, we use a small scale model that represents a local interaction. In a 2D grid configuration (each agent is externally constrained with four neighbors except for the ones on the grid boundary), the small scale model consists of five agents (A_1, A_2, A_3, A_4, A_5) with a middle agent (A_3) surrounded by the other four agents. Thus, a state in the COM-MTDP model is the tuple of the five agents' local states.

In the mapping, S_{low}, S_{high}, S_{all}, and $min - conflict$ are the actions for agents in the COM-MTDP model. A DCSP strategy such as $S_{low} - S_{high}$ is akin to a policy in COM-MTDP: S_{low} in the *good* state and S_{high} in the *nogood* state. The performance of DCSP strategies are compared by evaluating their mapped policies. Here, the evaluation of a policy is done by computing the value of an initial state of the COM-MTDP model under the policy. Note that we do not attempt to find an optimal policy but try to evaluate given policies.

In building a COM-MTDP model, the state transition can be derived by combining the local state changes of individual agents. The local state change for an agent is governed by the agent's local state, its neighboring agents' states, and the policies (strategies) selected by agents. Now, the state transition probability is defined as a product of the probabilities of local state changes:

- $P(s, a, s') = \Pi_{i=1}^{5} Pr(s_i'|s, a)$ where $s' = \langle s_1', s_2', s_3', s_4', s_5' \rangle$ denotes the next state after a state $s = \langle s_1, s_2, s_3, s_4, s_5 \rangle$ with an action a.

Note that the individual state transition probabilities are derived from the simulation of the whole system in a given problem setting, not from a simple experiment with only five agents.

Performance analysis is based on the fact that the best performing strategy has less chance of forcing neighboring agents into the *nogood* case than other strategies. Here, rewards (costs) are given to a state in proportion to the number of agents in the *nogood* cases. Therefore, as a policy (DCSP strategy) performs worse, its evaluation value increases. In comparing two strategies, a strategy with a smaller evaluation value is better than that with a larger evaluation value.

Analytical Results of DCSP Strategy Performance: Figure 2 shows the analytical results of three different strategies ($S_{low} - S_{low}$, $S_{low} - S_{high}$, and $S_{high} - S_{high}$) and the experimental results in two different problem settings (shown in [1]). In the analytical results (Figure 2-a & c), the vertical axis plots the evaluation value of each strategy computed from the COM-MTDP model. In the experimental results (Figure 2-b & d), the vertical axis plots the number of cycles until a solution in DCSP is found. Note that the lower evaluation values and cycles indicate the better performance in the analysis and the experiments respectively.

Here, the analytical results in Figure 2 match to the real experimental results in two different problem settings. That is, the ordering of strategies in analytical results is same with the empirical performance ordering. For instance, in the problem setting 1 (Figure 2-a & b), the experimental results (Figure 2-b) show that $S_{low} - S_{high}$ is the best with the least number of cycles, and $S_{low} - S_{low}$ and $S_{high} - S_{high}$ performs worse. The analytical results (Figure 2-a) clearly show that $S_{low} - S_{high}$ has the least evaluation value, and $S_{low} - S_{low}$ and $S_{high} - S_{high}$ have larger values. Note that, as a strategy performs worse, the evaluation value increases in the COM-MTDP model.

Our initial results illustrate that the strategy analysis with the COM-MTDP model match the actual experimental performance comparisons. Thus, the model could potentially form a basis for predicting strategy performance in a given

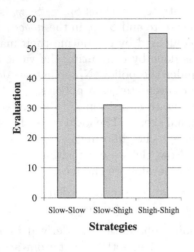

(a) Analytical results from setting 1

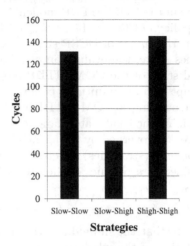

(b) Experimental results from setting 1

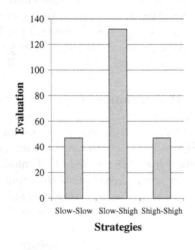

(c) Analytical results from setting 2

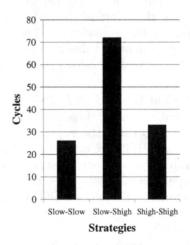

(d) Experimental results from setting 2

Fig. 2. DCSP strategy analysis with COM-MTDP

situation, and enable agents to flexibly adapt their strategies to changing circumstances.

6   Conclusion

In this paper, first we presented a formal model called R-COM-MTDP for modeling team formation and reorganization approaches by extending an existing formal model COM-MTDP that specializes in communication action analysis. R-COM-MTDP enables a rigorous and systematic analysis of complexity-optimality tradeoffs in team formation and reorganization approaches for different domain types. It provided: (i) worst-case complexity analysis of the team (re)formation under varying communication and observability conditions; (ii) illustrated under which conditions role decomposition can provide significant reductions in computational complexity.

In addition to the extension of COM-MTDP for team (re)formation, we proposed COM-MTDP as a formal framework for DCSP value selection strategy analysis. Different strategies are mapped onto COM-MTDP policies, and their performance can be compared by evaluating the policies. Thus, R-COM-MTDP could open the door to a range of novel analyses of multiagent coordination. The two extensions to COM-MTDP provided in this paper could open the door to a range of novel analyses of multiagent coordination.

Acknowledgement. The research in this paper was supported by National Science Foundation grant #0208580 and NASA Jet Propulsion Laboratory subcontract "Continual Coherent Team Planning". We thank David Pynadath for valuable discussion and feedback.

References

1. Jung, H., Tambe, M., Kulkarni, S.: Argumentation as Distributed Constraint Satisfaction: Applications and Results, *Proceedings of International Conference on Autonomous Agents* (2001)
2. Kitano, H., Tambe, M., Stone. P., Veloso, M., Coradeschi, S., Osawa, E., Matsubara, H., Noda, I., Asada, M.: The Robocup Synthetic Agent Challenge 97, *Proceedings of International Joint Conference on Artificial Intelligence* (1997)
3. Kitano, H., Tadokoro, S., Noda, I., Matsubara, H., Takahashi, T., Shinjoh, A., Shimada, S.: Robocup Rescue: Search and rescue for large scale disasters as a domain for multi-agent research, *Proceedings of IEEE International Conference on Systems, Man and Cybernetics* (1999)
4. Modi, P., Jung, H., Tambe, M., Shen, W., Kulkarni, S.: A Dynamic Distributed Constraint Satisfaction Approach to Resource Allocation, *Proceedings of International Conference on Principles and Practice of Constraint Programming* (2001)
5. Nair, R., Tambe, M., Marsella, S.: Team formation for reformation in multiagent domains like RoboCupRescue, *Proceedings of the International Symposium on RoboCup* (2002)
6. McDermott, D.: The 1998 AI Planning Systems Competition, *AI Magazine*, 21(2) (2000)
7. Minton, S., Johnston, M. D., Philips, A., Laird, P.: Solving Large-scale Constraint Satisfaction and Scheduling Problems Using a Heuristic Repair Method, *Proceedings of National Conference on Artificial Intelligence* (1990)

8. Peshkin, L., Meuleau, N., Kim, K., Kaelbling, L.: Learning to cooperate via policy search, *Proceedings of International Conference on Uncertainty in Artificial Intelligence* (2000)
9. Pynadath, D., Tambe, M.: Multiagent teamwork: analyzing the optimality complexity of key theories and models, *Proceedings of International Conference on Autonomous Agents and Multi Agent Systems* (2002)
10. Tambe, M.: Towards flexible teamwork, *Journal of Artificial Intelligence Research* 7:83-124 (1997)
11. Wellman, M., Greenwald, A. Stone, P., Wurman, P.: The 2001 Trading Agent Competition, *Proceedings of Innovative Applications of Artificial Intelligence Conference* (2002)
12. Yokoo, M.: Asynchronous Weak-commitment Search for Solving Distributed Constraint Satisfaction Problems, *Proceedings of International Conference on Principles and Practice of Constraint Programming* (1995)
13. Yokoo, M., Hirayama, K.: Distributed constraint satisfaction algorithm for complex local problems, *Proceedings of International Conference on Multi Agent Systems* (1998)
14. Yoshikawa T.: Decomposition of dynamic team decision problems, *Proceedings of IEEE Transactions on Automatic Control* (1978)
15. Xuan, P., Lesser, V., Zilberstein, S.: Communication decisions in multiagent cooperation, *Proceedings of Autonomous Agents* (2001)

Bounded Model Checking for Interpreted Systems: Preliminary Experimental Results*

A. Lomuscio[1], T. Łasica[2], and W. Penczek[2,3]

[1] Department of Computer Science
King's College London, London WC2R 2LS, United Kingdom
alessio@dcs.kcl.ac.uk
[2] Institute of Computer Science, PAS
01-237 Warsaw, ul. Ordona 21, Poland
tlasica@life.pl, penczek@ipipan.waw.pl
[3] Podlasie Academy, Institute of Informatics, Siedlce, Poland

Abstract. We present experimental results relating to a bounded model checking algorithm applied to the attacking generals problem. We use interpreted systems semantics and a logical language comprising knowledge and time.

1 Introduction

The field of MAS is concerned with the study of open, distributed systems, where the entities (processes or *agents*) show highly flexible and autonomous behaviour. MAS research spans from theoretical foundations to architectures, and applications. The problems and techniques used in MAS have much in common with the literature of distributed systems and software engineering, but contrary to these disciplines, the emphasis here is on the prominence given to concepts such as knowledge, beliefs, obligations, etc., that are used to model the agents in the system. Since information technology is facing the task of delivering ever more complex distributed applications, MAS researchers argue that much is to be gained from an approach that focuses on high-level macroscopic characteristics of the entities, at least in the modelling stage. These considerations are not new by any means, and indeed represent the traditional response that computer science offers when the intrinsic complexity of the application increases.

MAS theories involve the formal representation of agents' behaviour and attitudes. To this end various modal logics have been studied and developed, including logics for knowledge, beliefs, actions, obligations, intentions, as well as

---

* Partly supported by the State Committee for Scientific Research under the grant No. 7T11C 00620, and by the EU Framework V research project ALFEBIITE (IST-1999-10298). The first author also acknowledges support from the UK Royal Academy of Engineers for funding to present this paper to the FAABS workshop, organised by NASA.

M.G. Hinchey et al. (Eds.): 'FAABS 2002, LNAI 2699, pp. 115–125, 2003.

combinations of these with temporal operators. These logics are seen as *specifications* of particular classes of MAS systems. Their aim is to offer a precise description of the mental or behavioural properties that a MAS should exhibit in a specific class of scenarios.

While these investigations are conceptually valuable, they can seldom be applied *in practice*. In particular, the computational complexity of such logics is so hard [HV86] that current theorem provers seem to offer no easy solution to the problem of verification of MAS. Following a very influential paper by Halpern and Vardi [HV91], attempts have been made to use model checking techniques [CGP99] to tackle the verification problem of MAS. In particular, interpreted system semantics has been exploited to verify simple epistemic properties of MAS. Specifically, [vdHW02a,vdHW02b] analyse respectively the application of SPIN and MOCHA to model checking of LTL and ATL extended by epistemic modalities, whereas [vdMS99] studies the complexity of the model checking problem for systems for knowledge and time.

One recent attempt by the authors of this paper has involved extending bounded model checking [PWZ02] to knowledge and time [PL03a]. Bounded model checking, originally proposed in [BCCZ99,CBRZ01], is a technique based on SAT translation, that attempts to ease the problem of state-explosion by exploring only a part of the model that is sufficient to validate the particular formula that needs to be checked. The aim of this paper is to evaluate the technique presented in [PL03a], by reporting and commenting upon experimental results based on a typical MAS scenario.

The rest of the paper is organised as follows. Section 2 fixes the notation of the basic formal concepts on which this paper is based upon. Section 3 describes a BMC algorithm for **ECTLK**. In Section 4 we present an implementation for the bounded model checking algorithm. There we also discuss experimental results concerning an example in the MAS literature: the "attacking generals problem". In the final section we point to future and related work.

2   Basic Concepts and Notation

We assume knowledge of interpreted systems semantics [FHMV95], and the bounded checking algorithm developed for it in [PL03a]. What follows serves the purpose of fixing the notation, and providing a brief summary of the two above publications.

Assume a set of agents $A = \{1, \ldots, n\}$, a set of local states L_i and possible actions Act_i for each agent $i \in A$, and a set L_e and Act_e of local states and actions for the environment. The set of global states for the system is defined as $G \subseteq L_1 \times \ldots \times L_n \times L_e$, where each element $(l_1, \ldots, l_n, l_e)$ of G represents a computational state for the whole system. Further assume a set of protocols $P_i : L_i \to 2^{Act_i}$, for $i = 1, \ldots, n$, representing the functioning behaviour of every agent, and a function $P_e : L_e \to 2^{Act_e}$ for the environment. Note that this defines a non-deterministic system. We can model the computation taking place in the system by means of a transition function $t : G \times Act \to G$, where

$Act \subseteq Act_1 \times \ldots \times Act_n \times Act_E$ is the set of joint actions. Intuitively, given an initial state ι, the sets of protocols, and the transition function, we can build a (possibly infinite) structure that represents all the possible computations of the system. Many representations can be given to this structure; since in this paper we are only concerned with temporal epistemic properties, we shall find the following to be a useful one.

Definition 1. *Given a set of agents $A = \{1, \ldots, n\}$ a temporal epistemic model (or simply a model) is a pair $\mathrm{M} = (\mathcal{K}, \mathcal{V})$ with $\mathcal{K} = (W, T, \sim_1, \ldots, \sim_n, \iota)$, where*

- *W is a finite set of reachable global states for the system (henceforth called simply "states"),*
- *$T \subseteq W \times W$ is a total binary (successor) relation on W,*
- *$\sim_i \subseteq W \times W$ ($i \in A$) is an epistemic accessibility relation for each agent $i \in A$ defined by $s \sim_i s'$ iff $l_i(s') = l_i(s)$, where the function $l_i : W \to L_i$ returns the local state of agent i from a global state s. Obviously $\sim_i$ is an equivalence relation.*
- *$\iota \in W$ is the initial state,*
- *$\mathcal{V} : W \longrightarrow 2^{\mathcal{PV}}$ is a valuation function for a set of propositional variables $\mathcal{PV}$ such that $\mathbf{true} \in \mathcal{V}(s)$ for all $s \in W$. $\mathcal{V}$ assigns to each state a set of propositional variables that are assumed to be true at that state.*

Interpreted systems are traditionally used to give a semantics to an epistemic language enriched with temporal connectives based on linear time [FHMV95]. Here we use CTL by Emerson and Clarke [EC82] as our basic temporal language and add an epistemic component to it. We call the resulting logic Computation Tree Logic of Knowledge (**CTLK**).

Definition 2 (Syntax of CTLK). *Let $\mathcal{PV}$ be a set of propositional variables containing the symbol $\mathbf{true}$. The set of **CTLK** formulas $\mathcal{FORM}$ is defined inductively as follows:*

- *every member p of $\mathcal{PV}$ is a formula,*
- *if α and β are formulas, then so are $\neg\alpha$, $\alpha \wedge \beta$ and $\alpha \vee \beta$,*
- *if α is formula, then so are $\mathrm{EX}\alpha$, $\mathrm{EG}\alpha$ and $\mathrm{E}(\alpha\mathrm{U}\beta)$,*
- *if α is formula, then so is $\overline{\mathrm{K}}_i\alpha$, for $i \in A$,*
- *if α is formula, then so are $\overline{\mathrm{D}}_\Gamma\alpha$, $\overline{\mathcal{C}}_\Gamma\alpha$, and $\overline{\mathrm{E}}_\Gamma\alpha$, for $\Gamma \subseteq A$.*

The basic modalities are defined by derivation as follows: $\mathrm{F}\alpha \stackrel{def}{=} \mathbf{true}\mathrm{U}\alpha$, $\mathrm{A}(\alpha\mathrm{R}\beta) \stackrel{def}{=} \neg\mathrm{E}(\neg\alpha\mathrm{U}\neg\beta)$, $\mathrm{AX}\alpha \stackrel{def}{=} \neg\mathrm{EX}\neg\alpha$, $\mathrm{AG}\alpha \stackrel{def}{=} \neg\mathrm{EF}\neg\alpha$, $\mathrm{D}_\Gamma\alpha \stackrel{def}{=} \neg\overline{\mathrm{D}}_\Gamma\neg\alpha$, $\mathcal{C}_\Gamma\alpha \stackrel{def}{=} \neg\overline{\mathcal{C}}_\Gamma\neg\alpha$, $\mathrm{E}_\Gamma\alpha \stackrel{def}{=} \neg\overline{\mathrm{E}}_\Gamma\neg\alpha$. Moreover, $\alpha \to \beta \stackrel{def}{=} \neg\alpha \vee \beta$. We omit the subscripe Γ of the epistemic modalities if $\Gamma = A$, i.e., Γ is the set of all the agents.

The logic **ECTLK** is the restriction of **CTLK** such that negation can be applied only to elements of $\mathcal{PV}$ — the definition of **ECTLK** is identical to Definition 2 except for $\neg p$ replacing $\neg\alpha$ in the second itemised paragraph.

The logic **ACTLK** is the restriction of **CTLK** such that its language is defined as $\{\neg\varphi \mid \varphi \in \mathbf{ECTLK}\}$. It is easy to see that **ACTLK** formulas can be written as follows: $\mathrm{AX}\alpha$, $\mathrm{A}(\alpha\mathrm{R}\beta)$, $\mathrm{AF}\alpha$, $\mathrm{K}_i\alpha$, $\mathrm{D}_\Gamma\alpha$, $\mathcal{C}_\Gamma\alpha$, and $\mathrm{E}_\Gamma\alpha$.

Satisfaction and validity for **CTLK** is defined as standard [FHMV95,PL03a]. These can be defined also on a bounded model. This is essentially a temporal epistemic model as above, where the computational paths have been truncated at length k; we call them the k-computations.

Definition 3 (k-model). *Let* $M = (\mathcal{K}, \mathcal{V})$ *be a model and* $k \in \mathbb{N}_+$. *A* k-model *for* M *is a structure* $M_k = ((W, P_k, \sim_1, \ldots, \sim_n, \iota), \mathcal{V})$, *where* P_k *is the set of all the* k-computations *of* M, *i.e.,* $P_k = \bigcup_{s \in W} \Pi_k(s)$.

Satisfaction for the temporal operators in the bounded case depends on whether or not the computation π defines a loop, i.e., there is a transition from the last state of π to its earlier one. We refer to [PL03a] for more details.

The model checking problem ($M \models \varphi$) can be reduced to the bounded model checking problem ($M \models_k \varphi$) (see [PL03b] for details.)

3   A BMC Algorithm for ECTLK

In [PL03a] a method based on bounded semantics for a temporal epistemic language defined above was presented. The main idea of the method is that we can check φ over M_k by checking the satisfiability of a propositional formula $[M, \varphi]_k = [M^{\varphi, \iota}]_k \wedge [\varphi]_{M_k}$, where the first conjunct represents (part of) the model under consideration and the second a number of constraints that must be satisfied on M_k for φ to be satisfied. Once this translation is defined, checking satisfiability of an **ECTLK** formula can be done by means of a SAT-checker. Although from a theoretical point of view the complexity of this operation is no easier, in practice the efficiency of modern SAT-checkers makes the process worthwhile in many instances. In this process, an important decision to take is the size k of the truncation. We do not discuss this issue in this paper, but we do point out the fact that there are heuristics that can be applied in particular classes of examples.

A trivial mechanism, for instance, would be to start with $k := 1$, test SAT-satisfaction for the translation, and increase k by one either until $[M^{\varphi, \iota}]_k \wedge [\varphi]_{M_k}$ becomes satisfiable or k reaches $|M|$, i.e., the number of states of M.

Definition 4. *BMC algorithm for* **ECTLK**:

- *Let* $\varphi = \neg\psi$ *(where* ψ *is an* **ACTLK** *formula).*
- *Iterate for* $k := 1$ *to* $|M|$.
- *Select the* k-model M_k.
- *Select the submodels* M'_k *of* M_k *with* $|P'_k| \leq f_k(\varphi)$.
- *Translate the transition relation of the* k-computations *of all of the submodels* M'_k *into a propositional formula* $[M^{\varphi, \iota}]_k$.
- *Translate* φ *over all* M'_k *into a propositional formula* $[\varphi]_{M_k}$.
- *Check the satisfiability of* $[M, \varphi]_k := [M^{\varphi, \iota}]_k \wedge [\varphi]_{M_k}$.

The framework described in the previous sections allows us to verify the temporal epistemic properties of MAS. In principle, by means of BMC on **CTLK** we can check formulas representing:

- Private and group knowledge of a MAS about a changing world,
- Temporal evolution of knowledge in a MAS,
- Any combination of the above.

In practice the technique above is most useful when the following prerequisites are observed. First we should be able to specify fully the system under consideration. This can be done for instance by giving its complete description in terms of interpreted systems, i.e., by spelling out the sets of local states, actions, protocols, and transition relations. In this way we can build the model in an automatic way (details of how this can be done are not presented in this paper). Second, the benefits of the BMC machinery are more evident when the task is to check:

1. that an **ACTLK** formula is false (on an interpreted system),
2. that an **ECTLK** formula is true (on an interpreted system).

We perform 1) when we would like to check the model for faults, i.e., we would check whether some particular formula is actually false in the model. We perform 2) when we would like to check whether the model provides for a realisation of a formula.

4   Implementation and Experimental Results

In this section we introduce an implementation of the algorithm above as well as present and evaluate some experimental results obtained with it.

The tool, BMCIS (Bounded Model Checking for Interpreted Systems), is an extension of BBMC [PWZ02]. BMCIS is a bounded model checker for **ECTLK**. It computes translations into propositional formulas mentioned in the section above, and checks them for satisfaction by means of a SAT-checker. More precisely, BMCIS takes as input an interpreted system, an **ECTLK** formula to be checked, and an integer k representing the length of the model to be generated. The output is a propositional formula that is given to the Zchaff SAT-Checker [Zha01] to test for satisfaction. If the translated formula is not satisfied, k is increased until either the translated formula is satisfiable, or k reaches the size of the model.

In the description of the interpreted system, the user is required to provide the set of local states, actions, and a protocol for each agent of the system. Synchronisation among agents is achieved by locking each local transition to a global transition for the whole system. To describe state of affairs of the system, local propositions, i.e., propositions whose truth value depend on the local state of some agent, are used. Since we are concerned with modelling properties of the agents we do not see this as a limitation.

BMCIS is written in C++ making use of STL libraries. It runs both on Unix, and Windows machines. The tests presented below were produced by using a workstation equipped with a Pentium III 1GHz and 512 RAM under Linux RedHat 7.3.

4.1 Attacking Generals

We now give experimental results for an often analysed scenario: the coordinated attack problem. This is an example discussed in MAS, in distributed computing, as well as in epistemic logic. It concerns coordination of agents in the presence of unreliable communication. It is also known as the coordinated attack problem:

Two divisions of an army, each commanded by a general, are camped on the hilltops overlooking a valley. In the valley awaits the enemy. It is clear that if both divisions attack the enemy simultaneously, they will win the battle. While if one division attacks, it will be defeated. As a result neither general will attack unless he is absolutely sure the other will attack with him. In particular, one general will not attack if he receives no messages. The commander of the first division wishes to coordinate a simultaneous attack (at some point the next day). The generals can only communicate by means of messengers. Normally it takes a messenger one hour to get from one encampment to the other. However, it is possible that he will get lost in the dark or, worse yet, be captured by the enemy. Fortunately, on this particular night, everything goes smoothly. How long will it take them to coordinate an attack? ([FHMV95] page 176).

This example is appealing for at least two reasons. First, it is an instance of a recurring problem in coordination for action in MAS. Second, it can be formally analysed by means of interpreted systems and temporal epistemic logic. Crucially two key properties can be proven about the scenario above.

- No general will attack before it is common knowledge that they will both attack.
- No joint protocol can establish common knowledge, unless the delay with which the messages may be delivered is bounded.

From this one can infer that the generals will not attack on the night, even though the messengers do deliver the messages in exactly one hour. We refer to the literature [HM90] for a comprehensive analysis of the example, which turns out to be more subtle than it may appear at first. What we point out here is that the problem resides with the agents being forced to contemplate the possibility of the messenger getting lost at each round. This makes it impossible for common knowledge to be obtained in this circumstance[1].

Obviously it is problematic to perform model checking on the scenario as described above. The reason is that it is, in fact, a description for a *family* of joint protocols for the generals (the question of how long it will take to coordinate is more technically posed as "what joint protocol should the generals be running"). Indeed it looks difficult to prove in any way other than analytically as in the literature impossibility results of the kind mentioned above.

---

[1] One should not infer from this, as it is sometimes mistakenly done, that common knowledge can *never* been achieved by message passing. The key element here is that messages may be delayed without a bound.

For the purpose of this paper, we chose a particular joint protocol for the scenario above and verify the truth and falsity of particular formulas that capture its key characteristics. The variant we analyse is the following:

After having studied the opportunity of doing so, general A may issue a request-to-attack order to general B. A will then wait to receive an acknowledgement from B, and will attack immediately after having received it. General B will not issue request-to-attack orders himself, but if his assistance is requested, he will acknowledge the request, and will attack after a suitable time for his messenger to reach A (*assuming no delays*) has elapsed. A joint attack guarantees success, and any non-coordinated attack causes defeat of the army involved.

We can model the example above with the interpreted system which results from the product of the local protocols for *general A*, *general B*, and *the environment*. These are shown in Figures 1, 2, and 3, respectively. The global states are defined as 3-tuples of the local states of the above agents, whereas the global transitions are obtained by synchronising the local transitions with the same labels. The agent, which does not contribute to the synchronisation is assumed not to change its present local state.

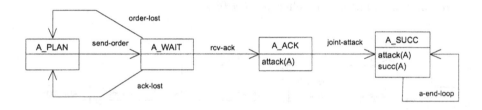

Fig. 1. Attacking generals: the local transition structure for general A

Figure 1 shows the transition structure for general A. *General A* begins by sending a request-to-attack order to *general B*, where the environment is used as a communication channel. After sending the order, A waits for the acknowledgement from B to come. Three things may happen at this stage. Either the order or the acknowledgement sent by B may be lost (this is represented by the transitions labelled *order-lost* and *ack-lost*, resp.). In this case, A goes back to state *A_PLAN*. If the message does get through together with the acknowledgement, A moves to state *A_ACK*. The proposition **attack(A)** is true in that state meaning that *general A* will attack the enemy.

Figure 2 shows the transition structure for general B. *General B* begins by receiving a request-to-attack order from *general A* (represented by transition labelled *rcv-order*). In fact, B receives the order from the environment, which is used as a communication channel. After receiving the order, B sends an acknowledgement to A and moves to state *B_READY*. The proposition **attack(B)**

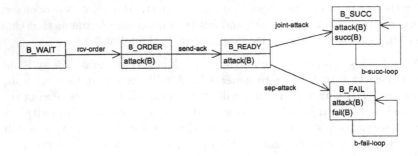

Fig. 2. Attacking generals: the local transition structure for general B

is true in that state meaning that *general B* will attack the enemy. Two things may happen at this stage.

Agent B may attack on its own. This occurs when the acknowledgement is lost, and results in a transition of B to state *B_FAIL* (represented by transition labelled *sep-attack*). B's attack is joint with A's; this occurs when the acknowledgement does get through, and results in B moving to state *B_SUCC* (represented by transition labelled *joint-attack*).

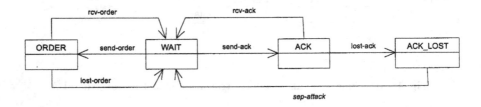

Fig. 3. Attacking generals: the local transition structure for the environment

Figure 3 shows the transition structure for the environment, which may deliver messages or lose them. The initial local state is *WAIT*. After receiving the order from A (represented by transition labelled *send-order*), the environment may pass it to B (transition labelled *rcv-order*) or lose it (transition labelled *lost-order*), and moves to state *WAIT*. There, after receiving an acknowledgement from B (represented by transition labelled *send-ack*), the environment goes to state *ACK*. Notice that this only happens where B has received the order, i.e., B moved to state *B_ORDER*. From *ACK* two things are possible. Either the environment chooses to pass the acknowledgement to B by executing the transition labelled *rcv-ack* or to lose it by executing the transition labelled *lost-ack*, which results in reaching state *WAIT* or *ACK_LOST*, resp. If the acknowledgment is lost, the environment moves to state $WAIT$ (transition labelled *sep-attack*), which represents a separate attack of B.

Some **properties** we may be interested in checking for the example above are the following:

1. $M \models AG(\text{attack}(\mathbf{A}) \Rightarrow K_B\text{attack}(\mathbf{A}))$,
2. $M \models AG(\text{attack}(\mathbf{B}) \Rightarrow K_A K_B\text{attack}(\mathbf{A}))$,
3. $M \models EF\text{fail}(\mathbf{B}) \wedge EF(succ(A) \wedge \text{succ}(\mathbf{B}))$,
4. $M \models EF(\text{attack}(\mathbf{B}) \wedge E\overline{GC}_{\{A,B\}}\neg\text{attack}(\mathbf{B}))$,
5. $M \models AG(\text{attack}(\mathbf{B}) \Rightarrow AF(K_B K_A\text{attack}(\mathbf{B})))$.

In the above, the proposition **attack(A)** is true on all the global states of the model M (for the interpreted system) having A's local state equal to A_ACK or A_SUCC. The proposition **attack(B)** is true on all the states of the model M having B's local state equal to A_ACK or A_SUCC. The proposition **fail(B)** is true on all the states with B's local state equal to B_FAIL, whereas **succ(A)** on all the states where A's local state is equal to A_SUCC. Similarly, **succ(B)** holds on all the states where B's local state is equal to B_SUCC.

Property 1) states that whenever general A decides to attack, then general B knows about it. Property 2) says that if B decides to attack, then A knows that B knows that A will attack. Property 3) states that there exist (separate) evolutions leading to success and failure. Property 4) states that it is possible that A and B will never achieve the common knowledge about B's attack. Property 5) specifies that if B decides to attack, then he will always eventually know that A knows that B had decided to attack

Formulas 1,2 and 5 are not true on the interpreted system in consideration, whereas formulas 3-4 are. This means that we can show that the negations of the formulas 1,2, and 5, and formulas 3,4 (which are all **ECTLK** formulas) are valid in the model. In all of the experiments the satisfiability of the corresponding translation of an **ECTLK** formula was found to be reasonably fast.

For each tested formula the experimental results are presented in the following form:

K	the bound of the bounded model
CNF clauses	the number of the CNF clauses
BMC-memory	memory in kB used by BMCIS
BMC-time	time in seconds used by BMCIS
SAT-time	time in seconds for SAT-checking, Zchaff

The **property 1** in **ACTLK** : $AG(\text{attack}(\mathbf{A}) \Rightarrow K_B\text{attack}(\mathbf{A}))$
Its negation in **ECTLK** : $EF(\text{attack}(\mathbf{A}) \wedge \overline{K}_B\neg\text{attack}(\mathbf{A}))$

K	CNF clauses	BMC-memory	BMC-time	SAT-time	Satisfiable
1	514	68	<0.01	<0.01	N
2	909	88	0.01	<0.01	N
3	1352	116	0.01	<0.01	N
4	1843	140	0.02	<0.01	Y

The **property 2** in **ACTLK** : $AG(\text{attack}(\mathbf{B}) \Rightarrow K_A K_B \text{attack}(\mathbf{A}))$

Its negation in **ECTLK** : $EF(\text{attack}(\mathbf{B}) \wedge \overline{K}_A \overline{K}_B \neg \text{attack}(\mathbf{A}))$

K	CNF clauses	BMC-memory	BMC-time	SAT-time	Satisfiable
1	561	72	<0.01	<0.01	N
2	1023	100	0.01	<0.01	Y

The **property 3** in **ECTLK** : $EF\text{fail}(\mathbf{B}) \wedge EF(\text{succ}(\mathbf{A}) \wedge \text{succ}(\mathbf{B}))$

K	CNF clauses	BMC-memory	BMC-time	SAT-time	Satisfiable
1	909	88	0.01	<0.01	N
2	1533	120	0.02	<0.01	N
3	2157	156	0.02	<0.01	N
4	2781	188	0.03	<0.01	N
5	3405	224	0.04	<0.01	Y

The **property 4** in **ECTLK** : $EF(\text{attack}(\mathbf{B}) \wedge EG\overline{C}_{\{A,B\}} \neg \text{attack}(\mathbf{B}))$

K	CNF clauses	BMC-memory	BMC-time	SAT-time	Satisfiable
1	2113	152	0.04	<0.01	N
2	4087	256	0.29	0.02	N
3	6353	372	1.96	0.02	Y

The **property 5** in **ACTLK** : $AG(\text{attack}(\mathbf{B}) \Rightarrow AF(K_B K_A \text{attack}(\mathbf{B})))$

Its negation in **ECTLK** : $EF(\text{attack}(\mathbf{B}) \wedge EG(\overline{K}_B \overline{K}_A \neg \text{attack}(\mathbf{B})))$

K	CNF clauses	BMC-memory	BMC-time	SAT-time	Satisfiable
1	2173	156	0.06	<0.01	N
2	3979	248	0.22	0.02	N
3	6113	352	0.57	0.02	N
4	8575	484	1.24	0.07	N
5	11365	624	2.43	0.02	Y

5   Conclusions

While theoretical studies in MAS have long been focused on theories, i.e., *specifications* of MAS, a growing number of researchers have now started investigating the issue of concrete verification of MAS. In this work we have described an implementation of the framework of bounded model checking for knowledge and time discussed in [PL03a]. A variant of the attacking generals problem has been implemented and various formulas verified. The tables of the previous section show that the implementation performed as intended for the task. We feel the methodology of bounded model checking can tackle examples that are considerably more complex than the one explored here. Indeed, the purpose of the work presented in this paper is simply illustrative of the kind of problems we can solve. In future work we plan to test the methodology above to complex scenarios with large number of states.

References

[BCCZ99]   A. Biere, A. Cimatti, E. Clarke, and Y. Zhu. Symbolic model checking without BDDs. In *Proc. of TACAS'99*, volume 1579 of *LNCS*, pages 193–207. Springer-Verlag, 1999.

[CBRZ01]   E. Clarke, A. Biere, R. Raimi, and Y. Zhu. Bounded model checking using satisfiability solving. *Formal Methods in System Design*, 19(1):7–34, 2001.

[CGP99]   E. M. Clarke, O. Grumberg, and D. A. Peled. *Model Checking*. The MIT Press, Cambridge, Massachusetts, 1999.

[EC82]   E. A. Emerson and E. M. Clarke. Using branching-time temporal logic to synthesize synchronization skeletons. *Science of Computer Programming*, 2(3):241–266, 1982.

[FHMV95]   R. Fagin, J. Y. Halpern, Y. Moses, and M. Y. Vardi. *Reasoning about Knowledge*. MIT Press, Cambridge, 1995.

[HM90]   J. Halpern and Y. Moses. Knowledge and common knowledge in a distributed environment. *Journal of the ACM*, 37(3):549–587, 1990. A preliminary version appeared in *Proc. 3rd ACM Symposium on Principles of Distributed Computing*, 1984.

[HV86]   J. Y. Halpern and M. Y. Vardi. The complexity of reasoning about knowledge and time. In *ACM Symposium on Theory of Computing (STOC '86)*, pages 304–315, Baltimore, USA, May 1986. ACM Press.

[HV91]   J. Halpern and M. Vardi. *Model checking vs. theorem proving: a manifesto*, pages 151–176. Artificial Intelligence and Mathematical Theory of Computation. Academic Press, Inc, 1991.

[vdHW02a]   W. van der Hoek and M. Wooldridge. Model checking knowledge and time. In *Proc. of the 9th Int. SPIN Workshop (SPIN'02)*, volume 2318 of *LNCS*, pages 95–111. Springer-Verlag, 2002.

[vdHW02b]   W. van der Hoek and M. Wooldridge. Tractable multiagent planning for epistemic goals. In *Proc. of the 1st Int. Conf. on Autonomous Agents and Multi-Agent Systems (AAMAS'02)*, July 2002. To appear.

[vdMS99]   R. van der Meyden and H. Shilov. Model checking knowledge and time in systems with perfect knowledge. In *Proceedings of Proc. of FST&TCS*, volume 1738 of *Lecture Notes in Computer Science*, pages 432–445, Hyderabad, India, 1999.

[PL03a]   W. Penczek and A. Lomuscio. Verifying epistemic properties of multi-agent systems via model checking. In T. Sandholm, editor, *Proceedings of AAMAS03*, 2003. To appear.

[PL03b]   W. Penczek and A. Lomuscio. Verifying epistemic properties of multi-agent systems via bounded model checking. *submitted to Fundamenta Informaticae*, 2003.

[PWZ02]   W. Penczek, B. Woźna, and A. Zbrzezny. Bounded model checking for the universal fragment of CTL. *Fundamenta Informaticae*, 51(1-2):135–156, 2002.

[Zha01]   L. Zhang. Zchaff. http://www.ee.princeton.edu/~chaff/zchaff.php, 2001.

Verifiable Middleware for Secure Agent Interoperability*

Dr. Ramesh Bharadwaj

Center for High Assurance Computer Systems
Na val Researh Laboratory
Washington DC, 20375
ramesh@itd.nrl.navy.mil

Abstract. There is an increasing need, within organizations such as the
Department of Defense and NASA, for building distributed applications
that are rapidly re-configurable and survivable in the face of attacks and
changing mission needs. Existing methods and tools are inadequate to
deal with the multitude of challenges posed by application development
for systems that may be distributed over multiple physical nodes separated by vast geographical distances. The problem is exacerbated in a
hostile and unforgiving en vironment such as space where, in addition,
systems are vulnerable to failures. It is widely believed that intelligen t
softw are agen ts are cen tral to the delopment of agile, efficient, and robust distributed applications. This paper presents details of agent-based
middleware that could be the basis for developing such applications. We
pa y particular attention to the correctness, survivabilit y, and efficiency
of the underlying middleware architecture, and dev elop a middleware
definition language that permits applications to use this infrastructure
in a scalable and seamless manner.

1 Introduction

There is an increasing need, both within Gov ernment and Industry, for methods
and tools to dev elop highly distributed and robust computer-based systems.
Moreov er, soft w are-in tensiv e systems in safetand mission-critical areas, such
as soft w arefor manned and unmanned space missions within NASA, or the
Net w ork-Cetric Warfare [6], Total Ship Computing, and FORCEnet initiatives
of the Department of Defense (DoD), are of exceedingly high complexity and
must in addition be dependable, robust, and adaptive. A recen t Department
of Defense (DoD) report to Congress [10] iden tifiesthe lac k of secure, robust
connectivity and in teroperability as one of the major impediments to progress
in Netw ork Cetric Warfare.

2 Why Software Agents?

It is widely ackno wledgedthat intelligen t soft w areagents are central to the
development of the capabilities required to write robust, reconfigurable, and

---

* This work is sponsored by the Office of Naval Research

M.G. Hinchey et al. (Eds.): 'FAABS 2002, LNAI 2699, pp. 126–132, 2003.

surviv abledistributed applications. This is because agents are an efficient, effectiv e, and surviable means of information distribution and access. Agents are efficient because only relevan t information needs to be passed along. Agents are effective because they allow local control over updates and the dissemination of data. Agents are survivable because their control is distributed. This new technology, which includes both autonomous and mobile agents, addresses many of the c hallenges posed by distribution of applications and is capable of achieving the desired quality of service especially over unreliable, low-bandwidth communication links. How ever, agents technology carries with it associated securit y vulnerabilities. Distributed computing in general carries with it risks such as denial of service, Trojan horses, information leaks, and malicious code. Agents technology, by introducing autonomy and code mobility, may exacerbate some of these problems. In particular, a malicious agent could do serious damage to an unprotected host, and malicious hosts could damage agents or corrupt their data. Such threats become very real in a distributed computing environment, in which a malicious intruder may be actively trying to disrupt communications.

The Secure Agents Middleware (SAM) is being designed to provide the required degree of trust in addition to meeting a set of achievable securit y requirements. Such an infrastructure is central to the successful deployment and transfer of agents technology to industry because securit y is a necessary prerequisite for distributed computing. To make agent-based systems economically viable, it is imperative that their development, upgrade, in tegration, testing, certification, and delivery be rapid and cost-effective. How ever, immense and profound challenges of softw are trust w orthiness remain. Methods and tools for software development that are available commercially are not sufficient to meet the challenges posed by the distribution of processing functions, real-time and non-real-time integration, multi-lev el securit,yand issues characteristic of COTS products, such as malicious code, viruses, worms, and Trojan horses.

3   Requirements for Secure Mobile Agents

Security is a **fundamental concern** in SAM. By building securit y from the ground up into SAM, we gain efficiency by identifying and dealing with potential bottlenecks early , i.e., at the design state. SAM proides an efficient architecture *and* ensures security by eliminating unnecessary and/or insecure communication among agents and hosts. Our classification of requirements for secure mobile agents is from FGS96[1]. For the initial release of SAM we shall assume a degree of trust among the participants. This is reasonable in a large organization such as the DoD or NASA where it may be assumed that other policing methods and techniques for intrusion detection and tolerance will identify and sift out casual in truders and eav esdroppers or programs carrying malicious payloads. How ev er, w eplan to address this very important research issue in greater detail in the later stages of this effort.

---

[1] "Security for Mobile Agents: Issues and Requirements," William N. Farmer, Joshua
   D. Gutman, and Vipin Swarup, The MITRE Corporation, Bedford, MA.

This project addresses the following security requirements:

- The author and sender of an agent are authenticated.
- The correctness of an agent's code is chec ked.
- Privacy is maintained during transmission by encrypting agent data.
- Hosts protect themselves against malicious agents b y first authenticating an agent and chec king that its proposed activities are authorized.
- Host safety is ensured by created agents in a language SOL [2] that promotes the development of safe programs.
- Senders have control o ver their agents, e.g., they may restrict or increase an agent's authorization in particular situations.
- By equipping each agen t with a state appraisal function, hosts can ensure that an agent is always in a safe state.
- Senders have control o ver which hosts hav e the authority to execute an agent.

4   A Brief Introduction to SOL

Agents are created in a special purpose synchronous programming language called Secure Operations Language (SOL) [2, 4, 1]. A SOL application comprises a set of agent modules, each of which runs on a given host. The host executes an agent module in compliance with a set of locally enforced security policies. A SOL multi-agent system may run on one or more hosts, spanning multiple net w orks and mltiple administrative domains.

A mote is   the unit of specification in SOL and comprises variable declarations, assumptions and guarantees, and definitions. The **assumptions** section typically includes assumptions about the en vironmert of the agent. Execution aborts when any of these assumptions are violated b y the en vironmert. The required safety properties of an agent are specified in the **guarantees** section. The **definitions** section specifies updates to internal and controlled variables.

A v ariable definition is either a *one-state* or a *two-state* definition. A one-state definition, of the form $x = expr$ (where $expr$ is an expression), defines the value of variable x in terms of the values of other variables *in the same state*. A tw o-state v ariable definition, of the form $x =$ **initially** $init$ **then** $expr$ (where $expr$ is a tw o-state expression), requires the initial alue of x to equal expression $init$; the v alue of x in eac h subsequent state is determined in terms of the values of variables in that state *as well as the previous state* (specified using operator **PREV**). A *conditional expression*, consisting of a sequence of branches "[] guard $\rightarrow$ expression", is introduced by the keyword "if" and enclosed in braces ("{" and "}"). A guard is a boolean expression. The semantics of the conditional expression if { $[]g_1 \rightarrow expr_1$ $[]g_2 \rightarrow expr_2 \ldots$ } is defined along the lines of Dijkstra's *guar ded commands* [7] – in a given state, its value is equivalent to expression $expr_i$ whose associated guard g_i is true. If more than one guard is true, the expression is nondeterministic. It is an error if none of the guards evaluates to **true**, and execution aborts. The *case expression* **case** $expr$ { $[]v_1 \rightarrow expr_1$ $[]v_2 \rightarrow expr_2 \ldots$ } is equivalen tto the conditional expression if { $[](expr == v_1) \rightarrow expr_1$ $[](expr == v_2) \rightarrow expr_2 \ldots$ }. The conditional expression and the case expression may optionally have an **otherwise** clause with the obvious meaning.

```
deterministic reactive module SecureRead {

interfaces
  string file_read(string filename, int position, int size);
  void   send(string address, string data);

internal variables
  {no_reads, read_performed} status;

definitions
  status = initially no_reads then
  case PREV(status) {
    [] no_reads ->
      if {
        [] @send        -> PREV(status)
        [] @file_read -> read_performed
      }
    [] read_performed ->
      if {
        [] @file_read -> read_performed
        // @send illegal!
      }
  }; // end case
} // end module SecureRead
```

Fig. 1. A SOL agent module that implements safe access to local files.

5   Enforcement Automata

In this section, we shall examine how *enforceable* safet y and security policies [11]
are expressed in SOL as *enfor ement automata* (also known as *security agents*
[3]). The enforcement mechanism of SOL works by terminating all executions of
a program for which the policy being enforced no longer holds. For reasons of
readability and maintainability, we prefer to use explicit automata for enforcing
safet y properties and securit y policies, although any language that allows references to previous values of variables may suffice. Unlike assertions, where no
additional state is maintained, SOL enforcement automata may include additional variables that are updated during the transitions of the automata.

5.1   Security Automata

We use the example from [11] to illustrate how w emay implement a security
policy that allows a softw are ageɪt to send data to remote hosts (using method
send) as well as read local files (using method **file_read**). How ev er, inocations
of **send** subsequent to **file_read** are disallow ed. It is difficult, if not impossible,
to configure current systems to implement such a policy. For example, it cannot
be implemented in the "sandbox" model of Ja va[8] in which one may either
always or nev er allo w access to a system resource. As shown in Figure 1, this
policy is easily implemented in SOL.

6   F ormalSemantics of SOL

State Machines A SOL agent module describes a state machine [2]. A *state machine* Σ is a quadruple (V, S, Θ, ρ), where $V = \{v_1, v_2, \ldots, v_n\}$ is a finite set of *state variables*; S is a nonempty set of *states* where each state $s \in S$ maps each $v \in V$ to its range of legal v alues;$\Theta : S \rightarrow$ *bo ol an* is a predicate characterizing the set of *initial states*; $\rho : S \times S \rightarrow$ *bo ole an*is a predicate characterizing the *transition relation*. We write Θ as a logical formula inv olving the names of variables in V. Predicate ρ relates the values of the state variables in a previous state $s \in S$ to their values in the current state $s' \in S$. We write ρ as a logical formula inv olving the v alues of state v ariables in the previous state (specified using operator PREV) and in the current state.

SOL Predicates Given a state machine $\Sigma = (V, S, \Theta, \rho)$ we classify a predicate $p : S \rightarrow$ *bo ol an* as a *one-state* predicate of Σ and a predicate $q : S \times S \rightarrow$ *bo ol an* as a *two-state* predicate of Σ.

More generally, *SOL predicate* refers to either a one-state or tw o-state predicate, and *SOL expression* refers to logical formulae or terms containing references to current or previous values of state variables in V.

*R eachability*Given a state machine $\Sigma = (V, S, \Theta, \rho)$, a state $s \in S$ is *reachable* (denoted R *eachabl*$_{\Sigma}(s)$) if

(i) $\Theta(s)$ or
(ii) $\exists s' \in S : Reachable_{\Sigma}(s')$ and $\rho(s', s)$

Invariants A one-state predicate p is a *state invariant* of Σ if and only if

$$\forall s : R \ eachabl_{\Sigma}(s) \Rightarrow p(s)$$

A tw o-state predicate$q$ is a *transition invariant* of Σ if and only if

$$\forall s, s' : (R \ eachabl_{\Sigma}(s) \wedge \rho(s, s')) \Rightarrow q(s, s')$$

More generally, a SOL predicate x is an *invariant* of Σ if x is a state invariant or transition inv ariant of Σ.

*V erific ation*For a SOL agent module describing a state machine Σ, and a set of SOL predicates $X = x_1, x_2, \ldots$, verification is the process of establishing that each SOL predicate $x_i \in X$ is an invariant of Σ.

7   SOL Agent Modules

A SOL agent module describes both an agent's en vironmert, which is usually nondeterministic, and the required agent behavior, which is usually deterministic [5,9]. A SOL agent module describes the required relation betw een*monitored variables*, environmental quantities that the agent monitors, and *contr olld* *variables*, environmental quantities that the agent controls. Additional internal variables are often introduced to make the description of the agent concise. In this paper, we only distinguish betw een monitored variables, i.e., variables whose values are specified by the environment, and *dep endent variables* i.e., variables whose values are dependent on the values of monitored variables. Dependent variables include all the con trolled variables and internal variables of a agen t module. In the sequel, we assume that variables $v_1, v_2, \ldots, v_I$ are an agent's monitored variables, and that variables $v_{I+1}, v_{I+2}, \ldots, v_n$ are the agent's dependent variables. The notation $NC(v_1, v_2, \ldots, v_k)$ is used as an abbreviation for the SOL predicate $(v_1 = PREV(v_1)) \land (v_2 = PREV(v_2)) \land \ldots \land (v_k = PREV(v_k))$.

Components of the state machine $\Sigma = (V, S, \Theta, \rho)$ are specified in the section **definitions** of a SOL agent module. The initial predicate Θ is specified in terms of the initial values for each variable in V, i.e., as predicates $\theta_{v1}, \theta_{v2}, \ldots, \theta_{vn}$, so that $\Theta = \theta_{v1} \land \theta_{v2} \land \ldots \land \theta_{vn}$. The transition relation ρ is specified as a set of assignments, one for eac h dependent variable of Σ, i.e., as SOL predicates $\rho_{vI+1}, \rho_{vI+2}, \ldots, \rho_{vn}$, each of which is of the form:

$$v_i = \begin{cases} e_1 \ if \ g_1 \\ e_2 \ if \ g_2 \\ \vdots \end{cases}$$

where $1 \leq i \leq n$, and $e_1, e_2, \ldots$ are SOL expressions, and $g_1, g_2, \ldots$ are SOL predicates. To av oid circular definitions, we impose an additional restriction on the occurrences of state variables in these expressions as below:

Define *dependency relations* D_{new}, D_{old}, and D on V × V as follows: For variables v_i and v_j, the pair $(v_i, v_j) \in D_{new}$ iff v_j occurs outside a $PREV()$ clause in the SOL expression defining v_i; the pair $(v_i, v_j) \in D_{old}$ iff $PREV(v_j)$ occurs in the SOL expression defining v_i; and $D = D_{new} \cup D_{old}$. We require D_{new}^+, the transitive closure of the D_{new} relation, to define a partial order.

7.1   Composition of SOL Agent Modules

Consider tw o SOL agent modules describing the state machines $\Sigma_1 = (V_1, S_1, \Theta_1, \rho_1)$ and $\Sigma_2 = (V_2, S_2, \Theta_2, \rho_2)$. We define the *composition* of the tw o SOL agents $\Sigma = (V, S, \Theta, \rho)$ as $\Sigma = \Sigma_1 \| \Sigma_2$ where

$$\begin{aligned} V &= V_1 \cup V_2 \\ \Theta &= \Theta_1 \land \Theta_2 \\ \rho &= \rho_1 \land \rho_2 \end{aligned}$$

Each $s \in S$ maps each $v \in V$ to its range of legal values

provided that there is no circularity in the occurrences of variables in ρ. Also in practice, it is the case that ρ_1 and ρ_2 define disjoint sets of state variables.

8   Conclusions

We plan to continue the development of design and analysis tools for SOL agents, and verification tools such as automatic invarian t generators and checkers, theorem provers, and model checkers. We currently have a compiler for SOL which generates Java code suitable for execution on multiple hosts. Planned extensions to the compiler include support for fine-grained security and problems associated with survivability such as fault-tolerance, load balancing, and self-stabilization.

The goal of the NRL secure agents project is to develop enabling technology that will provide the necessary securit y infrastructure to deploy and protect time- and mission-critical applications on a distributed computing platform. Our inten tion is to create a *robust* and *survivable* information grid that will be capable of resisting threats and surviving attac ks. One of the criteria on which this technology will be judged is that critical information is convey ed to principals in a manner that is secure, safe, timely, and reliable. No malicious agencies or other threats should be able to compromise the integrit y or timeliness of delivery of this information.

References

1. R. Bharadwaj. SINS: a middleware for autonomous agents and secure code mobility. In *Proc. Second International Workshop on Security of Moble Multi-Agent Systems (SEMAS-02), First International Joint Conference on A utonomous A gents and Multi-Agent Systems (AAMAS'02)*, Bologna, Italy, July 2002.
2. R. Bharadwaj. SOL: A verifiable sync hronous language for reactiv e systems. In *Proc. Synchr onousL anguages, Applications, and Programming, ETAPS 2002*, Grenoble, France, April 2002.
3. R. Bharadwaj. An infrastructure for secure interoperability of agents. T echnical report, Naval Research Laboratory, Washington, DC, To appear.
4. R. Bharadwaj et al. An infrastructure for secure interoperability of agents. In *Proc. Sixth World Multiconfer enc e on Systemics, Cybernetics, and Informatics*, Orlando, Florida, July 2002.
5. R. Bharadwaj and C. Heitmeyer. Model chec king complete requirements specifications using abstraction. *A utomated Software Engineering*, 6(1), Jan uary 1999.
6. A. K. Cebrowski and J. J. Garstka. Netw ork-Centric Warfare: Its origin and future. In *Pr oc. United States Naval Institute*, January 1998.
7. E. W. Dijkstra. *A Discipline of Programming*. Prentice-Hall, 1976.
8. L. Gong. Java Security: Present and near future. *IEEE Micro*, 15(3):14–19, 1997.
9. C. Heitmeyer, J. Kirby, B. Labaw, M. Archer, and R. Bharadwaj. Using abstraction and model checking to detect safety violations in requirements specifications. *IEEE T ransactions on Softwar Engineering*, 24(11), Novem ber 1998.
10. Secretary of Defense et al. Network centric w arfare. T echnical report, Departmen of Defense, www.c3i.osd.mil/NCW, July 2001.
11. F. B. Schneider. Enforceable security policies. *ACM Transactions on Information and System Security*, 3(1):30–50, February 2000.

Distributed Implementation of a Connection Graph Based on Cylindric Set Algebra Operators

Silvana Zappacosta Amboldi

Imperial College, Department of Computing
sza@doc.ic.ac.uk   http://www.doc.ic.ac.uk/{ sza

Abstract. The Connection Graph structure is transformed into another type of graph that reflects the inter-relationship of the most general unifiers, by using elements of Cylindric Set Algebras, and the computation of a solution is redefined in term of computing the Transitive Closure of the graph based on this new structure, thus providing an environment for a distributed implementation.

1 Introduction

The principal aim in the construction of a connection graph in Kowalski's resolution proof procedure [Kow75] was to expose in a concise form the search space where the proof, if any, is to be found. The edges of the graph or links indicate the axioms that could take part in the proof as well as indicating the particular instance of those axioms by means of the most general unifier that labels each link. Essentially, the links contain all the information needed to establish a proof. Much of the effort in this area has been oriented towards the development of heuristics to control the selection of links. Two of the major problems such heuristics have to deal with are the incompatibility of links and the unfolding of recursions.

The motivation behind the work presented here is to use Cylindric Algebra [LHT71] as set theoretical model to express the unifiers in terms of distinct elements and operators of this algebra. This allows to redefine the connection graph in terms of an Instantiation Graph (encapsulating the inter-relations of all unifiers) and express the computation of a solution not as the dynamic transformation of the connection graph but as the computation of the Transitive Closure of the graph, generating a natural environment for a distributed implementation of the later computation.

Part of this approach has been inspired by work done in the area of path-finding problems by Backhouse and Carre [BC75] and by suggestions put forward by Bibel in [Bib82].

2 Instantiation Graph

The Instantiation Graph is the structure that encapsulates the information of the most general unifiers labelling the links of the connection graph. Its underlying

M.G. Hinchey et al. (Eds.): 'FAABS 2002, LNAI 2699, pp. 133–145, 2003.
© Springer-Verlag Berlin Heidelberg 2003

model is the Cylindric Set Algebra defined by the Herbrand Lattice, as defined later.

2.1   Herbrand Universe and Partial Terms

The Herbrand Universe (HU) of ground terms for a first order predicate calculus expression is generated from the set of constants and function symbols appearing in it.

Definition : A *partial term* is obtained by omitting one or more sub-terms from a term, without altering the arity of the embedding function. To this effect, the place of the eliminated sub-term is filled with an underscore symbol. Since each element of HU is finite, the set of partial terms obtained from that element is also finite. The null term is a partial term of every element of HU.

Lemma : Partial terms are partially ordered by *term inclusion* (denoted $\leq$), i.e. given partial terms p_1 and p_2, $p_1 \leq p_2$, iff p_1 is obtained by omitting zero or more sub-terms from p_2. e.g. the term $f(g(a), b)$ has $_-$, $f(_-, _-)$, $f(g(_-), b)$, $f(g(_-), _-)$, $f(_-, b)$ and $f(g(a), _-)$ as lesser partial terms.

Clearly, $\leq$ is reflexive, transitive and antisymmetric. The null term is the least element for this ordering.

Definition : A *common partial term* for a finite subset of HU is a partial term which is included in every element of the set. There can be more than one common partial term for a set, but there is a unique greatest common partial term.

2.2   Herbrand Lattice

Taking the Herbrand Universe as isomorphic, cardinality wise, to the set of natural numbers, it follows that the power set of HU, is a lattice isomorphic to the power set of the natural numbers described in [Sco76]

Therefore, the Herbrand Lattice (HL), partially ordered by set inclusion, forms a boolean lattice in which the least upper bound is set union and the greatest lower bound is set intersection. The maximal and minimal element are HU and the empty set respectively.

The namability of the elements of HL is determined by the greatest common partial term. The cardinality of each element is determined according to the following rules:

- singleton sets are named by the ground term they contain;
- HU is the only element named by the null term;
- a partial term (other than the null element) names the subset of HU containing all the possible instances of this partial term.
- any other remaining element, i.e. infinite elements with null term as greatest common partial term or finite elements other than singleton sets, is named by the (possibly infinite) collection of names of its proper subsets. Such partition can always be established on a boolean lattice.

e.g. the element $\{f(a), f(b)\}$ is named by $f(a) \sqcup f(b)$ while the element $\{a, f(a), f(b), f(f(a)), \ldots\}$ i.e. containing a and all applications of f, is named by $a \sqcup f(\_)$.

2.3   Normal Form of a Substitution Equivalent Class

Substitutions are defined as finite set of pairs of the form $< term/variable >$ such that there is only one such pair per variable being replaced.

Sometimes, for a given variable, the substituting term is hidden in more than one pair e.g. $\{< f(y)/x >, \ < g(u)/y >\}$. This lack of clarity is avoided by normalising the substitution. Lets denote LV the set of variables appearing on the left hand side of the pairs and RV the set of variables appearing on the right hand side of the pairs:

- If $LV \cap RV = \emptyset$ the substitution is said to be in *normal form*. All well-formed substitutions have a normal form. This is the case of the most general unifiers labelling the links of a connection graph.
- If $LV \cap RV \neq \emptyset$ the substitution is said to be *cyclic*. This can be the case for some of the substitutions labelling pseudo-links in a connection graph e.g. $\{< f(y)/y >\}$ is the unifier labelling the pseudo-link between the literal of the clause $P(y) \vee \sim P(f(y))$.

The presence of pairs of the form $< v_i/v_j >$ in a normalised substitution, where v_i, v_j are interchangeable, gives origin to an equivalence class. The choice of $< v_i/v_j >$ or $< v_j/v_i >$ in the substitution is irrelevant to the final result and therefore it therefore essential to work with a normalised representative of the class.

This representative is obtained from any element of the class by means of a vectorial representation and the introduction of normalisation bindings.

Let S be a normalised substitution such that

$$S = \{< t_i/v_i >\}$$

where $v_i \in LV$ and t_i is either a ground term or a non-ground term whose variables belong to RV. The normalised representative for the class of S, denoted $\vec{S}$, is obtained by the following steps:

- create $\vec{S} = \{< *i/v_i > | v_i \in LV \sqcup RV\}$ where $*i$ is a normalised binding, i.e. the variable is replaced by something whose value is not yet defined.
- for all pairs of the form $< v_i/v_j > \in S$ transform $\vec{S}$ as

$$\vec{S} = \vec{S} - \{< *j/v_j >\} \sqcup \{< *i/v_j >\},$$

   that is, the two variables have now the same normalised binding.
- for pairs of the form $< t_i/v_i > \in S$ such that t_i is ground

$$\vec{S} = \vec{S} - \{< *i/v_i >\} \sqcup \{< t_i/v_i >\},$$

- for pairs of the form $< t_i/v_i > \in S$ such that $t_i = f(v_k)$,

$$\vec{S} = \vec{S} - \{< *i/v_i >\} \sqcup \{< f(*l)/v_i >\},$$

where $*l$ appears already in the pair $< *l/v_k >$ of $\vec{S}$.

Notice that because $\vec{S}$ is normalised v_k is at most replaced by another variable, hence the normalised binding associated to it. Entities such as $f(*l)$ will be called *normal terms* .

The right and left hand sides of this representative contain totally independent elements: variables on one side and normalised bindings and normal terms on the other e.g. the normal form of $\{< f(y)/x >, \quad < g(u)/y >\}$ is $\{< f(g(*1))/x >, \quad < g(*1)/y >, \quad < *1/u >\}$.

By imposing an ordering on the pairs, or more precisely, on the variables, the normalised representative is seen as a vector of normal terms with respect to the ordering. Extending the vectors as to include all the variables appearing in a connection graph, renaming as necessary to ensure nodes do not have common variables, will provide a graph/matrix representation for the links, whose elements are normal terms. The number of such variables determines the cardinality (α) of the Cartesian space of base HL where the solution is to be found. This approach was fundamental in the establishment of the new structures presented in the next subsection.

2.4   Most General Unifiers Amalgamation

As mentioned in [Kow75], look-ahead techniques assume that all substitutions are, and will be, compatible i.e. there is no information a-priori about the effect of transmitting values through the clauses by means of variables. By amalgamating all the links of a connection graph into a single structure, the **Instantiation Graph**, the search space is effectively reduced by pointing out potential term incompatibilities.

The most general unifiers labelling the links in a connection graph are, by definition, well formed substitutions. Their normalisation provides a means for separating the variables from the elements of the Herbrand Universe, which are the domain related items of information to be handled. These variables and elements give rise to 3 structures:

- A graph of variables VG : this is a multi-edge (undirected) graph, every node corresponds to a distinct variable of the vector; every edge is labelled with the identifier of the link which connects both variables, hence there can be more than one edge between two given nodes. As described, this graph represents the pairs of the form $< v_i/v_j >$ of an unnormalised substitution; in the context of Cylindric Set Algebra (CSA), every edge denotes the **diagonal** element $\mathbf{D}_{ij}$ of the HL^α space (first type of narrowing of the domain).

  In an unnormalised substitution with pairs $\{< v_k/v_i >, < v_k/v_j >\}$, the normalisation process described in section 2.3 will produce $\{< *1/v_i >, < *1/v_j >, < *1/v_k >\}$; when put into the context of the underlying CSA, the value $*1$ corresponds to the element $\mathbf{D}_{ij} \cap \mathbf{D}_{ik}$.

- A sub-lattice of the Herbrand Lattice SHL : the meta terms belonging to RV determine the elements of SHL in the following way:
  - The sets HU and $\emptyset$ are always included;
  - normalised bindings, i.e. *i, are equated with HU; in the context of the underlying CSA, a pair $< *i/v_k >$ in the normalised vector is defined as $< \mathbf{D}_k/v_k >$ by the postulates of CSA ($\mathbf{D}_k = HU$, for all k).
  - a ground term is represented by the singleton set containing it;
  - a semi ground term of the form $f(*i)$ is represented by the set containing the partial term naming it. e.g. an unnormalised pair $\{< f(v_k)/v_i >\}$ is normalised to $\{< f(*1)/v_i >, < *1/v_k >\}$; the later, in terms of CSA, becomes $\{< f(\mathbf{D}_k)/v_i >, < \mathbf{D}_k/v_k >\}$.

  The meet and join operators are preserved from HL.
- Instantiation arrows IA : This part will represent the pairs of the form $< groundterm/var_i >$ and $< semigroundterm/var_i >$ of an unnormalised substitution. An arrow departs from the node of VG i.e. variable being replaced, and points to the subset of SHL representing the ground or semi ground term; in the later case, the variables appearing in the unnormalised unifier are part of the information of the arrow.

  In the context of CSA, an instantiation arrow determines the subset of HL to which any **inner cylindrification** operation for a variable other than var_i is applied to (second type of narrowing). This is because we regard the finding of a solution as finding a non-empty cylindrification for every variable taking into account the 2 types of narrowing applied to HL^α.

Example. Give the connection graph shown in Figure 1:

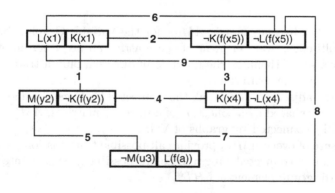

Fig. 1. Connection Graph G_1.

Its corresponding Instantiation Graph is given in Figure 2.

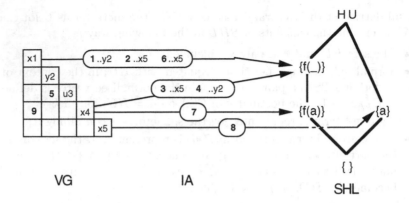

Fig. 2. Instantiation Graph corresponding to G_1

2.5   Determining Incompatibilities

Incompatibilities amongst links will not arise in a connection graph whose clauses contain either no variables or only variables; in the first case all links are labelled with the empty substitution, in the second case all the m.g.u.'s are renaming substitutions. In both cases, the problem of finding a proof is equivalent to the one of finding a proof in the propositional case.

Furthermore, the Instantiation Space Graph for the first case simply consists of the SHL part while in the second case it consists of only the VG part. The cases that really matter are those where the IG is complete i.e. all three parts exists. A separate study of each part and their interrelation provides the information needed to the establishment of all latent incompatibilities.

VG. First, the adjacency matrix AM_{VG} for the Variable Graph is built. As the graph is multi-edge, every element of the matrix can be either empty, a single identifier or a set of them; as the graph is undirected, only a triangular matrix is needed for the representation.

Having the adjacency matrix, all the connected parts can be determined and AM_{VG} can be replaced by a collection of adjacency matrices, AM_{VG}^i, representing each of the connected subgraphs of VG.

The closure of every AM_{VG}^i provides all possible transmission paths between two variables in a connected subgraph i.e. all possible necessary intersections of the named **diagonal** elements of HL^α.

IA. The connected subparts of VG can be ordered according to their variables dependency. This is indicated by the variables labelling the arrows directed towards subsets of SHL named by a partial term. So, for every subgraph VG^i there is a, possibly empty, set D^i of dependable variables.

Hence, VG^i is said to depend upon VG^j iff there is a variable $v \in D^i$ such that $v \in VG^j$.

In the best case, the dependencies will constitute a linear order; otherwise, the existence of cycles in the dependencies indicates the presence of recursive functions; their induction schema can be determined by looking at the partial terms being pointed at by the instantiation arrows.

Every variable is then examined individually to determine incompatibilities:

- two pointers to sets HL_i and $HL_j \in HL$ such that
  - $HL_i \sqcap HL_j = \emptyset \Rightarrow$ links incompatible
  - $HL_i \sqcap HL_j \neq \emptyset \Rightarrow$ links compatible;

  since the **inner cylindrification** of the empty set produces the empty set.
- pointer to set HL_i which is an abstract representation, hence has a variable name as label:
  - if variable belongs to another subgraph then pointer is acceptable,
  - if variable belongs to the same subgraph then pointer plus path(s) from pointer to variable constitute an incompatible set of links i.e. recursion;
- an acceptable pointer to HL_i and a pointer to HL_j such that
  - $HL_i \sqcap HL_j = \emptyset \Rightarrow$ links incompatible
  - $HL_i \sqcap HL_j \neq \emptyset \Rightarrow$ links compatibility depends on value of labelling variable.

Figure 3 shows the dependencies of the VG component for G_1 form a linear order.

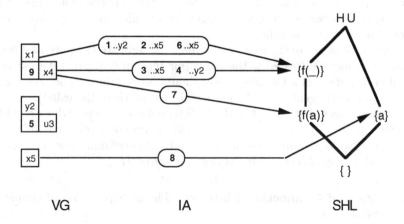

Fig. 3. Dependencies within the Instantiation Graph of G_1

3   Search of a Solution

3.1   Partial Coverings and Partial Unifiers

When a link is selected, the two literals connected by it are said to be covered and the nodes containing those literals are said to be partially connected. When all the literals in a node are covered, then the node becomes totally connected.

A partial covering of the original connection graph is determined by the selection of a set of compatible links such that:

- at least one node is totally connected,
- the covering is continuous.

The combination of the links corresponding to a partial covering constitute a partial unifier.

If all the nodes in a partial covering are totally connected, then the covering is said to be total.

3.2   Search Space

Transitive Closure of the Connection Graph. The matrix representation of the connection graph can be handled like a normal mono-node graph by slightly modifying the multiplication operation on matrices so that the transitive closure of the graph can be computed.

For a graph with n nodes, only the powers of M up to level n are of interest.

M^1 represents the connecting links of the connection graph. The main diagonal (MD) is null (no literal never links to itself) while the mail block diagonal (MBD) contains the pseudo links present in the graph.

M^n the blocks other than the MDB are null.

M^p for $1 < p < n$, the main diagonal indicates the vertices (sometimes called hinges) of factorisation loops. The combined unifiers of a factorisation loop should be $\neq \perp$ and a-cyclic.

The other elements in the main block diagonal indicate the potential pseudo links that may be created if the corresponding unifications take place: the combined unifiers of a tautology loop should be $\neq \perp$ but cyclic (the a-cyclic ones would only create tautologies, which will be then discarded).

The other blocks that are not in the MBD contain elements whose combined unifiers are $\neq \perp$ and a-cyclic. These elements represent proper acyclic paths in a graph, so they cannot contain any combination of links that have already appeared in the MBD of any previous power of M.

Multiplication of Connection Matrices. The multiplication of simple matrices is expressed as

$$M_{ij}^p = \sum_{k=1}^{n} M_{ik}^1 \times M_{kj}^{p-1} \qquad \text{for } 2 \leq p \leq n \text{ and } 1 \leq i,j \leq n$$

where $\times$ is the multiplication operation on $\Re$.

- First of all, we need to define a similar multiplication operation in our domain i.e. MGU (most general unifiers) to indicate the combination ($\circ$) of normalised most general unifiers such that, for $nmgu$ σ, we have

$$
\begin{aligned}
\sigma \circ \sigma &= \sigma && \text{idempotency} \\
\varepsilon \circ \sigma &= \sigma \circ \varepsilon = \sigma && \text{unit element (empty unifier)} \\
\bot \circ \sigma &= \sigma \circ \bot = \bot && \text{zero element}
\end{aligned}
$$

- Second, we are trying to form an a-cyclic path hence we don't want to extend paths by looping upon themselves so the main block diagonal sub-blocks will not be taken into account for the block matrix multiplication:

$$
M_{IJ}^p = \sum_{K=1}^{n} M_{IK}^{p-1} \circ M_{KJ} \qquad \text{for } p \in [2, n], I, J \in [1, n], I \neq K \text{ and } K \neq J.
$$

Each element within a block is calculated as follows:

$$
(M_{IJ}^p)_{ij} = \sum_{K=1}^{n} \sum_{k=1}^{|N_K|} \sum_{k'=1}^{|N_K|} \left(M_{IK}^{p-1} \right)_{ik} \circ (M_{KJ})_{k'j}
$$

$$
\text{for } i \in [1, |N_I|], j \in [1, |N_j|], I \neq K, J \neq K \text{ and } k \neq k'.
$$

Given the symmetry of M, the block matrix multiplication can be rewritten in terms of the lower triangular matrices as:

$$
M_{IJ}^p = \sum_{K=1}^{J-1} M_{IK}^{p-1} \circ M_{JK} + \sum_{K=J}^{I-1} M_{IK}^{p-1} \circ M_{KJ} + \sum_{K=I}^{n} M_{KI}^{p-1} \circ M_{KJ}
$$

$$
\text{for } p \in [1, n], I, J \in [1, n] \text{ and } J \leq I.
$$

The formula to calculate each element within a block remains the same.

4   Distributed Implementation

The implementation under progress makes use of the programming language Qu-Prolog. [CRH98,CRH99]. This was conceived as a tool for implementing theorem provers and has recently been enriched with multi-threading and message passing capabilities. In this framework, there is a main process that simply initiates the triggering of stand alone processes, one for each node in the graph. This main process is then relegated to the function of gathering the final result for information purposes. Qu-Prolog also offers an interface for the interaction with Tcl/Tk processes; this facility has been used in the tool here presented, as an option, to show the evolution of the computations in each node process and reflect all the narrowing operations taking place (see Figure 5).

Each node process will initiate communication with the other processes in order to establish the existence of links; this creates the equivalent of matrix M^1.

The information kept in each node process has 2 parts:

– the vector of variables that appear in the node
– a second vector, same length as the number of literals in the node, to keep track of the covering of the literals i.e. when an incident link has been chosen.

There will be as many of these tuples as necessary depending on the messages received. They encapsulate the instances of the node that contribute to the solution.

The messages received by the nodes are basically of two types:

– initial confirmation of a link existence: the variable vector elements are set with the sets of HL^α reflecting the narrowing embedded in the most general unifier.
– further narrowing of domains: this is equivalent to the computation of the transitive closure of M. As unifiers are further combined with others, there will be more narrowing being applied to the domains; sub-threads will keep track of these further narrowing as the partial coverage of the node is effectively computed. Any narrowing leading to the empty set will not trigger a sub-thread (incompatible links).

Once the closure has been completed, each node examines the vectors thus created: only those that reflect a complete coverage of the node will be reported back to the initiator node.

Examples. Figure 4 shows the result of computing the transitive closure of graph G_1 by using this distributive approach.

The computation is not shown is full, but the final result for each node is shown. The vertical boxes represent the vector of variables, containing elements of HU from the normalised (in the sense of the underlying CSA) form of the instantiation arrows. To the right of the vertical boxes, on each line, it is indicated the covering of literals, a • shows a literal is not covered and a number indicates the link identifier covering the corresponding literal.

One of the lines of the right-bottom node shows that taking links **3** and **7** for a complete covering of this node results in the narrowing of the domain for x_4 to element $f(a)$; this induces a narrowing of element $\mathbf{D}_5$ to be propagated via link **3**. The latter propagation produces a new instance of the second line of the right-top node, where variable x_5 is reduced to value a, with a partial covering **3** •. This latter narrowing, together with the partial covering of link **6**, produces a total coverage **3 6**, with value a for x_5.

Factorisation loops are shown by the presence of sets of link identifiers as covering for literals.

Figure 5 shows the result of the execution of the distributed tool on graph G_1 when the visualisation option is active. The red boxes on the left hand side of each window indicate the incomplete coverages of literals, while the green ones indicate the total coverages; the latter are the coverages analysed for the establishment of the solution.

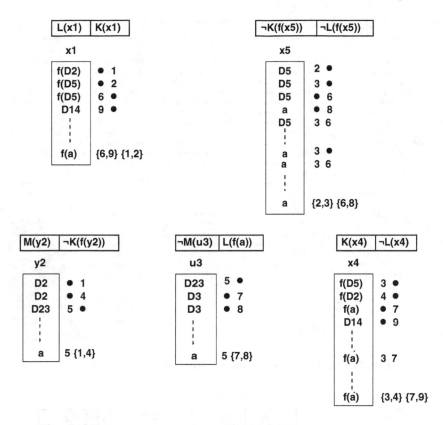

Fig. 4. Computed distributive transitive closure of G_1

Figure 6 shows the full computation for the connection graph, shown at the top of the figure, defined by the set of clauses $\{P(f(a)), \sim P(x) \vee P(f(x)), \sim P(f(f(f(a))))\}$.

The two nodes on the extreme sides of the figure contain ground literals, hence the vector of variables for each is empty; nevertheless, a link is connected in each case, rendering both literals completely covered.

The central node contains the pseudo link labelled **3**. For a pseudo link to be resolved upon, two copies of the same clause need to be present in the graph; we represent this notion by creating 2 coverages for each pseudo link in the node. In this example, the link derived from the pseudo link resolving with the literal on the right will have value $\mathbf{D}_2$ for variable x_2 and partial coverage • **3**; similarly, the link resolving with the literal on the left has value $f(\mathbf{D}_2)$ and partial coverage **3** •.

The first white arrow indicates the total coverage obtained by combining link **1** with the right edge of link **3**; the narrowing applied to $\mathbf{D}_2$ produces value a for x_2. By propagating this narrowing to the partial coverages for the pseudo link (first 2 lines) we obtain the next 2 lines below the first white arrow. When

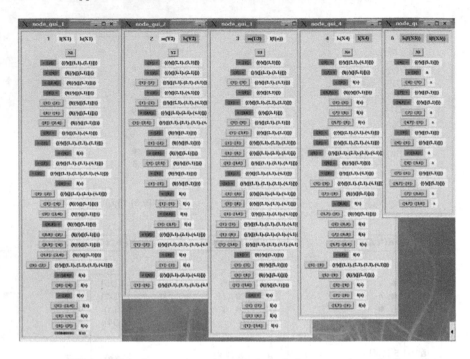

Fig. 5. Visual execution of multi-threaded prover of graph G_1

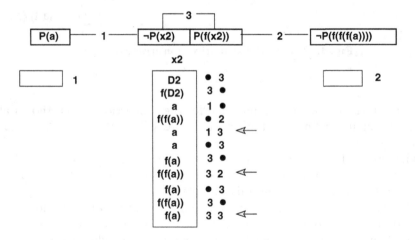

Fig. 6. Computed distributive transitive closure including a pseudo-link

all possible combination, narrowing and propagations have been applied, there are 3 complete coverages that correspond to the clauses $\{\sim P(a) \vee P(f(a)), \sim P(f(a)) \vee P(f(f(a))), \sim P(f(f(a))) \vee P(f(f(f(a))))\}$; these, together with the original clauses $\{P(a), \sim P(f(f(f(a))))\}$ provide the necessary model for the contradiction.

5   Further Work

One area of further work is to investigate the use of the implementation here sketched as part of the problem solving capabilities for a rational agent, as suggested by Fisher and Wooldridge [FW97]. The distributed approach taken in the present work allows for cooperative work to be carried out by various agents, since the transitive closure computation, as performed by the threads, follows the same strategy, so the overhead of communication costs is compensated by the uniformity of the algorithm.

A second area to explore is potential use of this work in the field of Abduction. As the threads keep track of incomplete vectors of literals, in absence of a solution, these incomplete coverages and the unifier of the associated vector of variables indicate potential axioms that could be added.

Another avenue is to explore the model of the Instantiation Graph and the Transitive Closure as basis to explain other resolution based heuristics that do perform the actual creation of resolvants.

Acknowledgements. The author wishes to thank Prof. Keith Clark for his valuable feed-back on the preparation of this document and Dr. William Knottenbelt for his untimely help with the "obscure" side of LATEX.

References

[BC75]   R C Backhouse and B A Carre. Regular algebra applied to path-finding problems. *J. Inst. Maths. Applics.*, 15:161–186, 1975.

[Bib82]   W Bibel. *Automated Theorem Proving.* Vieweg and Sohn, Wiesbaden, 1982.

[CRH98]   Keith Clark, Peter J. Robinson, and Richard Hagen. Programming internet based DAI applications in Qu-Prolog. In Chengqi Zhang and Dickson Lukose, editors, *Multi-Agent Systems: Theories, Languages and Applications*, pages 137–151, Heidelberg, 1998. Springer-Verlag.

[CRH99]   K Clark, P J Robinson, and R A Hagen. Multi-threading and message communication in Qu-Prolog. Technical Report 99-41, Software Verification Research Centre, School of Information Technology, The University of Queensland, Brisbane 4072, Australia, December 1999.

[FW97]   M Fisher and M Wooldridge. Distributed problem-solving as concurrent theorem-proving. In Boman and van de Velde, editors, *Multi-Agent Rationality*. Springer-Verlag, 1997.

[Kow75]   R A Kowalski. A proof procedure using connection graphs. *J. ACM*, 22(4): 572–595, Oct 1975.

[LHT71]   J D Monk L Henkin and A Tarski. *Cylindric Algebra, part 1.* North-Holland, 1971.

[Sco76]   D Scott. Data type as latices. *Siam Journal of Computing*, 5(3):522–587, Sep 1976.

Using Statecharts and Modal Logics to Model Multiagent Plans and Transactions

Albert C. Esterline

Dept. of Computer Science and NASA ACIT Center, North Carolina A&T State University,
Greensboro, NC 27411, USA
esterlin@ncat.edu

Abstract. We use a version of Statecharts to represent multiagent plans and transactions. Although epistemic and deontic logic are abstract and appropriate for specification, we argue that an agent must know that abstract modal properties apply to it and its collaborators. We develop a language that describes Statechart features but also expresses knowledge, common knowledge, and obligations. The hierarchical and concurrent structure of plans and transactions can hereby be exploited by modal logics.

1 Introduction

Concurrency formalisms differ on how abstract or concrete they are [1]. The most concrete are automata (such as Petri nets), which describe processes as concurrent, interacting machines with the full details of their operational behavior. More abstract are process algebras (such as CSP, CCS, and the π-calculus), term algebras that use process terms as an abstract concurrent programming language that emphasizes compositionality, that is, how complex processes are composed from simpler ones using a small set of combinators. The most abstract concurrency formalisms are logics, either ordinary predicate logic (where variables range over such things as finite sequences of communication actions) or some modal logic. A logic is used to *specify* the communication behavior of processes by asserting properties that should hold of this behavior. In the work reported here, we use both an automaton formalism and modal logics. In particular, we use Statecharts [2], which generalize finite-state automata with hierarchy and concurrency. And we use epistemic logic (the modal logic of knowledge) and deontic logic (the modal logic of obligation, prohibition, and permission).

The different levels of abstraction of these formalisms suggest a design approach: one starts with a specification in the form of assertions in epistemic or deontic logic (or both), and one refines a Statechart design, incrementally adding detail, always ensuring that the modal-logic assertions are not violated by the behavior of the Statechart. Normally, the implemented system directly reflects only the final design. The specification is relevant for verification, testing, and maintenance but has no direct realization in the computational entities that realize the design. The situation, however, is different when multiagent systems are developed. An agent, if it is to coordinate its behavior with other agents, must in some sense know that (and perhaps to some extent how) the abstract notions used in the specification apply to it and its

M.G. Hinchey et al. (Eds.): FAABS 2002, LNAI 2699, pp. 146–161, 2003.
© Springer-Verlag Berlin Heidelberg 2003

collaborators. Also, an agent should be able to determine whether its behavior or the behavior of one of its collaborators violates an obligation or prohibition (as per the specification) and, if so, to take appropriate corrective behavior.

Here we consider semantics of epistemic and deontic logic in terms of Statecharts. Such semantics must be understood to some degree if we are to determine whether Statechart designs violate modal-logic specifications. We shall consider how multiagent plans and transactions may be represented with Statecharts in a way that manifests the abstract, modal properties characteristic of a specification. We introduce Statecharts in section2 and epistemic and deontic logic in section 3. In section 4, we introduce a language that refers to Statechart features but allows us to formalize knowledge about plans and to make deontic statements relating to plans. Section 5 addresses multiagent transactions especially as they relate to obligations. Section 6 concludes and mentions future work.

2 Statecharts

A Statechart [2] allows one to represent hierarchies of states and states that are concurrently active. A superstate that contains substates and transitions that elaborate its sequential behavior is called an XOR state since, when it is active, exactly one of its substates is active. A superstate that contains concurrent substates – "orthogonal components" – is called an AND state. A basic state has no substates so is neither an XOR nor an AND state. A transition has a label e/a indicating that, when the system is in the source state and event e happens, it can move to the target state on performing action a; the action part is optional. A transition may have a non-basic state as either its source or target. In fact, it may have several source states (in different orthogonal components) or several target states (again in different orthogonal components).

For example, consider the Statechart in Figure 1. The overall state, s, is an AND state: the system must be in both its ("orthogonal") substates, u and v. States u and v are XOR states. In state u, the system must be in either m or k (but not both). Similarly for states m (substates n1-2) and v (substates p1-4). An arrow starting from a darkened circle points to the default initial substate of an XOR state. The label on the transition from k to m indicates that, in state k, if event a1 happens, the system can move to state m on performing action b1. Likewise for the other transitions. An action done by one orthogonal component can be a triggering event for another. E.g., when component u transitions from k to m, it performs action b1, which is the triggering event for component v when in state p1 (which may then transition to state p2). This chart is *zoomed in* on all components. If, for example, we *zoom out* on component u, the substates of m and the transitions among them are suppressed.

A transition label more generally may be of the form $e[c]/a$ (a again being optional), where c is a condition that must be true for the transition to fire. Finally, a history mechanism (denoted by H) may be included in a state. This indicates that, when the state is re-entered, the substate that was last active should again become active. This is useful for us for returning from the repair done in a violation state.

Orthogonal components in a Statechart coordinate by broadcast communication: an action in one component can serve as a triggering event in any other orthogonal component. This implicit coordination, however, eliminates encapsulation. We thus adopt Pazzi's Part-Whole Statecharts [3]. Here an additional orthogonal component – a "whole" – is added so that the original orthogonal components – the "parts" – communicate only with the whole, never with each other. If we add a new part to the Part-Whole Statechart, only the whole needs to change. We can sometimes factor the coordination of the parts so that it is handled by several parts. Also, when several Part-Whole Statecharts are combined, it is natural to introduce a new whole that coordinates the behavior of the wholes of these components. This is quite a natural way to achieve hierarchy among a collection of agents with an interesting communcal structure.

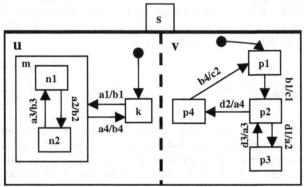

Fig. 1. An XOR state with two communicating substates

3   Epistemic and Deontic Logic

The presentation of epistemic logic here follows [4] and that of deontic logic follows [5] and [6]. We present the basic notions and syntax first of epistemic logic (subsection 3.1) then of deontic logic (subsection 3.2). The semantics of both is presented in subsection 3.3.

3.1   The Basic Notions and Syntax of Epistemic Logic

Consider a set $A = \{1, 2, ..., n\}$ of agents and a group $G \subseteq A$ of these agents. We are interested in propositional epistemic logic, which, besides the familiar propositional connectives, includes the epistemic operators K_i, $i \in A$, E_G, and C_G, where (for proposition φ)

$K_i \varphi$ is read "agent i knows that φ,"

$E_G \varphi$ is read "everyone in group G knows that φ," and

$C_G \varphi$ is read "it is common knowledge in group G that φ."

We expect $E_G \varphi$ to be true iff $\wedge_{i \in G} K_i \varphi$ is true (i.e., iff $K_1 \varphi$ and $K_2 \varphi$ and ... and $K_n \varphi$). To characterize common knowledge, let $E_G^{\,j}$ be the iteration of the E_G operator

j times, We then expect $C_G \varphi$ to be true iff $\wedge_{j \in \omega+} E_G^j \varphi$ is true. That is, it is common knowledge in group G that φ iff everyone in G knows that φ, everyone in G knows that everyone in G knows that φ, and so on, for arbitrarily deep nestings of the "everyone in G knows that" operator. In fact, common knowledge can be characterized with purely finite means as a fixed point since we have

$$C_G \varphi \Leftrightarrow E_G (\varphi \wedge C_G \varphi)$$

Several axiom systems for epistemic logic have been proposed. The S5 system, however, is more or less standard. A characteristic axiom of particular note is a version of the T axiom of general modal logic, called here the Knowledge Axiom:

$$K_i \varphi \Rightarrow \varphi$$

That is, if agent i knows that φ, then φ is true (reflecting the success nature of "to know"). If this axiom is dropped, we get a logic that characterizes belief (a "doxastic" logic): agent i might believe that φ even when φ is false.

The notion formalized by epistemic logic that is of particular interest for the study of collaborating systems of agents is that of common knowledge since common knowledge is a necessary and sometimes also sufficient condition for coordination. To see this, consider the simple example of what is needed on the part of the driving public for traffic lights to serve their intended role. It is not enough that everyone knows that red means stop and green means go. It must also be the case that everyone knows that everyone knows these facts. Otherwise, we could not proceed with confidence through a green light (since, for all we know, the people coming in the conflicting directions would not know that red means stop) and stopping for a red light would often be pointless (since those coming in the conflicting directions might stop since they might not know that I know that red means stop).

3.2 The Basic Notions and Syntax of Deontic Logic

Deontic logic is the logic of obligation, prohibition, and permission. It was first developed for the general version of these notions – for example, obligations that hold of everyone and are not specific to some group and are not obligations one agent has to another. So, in our initial account here, the modal operators are not indexed (as they are in epistemic logic) with agent or group names. Standard deontic logic, besides the familiar propositional connectives, includes modal operators O, P, and F, where (for proposition φ)

O φ is read "φ is obligatory,"
P φ is read "φ is permitted," and
F φ is read "φ is forbidden (or prohibited)."
Usually the following equivalences are valid:

$$P \varphi \Leftrightarrow \neg O \neg \varphi \Leftrightarrow \neg F \varphi$$

One could, therefore, take only one of the deontic operators as primitive.

The development of deontic logic has been driven by certain paradoxes. Such a paradox exists when the status (valid, satisfiable, etc.) of a deontic-logic formula conflicts with the intuitive understanding of the natural-language reading of the formula. One response to the paradoxes has been the introduction of dyadic deontic logic, where each operator is indexed with a proposition (essentially, a second propositional argument) expressing the condition under which the modality holds. For example, $O_\psi \, \varphi$ indicates that, given that ψ, it is obligatory that φ.

In many situations, we must analyze not obligations, prohibitions, and permissions that apply generally but rather these modalities restricted to specific individuals or groups. Let A denote an agent or a group of agents. Then, for example, $O_A \, \varphi$ indicates that it is obligatory for A that φ. These deontic modalities are known as *special* obligations, etc. [7]. There are also *directed* obligations, etc. [7]. For example, where A and B denote agents or groups of agents, $O_{A,B} \, \varphi$ indicates that A is obligated to B that φ.

Thus far, we have viewed deontic operators as operators that apply to propositions to produce propositions. This view often gives translations of formulas that are contorted English. For example, suppose that "B" denotes Bill and that "φ" expresses that the door is open. Then, to capture that Bill is obligated to open the door, we would use the encoding $O_B \, \varphi$, which literally translated is "It is obligatory for Fred that the door is open." Obligations are more naturally stated with infinitive clauses than with dependent declarative clauses. Such linguistic features have suggested to some [8] that deontic operators in the first instance apply to something other than propositions. Some have derived deontic modalities from operators that make action explicit, such as A *sees-to-it-that* φ [9] and the operators of dynamic logic.

Deontic logic has found quite wide application in computer science [10]. In general, deontic notions are appropriate whenever we distinguish between what is ideal (obligatory) and what is actual. Note that we reject the deontic version of the T axiom, viz., $O \, \varphi \Rightarrow \varphi$, since an obligation may be violated: $O \, \varphi$ is true but φ is false. Some areas of computer science in which deontic logic has been used include formal specification (since modern software is so complex, we must cover non-ideal cases too in specifications), fault tolerance (non-ideal behavior introduces obligations to correct the situation), and database integrity constraints (where we distinguish between deontic constraints, which may be violated, from necessity constraints, which largely are analytically true). There is also an active area that relates to legal reasoning and modeling, which sometimes captures legal status with deontic modalities.

In most of these areas, we would like to say that a violation gives rise to new obligations. Modeling such situations, however, leads straight to the contrary-to-duty paradoxes [11]. Still, several promising resolutions of these paradoxes have been proposed in these areas.

3.3 Possible-Worlds Semantics

Most work on the semantics of modal logics involves the notion of possible worlds. We first sketch a possible-worlds semantics for epistemic logic [4] then, with the key ideas already introduced, briefly indicate how a possible-worlds semantics for deontic logic is defined.

Given a set $A = \{1, 2, \ldots, n \}$ of agents and a set of primitive propositions, a *Kripke structure* is a tuple $M = (\, S, \pi, R_1, R_2, \ldots, R_n \,)$, where

S is a set of possible worlds (states),

π is a truth assignment that assigns truth values to primitive propositions in possible worlds, and

R_i, $i \in A$, is the accessibility relation (a binary relation on S) for agent i.

In [4], which has a distributed-systems orientation, a state $s \in S$ is a global state $(s_e, s_1, s_2, ..., s_n)$, where s_e is the state of the environment and s_i, $i \in A$, is the local state of agent i. $(s, t) \in R_i$ indicates that, in state s, state t is accessible by agent i. Stated in other terms, in state s, agent i considers it possible that it is in state t, or agent i cannot distinguish between states s and t when in state s. The accessibility relations needed to make the S5 axioms valid must be equivalence relations. In that case, it is natural to have $(s, t) \in R_i$ iff $s_i = t_i$. If we think of the local state of an agent as encoding the information it has, then $s_i = t_i$ means that agent i has the same information in states s and t.

Where $M = (S, \pi, R_1, R_2, ..., R_n)$, $s \in S$, and φ is a proposition, let $(M, s) \models \varphi$ mean that φ is true in state s for Kripke structure M. This notion is defined inductively, with the base case furnished by the truth assignment for primitive propositions p:

$(M, s) \models \varphi$ iff $\pi(s)(p) = \text{true}$

The definition of $\models$ is as usual for the propositional connectives. For modal operator K_i, we have

$(M, s) \models K_i \varphi$ iff $(M, s) \models \varphi$ for all t such that $(s, t) \in R_i$.

That is, in state s, agent i knows that φ iff φ is true in all possible worlds accessible by i from s, i.e., in all states i cannot distinguish from s (when in s). Intuitively, i knows that φ if i has enough information to rule out all cases where φ would be false. Figure 2 shows a case where $(M, s) \models K_1 p$ but $(M, s) \not\models K_2 p$. The Kripke structure is portrayed here as a labeled directed graph, with states as nodes. An edge from s to t that includes i in its label indicates that $(s, t) \in R_i$. Nodes are labeled with the primitive propositions or their negations that are true in the corresponding states. We see that, in both states accessible by agent 1 from s, p is true – so $(M, s) \models K_1 p$. There is, however, a state accessible by 2 from s where p is false – so $(M, s) \not\models K_2 p$.

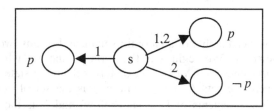

Fig. 2. A Kripke structure M and state s such that $(M, s) \models K_1 p$ but $(M, s) \not\models K_2 p$

It is relatively easy to establish from the definitions given that $(M, s) \models C_G \varphi$ iff $(M, t) \models \varphi$ for all states t reachable from s along paths labeled with members of G (where we interpret a Kripke structure in a graph-theoretic fashion, as in Figure 2).

Concerning the semantics of deontic logic, consider the simple, monadic case. A Kripke structure is now a tuple $M = (S, \pi, R)$, where S and π are as before and R, the accessibility relation, is a binary relation on S but now not indexed by an agent name.

The definition of $\models$ is similar to its definition in epistemic logic. In particular, similar to the $K_i \varphi$ case in epistemic logic is

$(M, s) \models O \varphi$ iff $(M, t) \models \varphi$ for all t such that $(s, t) \in R$.

We can take $(s, t) \in R$ to indicate that t is an ideal alternative to s. Since we generally reject the T axiom for deontic logic, we do not generally expect R to be reflexive. From the O φ case, we can derive the rules for the other deontic operators. For example,

$(M, s) \models P \varphi$ iff $(M, t) \models \varphi$ for some t such that $(s, t) \in R$.

In the semantics for dyadic deontic logic, we have a family of accessibility relations, relativized to the propositions that serve as conditions. For special deontic modalities, the simplest approach is again to have a family of accessibility relations, relativized this time to the agents (as in epistemic logic) or groups of agents. Directed deontic modalities are more complex. One approach [7] is to have one family of relations that is essentially the accessibility relations from the special-modalities case and another family of binary relations relativized to the agents to whom obligations are due (providing semantics for a notion like an agent benefiting from φ).

4   A Sentential Statechart Languages

We accept here that a Statechart can represent a multiagent plan. We would like to talk about agents in a group *knowing* their plans. But *know* applies to sentences, so we need a language that represents Statecharts with sentences – a sentential language. (See [12] for the details omitted here. See also [13].) We begin with the Statechart language presented in [14]. Expressions in this language denote things in the real world whereas expressions in the sentential language denote elements in the Statechart language. For a language, we view a Statechart as a four-tuple (Π, N, T, r), where Π is a finite set of primitive events, N is a finite set of names, T is a finite set of transitions, and $r \in N$ is the root state.

4.1   Syntax

The basic concept we need is that of an atomic sentence. For this, we introduce some sets of syntactic elements. We begin with the sorts Ev and Na, where Ev is a set of terms denoting event names, and Na is a set of terms denoting state (or plan) names. Correspondingly, there are sets $\underline{E}$ and $\underline{N}$, where $\underline{E}$ is the set of constants denoting event names (names of elements of Π – see below) and $\underline{N}$ is the set of constants denoting state (or plan) names (names of elements of N – see below). Furthermore, there are two variable sets: V_E is a set of variables of sort Ev, and V_N is a set of variables of sort Na. We can now recursively define the terms of sort Ev:

If $t \in \underline{E}$, then $t : Ev$.

If $t \in V_E$, then $t : Ev$.

If $f: T_1 \times \ldots \times T_n \rightarrow Ev$, and $t_i : T_i$ for $1 \le i \le n$, where T_i is Ev or Na, then $f(t_1, \ldots, t_n) : Ev$

Nothing else is in Ev.

and the terms of sort Na:

If $t \in \underline{N}$, then $t : Na$.

If $t \in V_{\underline{N}}$, then $t : Na$.

If $f: T_1 \times \ldots \times T_n \rightarrow Na$, and $t_i : T_i$ for $1 \leq i \leq n$, where T_i is Ev or Na, then $f(t_1, \ldots, t_n) : Na$.

Nothing else is in Na.

We can now define an atomic sentence. Given a predicate $Pred : T_1 \times \ldots \times T_n \rightarrow Boolean$, and $t_i : T_i$ for $1 \leq i \leq n$, where T_i is Ev or Na, then $Pred(t_1, \ldots, t_n)$ is an atomic sentence. (Nothing else is an atomic sentence.) We use the symbol Φ to stand for the set of atomic sentences. Based on the operators $\wedge$, $\neg$, O_A, $O\,t_{e,\ A}$, and $Prev$ and the definition of an atomic sentence, we can define the set S of sentences inductively as follows.

If $\varphi \in \Phi$, then $\varphi \in S$.

If $t_e : Ev$, then $Prev(t_e) \in S$.

If $\varphi_1, \varphi_2 \in S$, then $(\varphi_1 \wedge \varphi_2) \in S$.

If $\varphi \in S$, then $(\neg \varphi) \in S$.

If $\varphi \in S$, then $O_A(\varphi) \in S$.

If $\varphi \in S$ and $t_e : Ev$, then $O_{te,\ A}(\varphi) \in S$.

If $t_e : Ev$ and $t_a : Na$, then $O_{te,\ A}(t_a) \in S$.

Nothing else is in S.

Here $Prev(t_e)$ means that event t_e occurred in the last step. $O_A\varphi$ means that group A is obligated that φ, and $O_{te,\ A}(\varphi)$ means that group A is obligated that φ will be the case under the condition t_e occurs. $O_{te,\ A}(t_a)$ means that group A is obligated to do t_a under the condition that t_e occurs. Other operators are introduced with the usual definitions. We use the usual conventions for dropping parentheses.

4.2 Semantics

We define the semantics of a sentence with a *sentential interpretation* I, which is a tuple $(\Pi, N, \mathsf{T}, r, Val_E, Val_N, I_{Fn}, I_{Pr})$. Here (1) Π, N, T, and r are the same as in the syntax of Statecharts, (2) $Val_E: \underline{E} \rightarrow \Pi$ is a function that assigns event names in the Statechart language to event names in the sentential language, (3) $Val_N: \underline{N} \rightarrow N$ is a function that assigns state names in the Statechart language to state names in the sentential language, (4) I_{Fn} is a function that assigns function symbols in the Statechart language to the function symbols in the sentential language, (5) I_{Pr} is a function that assigns predicate symbols in the Statechart language to the predicate symbols in the sentential language.

We define I_{Fn} as follows. If $f: T_1 \times \ldots \times T_n \rightarrow Na$, then $I_{Fn}(f)$ is some function $F: U_1 \times \ldots \times U_n \rightarrow Na$, where, for $1 \leq i \leq n$, U_i is Π if T_i is Ev and is N if T_i is Na. If $f: T_1 \times \ldots \times T_n \rightarrow Ev$, then $I_{Fn}(f)$ is some function $F: U_1 \times \ldots \times U_n \rightarrow \Pi$, where, for $1 \leq i \leq n$, U_i is Π if T_i is Ev and is N if T_i is Na.

We define I_{Pr} as follows. If $pred: T_1 \times \ldots \times T_n \rightarrow Boolean$, then $I_{Pr}(pred) \subseteq U_1 \times \ldots \times U_n$, where, for $1 \leq i \leq n$, U_i is Π if T_i is Ev and is N if T_i is Na.

The functions Val_N and Val_E handle only the constant cases, and we need functions to handle more complex cases. Therefore, we extend Val_N and Val_E to functions that agree with these in the simple cases and extend them in ways that respect the structures in the complex cases. The definition of the homomorphic extension F_{Na} : $Na \rightarrow N$ of Val_N is as follows. Let $t_a : Na$. If $t_a \in \underline{N}$, then $F_{Na}(t_a) = Val_{\underline{N}}(t_a)$. If $t_a = f(t_1, \ldots, t_n)$, where $f: T_1 \times \ldots \times T_n \rightarrow Na$, and $t_i : T_i$ for $1 \leq i \leq n$, where T_i is Na or Ev, then $F_{Na}(t_a) = I_{Fn}(f) (F_{Na}(t_1), \ldots, F_{Na}(t_n))$. Where $\mathcal{L}(\Pi)$ is the language generated by closing Π over the functions defined on Π, the definition of the homomorphic extension $F_{Ev}: E_v \rightarrow \mathcal{L}(\Pi)$ of Val_E is as follows. Let $t_e : Ev$. If $t_e \in \underline{E}$, then $F_{Ev}(t_e) = Val_{\underline{E}}(t_e)$. If $t_e = f(t_1, \ldots, t_n)$, where $f: T_1 \times \ldots \times T_n \rightarrow Ev$, and $t_i : T_i$ for $1 \leq i \leq n$, where T_i is Na or Ev, then $F_{Ev}(t_e) = I_{Fn}(f) (F_{Ev}(t_1), \ldots, F_{Ev}(t_n))$.

So far we have ignored variables. To give meanings to terms and sentences that contain variables, we need not just an interpretation I but also a *variable assignment* v that assigns elements of $\mathcal{L}(\Pi)$ and N to the elements of V_E and V_N, respectively. In more detail, a variable assignment v is a pair (v_{Ev}, v_{Na}), where $v_{Ev} : V_{Ev} \rightarrow \mathcal{L}(\Pi)$ assigns (possibly complex) Statechart events to event variables and $v_{Na} : v_{Na} \rightarrow N$ assigns Statechart names to name variables. We must then extend the bases of the inductive definitions of the homomorphisms F_{Ev} and F_{Na}. These extensions are quite routine by rather lengthy hence omitted here – see [13] for details.

To define what it is for a sentence to be true, we need, in addition to an interpretation I, a pair (σ, γ). Here σ is a state configuration of a Statechart, a maximal configuration of states that the system can be in simultaneously, and γ is a history at a state that is expressed by a sequence of (configuration, E-step) pairs, where an E-step is a nonempty finite set of events. The set of E-steps is denoted by $\wp^+(\Pi)$, the set of nonempty finite subsets of Π. Σ denotes the set of all configurations of the Statechart in question. We let $Tr = (\Sigma, \wp^+(\&))^*$, the set of finite sequences of (configuration, E-step) pairs. Such a sequence is called a *trace*, and has the form $(\sigma_0, S_0) \circ \ldots \circ (\sigma_n, S_n)$, where $\circ$ is the concatenation operator, $\sigma_0, \ldots, \sigma_n \in \Sigma$, and $S_0, \ldots, S_n \in \wp^+(\Pi)$. We use σ with or without superscripts or subscripts to denote configurations, S with or without superscripts or subscripts to denote E-steps, and γ with or without superscripts or subscripts to denote traces.

A function *ActiveStates* is defined over a configuration σ as

$ActiveStates(\sigma) = \{st \mid \exists n \in \sigma \text{ such that } n \in children^*(st)\}$,

where $children(st)$ is the set of children of state st and $*$ indicates the reflexive and transitive closure. That is, function *ActiveStates* applied to a configuration σ gives the set of states that are themselves in σ or are the ancestors of states in σ.

We use the notion $(I, (\sigma, \gamma)) \models \varphi$ to indicate that sentence φ is true in interpretation I at state σ with trace γ. Where $\tau \in T$ is a transition, $source(\tau)$ is the set of (often only one) source states of τ, $target(\tau)$ is the set of (often only one) target states of τ, and $label(\tau)$ is the label e/a of τ, where $e = trigger(label(\tau))$ and $a = action(label(\tau))$. In particular, we say

- $(I, (\sigma, \gamma)) \models active(t_n)$ if $t_n : Na$ and $F_{Na}(t_n) \in ActiveStates(\sigma)$. Here $active: Na \rightarrow Boolean$ is a predicate. Intuitively, $active(t_a)$ is true if the state denoted by t_a is currently active.

- $(l, (\sigma, \gamma)) \models Prev(t_e)$ if $t_e : Ev$ and there exist $\gamma' \in Tr$, $S \in \wp^+(\Pi)$, $\sigma' \in \Sigma$ such that $\gamma = \gamma' \circ (\sigma', S)$ and $F_{Ev}(t_e) \subseteq S$. That is, $F_{Ev}(t_e)$ happened on the previous step, S, from the previous configuration σ' (see Figure 3 a).

- $(l, (\sigma, \gamma)) \models O_A \varphi$ if $\gamma = \gamma' \circ (\sigma', S)$, and for all σ'', if there exists $\tau \in T$ such that $source(\tau) \subseteq ActiveStates(\sigma')$, $target(\tau) \subseteq ActiveStates(\sigma)$, and $trigger(label(\tau)) \cup action(label(\tau)) \subseteq S$, then $(l, (\sigma'', \gamma' \circ (\sigma', S''))) \models \varphi$, where $S'' \supseteq trigger(label(\tau)) \cup action(label(\tau))$. That is, group A is obligated that φ be the case if φ is true at any configuration σ'' reachable from the previous configuration σ' by a transition τ whose events are a subset of the E-step that led from σ' to the present configuration, σ (see Figure 3 b).

- $(l, (\sigma, \gamma)) \models O_{te, A}(\varphi)$ if for all $S \in \wp^+(\Pi)$ such that $F_{Ev}(t_e) \subseteq S$ and all $\sigma' \in \Sigma$, if there exists $\tau \in T$ such that $source(\tau) \subseteq ActiveStates(\sigma)$, $target(\tau) \subseteq ActiveStates(\sigma')$, and $F_{Ev}(t_e) \subseteq trigger(label(\tau)) \cup action(label(\tau)) \subseteq S$, then $(l, (\sigma', \gamma \circ (\sigma, S))) \models \varphi$. Recall that $O_{te, A}(\varphi)$ states that group A is obligated that φ will be the case under the condition that $F_{Ev}(t_e)$ occurs. This is true, then, if φ is true at any configuration σ' reachable from the current configuration σ by a transition whose events include $F_{Ev}(t_e)$ (see Figure 3 c).

- $(l, (\sigma, \gamma)) \models O_{te, A}(t_a)$ if for any $\tau \in T$ such that $source(\tau) \subseteq ActiveStates(\sigma)$, $target(\tau) \subseteq ActiveStates(\sigma')$, and $F_{Ev}(t_e) \subseteq trigger(label(\tau))$, we have $F_{Ev}(t_a) \subseteq action(label(\tau))$. Recall that $O_{te, A}(t_a)$ states that group A is obligated to do $F_{Ev}(t_a)$ under the condition that $F_{Ev}(t_e)$ occurs. This is true, then, if $F_{Ev}(t_a)$ should occur on any transition τ from the current configuration σ whose triggering events include $F_{Ev}(t_e)$, (see Figure 3 d).

Permission and forbiddance operators in the interpretation l can be defined in similar ways.

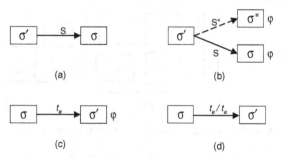

Fig. 3. The Transitions between states used in defining $(l, (\sigma, \gamma)) \models \varphi$

Obligations have been defined in terms of the normal transitions that happen in Statecharts – a Statechart shows what *ought* to be or *ought* to happen. In the real word, there exist non-ideal transitions, that is, Statecharts may show violation transitions, which lead to non-ideal states. The O operators defined above do not cover such non-ideal transitions and states in their semantics. This reflects the fact that what is actual need not to be ideal.

4.3 Representing Plans and Common Knowledge of Plans

A plan is formed based on agreements within an authority structure. The plan includes (1) the positions to be filed by the executive agents, (2) the subplans or tasks to be carried out, and (3) the rules governing the tasks and duties agents have in their positions. The agents, as position holders, form not only a joint intention but also an agreement to jointly perform the plan. It is common knowledge among the agents in the group that they have such a joint agreement and made such an agreement. The agents commit to doing their parts of the job. We locate the negotiation process in the whole component in a Part-Whole Statechart. Negotiation results in the agents filling plan positions, thereby establishing the bridge between a multiagent plan and a multiagent system.

In order to express that an agent knows a plan, we need to translate a plan to a conjunction of sentences. Here we define a translation function Tl as follows. The translation of a transition from state n_1 to n_2, illustrated in Figure 4 a, is

$$active(n_1) \wedge Cd \Rightarrow O_{te,A}(t_a) \wedge O_{AND(te,ta),A}(active(n_2)).$$

Here, $F_{Ev}(t_e) = e$, $F_{Ev}(t_a) = a$, and $Tl(C) = Cd$. The translation of a state n with XOR structure, illustrated in Figure 4 b, is

$$active(n) \Rightarrow active(n_1) \otimes \ldots \otimes active(n_m),$$

where $\otimes$ is the exclusive-or connective. The translation of a state n with AND structure, illustrated in Figure 4 c, is

$$active(n) \Rightarrow active(n_1) \wedge \ldots \wedge active(n_m).$$

Finally, for every $n \in children^*(m)$, we have

$$active(n) \Rightarrow active(m)$$

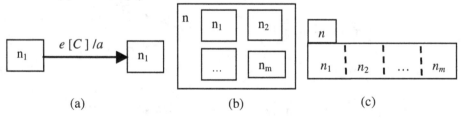

(a)   (b)   (c)

Fig. 4. The Statecharts used to illustrate the translation Tl

Concerning common knowledge of plans, let P_1, P_2, ..., P_n be the plans for positions p_1, p_2, ..., p_n of a multiagent plan. $M = (S, I, R_1, R_2, \ldots, R_n)$ is a Kripke structure for a system of agents 1, 2, ..., n that fill positions p_i, $1 \leq i \leq n$. We assume without loss of generality that agent i fills position p_i. Here S is a set of global states (possible worlds), an $n+1$-tuple containing the local states of the whole component and the parts (agents). I is the interpretation of the plan-Statechart. Note that this gives the truth values of the relevant propositions in the various global states. And R_i, $1 \leq i \leq n$, is the accessibility relation for agent i. We interpret R_i so that $(s, t) \in R_i$ iff agent i has the same local state in s and t. Note that I and $(R_1, R_2, \ldots, R_n)$ are not independent.

When $(M, s) \models \varphi$ holds for all $s \in S$, we write $M \models \varphi$ and say that φ is *valid* for the Kripke structure M. We want to have

$$M \models C_G K_i \, Tl(P_i), \quad G = \{1, 2, \ldots, n\}$$

That is, in any global state, it should be common knowledge among the agents in the system that each agent knows its part of the plan. Also, agents that fill positions obtain knowledge of the whole component, essentially the rules for coordinating. Let t_j, $1 \leq j \leq m$, be the transitions in the whole component and let *Comb* be a polyadic operator that combines transitions. We want to have

$$M \models C_G \, Tl(\, Comb(\, t_1, t_2, \ldots, t_m\,)),$$

where the translation of an application of *Comb* shows up as a conjunction.

Note that, although it should be common knowledge that each agent knows its plan, the details of the individual plans need not be common knowledge. In fact, the global states need not include as components basic states of the individual agents – we need zoom in only far enough that distinctions critical to the execution of the plan are respected. If we combine systems of agents, each executing its own multiagent plan, then the whole components of the various systems serve as parts for the new, all-inclusive system, for which a new whole component is introduce. The global states of the inclusive new system have component states for the wholes of the subsystems but need not have component states for their parts. This suggests a modular treatment of knowledge, especially common knowledge, with various levels of resolution.

5 Multiagent Transactions

We have also considered directed deontic modalities introduced by Ryu [15] of the form $O_{\rho,\sigma;T} \, \varphi$, where ρ and σ are roles. This means that ρ (the *obligee*) is obligated to σ (the *obligor*) that φ at T. (We ignore the fact that Ryu also includes a condition, giving a directed dyadic deontic logic.) Similar forms exist for permission and prohibition. T is a temporal reference, for example, an expression indicating before a certain action is performed by a given role. We take the default for T to be *eventually* and are not particularly concerned with it here. We apply these notions to model multiagent transactions, which we also model with Part-Whole Statecharts. Obligations, prohibitions, and permissions are held to be established by speech acts, and obligations are discharged by speech acts. The semantics for these deontic notions must look at traces possibly arbitrarily into the future (as when T is *eventually*).

In Statecharts for transactions, we explicitly represent some of the prohibited transitions and some of the violation states. (We cannot represent all such transitions or states since we lack complete control of the system.) Transitions out of a violation state are obligatory, involving sanctions in the form of recovery actions, which right what is wrong. Such transitions lead (at least eventually) to non-violation (ideal) states.

This work was done within the framework of our previously-developed deontic transaction model [16]. This is an extended transaction model intended for multiagent systems. It relaxes the ACID properties, especially atomicity. Figure 5 shows the possible sequences of high-level states an agent moves through in carrying out a subtransaction. Roughly, the *prepare* state is where the agent negotiates and commits to obligations, the *active* state is where it discharges these obligations, and it enters the *committed* state once it has met all its obligations relative to the subtransaction. If it violates an obligation or prohibition, it enters the *excepted* state to perform recovery actions. The *committed* and *excepted* states are depicted with dashed ovals to indicate that they are continuation states: from the *committed* state, the agent continues to another part of the overall transaction while, from the *excepted* state, it proceeds to a recovery task, which, from this point of view, is essentially a new subtransaction. Within the recovery task itself, the agent eventually reaches either the *aborted*, the *committed*, or the *excepted* state. The agent enters the *aborted* state when it fails to negotiate a subtransaction (in the *prepare* state) or (in the *active* state) it violates an obligation or prohibition with no hope of recovery. Such a violation often cascades from the violation by another agent of an obligation on which the first agent depended. What are generally considered failures in other transaction models are interpreted here as violations. The entire system is seen as having the same possible sequences of high-level states. It enters the *aborted* state from the *active* state, for example, if some of its agents have aborted and none can take up the unfinished subtransactions or if so many have entered their *excepted* states that progress is impossible.

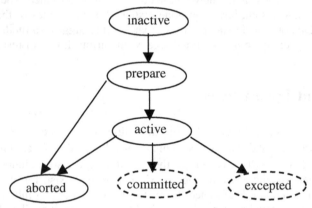

Fig. 5. The states in the deontic transaction model and transitions between them

The notion of spheres of control [17] has had a large impact on extended transaction models and relates to the dependence some processes (or agents) have on others because of the flow of data. When an error is detected and its source is not yet fully determined or the action required to correct it is not fully known, the effect of processing it is contained within a sphere of control until we determine whether releasing the effects will adversely affect subsequent processing. Singh [18] contends that, in a multiagent system, spheres of control unduly restrict agent autonomy. He instead suggests spheres of commitment, which encapsulate the obligations agents have to others. Singh gives the form of a commitment as $C(x, y, p, G, d)$, where x is the committer (obligee), y is the "committee" (obligor), p is the discharge condition, G is the context group, and d is the cancellation policy. The correctness condition is given as

If a commitment is created, then it must satisfactorily be discharged unless it is canceled in time.

Generally, however, there is no need to load so much into an obligation (commitment). In many situations, we are faced with several *prima facie* obligations (obligations that, considered in isolation, would be binding) that conflict. Only some of these *prima facie* obligations are actual obligations; the remainder are defeated by them. Defensible deontic logic [15,19] attempts to find principles to order obligations so as to account for the way some obligations defeat others in practice. Some of the more convincing principles order more specific obligations above less specific ones [15]. What counts as more specific can be, for example, more specific roles or (in the dyadic case) a stronger condition. Other principles depend on authority structure. For example, obligations to a higher authority take precedence over those to a lower authority.

Now, cancellation often reflects defeasibility. At the very least, an obligation or prohibition can often be defeated by a permission. Furthermore, defeasance helps explain the structure of a multi-level transaction in that obligations specific to subtransactions defeat conflicting obligations on their parent transactions until they are discharged, violated, or themselves defeated.

We experimented with some of these ideas by modeling a transaction scenario with a Statechart [20]. A simplified version was implemented with the Zeus multiagent toolkit [21]. We followed obligations from the speech acts that give rise to them to the speech acts that discharge them. The scenario is shown in Figure 6. There are three people, 0, 1, and 2, and two roles S (supplier) and C (consumer). Person 0 a supplier role (S[0]), 1 assumes both roles (S[1] and S[2]), and 2 assumes a consumer role (C[2]). S[0] and C[1] negotiate a deal whereby 0 will surrender a widget to 1 once 1 pays him. Likewise, S[1] and S[2] negotiate a deal whereby 1 will surrender the widget to 2 once 2 pays him. The design incorporated agents as representatives for the people in their roles and a broker agent to facilitate the negotiations, which are actually carried out by the representatives.

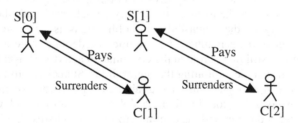

Fig. 6. The transaction scenario

The interesting case here is where S[0] and C[1] make a deal but do not complete the transaction until S[1] and C[2] make a deal and C[2] pays S[1]. (perhaps 1 is a dealer with little money of his own.) Then C[1] pays S[0], who surrenders the widget to C[1], whereupon S[1] surrenders it to C[2]. For a while, there is a chain of obligations creating a sphere that encompasses all three people. Now suppose that after, say, C[1] pays S[0] and before and before S[0] surrenders the widget to C[1], person 1 sees someone in a terrible car accident and only a will save him. The obligation to save the dying driver defeats the obligation to surrender the widget to

C[1]. But now S[1] cannot discharge his obligation to C[2] to turn over the widget. Some sanction is in place (e.g., returning the money).

Space limitations preclude presenting the Statechart design here. We found that the design was facilitated by including conditions that represent whether the system wass or was not in certain states. This enhancement allowed us to handle options and broken promises. The design actually had two whole components: an "inner" whole for coordinating the broker agent, the representative agents, and the people communicating with the representatives, and an "outer" whole for coordinating the exchange among the people alone (paying and turning over the widget).

6 Conclusion and Future Work

We began with the observation that epistemic and deontic logic are abstract and appropriate for specification whereas Statecharts are more concrete and appropriate for expressing designs. This suggests an obvious direction in development, but we also observed that an agent must know that the abstract modal properties apply to it and its collaborators. We developed the syntax and semantics of a language that asserts Statechart features with sentences and allows us to talk about knowing plans. In particular, it lets us describe the common knowledge of a group of agents to the effect that each agent knows its part of the plan (Statechart) and the sequences of coordination actions for the plan. This language also has deontic operators that address both what propositions ought to hold and what an agent ought to do. The modal properties are grounded in the plan Statechart. We also considered multiagent transactions from the point of view of our deontic transaction model but with the assumption that possible courses of action are described with Statecharts that support directed obligations. We considered spheres of commitment as a replacement in multiagent systems of the notion of spheres of control. We argued, however, that the desired results of these mechanisms could largely be achieved with the formalism of deontic logic as long as the defeasibility of obligations is accounted for. We are generally able to relate the semantics of epistemic and deontic logic to Statecharts so that modal properties still play a role in the coordinated activity of agents.

Future work will include exploiting the hierarchy in Statecharts to find the level of abstraction where just enough detail is available to support the common knowledge and obligations needed for coordination. Prohibited transitions and violation states should be characterized better and the contrary-to-duty paradoxes should be addressed directly. A proper account of directed deontic modalities must relate the content of speech acts to Statechart structure. Finally, we must experiment with more scenarios to maintain an accurate picture of agent behavior.

References

1. Olderog, E.R.: Nets, Terms, and Formulas: Three Views of Concurrent Processes and Their Relationship. Cambridge University Press, Cambridge, UK (1991)
2. Harel, David.: Statecharts: A Visual Formalism for Complex Systems. Science of Computer Programming 8 (1987), pp. 231–274

3. Pazzi, L.: Extending Statecharts for Representing Parts and Wholes. Proceedings of the 23rd EUROMICRO Conference (1997)
4. Fagin, R., Halpun, J. Y., Moses, Y., Vardi, M. Y.: Reasoning about Knowledge. The MIT Press: Cambrigde, MA: (1995)
5. Meyer, J.-J.Ch. and Wieringa, R.J.: Deontic Logic: A Concise Overview. In: Meyer, J.-J.Ch and Wieringa, R.J. (eds.): Deontic Logic in Computer Science: Normative System Specification. Wiley: New York: (1993) 3–16
6. Åquist, L.: Deontic Logic. In: Gobbay, D. and Guenther, F. (eds): Handbook of Philosophical Logic, Vol. II. Reidel: Dordrecht, The Netherlands (1984) 605-714.
7. Krogh, C.: Obligations in Multiagent Systems. In: Aamond, A. and Komorowski, J. (eds.): SCAI'95 – Fifth Scandinavian Conference on Artificial Intelligence. ISO Press: Amsterdam (1995) 4–16
8. Castañeda, H.-N.: Aspectual Actions and Davisdon's Theory of Events. In: LaPore E. and McLaughlin, B.P. (eds.): Actions and Events: Perspectives on the Philosophy of Donald Davidson. Basil Blackwell: Oxford, UK (1985) 294–310
9. Horty, J.F.: Agency and Deontic Logic. Oxford University Press, Oxford, UK (2001)
10. Wieringa, R.J. and Meyers, J.-J. Ch.: Applications of Deontic Logic in Computer Science. In: Meyers, J.-J. Ch. and Wieringa, R.J. (eds.): Deontic Logic in Computer Science: Normative System Specification. Wiley, Chichester, UK (1993) 17–40
11. Carmo, J. and Jones, A.J.I.: Deontic Logic and Contrary-to-Duties. In: Gabbay, D, and Guenthner, F. (eds.): Handbook of Philosophical Logic, 2nd Ed., Vol. 8. Kluwer: Dordrecht, The Netherlands (2002)
12. Wu, X.: The Formal Representation of Multi-Agent Plans. Masters thesis, Dept. of Comp. Science, North Carolina A&T State University, Greensboro, NC (1999)
13. Xiaohong Wu, Benny Cox, and Albert C. Esterline, "Representing and Interpreting Multiagent Plans with Statecharts," *WAC 2000* (World Automation Conference), Maui, Hawaii, 2000.
14. Harel D., Pnueli A., Schmidt J.P., and Sherman R.: On the Formal Semantics of Statecharts. Proc. 2nd IEEE Symposium on Logic in Computer Science (1987). 54–64,
15. Ryu, Y.U.: Conditional Deontic Logic Augmented with Defeasible Reasoning. Data & knowledge Engineering 16 (1995) 73–91
16. Yelena Tretyakova, Yingli Liu, and Albert C. Esterline, "A Deontic Transaction Model for Multiagent Systems," *WAC 2000* (World Automation Conference), Maui, Hawaii, 2000.
17. Davies, C.T., Jr.: Data Processing Spheres of Control. IBM Systems Journal, Vol. 17, No. 2 (1978) 179–198
18. Singh, M. P.: Multiagent Systems as Spheres of Commitment. Int. Conf. on Multiagent Systems (ICMAS), Workshop on Norms, Obligations, and Conventions. Kyoto, Japan (1996)
19. Nute, D. (ed.): Defeasible Deontic Logic. Kluwer: Dordrecht, The Netherlands (1997)
20. Anderton, D.E.: A Formal Representation of Spheres of Commitment. Masters thesis, Dept. of Comp. Science, North Carolina A&T State University, Greensboro, NC (2002)
21. Intelligent Systems Research Group. Zeus Technical Manual. British Telecommunications (1999)

Qu-Prolog: An Implementation Language for Agents with Advanced Reasoning Capabilities

Peter J. Robinson[1], Mike Hinchey[2], and Keith Clark[3]

[1] School of Information Technology and Electrical Engineering,
The University of Queensland, Australia
pjr@itee.uq.edu.au
[2] NASA Goddard Space Flight Center, Software Engineering Laboratory,
Greenbelt, MD, USA
Michael.G.Hinchey@nasa.gov
[3] Imperial College, London
klc@doc.ic.ac.uk

Abstract. Qu-Prolog is an extension of Prolog that was initially designed as an implementation language for interactive theorem provers. It provides built-in support for quantifiers, substitutions and object variables. Recently, Qu-Prolog has been further extended to support multiple threads and high-level communication. The combination of these features makes it ideal as an implementation language for intelligent agents with advanced reasoning capabilities.

1 Introduction

Qu-Prolog [4] is an extended Prolog designed as an implementation language for interactive theorem provers. It has built-in support for the kinds of data structures encountered in theorem proving such as quantifiers, substitutions and object variables. Qu-Prolog is the implementation language for the Ergo series of theorem provers [1,5].

In order to investigate the possibilities of implementing multi-threaded theorem provers and cooperative work environments for theorem proving, Qu-Prolog has been extended to include support for multiple threads and high-level communication.

Inter-thread communication uses the API of the InterAgent Communication Model (ICM) [3]. Addresses in this model are similar to email addresses and it allows a thread in one Qu-Prolog process to communicate with a thread in another Qu-Prolog process (or any other process using the ICM API) using these email like addresses.

We illustrate the combination of the reasoning capabilities and communication of QuProlog with a simple example of a reasoning agent that can be queried about its own beliefs and of the beliefs of other agents. Each agent contains a simple automatic prover for classical predicate calculus that it uses to reason about its own beliefs, and uses communication to query other agents about their beliefs.

M.G. Hinchey et al. (Eds.): 'FAABS 2002, LNAI 2699, pp. 162–172, 2003.

In section 2 we discuss the Qu-Prolog extensions for supporting reasoning involving quantifiers and give an implementation for the automatic prover for our reasoning agents. In section 3 we discuss the Qu-Prolog support for threads and high-level communication, and in section 4 we bring these ideas together with an implementation of our reasoning agents. Finally, in section 5, we provide some concluding remarks.

2 Reasoning

Qu-Prolog is an extended WAM based Prolog that will run most applications written in a standard Prolog virtually unchanged. The key difference is the extensions of terms to include quantifiers, substitutions and object variables and the consequent changes to the unification algorithm. In Qu-Prolog, the unification algorithm attempts to find instantiations of variables to make terms α-equivalent, rather than syntactically identical as is the case in standard Prolog. Qu-Prolog also allows arbitrary terms to appear in the functor position of structures, thus supporting reasoning in higher order logics. Note, however, that β-reduction is not carried out during unification.

Because Qu-Prolog's main area of interest is in theorem proving, the unification algorithm also carries out the occurs check. The implementation is careful to reduce the computational overhead of the occurs check by not applying it in cases where it knows the occur check cannot cause problems.

The extra reasoning capabilities of Qu-Prolog comes from the extension to the term structure (and unification algorithm) – the inference mechanism for Qu-Prolog itself is standard Prolog resolution with support for goal delaying.

We now look at Qu-Prolog terms in more detail and show how they support advanced reasoning capabilities.

The Herbrand universe (or object-level) of Qu-Prolog is essentially the same as that of standard Prolog except that it also includes higher-order terms, quantified terms and variables. The corresponding meta-level of Qu-Prolog also contains higher-order terms, quantified terms, object-variables (variables that range over variables at the object-level) and substituted terms.

Object variables use the same syntax as atom and are distinguished from atoms by declaration (or by using an exclamation mark as the first character of the name). Assuming x and y have been declared as object variable prefixes, **all**, **ex** and **lambda** have been declared as quantifiers, and **and**, **or**, **=>** and **not** have been declared as operators of the appropriate kind, then the following are legal terms of Qu-Prolog.

```
all x:nat (x > 1 => x > 0)
[A/x,B/y]T
(lambda x F)(A)
!!integral(A,B) x F
```

The first term is a quantified term whose bound variable is x and whose body is x > 1 => x > 0. The bound variable has an associated (optional) term which is typically used as a type. The second term is a substituted term that represents the term T with all the free occurrences of x and y respectively replaced by A and B. The third term is an example of a higher-order term whose functor is a quantified term.

The last example is a quantified term – the !! introduces a quantifier that is either not an atom , or an atom that has not been declared as a quantifier symbol. This term could represent the definite integral from A to B of the function F with respect to x.

As with function symbols, Qu-Prolog has no built-in semantics for quantifier symbols – the semantics of all symbols is determined by the program.

In the remainder of this section we describe an implementation of tableau style prover for predicate calculus that we later use as the reasoning component of our agent.

For this implementation, we need to choose a data structure to represent the state of a proof, predicates that define how rule applications modify the proof state, and a way of determining when a proof is complete.

This can be done in many different ways. For example, Ergo [5] is a sequent calculus prover whose proof state is a proof tree where the nodes are sequents. The dynamic database contains a collection of sequent calculus rules that apply to sequents, and Ergo uses this database to modify the proof tree.

The Qu-Prolog release comes with an simple example of a natural deduction prover which uses the same basic approach as Ergo, and the agent reasoner described in [2] is basically a tableau style reasoner with the proof state represented as a list of formulae and the rules are encoded directly as proof state transformers. This example prover is an automatic prover, which is more suited to reasoning agents than interactive provers. Here we take the same approach.

The proof state is a list of formulae and the object is to find a contradiction among the formulae of the list. We assume that the predicate

```
% T is in List and Rest is List without T
member_and_rest(T, List, Rest)
```

has been defined.

We provide a resource bound (the number of inference steps) to prevent the construction of infinite proofs. So a proof may fail if there is no contradiction, or if the resource bound is exceeded.

The implementation begins with some declarations for object-variables and operators.

```
?- obvar_prefix([x,y,z]). % declare x,x1,x2, etc as object-variables
?- op(860, quant, all).   % universal quantification
?- op(860, quant, ex).    % existential quantification
?- op(810, fx, ~).        % negation
?- op(820, xfy, and).     % conjunction
?- op(830, xfy, or).      % disjunction
?- op(840, xfy, =>).      % implication
?- op(850, xfy, <=>).     % logical equivalence
```

The predicate that attempts to find a contradiction is

```
find_contradiction(FormulaList,InResource,OutResource)
```

where `FormulaList` is the formula list of interest, `InResource` is the supplied resource bound as a count on the maximum number of inference rules that can be applied, and `OutResource` is the remaining resource bound at the completion of the proof. This is used to carry the resource bound from one sub-proof to the next.

The first five clauses are used to terminate the proof

```
% the resource bound has beed exceeded, so fail
find_contradiction(_,0,_):- !,fail.
% a contradiction has been found,
% so succeed but decrement the resource count
find_contradiction(Fs,R,RR) :-
    member(false, Fs),!,
    RR is R-1.
find_contradiction(Fs,R,RR) :-
    member(~true, Fs),!,
    RR is R-1.
find_contradiction(Fs,R,RR) :-
    member(X, Fs),
    member(~X, Fs),
    !,
    RR is R-1.
```

The next group of clauses simplify the proof without branching.

```
find_contradiction(Fs,R,RR) :-
    member_and_rest(A and B, Fs, Rst),
    !,
    NR is R-1,
    find_contradiction([A,B|Rst],NR,RR).
find_contradiction(Fs,R,RR) :-
    member_and_rest(A <=> B, Fs, Rst),
    !,
    NR is R-1,
    find_contradiction([A=>B,B=>A|Rst],NR,RR).
find_contradiction(Fs,R,RR) :-
    member_and_rest(~(A or B), Fs, Rst),
    !,
    NR is R-1,
    find_contradiction([~A,~B|Rst],NR,RR).
find_contradiction(Fs,R,RR) :-
    member_and_rest(~(A => B), Fs, Rst),
    !,
    NR is R-1,
    find_contradiction([A,~B|Rst],NR,RR).
find_contradiction(Fs,R,RR) :-
    member_and_rest(ex x A, Fs, Rst),
```

```
    x not_free_in Rst,
    !,
    NR is R-1,
    find_contradiction([A|Rst],NR,RR).
find_contradiction(Fs,R,RR) :-
    member_and_rest(~all x A, Fs, Rst),
    x not_free_in Rst,
    !,
    NR is R-1,
    find_contradiction([~A|Rst],NR,RR).
```

Note that the last two clauses (that deal with quantification) add a not_free_in constraint as is required for removing the quantifier.

The next group of clauses cause the proof to branch, and this is where we see the resource count being passed from one subproof to the next.

```
find_contradiction(Fs,R,RR) :-
    member_and_rest(A or B, Fs, Rst),
    !,
    NR is R-1,
    find_contradiction([A|Rst],NR,IRR),
    find_contradiction([B|Rst],IRR,RR).
find_contradiction(Fs,R,RR) :-
    member_and_rest(A => B, Fs, Rst),
    !,
    NR is R-1,
    find_contradiction([~A|Rst],NR,IRR),
    find_contradiction([B|Rst],IRR,RR).
find_contradiction(Fs,R,RR) :-
    member_and_rest(~(A and B), Fs, Rst),
    !,
    NR is R-1,
    find_contradiction([~A|Rst],NR,IRR),
    find_contradiction([~B|Rst],NR,IRR).
find_contradiction(Fs,R,RR) :-
    member_and_rest(~(A <=> B), Fs, R),
    !,
    NR is R-1,
    find_contradiction([A,~B|Rst],NR,IRR),
    find_contradiction([B,~A|Rst],IRR,RR).
```

The final clause given below is used to create instances of all universally quantified formulae appearing in the formula list. This is the step that can cause infinite proofs without using a resourse bound. Note that creating an instance is really done by the application of an inference rule, and so the resource count is decremented for each created instance.

```
find_contradiction(Fs,R,RR) :-
    make_instances(Fs, Fs, NewFs, R, NR),
    NR < R,
    !,
    find_contradiction(NewFs, NR, RR).
```

```
% Make an instance of all universally quantified formulae in the formula
                                                              list
% All the universally quantified formula are kept in the resulting list.
make_instances([], New, New, R, R).
make_instances([H|T], Fs, NewFs, R, NR) :-
    ( H = all x A ->
        IFs = [[_/x]A|Fs],
        IR is R-1
    ; H = ~(ex x A) ->
        IFs = [~[_/x]A|Fs],
        IR is R-1
    ;
        IFs = Fs,
        IR = R
    ),
    make_instances(T, IFs, NewFs, IR, NR).
```

The term [_/x]A is a substitution term where all free occurrences of the object-variable in A are replaced by a new (anonymous) variable. This variable is a new instance for x.

As we will see later, each agent maintains a collection of its beliefs in its dynamic database, and a request to do a proof for a formula causes the agent to collect its belief formulae into a list, add the negation of the formula it has been asked to prove, and call the above predicate to attempt a proof by contradiction.

3   Threads and Communication

Qu-Prolog is a multi-threaded Prolog, where a scheduler is responsible for time-slicing threads and managing blocking, messages and signals. Threads within a single Qu-Prolog process carry out independent computations but share the static and dynamic databases. The Qu-Prolog library contains several predicates that create and kill threads as well as controlling their execution.

The predicate thread_fork(ID, Goal) creates a new thread whose name is ID and sets the initial goal of the thread to Goal. If the name is supplied by the user, it will become the name of the thread, and if it is not supplied, the system will generate a name and instantiate ID to that name.

The execution of threads can be controlled in several ways, for example:

- thread_yield cause the thread to give up its timeslice;
- thread_sleep(Secs) cause the thread to sleep for the specified number of seconds; and
- thread_atomic_goal(Goal) cause the thread to call Goal without letting other threads get a timeslice.

Threads can also block in several ways – for example a thread doing a message read will block until a message arrives (see later) and a call on thread_wait_on_goal(Goal) will block until the dynamic database changes in such a way that Goal succeeds.

The high-level communication support of Qu-Prolog is based on the ICM. The ICM consists of one of more `icm` processes that act as message routers and an API that provides applications with ICM functionality. Using this, a process can register its name with an `icm` process and then send and receive messages via the `icm` processes.

ICM addresses have three main components: a thread name, a process name, and a machine address (the home of the process). An `icm` process uses the process name and home fields to determine the message destination. The process itself is responsible for managing the thread name field.

The Qu-Prolog implementation provides library support for the ICM API and manages an incoming message buffer for each thread within a Qu-Prolog process. The library provides two layers of support for ICM messages: a lower-level layer that provides the basic send and receive primitives, and a higher-level layer that further simplifies communication. In this paper we focus on the higher-level support.

In the higher-level layer the message send predicate is

```
Message ->> Address reply_to RTAddress
```

where `Message` is any Qu-Prolog term, `Address` is a Qu-Prolog term representing an ICM address. The reply-to part is optional and is used if the recipient of the message should forward a reply to some other process.

The most general form for a Qu-Prolog address is

```
ThreadName:ProcessName@MachineName
```

where the home part (`MachineName`) can be dropped if the message is to another process on the same machine. The process name (`ProcessName`) can also be dropped if the message is to another thread within the same process.

The special address `self` can be used for a thread to send a message to itself.

The message receive predicates are

```
Message <<- Address reply_to RTAddress
Message <<= Address reply_to RTAddress
```

where the reply-to fields are again optional. The first of the above predicate extracts the first message from the message buffer and tries to unify the arguments with information contained in this message. The second predicate searches the message buffer looking for a message that matches the supplied pattern and removes the first matching message. In either case, if no (matching) message is found, the call blocks until a new message arrives.

The library also contains a powerful extension of the second of the above predicates that provides case analysis on incoming messages by associating goals with messages. The example below shows this predicate in action.

```
message_choice(
  (echo(T) <<- Address) -> (T ->> Address)
  ;
  (process(Goal) <<- _) -> call(G)
  ;
  (exit <<- Address)::can_kill_me(Address) -> thread_exit
```

```
;
timeout(3) -> do_something_else
)
```

The argument of the `message_choice` predicate uses the same structure and similar semantics to the if-then-else construct in Prolog except that the test is replaced by a message pattern.

In the example, the first choice matches a message of the form `echo(T)` and simply sends the term back to the sender. The second choice matches a message of the form `process(Goal)` and calls the goal. The third choice has a test that must succeed before the message is consumed and this choice committed to. The last choice provides a timeout – if no message has arrived within three seconds then `do_something_else` will be called.

The timeout choice is optional, and `message_choice` will block until some matching message arrives if it is not supplied.

The `message_choice` predicate makes it very easy to write reactive agents. For example, simply by wrapping the above call to `message_choice` with a repeat-fail and forking a thread with that goal we produce a simple reactive agent that responds to the supplied message patterns.

4   A Reasoning Agent

The reasoning agent described in this section is a simple reactive agent that responds to messages from other reasoning agents and other processes (e.g., an agent server).

The main thread of the agent is simply a loop that reacts to messages. The prededicate `believes/1` is used to store beliefs of the agent.

```
message_loop :-
    message_choice
    (
        quit <<- thread0:server@MID ->
            exited ->> thread0:server@MID
    ;
        tell(Fact) <<- Address :: can_tell(Address) ->
            assert(believes(Fact)),
            message_loop
    ;
        ask(Fact) <<- Address    ->
            thread_fork(ID, try_proof(Fact, Address)),
            message_loop
    ).
```

When this agent receives a `quit` message from a process whose address matches the message pattern the message loop is exited (and the agent exits). `quit` messages from any other addresses are ignored.

When an agent receives a `tell` message from a process whose address satisfies the `can_tell` predicate then the agent asserts the supplied term as a fact that it believes. Again, `tell` messages from "untrusted" sources are ignored.

The agent will respond to an **ask** request (from anywhere) by forking a thread that attempts a proof of the supplied term. As we will see later, by forking a subthread to do the proof, rather than by doing the proof itself, the main thread can respond to messages while the subthread carries out the proof. This is particularly important if the proof requires feedback from another reasoning agent that in turn requires feedback from this agent.

This subthread attempts a proof and sends an appropriate message back to the querying agent as follows.

```
try_proof(Fact, Agent) :-
    ( can_prove(Fact) ->
        result(proved, Fact) ->> Agent
    ;
        result(not_proved, Fact) ->> Agent
    ).
```

The agent can prove the fact if

- it already believes this fact;
- the fact is of the form **believes(Agent, Fact)** and **Agent** believes **Fact**; or
- it can be proved from its "basic" beliefs (i.e. not a **believes** formula) using its prover.

```
can_prove(Fact) :-
    believes(Fact),!,
can_prove(believes(Agent, Fact)) :-
    !,
    ask(Fact) ->> agent:Agent,
    result(ProofResult, Fact) <<= _:Agent,
    ProofResult = proved,
    assert(believes(believes(Agent, Fact))).
can_prove(Fact) :-
    collect_basic_facts(Facts),
    find_contradiction([~Fact|Facts], 20, _).
```

Note that, in this example, we choose to cache beliefs of other agents beliefs (by asserting belief facts) but not proved facts of the agent itself.

As an example, assume we have an agent server that creates three reasoning agents called **alice**, **bob** and **carol** and further assume that the server has sent the following tell messages to **alice**.

```
tell(all x (b(x) => c))
tell(all x a(x))
tell(ex x (a(x) => b(x)))
```

If the server now sends the message **ask(believes(alice, c))** to **bob** then **bob** will send an **ask(c)** message to **alice**. The **alice** agent will then use her prover to prove **c** by contradiction using her stored beliefs and send a success message back to **bob** who will add the belief `believes(alice, c)` to his set of beliefs. **bob** will then send a success message back to the server.

If the server now sends the message
`ask(believes(carol, believes(bob, believes(alice,c))))`
to **bob**, then **bob** will send **carol** the message
`ask(believes(bob, believes(alice,c)))`
who will in turn send **bob** the message
`ask(believes(alice, c))`.

Now, **bob** believes this (from the previous interaction) and so sends a success message back to **carol** who then relays this back to **bob** who then sends the success message back to the server.

Note that this sort of query works because **bob**'s main thread is able to respond even though his subthread is blocked waiting on a reply from **carol**.

The simple reasoning agent described above could be modified or extended in several ways.

Firstly, the Qu-Prolog release comes with an extension of the Tcl/Tk interpreter that provides ICM message support. It is straightforward to write a Tcl/Tk GUI that, for example, could be used to debug a collection of reasoning agents, or show the message traffic between the agents. Simply be adding message sends to the GUI at appropriate points in the agent code, we can provide the GUI with information about the workings of individual agents. The sender address lets the GUI know which agent has sent the message.

Such a GUI could be further extended to communicate with an agent server, thus providing a complete interface to the agent community.

The agent described earlier included its own prover. Another possibility is to provide a collection of prover agents, perhaps with different capabilities or that support different logics. Our agents could then choose an appropriate prover agent and get the prover agent to do the proof on its behalf.

For our example, we choose to cache beliefs from other agent. This, however raises the question about what should happen when an agent dies, or even simply removes some of its beliefs. This could be avoided by not caching, or be storing queries from other agents so that when this agent changes it can send messages to other agents to warn them about changes.

5   Conclusion

The combination of multi-threading and high-level communication provided by Qu-Prolog makes it an ideal language for programming agents, particularly intelligent agents. Programming certain types of agents can be made even easier by using the OO layer described in [2]. This OO extension provides a class definition mechanism and a compiler to convert these definitions into Qu-Prolog code. Objects are threads whose methods are invoked via messages. An example of a mobile object (agent) class is given that shows how mobile agents with simple state can be coded.

The built-in support for reasoning in Qu-Prolog allows agents to be equipped with a wide-range of reasoning skills from standard Prolog inference through automatic propositional reasoning to sophisticated inference for predicate logics, higher-order logics and modal logics.

We contend that the Qu-Prolog extensions that support agents and reasoning provide application writers with simple and powerful techniques for implementing agents with advanced reasoning capabilities.

Qu-Prolog is freely available from the Software Verification Research Centre at http://www.svrc.uq.edu.au

References

1. Holger Becht, Anthony Bloesch, Ray Nickson and Mark Utting, Ergo 4.1 Reference Manual, Technical Report No. 96–31, Software Verification Research Centre, Department of Computer Science, University of Queensland, 1996.
2. Keith Clark and Peter J. Robinson, Agents as Multi-threaded Logical Objects, to appear
3. F.G. McCabe, The Inter-Agent Communication Model (ICM), http://www.nar.fla.com/icm/, Fujitsu Laboratories of America Inc, 2000.
4. Peter J. Robinson. Qu-Prolog 6.0 User Guide. Technical Report No. 00-20, Software Verification Research Centre, University of Queensland, 2000.
5. Mark Utting, Peter Robinson, Ray Nickson, Ergo 6: A generic proof engine that uses prolog proof technology, *JCM*, 5, pp 194–219 , 2002

A Model for Conformance Testing of Mobile Agents in a MASIF Framework

Mikaël Marche and Yves-Marie Quemener

France Télécom R&D, 2 Avenue Pierre Marzin
22300 Lannion cedex, France
{mikael.marche, yvesmarie.quemener}@rd.francetelecom.com

Abstract. This paper defines a formal framework for testing mobile agents based on the existing concepts of conformance testing. First, we introduce a model of mobile agent based on transition systems. Our goal is to propose a model which have the properties of abstraction required for the test, in the same way as test models based on transition systems for conformance testing. Then we propose an approach of observation of the behaviour of mobile agents in their environment to finally define a parametrized conformance relation between mobile agents. The relation is parametrized because the conformance depends on what can be observed on the agent in a mobile setting. We then define a test object named "observer" that fully characterizes the set of correct implementations according to the conformance relation, depending on a specification and the degree of observation available on the environment. A method to create this observer from a specification is given which we prove to embody a sound and exhaustive test suite for validating the conformance of an implementation. Last, we propose on this framework a solution to execute real tests on mobile agents, *i.e* how to execute an observer to prove the conformance of an implementation. This solution is already implemented through a simulation tool.

1 Introduction

The changing nature of distributed computing, the availability of common middleware, the adaptability of software code to various environments due to the variety of terminals and the interlinking of servers on the Internet have raised the interest in the mobility of code over networks. Applications can be implemented as systems of mobile software agents executing upon dedicated execution sites [8]. A standard like MASIF [15] defines this framework, promising the interoperability of agent platforms. In this paper, we will describe those mobile agents as processes that travel on a heterogenous environment over a network. Those processes are code-containing objects whose code will execute itself upon different locations, also called execution sites, following users' demands or its own internal logic.

Just as the need for interoperability in distributed networks raised interest for testing protocols in the 1980's, the need for solutions in testing new types

M.G. Hinchey et al. (Eds.): 'FAABS 2002, LNAI 2699, pp. 173–192, 2003.

of distributed communicating software based on mobile code should come up rapidly. We found that software developers at France Telecom using agent technology were lacking test methods and tools, because very little research has been done on the specific problems implied by code mobility. Of course, applications based on mobile agents are distributed software applications, and much of the theory and practice on software testing, as well as the theory of testing in distributed contexts (such as embodied in the ITU Z.500 standard for instance [10]) is relevant. But there are specific problems in testing mobile applications.

We are interested in addressing those problems in the testing of mobile agents. In fact, a lot of work has been done in the area of conformance testing [4,11] leading to a precise definition of conformance. Unfortunately, this work does not address mobile agent testing. But it is clear that most of the concepts, methodologies and theory developed for conformance testing can be adjusted for black box testing (functional testing) of mobile agents. Following this idea, the work presented in this paper proposes a formal framework in conformance testing for mobile agents. In particular, we address the following questions:

- What can be the level of observation and control for a given mobile agent in a given environment?
- How should we define a conformance relation between a specification and an implementation taking into account mobility actions, and more generally actions taking place in the environment?
- How to define tester processes, and their execution, such that they can bring a verdict of conformance following a given relation?

In another paper [12], we studied this question on a practical level, describing a tool which enables to test mobile agents by simulating their environment for ensuring a maximal control on it. In this paper, we present theoretical justifications to the approach we follow. Our main tool for this is a model of mobile agents based on labelled transition systems, enabling to formalize testing and conformance relation following the line of work pursued by Tretmans for describing conformance testing of distributed systems [17].

For this, we need to describe in an abstract way execution sites and mobile agents as labelled transition systems with dedicated actions for representing mobility. This will enable us to describe interactions between agents and between agents and execution sites, and finally execution traces of a given mobile agent in the context of a complete mobile agent system made of mobile agents and several execution sites. We then define conformance relation as a relation between the execution traces of a specification of a agent and its implementation (modeled in the same way as specifications). After that, test execution can be seen as the introduction, within the mobile agent system encompassing the tested agent, of a designated tester process. We show how it is possible to synthesize tests from a specification: the tester can detect all implementations in conformance with the specification, following a given conformance relation, like a canonical tester. Of course, the tester obtained in that way is typically not directly executable, hence the problem of test selection remains, for extracting from the complete tester agent simple test cases.

This brings us to the question of how we propose to put into action the theory. In particular, our modeling enables us to underline the problems raised by the control and the observation of mobile agents in a given environment. Our theoretical framework enables us to demonstrate a fundamental notion: environment constraints put a limit on the discriminating power of the conformance relation which can be checked when the test is executed directly in the original environment. We discuss this point in the light of the practical approach we have taken: our tool SAM enables to overcome those limitations by simulating and controlling various environments for the tested agent [12].

2 Mobility Framework Considered

Simple mobile code techniques are based on code on demand and remote evaluation (e.g. applets, RMI). This results in moving static code and/or data. As mentioned in the introduction, we consider in this paper a richer form of mobility corresponding to mobile agent techniques which combines several of those techniques and enables the autonomous migration of active agents under execution. This concept has been introduced by Telescript [19] to reduce network load and latency and to suit temporary network connectivity.

The technology supporting mobile agent takes a perspective which differs from classical distributed systems. In a mobile paradigm, as shown in Figure 1, the structure of the underlying computer network consists of execution sites layered upon the operating system. The purpose of these execution sites is to provide an execution context to agent applications which are able to dynamically relocate their execution. The concept of mobile agent raises two significant problems, related for the first one to the heterogeneity of the host systems (operating system and hardware) and for the second one to the management of the execution environment. More precisely, an environment for mobile agents must bring a solution to the following points: portability and code migration; mobility management; communication management; resources management; security management.

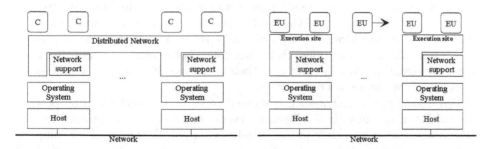

Fig. 1. Classical distributed structures vs Mobile distributed structures

Portability and code migration problems are solved by the use of *MCLs(mobile code languages)* [6], particularly adapted to the mechanisms of mobility. Indeed, these languages such as Java, Obliq, Objective Caml, Tcl, etc, are interpreted and offer a runtime allowing code insulation and migration, although some languages, for example Java, propose only a serialization mechanism of the code. In this case, the agent's state is not completely restored after its migration. The other problems which are linked to the agent's execution management (migration, communication, authorization, ...) are solved in an applicative way. A uniform solution is to consider the execution sites as a service-providing environment. The agent in this environment reaches the various services it needs by calling methods of an application which plays the role of the execution site.

MASIF [15] clearly defines this hierarchy between agent and execution sites. However, MASIF is limited to interoperability between execution sites. Hence, it addresses the site interface and concepts, but not the problems of language interoperability and the standardization of agents' actions, such as migration and communication. So, it can be said that MASIF defines the interfaces at the execution site level rather than at agent level. MASIF standardizes agent management primitives (creation, execution, suspension, termination..), agent transfer primitives (emission and reception of messages) and syntaxes and terms defining for example agent and execution site names, their characteristics and their properties.

In the rest of this paper, our study of test for mobile agents is based on the MASIF framework. In this framework, agents encapsulated by an execution unit act on behalf of a person and are executed by an execution site. Agents have the ability to move to other execution site and to communicate with other agents to perform their computation task.

3   Modeling Mobile Agent Systems

Our model of mobile agent systems is influenced by our goal: we want to describe the conformance testing of a mobile agent which can be executed in a variety of settings, but close of the notions described in the MASIF standard. In particular, this implies that we will need a primitive notion of execution site which offers a set of functionalities to mobile agents which can migrate from site to site. Thus, the two key notions of the model are *execution sites* and *mobile agents*. Execution sites are located computational environments where mobile agents can reside. Mobile agents have their own code (behaviour), can move between different execution sites, interact with their execution site, and can communicate with each other by means of messages.

To design such a test model, it seemed to us more judicious to propose an alternative of test models developed for communicating systems, rather than to use a model based on mobile process algebras. Indeed, the higher order complexity of those process algebras (Join-Calculus [7], $\pi-$Calculus [13]) makes difficult to express the notion of conformity on processes. For example, in a study on bisimulation of processes in Join-Calculus [3], the author cannot conclude about the possibility to define a canonical tester in this framework. Finally, let us note that those process algebras seemed badly adapted to the modeling of mobile systems based on the MASIF standard. For example, in Join-Calculus, the definition of locality is regarded as a simple label and is confused with the definition of process, and in the π-calculus, the mobility of process is represented by a transmission of channels and the definition of locality is non-existent.

Thus, following Phalippou [16] and Tretmans [17], we represent specifications and implementations of agents as labelled transitions systems whose set of actions is partitioned into output actions (the observable ones) and input actions (the controllable ones), plus an internal unobservable action. Those input/output actions can also be seen as the emissions/receptions of messages. But, if this first approach is well adapted for describing interaction between agents, this is not enough for describing the interactions between agents and execution sites, for example when agents ask their execution site to migrate them to another one. We will use different notations for representing interactions between agents and interactions between agents and sites.

We first need to give a definition for transitions systems.

Definition 1. *A labelled transition system (in short, a LTS) is a tuple $< S, L, T, s_0 >$ where:*

- *S is a finite set of* states;
- *L is a finite set of* labels;
- *$T \subseteq S \times (L \uplus \{\tau\}) \times S$ is the* transition relation;
- *$s_0 \in S$ is the* initial state.

Labels in L represent observable actions, whereas the distinguished τ label represent unobservable internal actions. We use μ to denote labels. As usual, we note $s \xrightarrow{\mu} s'$ for $(s, \mu, s') \in T$. This defines an atomic action: the LTS in state s executes the action μ and arrives in state s'. We say that a state s' is *accessible* from s when there exists states $(s_1, \ldots, s_n = s')$ and labels $(\mu_1, \ldots, \mu_n)$ such that $s \xrightarrow{\mu_1} s_1 \xrightarrow{\mu_2} \cdots \xrightarrow{\mu_n} s_n = s'$. Denoting by σ the concatenation of n labels $\mu_1 \ldots \mu_n$, we also write $s \xrightarrow{\sigma} s'$. When we are not interested in target states, we note $s \xrightarrow{\mu}$ for $\exists s', s \xrightarrow{\mu} s'$ and $s \xrightarrow{\sigma}$ for $\exists s', s \xrightarrow{\sigma} s'$. We consider only labelled transition systems whose all states are accessible from s_0. For simplicity reasons, we have chosen to consider only finite labelled transitions systems.

Let *Messages* and *Sites* be finite sets enabling to derive identifiers for respectively the messages exchanged between agents (and between agents and execution sites) and the execution sites. Then, mobile agents are defined as transition systems following the definition 2.

Definition 2. *A mobile agent $P = (S_p, L_p, T_p, s_0)$ is a LTS where the set of labels L_p is included in $\{!, ?, !!, ??\} \times Messages \uplus \{\delta\} \times Sites$, i.e. a label is either an element of $\{!, ?, !!, ??\} \times Messages$, either an element of $\{\delta\} \times Sites$.*

Let $a \in Messages$ and $f \in Sites$. The label $!a$ represents the action of emitting the message a to another agent whereas $?a$ represents the reception of such a message. The label $!!a$ represents the emission of the message a from the agent to its own execution site, whereas $??a$ represents the reception of a from this site. Last, δf represents the action of asking the migration of the agent to the execution site f.

We will partition the set of actions L_p in input actions L_{p_i} and output actions L_{p_u}. We define L_{p_i} as $L_{p_i} = L_p \cap \{?, ??\} \times Messages$ and L_{p_u} as $L_p \cap (\{!, !!\} \times Messages \uplus \{\delta\} \times Sites)$. We of course have $L_p = L_{p_i} \uplus L_{p_u}$.

Let P be a agent. When P executes itself, this is represented by a notion of current state, which is at first the initial state, and afterwards one of the states of the underlying LTS. When we want to represent explicitly this notion of current state, we use the following notation:

Definition 3. *Let* $P = (S_p, L_p, T_p, s_0)$ *be a mobile agent, and* $p \in S_p$ *be a state of* P. *We note* $P \triangleright p$ *for expressing that, during the execution of* P *its current state is* p.

Also, we will sometimes identify a agent P with its initial state s_0. For example, when σ is a sequence of actions, we will note $P \overset{\sigma}{\Rightarrow}$ instead of $s_0 \overset{\sigma}{\Rightarrow}$. We also define the set of traces of a mobile agent, independently of any context, as follows:

Definition 4. *Let* $P = (S_p, L_p, T_p, s_0)$ *be a mobile agent. We will note* $Trace(P)$ *and we will call the set of traces of* P *the subset of* L_p^* *such that:*

$$Trace(P) = \{\sigma \in L_p^* | P \overset{\sigma}{\Rightarrow}\}$$

We now define execution sites as located (named) computational environments inside which agents can execute.

Definition 5. *An* execution site *is a tuple* $ES = (n, F_{es}, A)$ *where:*

- $n \in Sites$ *is the name of the site;*
- $F_{es} = (S_{es}, L_{es}, T_{es}, s_0)$ *is a LTS defining the behaviour of the site. The labels* L_{es} *are in* $\{!!, ??\} \times Messages \uplus \{\Delta\} \times Sites;$
- A *is a multi-set of agents currently executing upon the execution site.*

As for agents, labels $!!a$ and $??a$ represent the emission and reception of messages between an execution site and a agent executing on it. The label Δf represent the execution of a migration action for a mobile agent to the site f. Also, an execution site embodies in its LTS defining its behaviour a notion of current state, and we will note $F \triangleright f$ for expressing that the execution site F is in current state f.

We can remark that this definition doesn't specify what is the initial distribution of agents on the execution site, before it begins to execute. This is precised in the complete definition for a mobile agent system.

Definition 6. *A* mobile agents system *is a finite set of execution sites, whose names are pairwise distinct, given with a mapping which, for each execution site, gives the multi-set of agents initially executing upon the site.*

Now, we can define the operational semantics of such a mobile system.

Definition 7. *The operational semantics of a mobile agents system are given as a labelled transition system. A state of this LTS is made of the states of all agents, of the states of the LTS defining the behaviour of the execution sites, and of the repartition of the agents upon the sites; the initial state of this LTS is given by the initial states of agents and sites, and the initial mapping of agents upon sites; and the transition relation is given by the application of the composition rules given in table 1, which uses the following notations:*

- $F_{es} \vdash_n A$ *denotes the execution site* $ES = (n, F_{es}, A)$;
- $P_1|P_2$ *denotes the multi-set of agent* $A = \{P_1, P_2\}$ *defining the parallel composition of the agents* P_1 *and* P_2 *on the same execution site;*
- $F_{es} \vdash_n A \parallel F'_{es} \vdash_{n'} A'$ *the parallel execution of two execution sites.*

Table 1. Operational semantics of a mobile system

$$(\text{int}_1)\ \frac{S \xrightarrow{\tau} S'}{S \vdash_n P \xrightarrow{\tau} S' \vdash_n P} \qquad (\text{int}_2)\ \frac{P \xrightarrow{\tau} P'}{S \vdash_n P \xrightarrow{\tau} S \vdash_n P'}$$

$$(\text{int}_3)\ \frac{P_1 \xrightarrow{\tau} P'_1}{S \vdash_n P_1|P_2 \xrightarrow{\tau} S \vdash_n P'_1|P_2} \qquad (\text{com-p}_1)\ \frac{P_1 \xrightarrow{(!/?)a} P'_1 \wedge P_2 \xrightarrow{(?/!)a} P'_2}{S \vdash_n P_1|P_2 \xrightarrow{\tau} S \vdash_n P'_1|P'_2}$$

$$(\text{com-p}_2)\ \frac{P_1 \xrightarrow{(!/?)a} P'_1 \wedge P_2 \xrightarrow{(?/!)a} P'_2}{S_1 \vdash_n P_1 \parallel S_2 \vdash_n P_2 \xrightarrow{\tau} S_1 \vdash_{n_1} P'_1 \parallel S_2 \vdash_{n_2} P'_2} \qquad (\text{com-sp})\ \frac{S \xrightarrow{(!!/??)a} S' \wedge P \xrightarrow{(??/!!)a} P'}{S \vdash_n P \xrightarrow{\tau} S' \vdash_n P'}$$

$$(\text{mig}_1)\ \frac{P \xrightarrow{\delta n} P' \wedge S \xrightarrow{\Delta n} S'}{S \vdash_n P \xrightarrow{\tau} S' \vdash_n P'} \qquad (\text{mig}_2)\ \frac{P \xrightarrow{\delta n_2} P' \wedge S_1 \xrightarrow{\Delta n_2} S'_1}{S_1 \vdash_{n_1} P \parallel S_2 \vdash_{n_2} Q \xrightarrow{\tau} S'_1 \vdash_{n_1} \parallel S_2 \vdash_{n_2} Q|P'}$$

As embodied in the semantics rule, we consider as composition between agents a synchronization between inputs and outputs. We use a similar notion for describing the interaction between agents and sites, whether it concerns exchange of messages or migration actions.

4   A Conformance Relation for Mobile Agents

After having presented our model of mobile execution, we study now the observation of the agent execution, and consequently the notion of conformance between agents which depends on the possible observations of their behaviours.

4.1   Observation and Execution Context

We call execution context the environment where a agent is carried out. An execution context is formed by the set of the execution sites which take part into the computation of the observed agent. In this way, a computation of the agent in an execution context corresponds to a global computation of the environment following the operational semantics rules given in table 1. However, in order to focus on the agent execution, we extract an internal observation of the agent in its environment following the actions which take place on the observed agent. This idea comes from the line of work initiated by [14].

Definition 8. *Let P be a mobile agent, p and p' states of P and $C = \{(n_i, F_i, A_i)\}$ a system of mobile agents. Let a be a message. We define the following notations:*

- $C[P]_{n_i} =_{def} \exists (n_i, F_i, A_i) \in C, P \in A_i$
- $C[p]_{n_i} \xrightarrow{(!/?)a} C[p']_{n_i} =_{def} p \xrightarrow{(!/?)a} p' \wedge \exists (n_j, F_j, A_j) \in C, Q \in A_j, (Q \triangleright q \wedge q \xrightarrow{(?/!)a})$
- $C[p]_{n_i} \xrightarrow{(!!/??)a} C[p']_{n_i} =_{def} p \xrightarrow{(!!/??)a} p' \wedge F_i \triangleright f_i \wedge f_i \xrightarrow{(??/!!)a}$
- $C[p]_{n_i} \xrightarrow{\delta n_j} C[p']_{n_j} =_{def} p \xrightarrow{\delta n_j} p' \wedge \exists (n_j, F_j, A_j) \in C \wedge F_i \triangleright f_i \wedge f_i \xrightarrow{\Delta n_j}$

In plain words, we note $C[P]_n$ when the agent P executes in the system C upon the site of name n, and $C[p]_n \xrightarrow{\mu} C[p']_{n'}$ when this agent, in the current state p is able to fire the action μ, which brings it to the state p', upon the execution site of name n' (if the action implies a change of site).

As with precedent notations, we will extend this one. First, when we don't need to take note of the state reached by the agent P in state p after executing μ, we note $C[p]_n \xrightarrow{\mu}$. We also enable to extend the previous notations to sequences of actions: $C[p]_n \xRightarrow{\sigma}$ means that the agent P, in state p in the context C upon the site n can execute the sequence of actions σ. Also, we will identify a agent and its initial state by writing $C[P]_n \xRightarrow{\sigma}$ instead of $C[s_0]_n \xRightarrow{\sigma}$.

Whatever the kind of action, we can make the following remark:

Remark 1. Let P a agent which executes in the context C, p a state of P, and μ an action. We can write the predicate $C[p]_n \xrightarrow{\mu} C[p']_n$ in the form $p \xrightarrow{\mu} p' \wedge Cond(C)$ where $Cond$ is a predicate which is independent of P. By combining this remark for sequence of actions, we can write $C[p]_n \xRightarrow{\sigma}$ in the form $p \xRightarrow{\sigma} \wedge Cond(C)$, where $Cond$ is a predicate independent of P.

This means that an action can be fired by a agent in a given execution context if and only if this action can be fired independently of any context **and** the current context of the agent enables the firing of this action. This is also true for sequences of actions.

For defining a conformance relation between specifications and implementations of mobile agents, we will also need the following definitions, inspired by similar ones introduced by Tretmans in [17]:

Definition 9. *Let P be a mobile agent, p a state of P, and $\mathcal{P}$ a subset of states of P. Let C be a mobile system, and n a site name. Let σ be a sequence of actions. We define:*

- $out(C[p]_n) =_{def} \{\mu \in L_{p_u} \mid C[p]_n \xrightarrow{\mu} \}$
- $Out(\{C[p]_n \mid p \in \mathcal{P}\}) =_{def} \bigcup \{out(C[p]_n) \mid p \in \mathcal{P}\}$
- $C[P]_n$ **after** $\sigma =_{def} \{C[p']_{n'} \mid C[P]_n \xRightarrow{\sigma} C[p']_{n'}\}$
- $Trace(C[P]_n) =_{def} \{\sigma \in L_p^* \mid C[P]_n \xRightarrow{\sigma}\}$

We have the following results:

Lemma 1. *Let P be a agent, executing in the system C, upon the site n. We have:*

$$Trace(C[P]_n) \subset Trace(P)$$

Proof. Let $\sigma \in Trace(C[P]_n)$. Following the definition 9, we have $C[P]_n \overset{\sigma}{\Rightarrow}$. Following the remark 1, we have $P \overset{\sigma}{\Rightarrow} \wedge Cond(C)$, hence $\sigma \in Trace(P)$.

Lemma 2. *Let P and Q be agents executing in the mobile system C, and n a site name. We have:*

$$(C[P]_n \overset{\sigma}{\Rightarrow} \wedge Q \overset{\sigma}{\Rightarrow}) \Rightarrow C[Q]_n \overset{\sigma}{\Rightarrow}$$

Proof. Following remark 1, we have:

$$(C[P]_n \overset{\sigma}{\Rightarrow} \wedge Q \overset{\sigma}{\Rightarrow}) \Leftrightarrow (P \overset{\sigma}{\Rightarrow} \wedge Cond(C) \wedge Q \overset{\sigma}{\Rightarrow})$$

This implies $(Cond(C) \wedge Q \overset{\sigma}{\Rightarrow})$, and, since the predicate $Cond(C)$ is independent of any agent, this is equivalent to $C[Q]_n \overset{\sigma}{\Rightarrow}$.

In other words, if a agent P can execute a given sequence of actions in a given context, and a agent Q can execute the same sequence of actions independently of any context, Q can execute this sequence in the context which enables P to execute it.

Lemma 3. *Let P be a agent executing in the mobile system C, and n a site name. We have:*

$$(\neg C[P]_n \overset{\sigma}{\Rightarrow} \wedge \exists Q, C[Q]_n \overset{\sigma}{\Rightarrow}) \Rightarrow (\neg P \overset{\sigma}{\Rightarrow})$$

Proof. Following remark 1, $\neg C[P]_n \overset{\sigma}{\Rightarrow}$ is equivalent to $\neg P \overset{\sigma}{\Rightarrow} \vee \neg Cond(C)$, where $Cond$ is a predicate independent of P. But since there exists Q such that $C[Q]_n \overset{\sigma}{\Rightarrow}$, this implies that $Cond(C)$ is true. Hence, we have $\neg P \overset{\sigma}{\Rightarrow}$.

In other words, if a agent P can not execute a given sequence of actions in a given context whereas there exists a agent Q which can execute the same sequence of actions in the same context (*i.e.*, the context enables at least one agent to execute this sequence), this implies that P can not execute this sequence independently of any context.

Depending on the nature of the execution context in which the agent to be tested is executed, different levels of control and observation on the agent execution are possible. Indeed, it is clear that the observation of all the actions of a agent depends on the observation level which one can have on its execution environment. And in this case, the practice shows, for example in interoperability testing [18], that only certain actions are observable in a test environment. Thus, we are reduced to be able to observe some specific events among all the possibles traces of the implementation. These traces, reduced to the observable messages in a context, can be obtained by a projection of complete traces on a set representing the degree of observation we are able to have.

In this way, to observe a agent in an execution context, we define, according to the degree of observation which we are able to have on the agent in this context, the set of its observable behaviour. For example, if we consider the trace σ of a agent P in an execution context where only the actions defined in a subset X are observable, then the observable trace σ' in this context is reduced to some actions obtained by projecting σ over X.

Definition 10. *Let $\sigma \in L_p^*$ denote a sequence of actions, and $\mu \in L_p$ an action. Let $X \subseteq L_p$ be a set of actions, called the* observable actions. *The projection of σ on X, denoted σ/X is defined by induction as follows:*

- *For the empty sequence: $\epsilon/X =_{def} \epsilon$*
- *Else: $\mu.\sigma/X =_{def} \sigma/X$ if $\mu \notin X$*
- *And: $\mu.\sigma/X =_{def} \mu.(\sigma/X)$ if $\mu \in X$*

According to a set of observable actions X in an execution context C, we complete the previous definitions 9 and the lemma 1.

Definition 11. *Let P be a mobile agent, p a state of P, and $\mathcal{P}$ a subset of states of P. Let C be a mobile system, and n a site name. Let σ be a sequence of actions and X a set of observable actions. We define:*

- $out_X(C[p]_n) =_{def} \{\mu \in L_{p_u} \cap X \mid C[p]_n \overset{\mu}{\rightarrow} \}$
- $Out_X(\{C[p]_n \mid p \in \mathcal{P}\}) =_{def} \bigcup\{out_X(C[p]_n) \mid p \in \mathcal{P}\}$
- $C[P]_n$ **after** $_X\sigma =_{def} \{C[p']_{n'} \mid C[P]_n \overset{\sigma'}{\Rightarrow} C[p']_{n'} \wedge \sigma = \sigma'/X\}$
- $Trace_X(C[P]_n) =_{def} \{\sigma \in (L_p \cap X)^* \mid C[P]_n \overset{\sigma'}{\Rightarrow} \wedge \sigma = \sigma'/X\}$

Lemma 4. *Let P be a mobile agent, C a mobile system, and n a site name. Let X be a set of observable actions. We have:*

$$Trace_X(C[P]_n) \subseteq Trace_X(P)$$

Proof. This comes directly from the result of lemma 1 ($Trace(C[P]_n) \subseteq Trace(P)$) and the definition 10 of the projection of traces on X.

4.2   Conformance Relation

In this section, we give a formal definition of the notion of conformance based on the model of mobile agent introduced. Typically, a conformance relation states that an implementation I is conformant to its specification S if, after a trace of S, outputs of I are foreseen in S. For example, let us consider the most commonly used *ioconf* conformance relation, defined by Tretmans in [17]:

Definition 12. *Let I and S be labelled transition systems representing respectively an implementation and a specification. The conformance relation ioconf is defined as follows:*

$$ioconf(I, S) \Longleftrightarrow_{def} \forall \sigma \in Trace(S), \ Out(I \textbf{ after } \sigma) \subseteq Out(S \textbf{ after } \sigma)$$

It is natural to study how this conformance relation can be adapted to our model. However, it is clear that this relation is not directly adaptable in our study. Indeed, we have to take into account the influence of the execution context in the observable behaviour of the implementation and also all the possible behaviours of the specification in a context. For example, how to conclude on conformance of an implementation if some traces envisaged in the specification are not executable in a context?

We already introduced a way to represent that the execution context interfere with the possible observations of the agent' actions. Within this framework, it is necessary to take into account this incidence on the traces described in the specification. In short, it is clear that the concept of execution context is significant in the definition of conformance and then it is necessary to compare an implementation with a specification in a same context of execution and observation to conclude on their conformance.

Definition 13. *Let I and S be mobile agents representing respectively an implementation and a specification. Let X be a set of observable actions. We define the conformance relation $\mathcal{R}_X$ as follows:*

$$\mathcal{R}_X(I,S) \Longleftrightarrow_{def}$$
$$\forall C, \forall n, \forall \sigma \in Trace_X(C[S]_n), \sigma \in Trace_X(C[I]_n) \Rightarrow Out_X(I \; \mathbf{after}_X \; \sigma) \subseteq$$
$$Out_X(S \; \mathbf{after}_X \; \sigma)$$

This relation is close to the idea of definition 12: it is said that an implementation I is in conformance with a specification S if, in all possible contexts, the behaviour of I in these contexts is included in the behavior of S in same contexts.

Finally, like *ioconf*, the relation $\mathcal{R}_X$ can be refined to behaviour equivalence or by authorizing the addition of behaviour. For example, as the figure 2 shows it, this relation does not authorize the functionality extensions as the non-conformance of $I3$ shows it, if all the actions are observable. Also let us note that, if the absence of action is not observable, this relation authorizes an implementation to do nothing, even if the specification plans one or more actions, as the conformity of $I2$ shows it. More generally, if all observations are possible, this relation safeguards that in any environment, all that can be realized by the implementation in response to a given input is planned by the specification in this environment for the same input, as the conformance of $I1$ shows it. However, if the observation is too much restricted in the environment, this relation loses its power of non-conformance detection, as the conformance of $I4$ shows when the observation is restricted.

This remark should point the attention of the reader on the fact that if the degree of observation is too restricted the conformance relation will lose its power of non-conformance detection. And we will see in section 6 that in a real mobile environment the observation of events on the execution site are almost impractical.

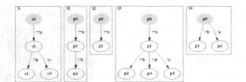

$\mathcal{R}_X^2$	$X = \{x, b, c\}$	$X = \{x, b, c, d\}$	$X = \{b, c\}$
I1	conform	conform	conform
I2	conform	conform	conform
I3	conform	not	conform
I4	not	not	conform

Fig. 2. Example of the conformance relation $\mathcal{R}_X$

5   Observer Processes and Test Synthesis

After having modeled the mobile execution of agents, as well as the concept of conformance, we now propose to present the test activity in this model and thus answer to the question of which type of "tester" is needed to check the conformance relation we just presented.

5.1   Observer

In the differents works [16,17] on test conformance on which this study is based, a single object called *tester*, assimilated itself to a process, is used to represent the test activity. This approach already proposed by [5] has the advantage of presenting in a global way the tests and their execution. Intuitively, this tester object represents the execution of all exchanges of messages between the tester and the implementation corresponding to all execution traces needed to check the conformance relation. In a more pragmatic way, the tester defines the interface offered to the implementation and its execution with the implementation is synchronized on the input-output actions of this one, to observe and control it and then check its execution.

This homogeneous vision of test activity including the contextual and the operational definition of the test is valid in those studies because the concept of test context is comparable to the concept of process. However, in case of mobile execution, the notion of context is not comparable to a process, but to a composition of execution sites carrying out agents. Thus, in case of mobile execution, the tester would be considered as a very complex object which would have to play at the same time the role of "test driver" and the role of several execution sites. Moreover, as in embedded systems, the role of the execution site is needed to execute the agents, and cannot be replaced by a simple *stub*. Hence, it is more reasonable to think that a particular object can observe a part of the interactions between the tested agent and execution sites at the interface of the execution sites. Such an object, considered as a agent, could synchronize its execution on a part of the interactions between the tested agent and the execution sites by observing those interfaces, and control the tested agent through its inputs and outputs between agents. We propose to name this object an "observer".

An observer is represented in our model by an individual process, which has the possibility to observe certain messages defined in definition 14 at the interface of the execution sites, and has a mechanism of verdict assignment at its terminal state.

Definition 14. *We define OBS the set of all possible observable messages between agents and execution sites as follows:*

$$OBS \;=\; \{!!, ??\} \times Messages \cup \{\delta\} \times Sites$$

Definition 15. *Let $P = (S, L, T, s_0)$ be a agent where L is partitioned into inter-agent actions L_{pp} and agent-site actions L_{ps}:*

- $L_{pp} = \{(!/?)a \mid (!/?)a \in L\}$
- $L_{ps} = \{(!!/??)a \mid (!!/??)a \in L\} \cup \{\delta n \mid \delta n \in L\}$

And let $A \subseteq L_{ps} \subseteq OBS$ be a set of observable actions over L_{pp}, we define X_P^A the set of all observable action over P as follows: $X_P^A = A \cup L_{pp}$

In other words, we consider that, for a given agent, all its inter-agent actions are observable, whether only a subset of its interactions with the execution sites is observable.

Definition 16. *An observer O is a particular agent (S_o, L_o, T_o, s_0) where :*

- ***fail*** $\in S_o$ *is a final state of verdict;*
- $L_o \subseteq \{!, ?, !!, ??\} \times Messages \cup \{\delta\} \times Sites \cup \{Obs(\mu) \mid \mu \in OBS\}$

In the proposed definition of observer, the labels $(!/?)a \in L_o$ represent interactions between agents and the special label $Obs(\mu)$ represents the observation of the action μ from a agent to its execution site. Thus, the execution of an observer is defined by a set of transitions synchronized on the one hand on the execution of the agent, and on the other hand on the observation of actions between agents and execution sites. The execution of the transitions of observers are based on the semantics proposed in section 3, according to the parallel composition rule of agent (see table 1), in addition with observation rules defined in table 2.

Table 2. Observation rules

$$(com_{o1}) \quad \frac{S \xrightarrow{(!!/??)a} S' \;\wedge\; P \xrightarrow{(??/!!)a} P' \;\wedge\; O \xrightarrow{Obs((!!/??)a)} O'}{S \vdash_n P|O \xrightarrow{\tau} S' \vdash_n P'|O'}$$

$$(com_{o2}) \quad \frac{S_1 \xrightarrow{(!!/??)a} S_1' \;\wedge\; P \xrightarrow{(??/!!)a} P' \;\wedge\; O \xrightarrow{Obs((!!/??)a)} O'}{S_1 \vdash_{n_1} P \parallel S_2 \vdash_{n_2} O \xrightarrow{\tau} S_1' \vdash_n P' \parallel S_2 \vdash_{n_2} O'}$$

$$(mig_{o1}) \quad \frac{P \xrightarrow{\delta n} P' \;\wedge\; S \xrightarrow{\Delta n} S' \;\wedge\; O \xrightarrow{Obs(\delta n)} O'}{S \vdash_n P|O \xrightarrow{\tau} S' \vdash_n P'|O'} \qquad (mig_{o2}) \quad \frac{P \xrightarrow{\delta n} P' \;\wedge\; S_1 \xrightarrow{\Delta n} S_1' \;\wedge\; O \xrightarrow{Obs(\delta n)} O'}{S_1 \vdash_n P \parallel S_2 \vdash_{n_2} O \xrightarrow{\tau} S_1' \vdash_n P' \parallel S_2 \vdash_{n_2} O'}$$

$$(mig_{o3}) \quad \frac{P \xrightarrow{\delta n_2} P' \;\wedge\; S_1 \xrightarrow{\Delta n_2} S_1' \;\wedge\; O \xrightarrow{Obs(\delta n_2)} O'}{S_1 \vdash_{n_1} P|O \parallel S_2 \vdash_{n_2} \xrightarrow{\tau} S_1' \vdash_{n_1} O' \parallel S_2 \vdash_{n_2} P'} \qquad (mig_{o4}) \quad \frac{P \xrightarrow{\delta n_2} P' \;\wedge\; S_1 \xrightarrow{\Delta n_2} S_1' \;\wedge\; O \xrightarrow{Obs(\delta n_2)} O'}{S_1 \vdash_{n_1} P \parallel S_2 \vdash_{n_2} O \xrightarrow{\tau} S_1' \vdash_{n_1} \parallel S_2 \vdash_{n_2} P'|O'}$$

Each of those observation rules means that an observer O can observe and synchronize its execution on actions between agents and execution sites according to the transition $(s, Obs(a), s')$. The introduction of those new rules brings us to define the concept of observation context, as being a context C containing only an observer O on its execution sites.

Definition 17. *Let* $C = \{ES_i = (n_i, F_{es_i}, A_i)\}$ *be a mobile system and* O *an observer. We define the* observation context *built from* C *with* O*, and we note* $C_O = \{ES'_i\}$ *the mobile system such that:*

- *there is one and only one site* $ES'_i = (n_i, F_{es_i}, \{O\})$ *upon which* O *is executed;*
- *and for all the other sites,* $ES'_j = (n_j, F_{es_j}, \emptyset)$*, i.e. no other agent is executed.*

The concept of the observation context introduces the notion of a minimum context where an observer can observe the execution of a agent P.

5.2   Observer and Conformance Relation

According to the approach followed in [17,16], we present now how, starting from any specification, to calculate an observer which characterizes all implementations in conformance with this specification according to the conformance relation R_X. In fact, the test approach by an observer has a common point with the approach of testing communicating systems, in synchronising the tester on the input and outputs of the implementation. The structure of such a tester in these approaches is obtained by inversion of the input and outputs transitions of the specification. The principle of the observer remains identical in the synchronisation of the input and outputs of the implementation between agents, to which we add observation transitions in relationship with interactions between the implementation and execution sites.

Definition 18. *Let* σ *be a trace of a mobile agent. We define inductively* σ^{-1} *the* inverted trace *of* σ *as follows:*

- $\epsilon^{-1} = \epsilon$
- $(?a.\sigma)^{-1} = !a.(\sigma)^{-1}$
- $(!a.\sigma)^{-1} = ?a.(\sigma)^{-1}$
- $(!!a.\sigma)^{-1} = Obs(!!a).(\sigma)^{-1}$
- $(??a.\sigma)^{-1} = Obs(??a).(\sigma)^{-1}$
- $(\delta n.\sigma)^{-1} = Obs(\delta n).(\sigma)^{-1}$

Definition 19. *Let* $S = (S_s, L_s, T_s, s_0)$ *be a specification and* $A \subseteq OBS$ *be a set of observable actions between* S *and execution sites. Let* X_S^A *be the set of all observable actions of* S*. We call an observer for* S *on* X_S^A*, and we note* $O_{X_S^A}(S)$*, an observer* O *whose transition relation is defined by the recursive application of the following rules:*

$\forall \sigma \in Trace(S)$ *such that* $S \stackrel{\sigma}{\Rightarrow} s$

- $(\sigma / X_S^A)^{-1} \in Trace(O)$
- $\neg \exists\, s', s \stackrel{!!a}{\Rightarrow} s' \wedge !!a \in X_S^A \Rightarrow ((\sigma / X_S^A)^{-1}.Obs(!!a).\textbf{\textit{fail}}) \in Trace(O)$
- $\neg \exists s', s \stackrel{\delta n}{\Rightarrow} s' \wedge \delta n \in X_S^A \Rightarrow ((\sigma / X_S^A)^{-1}.Obs(\delta n).\textbf{\textit{fail}}) \in Trace(O)$

$$- \neg \exists s', s \overset{!a}{\Rightarrow} s' \wedge !a \in L_s \Rightarrow ((\sigma/X)^{-1}.?a.\textbf{fail}) \in Trace(O)$$

We note O_X an observer of a specification when there is no ambiguity on the observed specification.

Remark 2. $\forall \sigma, \sigma \in Trace_X(S) \Rightarrow \sigma^{-1} \in Trace(O_X)$

Intuitively, an observer O_X synchronises itself on an implementation I following the traces σ defined in the specification S and observable over X, and checks the outputs of the implementation by the presence of the **fail** state if the output of the implementation does not correspond to those awaited.

From this definition, we can now prove a significant property of the observation contexts, which is that if a agent S is executable in a context C, then S is executable in the observation context C_{O_X}, defined from C with an observer O_X of S.

Lemma 5. *Let S be a agent, C a context, and n a site name. Let O_X be an observer for S. We have:*

$$(C[S]_n \overset{\sigma}{\Longrightarrow}) \Rightarrow (C_{O_X}[S]_n \overset{\sigma}{\Longrightarrow})$$

Proof. We suppose $C[S]_n \overset{\mu}{\rightarrow}$, and according to the case of μ, we have:

1. $\mu = \delta n_j$: $(S \overset{\delta n_j}{\longrightarrow} s') \wedge \exists (n_j, F_{es_j}, A_j) \in C \wedge F_{es_i} \overset{\Delta n_j}{\longrightarrow}$. And, following the definition 17, $(n_j, F_{es_j}, A'_j) \in C_{O_X}$ and $(n_i, F_{es_i}, A'_i) \in C_{O_X}$. Hence, the conditions imposed on the context C for enabling the action δn_j to execute are satisfied for the context C_{O_X}. So, we have $C_{O_X}[S]_n \overset{\mu}{\rightarrow}$ according to the definition 8.

2. $\mu = (!!/??)a$: $(S \overset{(!!/??)a}{\longrightarrow} s') \wedge F_{es_n} \overset{(??/!!)a}{\longrightarrow}$. Then, following the definition 17, $(n, F_{es_n}, A_n) \in C_{O_X}$. Hence, the condition imposed on the context C for enabling the action $(!!/??)a$ is satisfied by C_{O_X}. So, $C_{O_X}[S]_n \overset{\mu}{\rightarrow}$, according to the definition 8.

3. $\mu = (!/?)a$: $(S \overset{(!/?)a}{\longrightarrow} s') \wedge \exists (n_j, F_{es_j}, A_j) \in C, (Q \in A_j) \wedge Q \overset{(?/!)a}{\longrightarrow}$).
   Following the definition 19, if $S \overset{\mu}{\rightarrow}$ then $O_X \overset{\mu^{-1}=(!/?)a}{\longrightarrow}$. And, according to definition 17, $\exists (n_j, F_{es_j}, A_j) \in C_{O_X}$ such $A_j = \{O_X\}$, and consequently $C_{O_X}[S]_n \overset{\mu}{\rightarrow}$ following the definition 8.

Thus, by induction over the length of σ, we have: $(C[S]_n \overset{\sigma}{\Rightarrow}) \Rightarrow (C_{O_X}[S]_n \overset{\sigma}{\Rightarrow})$.

Last, to be able to decide about the success of a test executed by an observer, we define the notion of verdict provided by an observer O_X on an implementation I. According to the conformance relation $\mathcal{R}_X$, in term of execution trace, an implementation is not in conformance with a specification if there is a context in which the observed execution traces of the implementation are not in conformance (not included) with the execution traces of the specification, and in this case, the observer must reach the state **fail**.

Definition 20. *Let O_X be an observer for a given specification on X, and I a mobile agent representing an implementation of the specification. We define the test verdict as follows:*

- $Fail(O_X, I) \quad \Leftrightarrow \quad (\exists(C,n), \exists\sigma \quad \in \quad Trace(O_X)), \sigma^{-1} \quad \in$
  $Trace_X(C_{O_X}[I]n) \wedge O_X \overset{\sigma}{\Rightarrow} \textbf{fail}$
- $Pass(O_X, I) \Leftrightarrow \neg Fail(O_X, I)$

The idea of this definition is that by composing the execution of the implementation with an observer in an observation context, if the observer reaches the **fail** state while synchronising itself on the implementation, that means that the implementation is not in conformance with the specification characterized by the observer.

Now, all ingredients are there to present the aim of this paper, *i.e* prove that an observer O_X of a specification S is able to distinguish all implementations in conformance with S, following the meaning of the conformance relation R_X.

Theorem 1. *Let S be a mobile agent, and O_X be the observer for S on the set of observable actions X. For all mobile agents I representing potential implementations of S, we have:*

$$Pass(I, O_X) \Leftrightarrow R_X(I, S)$$

Proof. First, we will prove $\neg R_X(I, S) \Rightarrow \neg Pass(I, O_X)$ and then we will prove $\neg Pass(I, O_X) \Rightarrow \neg R_X(I, S)$.

- If $R_X(I, S)$ is false, then there exists C, n and $\sigma \in Trace_X(C[S]_n)$ such that $\sigma \in Trace_X(C[I]_n)$ and:
  $Out_X(C[I]_n \textbf{ after}_X \ \sigma) \not\subseteq Out(C[S]_n \textbf{ after}_X \ \sigma)$. So, there exists $\mu = (!a \vee !!a \vee \delta n)$ such that $\sigma.\mu \in Trace_X(C[I]_n)$ and $\sigma.\mu \notin Trace_X(C[S]_n)$. However, since $\sigma \in Trace_X(C[S]_n)$, $\sigma \in Trace_X(S)$ according to lemma 1. And following the definition 19, $\sigma^{-1} \in Trace(O_X)$. In consequence of the lemma 3, if $\sigma.\mu \notin Trace_X(C[S]_n)$ and $\sigma.\mu \in Trace_X(C[I]_n)$ then $\sigma.\mu \notin Trace_X(S)$. Thus, following the definition of observer 19, if $\sigma.\mu \notin Trace_X(S)$ then there exists $\sigma' = (\sigma.\mu)^{-1} \in Trace(O_X)$ such that $O_X \overset{(\sigma.\mu)^{-1}}{\Rightarrow} fail$.
  However, according to the lemma 5, if $C[S]_n \overset{\sigma}{\Rightarrow}$ then $C_{O_X}[S]_n \overset{\sigma}{\Rightarrow}$ and following the lemma 2, $C_{O_X}[I]_n \overset{\sigma}{\Rightarrow}$. Moreover, since $\sigma' = (\sigma.\mu)^{-1} \in Trace(O_X)$, we have $C_{O_X}[I]_n \overset{\sigma.\mu}{\Rightarrow}$.
  Finally, there exists C and n such that $\sigma.\mu \in Trace_X(C_{O_X}[I]_n)$ and $(\sigma.\mu)^{-1} \in Trace(O_X)$ such that $O_X \overset{(\sigma.\mu)^{-1}}{\Rightarrow} \textbf{fail}$, so according to the definition 20, we have $Fail(O_X, I)$.
- If $Fail(O_X, I)$, then there exists C, n and $\sigma \in Trace(O_X)$ such that $\sigma^{-1} \in Trace_X(C_{O_X}[I]_n)$ and $O_X \overset{\sigma}{\Rightarrow} \textbf{fail}$.
  However, according to the definition 19, only the reception of a message or an observation can put the observer in the state **fail**. Consequently, the trace σ of O_X can be written $\sigma_1.\mu$ with $\mu =?a \vee Obs(!!a) \vee Obs(\delta n)$.

Following the construction of an observer (see definition 19), we can deduce that $\sigma_1^{-1} \in Trace_X(S)$, but $\sigma^{-1} \notin Trace_X(S)$, with $\sigma^{-1} = \sigma_1^{-1}.\mu^{-1}$. From lemma 1, we can add that $\sigma^{-1} \notin Trace_X(C_{O_X}[S]_n)$. And the action μ^{-1} is one of the actions $!a \vee !!a \vee \delta n$, $i.e.$ one of those output actions which should be detected by the predicate out. Hence, we have: $\mu^{-1} \notin Out_X(C_{O_X}[S]_n \text{ after}_X \sigma_1^{-1})$.

But, on the contrary, we have $\sigma^{-1} \in Trace_X(C_{O_X}[I]_n)$. Hence, using the same decomposition of σ in $\sigma_1.\mu$, we can deduce: $\mu^{-1} \in Out_X(C_{O_X}[I]_n \text{ after}_X \sigma_1^{-1})$.

Hence, there exists a context C_{O_X}, a name n, and a trace $\sigma_1^{-1} \in Trace_X(C_{O_X}[S]_n)$ such that $Out_X(C_{O_X}[I]_n \text{ after}_X \sigma_1^{-1}) \not\subseteq Out_X(C_{O_X}[S]_n \text{ after}_X \sigma_1^{-1})$. This is equivalent, by definition, to $\neg\mathcal{R}_X(I,S)$.

Remark 3. Let us note that this theorem is true for the class of observer and observation context we define but if inter-agent actions are not observable, it becomes false. Indeed, it is a consequence of the lemma 5, which shows the correlation between the observation context and the observer. In our definition, this lemma is true because the observer interacts with the agent for all the actions between agents. So if those actions are not observable (can not be interpreted by an observer), one must define an observation context where P can be executed without interaction of an observer for those actions.

Intuitively, in terms of test execution, the theorem 1 stipulates that if all executions of the observer on all possible observation contexts, synchronised with the implementation, never reaches the state *fail*, then the implementation is in conformance with the specification characterized by the observer. In fact, it would not be necessary to execute the observer in all possible contexts but "only" to ensure that all the transitions of the observer (corresponding to all the transitions of the specification) have been executed. Let us note, that the mechanism of assignment of verdict of the observer given here is known as *global*, in reference to the work of [16]. Indeed, since the observer does not have a particular state **pass**, success is defined like the negation of the failure. On the other hand, in the case of a tester with local verdict, the tester can always associate a verdict to an execution trace, while the success or the failure being always a final state of the tester.

Typically, we have here only looked at the problem of test generation, but not at test selection. To derive from an observer as defined precedently executable tests, it would be necessary to select parts of the observer, able to provide a local verdict. But in this case, the success of a test would not guarantee the conformance of the implementation: nevertheless, the failure of such local tests would imply the non-conformance of the specification. However, it would be possible to provide an observer which defines a local verdict, but more assumptions would be needed on the specification and the implementation. For example, in case of non-deterministic implementations, we need to assume that the non-determinism satisfies some fairness rules. More generally, a whole set of assumptions of regularity, uniformity and fairness defined by [16], for conformance testing based on *LTS*, and initially proposed by [9], allows to provide a test object with local verdict. Such work could be extended to our framework for mobile systems.

6 Test Execution

We studied the observation of a mobile agent by a test object named "observer". This observer is built to be able to control and observe an implementation under test to check its validity, on the assumption that on one hand the coupling between the test and the implementation is modeled by a perfect synchronisation, and on the other hand the observation at the interface of the execution sites was practicable. But concretely, to execute the observer, it should be placed in the execution environment of the tested implementation, so in a system made of execution sites, where:

- the execution sites do not provide necessarily an observable interface for an observer, which considerably reduces the test power;
- the execution sites do not give to the observer the control of events triggered on the implementation, thus for example, it is difficult to test the robustness of an implementation over erroneous interactions;
- the execution sites can not allow the release of all transitions planned for the implementation by a specification, thus it is difficult to select a set of sound tests for some properties to check;
- the distribution of execution sites can create various problems of synchronization, in particular if the observer has to be distributed, it will be difficult to rebuild the order of the events emitted by the implementation;
- last, the execution sites are for the majority proprietary software, and therefore not easily modifiable in order be made observable.

Thus, the concrete test implementation of mobile agents is strongly bounded by the observation and control of the execution sites. If in practice observation rules defined in table 2 can not be applied, the test is then limited to the observation and control of the communications between agents of the implementation under test, which excludes, for example, all checks of the mobile behaviour. Similar problems of control and observation exist in the field of embedded software. Indeed, as soon as software is placed inside an embedded environment, it is very difficult to observe it thoroughly. Hence, prior testing is made using a simulator which will emulate the embedding context of such software. A simulator makes it easy to test the software in various different contexts which correspond to the different possible embedding contexts.

In the framework of testing mobile agent, a simulator, based on the abstraction of the execution sites proposed in 3, would allow, according to the theoretical method of construction of observers we just proposed, to execute tests for mobile agents in a formal framework. According to this fact, we have developed a simulation tool of execution sites, for testing mobile agents. The simulation model is directly deduced from the abstraction we presented. The mobile agents are connected to the simulator by an interface allowing the abstraction of the agent to its sequencing of actions. The test execution is carried out by observers which have the synchronisation properties we presented previously, and to which we add a mechanism defining a global instant of execution for writing distributed tests. Let us note that those test are written in a dedicated formalism, which makes it possible to abstract the test itself to the type of tested implementation. Last, the tool makes it possible to customize the simulation of the execution sites for a given platform, like for example Jade [2] and Grasshopper [1], such that we can execute agents implemented for those platforms upon our simulated environment without recompiling those implementations. We refer the interested reader to [12] where we present in detail this simulation tool.

7   Conclusion

In this paper we have proposed a formal framework for mobile agent conformance testing. First, we used existing concepts, methodologies and theory developed for conformance testing to propose an approach for mobile agent testing. We have defined an abstract model of mobile execution compliant with the MASIF standard and a widely used test model based on transition systems. Then, we have proposed a conformance relation between agents of the model. This conformance relation is based on the idea that the degree of observation on the agent behaviour in its environment is relevant when we try to show its conformance on a environment where all its actions are not observable. Indeed, it is clear that what can be tested depends on what can be observed in the mobile environment. To take into account this notion of observation in test definition, we draw a parallel between an test object named observer and the conformance relation, based on the assumption that an observer can observe possible actions between the implementation under test and its environment.

Last, we were interested in the question of the test execution, and its relevant question: how to establish the so-called Points of Control and Observation (PCOs) between the implementation and the observer? Indeed, for testing mobile agents it is necessary to define a testing context which will be able to fulfill two different goals. First, it will be used for the execution of mobile agents; second, it will enable the observation of those agents and their controllability by an observer.

To solve those problems, we decided to go for an approach based on the simulation of the mobile environment. This is a natural choice as it provides the needed level of observability, control of the configurations and some control over the execution. We have implemented those ideas in a tool called SAM [12]. Based on our formal framework, this simulator represents the locations and services typically offered by a mobile platform where an implementation can be carried out in order to be tested by an observer. SAM enables to execute agents designed for the Jade [2] and Grasshopper [1] platforms without recompiling them by mimicking the interfaces those platforms offer to mobile agents, and this result can be extended easily to platforms following the MASIF standard.

References

1. C. Bäumer, M. Breugst, S. Choy, and T. Magedanz. Grasshopper — A universal agent platform based on OMG MASIF and FIPA standards. In *First International Workshop MATA'99*. World Scientific Publishing Ltd., October 1999.
2. Fabio Bellifemine, Agostino Poggi, and Giovanni Rimassa. JADE — A FIPA-compliant agent framework. In *Proceedings of the 4th International Conference PAAM-99*, London, UK, 1999. The Practical Application Company Ltd.
3. Michele Boreale, Cédric Fournet, and Cosimo Laneve. Bisimulations for the join-calculus. In David Gries and Willem-Paul de Roever, editors, *Programming Concepts and Methods (PROCOMET '98)*. ifip, ch, 1998.
4. E. Brinksma and J. Tretmans. Testing Transition Systems: An Annotated Bibliography. In *Summer School MOVEP'2k – Modelling and Verification of Parallel Processes*, Nantes, July 2000.
5. Ed Brinksma. A theory for the derivation of tests. In *PSTV'VIII*. North Holland, 1989.
6. G. Cugola, C. Ghezzi, G.P. Pico, and G. Vigna. Analyzing Mobile Code Languages. In *Mobile Object Systems*, volume 1222 of *LNCS*, 1997.
7. Cédric Fournet and Georges Gonthier. The Reflexive Chemical Abstract Machine and the Join-Calculus. In Jr. Guy Steele, editor, *23rd Annual Symposium on Principles of Programming Languages (POPL) (St. Petersburg Beach, Florida)*, pages 372–385. ACM, jan 1996.
8. A. Fuggetta, G.P. Pico, and G. Vigna. Understanding Code Mobility. In *IEEE Transactions on Software Engineering*, volume 24, pages 342–360, May 1998.
9. Marie-Claude Gaudel. Testing can be formal, too. In *TAPSOFT '95*, volume 915 of *LNCS*. Springer, 1995.
10. ITU. Framework : Formal methods in conformance testing. In *ITU-T proposed recommendation Z.500*, 1996.
11. D. Lee and M. Yannakakis. Principles and Methods of Testing Finite State Machines – A Survey. In *Proceedings of the IEEE*, August 1996.
12. M. Marche, Y.M. Quemener, and R. Groz. Testing mobile agents : Sam, a tool based on a simulation approach. In *14th International Conference on Testing of Communicating Systems (TestCom 2002)*, Berlin, March 2002. IFIP, Kluwer.
13. Robin Milner. *Communicating and Mobile Systems: the π-Calculus*. Cambridge University Press, May 1999.
14. Rocco De Nicola and Matthew C. B. Hennessy. Testing equivalence for processes. In *ICALP'83*, volume 154 of *LNCS*. Springer, 1983.
15. OMG. Mobile Agent Systems Interoperability Facilities Specification (MASIF). Available from http://www.camb.opengroup.org/RI/MAF/.
16. M. Phalippou. Abstract testing and concrete testers. In *Protocol Specification Testing and Verification 'XIV*. North Holland, 1994.
17. J. Tretmans. Conformance testing with labelled transitions systems: Implementation relations and test generation. *Computer Networks and ISDN Systems*, (29):49–79, 1996.
18. C. Viho, S. Barbin, and L. Tanguy. Towards a formal framework for interoperability testing. In *FORTE 2001*, pages 53–68, Korea, August 2001. Kluwer.
19. James E. White. Telescript technology: Mobile agents. Available as General Magic White Paper.

Analysis of a Phase Transition in a Physics-Based Multiagent System

Diana F. Gordon-Spears and William M. Spears

Computer Science Department
College of Engineering
University of Wyoming
Laramie, WY 82071
{dspears, wspears}@cs.uwyo.edu

Abstract. This paper uses physics-based techniques to analyze a physics-based multiagent system. Both qualitative and quantitative analyses are provided to better understand and predict a system phase transition. These analyses yield deep insights into the system behavior. Furthermore, they have been tested in a practical context on actual robots and proven to be quite effective for setting system parameters.

1 Motivation

The objective of this research is to design rapidly deployable, scalable, adaptive, inexpensive, and robust networks (swarms) of autonomous distributed sensing agents (e.g., robots). The agents are to monitor, detect, track, report, and respond to environmental conditions within a specified physical region. This is done in a distributed manner by deploying numerous physical mobile robotic agents (each carrying one or more sensors), and then aggregating and fusing the distributed data collected from the agents into a single, coherent tactical picture. Potential applications for multiagent networks include search and rescue, virtual space telescopes consisting of micro-satellites, surveillance and perimeter defense, and distributed sensors for mapping biological hazards.

One of the most significant challenges when dealing with swarms of mobile agents is how to design and analyze the desirable collective behavior. It is assumed that there is no global controller for the multiagent system. The desired aggregate behavior must emerge from purely local interactions, despite restricted situational awareness and a limited communication range. In other words, the agents need to self-assemble (self-organize). Not only do we want desirable global behavior to emerge from local interactions between agents, but we also would like there to be some measure of fault-tolerance i.e., the global behavior degrades gradually if individual agents are damaged. Self-repair is also desirable, where the system repairs itself after being damaged. Finally, *formal (mathematical) behavioral assurances, i.e., predictions of how and when a system will behave in a certain manner, are crucial. Such assurances are the focus of this paper.*

M.G. Hinchey et al. (Eds.): 'FAABS 2002, LNAI 2699, pp. 193–207, 2003.

2   Relation to Alternative Approaches

System analysis enables behavioral assurance. Here, we adopt a physics-based approach to analysis. We consider this approach to fit under the category of "formal methods," not in the traditional sense of the term but rather in the broader sense, i.e., a formal method is a mathematical technique for designing and/or analyzing a system. The two main *traditional* formal methods used for this purpose are theorem proving and model checking. Why do we use a physics-based method instead of these more traditional methods? The gist of theorem proving (model checking) is to begin with a theorem (property) and prove (show) that it holds for the target system. But what if you don't know how to express the theorem or property in the first place? For example, suppose you visually observe a system behavior that you want to control, but you have no idea what causes it or how to express your property in concrete, logic-based or system-based terms? In particular, there may be a property/law relating various system parameters that enables you to predict or control the observed phenomenon, but you do not understand the system well enough to write down this law.

For such a situation, the traditional, logic-based formal methods are not directly applicable. One potentially applicable approach is empirical. Certainly machine discovery [5] and a vast array of statistical techniques could be applied to solve this problem of deriving laws empirically. We have instead chosen a theoretical (formal) physics-based approach for the following reasons:

- Empirical techniques can tell you *what* happens, but not *why* it happens. By gaining a deep, scientific understanding of a system, it is possible to generalize and extend analogies to a wide variety of aspects of the system in a way that is inconceivable to do with empirically derived laws. We have demonstrated this advantage by developing a deep, highly predictive, and practical framework using a physics potential energy analysis [10] in addition to the phase transition analysis presented here. The practicality of our framework has been validated on a set of actual robots. Minor modifications to the theory are trivial to implement once a deep understanding of the physics has been achieved.
- Other scientists (in other fields) tend to find theoretical results with a solid scientific rationale to be easier to understand and to apply than empirically derived results. Furthermore, a scientifically sound theory is easier for other scientists to build upon.
- Empirical methods can be combinatorially explosive.
- If a physics-based analysis technique is predictive of a system built on physics-based principles, then this analysis provides formal verification of the correctness of the system implementation. No such claims can be made for empirical results.

Note that we will not necessarily abandon empirical methods altogether. Empirical methods form a nice backup approach to apply when physics-based approaches become too difficult. So far, we have made a good deal of progress in analyzing our multiagent system using physics alone, and have not yet seen the need for an alternative. However, we may see such a need in the future.

3   The Physicomimetics Framework

We have created a framework for the design and analysis of multiagent systems that is grounded in natural laws of physics [9]. We call this framework "physicomimetics" or "artificial physics" (AP). In the AP framework, artificial (virtual) forces control agents. We use the term "artificial" because although we will be motivated by natural physical forces, we are not restricted to only natural physical forces. Although AP forces are virtual, agents *act* as if they are real. Thus the agent's sensors must see enough to allow it to compute the forces to which it is reacting. The agent's effectors must allow it to respond to this perceived force.

There are potential advantages to this approach. First, in the real physical world, collections of small entities yield surprisingly complex behavior from very simple interactions between the entities. Thus there is a precedent for believing that complex behavior can be achieved through simple local interactions. This is required for very small agents (such as nanobots), since their sensors and effectors will necessarily be primitive. Two, since the approach is largely independent of the size and number of agents, the results should scale well to larger agents and larger sets of agents. Finally, because this approach is physics-based, it is amenable to well-understood, physics-based analysis techniques.

In the AP framework, agents are treated as physical particles, which could range in size from nanobots to satellites. Particles move in response to the virtual forces that are exerted upon them by their neighbors – in essence the particles act as if they were part of a molecular dynamics simulation. Particles have a position, mass, velocity, and momentum. Friction is included, for self-stabilization. The net action of the system of particles is to reduce potential energy in a continuously changing virtual potential field.

Each particle i has position $p = (x, y)$ and velocity $v = (v_x, v_y)$. We use a discrete-time approximation to the continuous behavior of the particles, with time-step Δt. At each time step, the position of each particle undergoes a perturbation Δp. The perturbation depends on the current velocity $\Delta p = v \Delta t$. The velocity of each particle at each time step also changes by Δv. The change in velocity is controlled by the force on the particle $\Delta v = F \Delta t / m$, where m is the mass of that particle and F is the force on that particle. Our simulation is written in Java and is Web-accessible at http://www.cs.uwyo.edu/~wspears/ap.html. For a detailed description of how AP relates to prior research, see [9].

Given a problem, by defining it within the AP framework, we map the problem to one of minimizing potential energy (PE). As constraints are violated or performance degrades, PE increases, thus triggering a reactive response. *However, the PE field is never computed by the agents – it is an intellectual framework. The particles respond only to forces. Global patterns are automatically self-assembled via local force interactions between agents.* Given a set of initial conditions and some desired global behavior, it is necessary to define what sensors, effectors, and force laws are required for the desired global behavior to emerge. We call this the "design problem."

4   Hexagonal Lattice Sensing Grids

Let us consider an example of design. In this example, AP is applied to a swarm of micro-air vehicles (MAVs) whose mission is to form a hexagonal lattice, which acts as a distributed sensing grid [2]. Such a lattice creates a virtual antenna or synthetic aperture radar to improve the resolution of radar images.

Since MAVs have simple sensors and primitive CPUs, our goal is to provide the simplest possible control rules that require minimal sensors and effectors. At first blush, creating hexagons would appear to be somewhat complicated, requiring sensors that can calculate range, the number of neighbors, their angles, etc. However, it turns out that only range and bearing information are required. To understand this, recall an old high-school geometry lesson in which six circles of radius R can be drawn on the perimeter of a central circle of radius R (the fact that this can be done with only a compass and straight-edge can be proven with Galois theory). Figure 1 illustrates this construction. If the particles (shown as small circular spots) are deposited at the intersections of the circles, they form a hexagon with a particle in the middle.

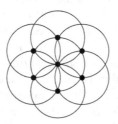

Fig. 1. How circles can create hexagons.

The construction indicates that hexagons can be created via overlapping circles of radius R. To map this into a force law, imagine that each particle repels other particles that are closer than R, while attracting particles that are further than R in distance. Thus each particle can be considered to have a circular "potential well" around itself at radius R – neighboring particles will want to be at distance R from each other. The intersection of these potential wells is a form of constructive interference that creates "nodes" of very low potential energy where the particles will be likely to reside (again these are the small circular spots in the figure). Thus the particles serve to create the very potential energy surface they are responding to![1]

---

[1]   Again, potential energy is never actually computed by agents. Agents only compute local force vectors for their current location. PE is computed for visualization/analysis purposes only.

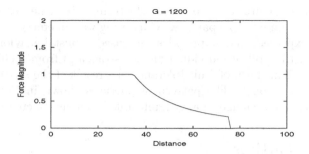

Fig. 2. The force law, when $R = 50$, $G = 1200$, $p = 2$ and $F_{max} = 1$.

With this in mind, we define a force law $F = Gm_im_j/r^p$, where F is the magnitude of the force between two particles i and j, r is the range between the two particles, and p is some power.[2] The "gravitational constant" G is set at initialization. The force is repulsive if $r < R$ and attractive if $r > R$. Each particle has a sensor that detects the range and bearing to nearby particles. The only effector is to be able to move with velocity v. To ensure that the force laws are local in nature, particles have a visual range of only $1.5R$. Also, due to the discrete-time nature of the model, it is important to define a maximum force F_{max} that can be obtained.

Figure 2 shows the magnitude of the force, when $R = 50$, $G = 1200$, $p = 2$, and $F_{max} = 1$ (the system defaults). There are three discontinuities in the force law. The first occurs where the force law transitions from F_{max} to $F = Gm_im_j/r^p$. The second occurs when the force law switches from repulsive to attractive at R. The third occurs at $1.5R$ ($= 75$), when the force goes to 0.

Figure 3 shows how an initial universe of $N = 200$ particles that began in a single small, random cluster has evolved over 1000 time steps into a hexagonal lattice, using this very simple force law. For a radius $R = 50$ and $p = 2$ we have found that a gravitational constant of $G = 1200$ provides good results.

Fig. 3. A hexagonal lattice ($t = 1000$).

---

[2] The default setting has $m_i = 1.0$ for all particles.

Note that in Figure 3 we observe a clustering effect, i.e., each node in the lattice may contain multiple particles. Clustering was an emergent property that we had not expected, and it provides increased robust behavior, because the disappearance (failure) of individual particles (agents) from a cluster will have minimal effect. This form of fault-tolerance is a result of the setting of G, which we explore in Section 6. The pattern of particles shown in Figure 3 is quite stable, and does not change to any significant degree as t increases past 1000.

5   Square Lattices

Given the success in creating hexagonal lattices, we were inspired to investigate square lattices also. The success of the hexagonal lattice hinges upon the fact that nearest neighbors are R in distance. Clearly this is not true for squares, since if the distance between particles along an edge is R, the distance along the diagonal is $\sqrt{2}R$. The problem is that the particles have no way of knowing whether their relationship to neighbors is along an edge or along a diagonal.

Once again we use a very simple approach. Suppose that at creation each particle is given another attribute, called "spin". Half of the particles are initialized to be spin "up", whereas the other half are initialized to be spin "down". Spins do not change during the evolution of the system.[3]

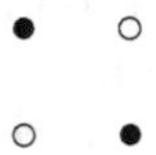

Fig. 4. Forming a square using two spins.

Consider the square depicted in Figure 4. Particles that are spin up are open circles, while particles that are spin down are filled circles. Particles of unlike spin are distance R from each other, whereas particles of like (same) spin are distance $\sqrt{2}R$ from each other. This "coloring" of the particles extends to square lattices, with alternating spins along the edges of squares, and same spins along the diagonals.

The construction in Figure 4 indicates that square lattices can be created if particles can sense not only range and bearing to neighbors, but also the spins of their neighbors. Thus the sensors need to be able to detect one more bit of information, spin. We use the same force law as before: $F = Gm_im_j/r^p$. In this case, however, the range r is renormalized to be $r/\sqrt{2}$ if the two particles have the same spin. Then once again the force is repulsive if $r < R$ and attractive if $r > R$. The only effector is to be able to move with velocity v. To ensure that the force laws are local in nature, particles cannot even see or respond to other particles that are further than $1.7R$.[4] Clustering also occurs in square lattices.

---

[3] Spin is merely a particle label, like a color.

[4] The constant is 1.3 if particles have like spin and 1.7 otherwise.

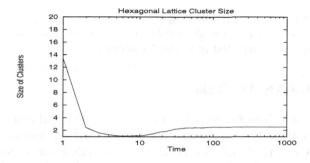

Fig. 5. The size of clusters as t increases.

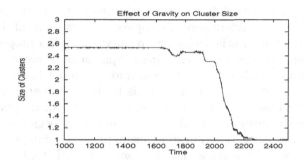

Fig. 6. Cluster size drops suddenly as G is decreased linearly after $t = 1000$.

6   Phase Transition

We decided to study the evolution of cluster size as a lattice emerges. In this section, we focus on hexagonal lattices, although the results with square lattices are a straightforward analogy. For each particle i, we count the number of particles that are close to i $(0 < r < 0.2R)$. The particle i is always included, so minimum cluster size is 1.0. This is averaged over all particles and displayed for every time step. Results are shown in Figure 5. At $t = 0$, all particles are very close to one another, yielding a high clustering. Immediately, the particles fly apart, due to the repulsive force, so that by $t = 6$ the particles are all effectively separated. However, after $t = 6$ clusters re-emerge, with the final cluster size being around 2.5. Clearly the re-emergence of clusters serves to lower the total potential energy of the system, and the size of the re-emerged clusters depends on factors such as G, R, and the geometry of the system.

Next, we summarize an interesting follow-on experiment. The previous experiment was repeated, evolving the system until $t = 2500$. However, after $t = 1000$ we lowered G by 0.5 for every time step. The results are shown in Figure 6. Our expectation was that the average cluster size would decrease linearly with G, but we were surprised. The average cluster size remained quite constant until about $t = 2000$, which is where G is 700. At this point (which is a phase transition), the cluster size dramatically dropped until roughly $t = 2200$ (where $G = 600$), where the particles are separated again.[5] This appears very similar to a phase transition in natural physics, demonstrating that AP can yield behavior very similar to that demonstrated in natural systems.

7   Qualitative Analysis

Recall that our primary objective is to provide behavioral assurance. Our goal is to model and analyze multiagent system behavior, thus enabling predictions and, if needed, corrections. Complex, evolving multiagent systems are notoriously difficult to predict. It is quite disconcerting when they exhibit anomalous behaviors for which there is no explanation. This is especially a concern when there are abrupt, radical shifts in their performance. Avoidance of abrupt, undesirable shifts in the performance of complex systems is one of the motivations for formally verifying invariance (safety) properties [3]. If a property can be expressed in temporal logic, model checking is applicable. However, the clustering property is spatial, rather than temporal, and we do not know how to express it. Therefore, we use physics-based methods for property derivation.

Consider the observed phase transition just described. It appears similar to real-world phase transitions. To gain initial insights, we began with a *qualitative* modeling and analysis of this transition, using physics techniques. In particular, we have explored mathematical visualizations of the PE fields, which are computed by performing a line integral over the forces. A line (path) integral is a measure of the work that would need to be done by a virtual particle to get to some position in the force field. By definition:

$$V = -\int_s \boldsymbol{F} \bullet d\boldsymbol{s}$$

where $\boldsymbol{s} = x\boldsymbol{i} + y\boldsymbol{j}$ is the path. The actual computation is done via the method of finite differences [4].

A line integral may be used to calculate PE if the force is (or is approximately) conservative because in that case the work to get from point a to point b is independent of the path taken (which is an assumption of the line integral). This can be verified by determining the *curl* of the force field [1]. More formally, V, the potential energy field, is a scalar. The gradient of V, i.e., $\nabla V = \boldsymbol{i} \, \partial V/\partial x + \boldsymbol{j} \, \partial V/\partial y$. ∇ is a vector operator, which in two dimensions is $\boldsymbol{i} \, \partial/\partial x + \boldsymbol{j} \, \partial/\partial y$. The curl of $\boldsymbol{F}$, $\nabla \times \boldsymbol{F}$, equals $\partial F_y/\partial x - \partial F_x/\partial y$. The interpretation is that the curl is a measure of rotation of the vector force field near a point. If the curl is 0 then the force field is conservative and the computation of the potential field is meaningful. As it turns out, due to the radial symmetry of our force law, the curl is 0 everywhere, except for small deviations from 0 at the three force law discontinuities.

Figure 7 illustrates the PE field, for a system of seven particles (there are three on the right that are hard to see) that have stabilized into a hexagonal

---

[5] We define the precise time of the phase transition to be when the average cluster size falls below 1.5.

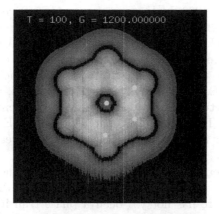

Fig. 7. The PE field when $G = 1200$.

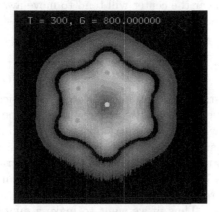

Fig. 8. The PE field when $G = 800$.

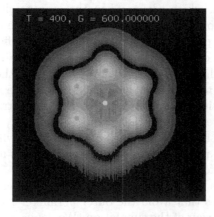

Fig. 9. The PE field when $G = 600$.

formation, where $G = 1200$. Light grey represents positive potential energy (the lightest shade represents the maximum), while dark grey represents negative potential energy. Black represents zero potential energy. A virtual particle placed in this field wants to move from regions of high potential energy to low potential energy. For example, consider the central particle, which is surrounded by a region of negative PE, followed by a region of zero PE, and then by a region of positive PE. A virtual particle that is close to the center will tend to move towards that center. Thus the central particle is in a PE well that can attract another particle. This is not surprising, since we showed earlier that a G of 1200 results in clustering.

Now consider lowering G to 800. Figure 8 illustrates the PE field. The central PE well is not as deep as it was previously, but it is still a PE well and can attract another particle. There has not yet been a phase transition. Finally, consider lowering G to 600. Figure 9 illustrates the PE field. Note that the central PE well no longer exists! The central particle is now surrounded by regions of lower PE – thus a particle near the center will tend to move away from that center. A phase transition has occurred and clustering ceases.

8   Quantitative Analysis

We have now set the stage for a more *quantitative* theoretical analysis of the cluster size phase transition. Specifically, we would like to be able to predict *when* the phase transition will occur. In particular, we want to predict the value of G in terms of other parameter settings for which the transition will occur. Before we do this, note that there are, in fact, multiple phase transitions occurring on the microscopic level. In other words, clusters break up in sub-phases, from the largest cluster size to the smallest (of size one). These mini-phase transitions occur at distinct times. Thus, if we want to make a quantitatively precise prediction, then we need to choose which mini-phase transition we wish to predict. The one of interest in this paper is the final mini-phase transition, i.e., the final cluster fragmentation, which occurs when the average cluster size prior to the phase transition is above 1.5, and the average cluster size after the phase transition is 1.0. This final phase transition is qualitatively different from the others, in that the formation changes behavior from a solid to a liquid.

Based on the qualitative analysis (above), we hypothesize that a standard physics *balance of forces* law will be predictive. In the context of our phase transition, this quantitative law states that the phase transition will occur at precisely those parameter values when the *cohesion force*, which keeps a particle within a cluster, exactly equals the *fragmentation force*, which repels the particle out of the cluster. To quantitatively specify this law, it is necessary to derive the expressions for these forces.

Figure 9 indicates that a particle placed near the central particle can escape along trajectories that avoid the outer perimeter particles. This has been confirmed via observation of the simulation. We depict these most likely escape paths in Figure 10. In this figure, which depicts a canonical scenario, there are two particles in the central cluster, and one particle in all other clusters (and all particles have a mass $m = 1$, although we can easily generalize our analysis). Let us focus on one of the two particles in the center, and call this particle "A." Due to the symmetry, without loss of generality we can focus on any of the escape paths for particle A. Let us arbitrarily focus on the escape path along the horizontal axis. Particle A can be expelled from its cluster along this axis by the other central particle, which exerts a repulsive force of F_{max}, because the range between particles, r, is very small. Therefore, the fragmentation force upon particle A is equal to F_{max}.

Fig. 10. How particles escape.

Next, we derive an expression for the cohesion force on A. Particle A is held near the center by the outer perimeter clusters/particles. Due to the geometry of the situation, it is simple to show that the cohesion force is $2\sqrt{3}G/R^p$. As above, without loss of generality we focus on the horizontal axis as the escape path of particle A. Consider the force exerted by one of the outer perimeter clusters just above this horizontal axis, on particle A. Because clusters are R apart, the magnitude of this force is G/R^p. The projection of this force on the horizontal axis escape path is $\sqrt{3}/2$ times the magnitude of this force – because the angle between the chosen outer perimeter cluster and the horizontal axis is 30 degrees. Since there are four outer perimeter clusters exerting this force (the remaining two have a force of 0 after projection), we multiply this amount by four to get a total cohesion force of $2\sqrt{3}G/R^p$.

When the cohesion force is greater than the fragmentation force, the central cluster will remain intact. When the fragmentation force is greater, the central cluster will separate. Thus, our law states that the phase transition will occur roughly when the two forces are in balance: $F_{max} = 2\sqrt{3}G/R^p$. We can now state that the phase transition will occur when $G = F_{max}R^p/2\sqrt{3}$. We denote this value of G as G_t. For the system described in the previous section $G_t = 722$, which is consistent with our visualizations. Our phase transition law is:

$$G_t = \frac{F_{max}R^p}{2\sqrt{3}}$$

We tested this law for varying values of R, F_{max}, and p. The results are shown in Tables 1 and 2, averaged over 10 independent runs, with $N = 200$. The system evolved until equilibrium with a high value of G. Then G was gradually lowered.

Cluster size was monitored, and we noted the value of G when the average cluster size dropped below 1.5. The observed values are very close to those that are predicted (within 6%), despite the enormous range in the magnitude of predicted values (approximately four orders). Plus, the variance is low.

Table 1. Predicted/observed values of G_t when $p = 2$.

R	F_{max}		
	0.5	1.0	2.0
25	90/87	180/173	361/342
50	361/355	722/687	1,440/1,430
100	1,440/1,410	2,890/2,840	5,780/5,630

Table 2. Predicted/observed values of G_t when $F_{max} = 1$.

R	p		
	1.5	2.5	3.0
25	36/35	902/874	4,510/4,480
50	102/96	5,100/5,010	36,100/35,700
100	289/277	28,900/28,800	289,000/291,000

These results are quite promising. We have provided a very good predictor of the phase transition G_t, which incorporates the most important system parameters p, R, and F_{max}. It is important to notice that N (the number of particles) does not appear in our equations. This is because the phase transition behavior is largely unaffected by N, which is a nice feature.

Table 3. Predicted/observed values of G_t when $p = 2$ for square lattices.

R	F_{max}		
	0.5	1.0	2.0
25	65/69	130/136	259/278
50	259/272	519/530	1,036/1,066
100	1,036/1,112	2,071/2,138	4,143/4,405

As with hexagonal lattices, square lattices also display a similar phase transition as G decreases. The derivation of a predictive, quantitative law for square lattices is a straightforward analogue of the analysis for hexagonal lattices. The one difference between the two analyses is that in a square lattice, one of the two particles in the central cluster is expelled along a path to one of the outer perimeter particles, rather than between them (see Figure 11). As with hexagonal lattices, square lattices also have mini-phase transitions. Again we focus on the final mini-phase transition, i.e., the final cluster fragmentation, which occurs

Table 4. Predicted/observed values of G_t when $F_{max} = 1$ for square lattices.

R	p		
	1.5	2.5	3.0
25	26/26	647/651	3,236/3,312
50	73/74	3,662/3,730	25,891/26,850
100	207/206	20,713/21,375	207,125/211,350

when the average cluster size prior to the phase transition is above 1.5, and the average cluster size after the phase transition is 1.0.

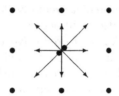

Fig. 11. How particles escape.

In Figure 11, there are two particles in the cluster at the center of the formation, and one particle in all other clusters. Let us focus on one of the two particles in the center, and call this particle "A." Using the same reasoning as with hexagons, the fragmentation force upon particle A is equal to F_{max}. Particle A is held near the center by the outer perimeter clusters/particles. Using the geometry of the situation as we did with hexagons, it is simple to show that the total cohesion force on A is $(2\sqrt{2}+2)G/R^p$. The phase transition will occur when $G = F_{max}R^p/(2\sqrt{2}+2)$. Our phase transition law for square lattices is:

$$G_t = \frac{F_{max}R^p}{2\sqrt{2}+2}$$

We tested this law for varying values of R, F_{max}, and p. The results are shown in Tables 3 and 4, averaged over 10 independent runs, with $N = 200$. The observed values are very close to those that are predicted (within 7%), and the variance among runs is low.

There are several uses for these equations. Not only can we predict the value of G_t at which the phase transition will occur, but we have observed that we can use G_t to help design our systems. For example, running the system at $G \approx 0.9G_t$ will yield the best unclustered formations, while a value of $G \approx 1.8G_t$ will yield the best clustered formations. In addition to empirical testing of our laws, we also tested them on a group of six actual robots. The goal of the robots was to get into geometric lattice formations. Using our laws, we were able to optimize robot behavior with or without clustering, whichever was desired. For details, see [10].

Finally, note that the predictiveness of the equations is a form of verification of the correctness (in a physics sense) of the AP code!

9   Summary and Related Work

This paper has presented both qualitative *and* quantitative analyses of a phase transition that occurs in a physics-based multiagent system. The qualitative analysis is based on a formal model of the potential energy and related fields, visualized using numerical analysis techniques. Observations of the field dynamics provided key insights into the physics phenomena precipitating the phase transition. We also present a novel quantitative analysis, that is inspired by traditional physics-style mathematical analyses of balance of forces. This analysis has resulted in *new laws*, which predict precisely (for a wide variety of parameter settings) *when* the phase transition will occur.

The significance of this work is that predictive analyses of swarm behavior are scarce. Multiagent swarms with emergent behavior are notoriously difficult to predict, and only a few researchers have tackled such an endeavor. Our advantage in this respect is that AP is physics-based, and thus we are able to employ traditional physics analysis techniques.

The most related analysis of a swarm under distributed control was presented by Lerman at FAABS'00 [6], and further developed in a subsequent technical report [7]. Lerman applied differential equations to mathematically analyze a multiagent system that uses behavior-based methods for control. Behavior-based multiagent systems assume that a subgroup of the agents will jointly and simultaneously perform a single behavior (such as flocking or homing) for a period of time, then switch to another behavior. Lerman formulated differential equations about state-to-state transitions that can be used to predict the fraction of agents that will be performing a given behavior after a specified time. The similarity to the work presented here is that both analyses predict a behavioral transition. The difference is that behavior-based systems are heuristic, rather than physics-based. Therefore, the full gamut of deep, knowledge-based physics techniques is not applicable to behavior-based systems. Because these systems are heuristic, it is unclear to what extent they will be amenable to further rigorous analyses – beyond predicting state transitions.

Numaoka has also done a related analysis on emergent collective behavior of swarms [8]. Like Lerman, Numaoka developed a model to predict when a heuristically controlled swarm would switch between strategies (which are like behaviors). The focus of Numaoka's analysis, unlike ours and Lerman's, however, was on how many "instigators" would be required to coerce the other agents into switching strategies.

In the future, we plan to formally analyze *all* important aspects of AP systems – for the purpose of developing behaviorally assured swarms.

Acknowledgements. We are grateful to David Book for much advice and guidance on selecting and representing the fields for visualization.

References

1. W. Fulks. *Advanced Calculus*. Wiley & Sons, 1978.
2. J. Kellogg, C. Bovais, R. Foch, H. McFarlane, C. Sullivan, J. Dahlburg, J. Gardner, R. Ramamurti, D. Gordon-Spears, R. Hartley, B. Kamgar-Parsi, F. Pipitone, W. Spears, A. Sciambi, and D. Srull. The NRL Micro Tactical Expendable (MITE) air vehicle. *The Aeronautical Journal, 106(1062)*:431–441, 2002.
3. R. Kurshan. *Computer-Aided Verification of Coordinating Processes*. Princeton University Press, 1994.
4. R. Landau and M. Paez. *Computational Physics*. Wiley & Sons, 1997.
5. P. Langley. *Data-driven discovery of physical laws*. *Cognitive Science 5*: 31–54, 1981.
6. K. Lerman. Design and mathematical analysis of agent-based systems. In Rash, Rouff, Truszkowski, Gordon, and Hinchey, editors. *Lecture Notes in AI, volume 1871*: 222–234. Springer-Verlag, 2001.
7. K. Lerman and A. Galstyan. A general methodology for mathematical analysis of multi-agent systems. Tech. Report ISI-TR-529, USC Information Sciences, 2001.
8. C. Numaoka. Phase transitions in instigated collective decision making. *Adaptive Behavior, 3(2)*:185–222, 1995.
9. W. Spears and D. Gordon. Using artificial physics to control agents. In *IEEE International Conference on Information, Intelligence, and Systems*: 281–288, 1999.
10. W. Spears and D. Gordon-Spears and R. Heil. Distributed, physics-based control of swarms of vehicles. In review.

You Seem Friendly, But Can I Trust You?

Tim Menzies, David Owen, and Bojan Cukic

Lane Department of Computer Science
West Virginia University
PO Box 6109 Morgantown, WV 26506-6109, USA
tim@menzies.com, {dowen|cukic}@csee.wvu.edu

Abstract. A "stranger agent" is an agent you did not build but may need to work with. Such strangers may come with a certificate saying "I have been tested, trust me". In the special case of nondeterministic agents built via FSMs, the level to which we can trust this certificate can be determined via a simple summary of topological features of the agent.

1 Introduction

> *A stranger is someone that you don't know.*
> *Most strangers will not try to harm you,*
> *but some strangers are dangerous,*
> *even if they dress nice or look friendly.*
> *Never take rides, candy, gifts, or money from strangers.*
> *It's okay to say "NO THANK YOU."*
> – *"Stranger Danger"*
> *http://www.ci.mesa.az.us/*
> *police/stranger.htm*

Two major trends in software engineering is the increased used of COTS (commercial-off-the-shelf) products and decentralized processing. In the near future, applications that work via the coordinated effort of many components, most of which we don't build ourselves but buy (or hire) from others. Can we trust such *stranger agents* to deliver the functionality we require?

To make this analysis interesting, we make five assumptions:

Nondeterminacy: The stranger agents may be nondeterministic. For example, agents conduct searches of complicated spaces may use heuristics to direct their processing. These heuristics may use random choice to (e.g.) break ties within the reasoning.

Safety: Somewhere within our collection of collaborating agents is a safety critical agent we are very concerned about. This assumption motivates us to make as detailed an analysis as possible of stranger agents.

Certified: Each new agent in our community arrives with a certificate saying "I have been thoroughly tested" (imagine the firm handshake of the smiling used-car sales-man). If we believe that certificate, then we might test other agents in our community before testing this agent.

M.G. Hinchey et al. (Eds.): 'FAABS 2002, LNAI 2699, pp. 208–219, 2003.

Benevolence: The agents we are assessing are not deliberately malicious agents. Our goal in assessing stranger agents is to check that the benevolent author of some other agent did not inadvertently miss something during their testing.

Need lightweight assessment: If the agents are COTS products, we must assume that they are true strangers; i.e. we can't examine them in great detail since such an examination may violate corporate confidentiality. Hence, any assessment we make of agent must be a *lightweight* assessment that does not require or reveal specifics of the internal of an agent.

How suspicious should we be of nondeterministic certified benevolent agents which we can't examine in detail and which are participating in an community of agents containing a safety critical agent? Can we assess our level of doubt? Is possible to assess how hard or easy it is to test a nondeterministic agent and, therefore, how much or little we should believe in those certificates? And can all the above be done in a *lightweight* manner so as to not intrude on the privacy of our agents?

While in the general case this assessment is difficult, for one definition of "testability" and for nondeterministic agents constructed from communicating finite state machines FSMs, we show here that that the assessment is simple. Further, since the assessment just relies on high-level summaries of FSM topology, it is *lightweight* in the above sense of the term.

The interesting point of this analysis is that, according to classical software reliability theory, it is impossible. For example Nancy Leveson says that "nondeterminism is the enemy of reliability" [5]. We must disagree. Like it or not, future software systems will be based on collaborations of distributed units, each with their own style of reasoning which may include nondeterministic inference. We demonstrate in this paper that we need not necessarily fear this future since nondeterministic agents can be tested and the probability that those tests will reveal errors can be determined from the topology of the agents.

The rest of this paper is structured as follows. After defining FSMs, we describe LURCH1, our *nondeterministic simulator*. This is followed by a definition of *testability* used for our study. We next describe a *model mutator* that can generate many FSMs and the TAR2 *treatment learner* that found the topological features of the FSMs that makes them more or less testable.

2   FSMs

Our analysis assumes agents are implemented or can be modelled as FSMs. We therefore start by defining an FSM.

An FSM has the following features:

- Each FSM $M \in S$ is a 3-tuple (Q, Σ, δ).
- Q is a finite set of states.
- Σ is a finite set of input/output symbols.
- $\delta : Q \times B \longrightarrow Q \times B$, where B is a set of zero or more symbols from Σ, is the transition function.

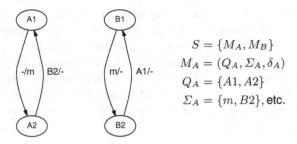

$$S = \{M_A, M_B\}$$
$$M_A = (Q_A, \Sigma_A, \delta_A)$$
$$Q_A = \{A1, A2\}$$
$$\Sigma_A = \{m, B2\}, \text{etc.}$$

Fig. 1. A system of communicating FSMs ("m" is a message passed between the machines).

Figure 1 shows a very simple communicating FSM model. States are indicated by labelled ovals, and edges represent transitions that are triggered by input and that result in output. Edges are labelled: *input / output*. An important distinction in Figure 1 is ebtween *consumables* and *non-consumables*. A transition triggered by a message *consumes* the message, so that it is no longer able to trigger another. But states are unaffected by transitions they trigger; they are good for an arbitrary number of transitions.

FSMs can be characterized via the following parameters:

1. The number of individual finite-state machines in the system. Figure 1 has two.
2. The number of states per finite-state machine. Figure 1 has two states per mission (true and false).
3. The number of transitions per machine. Figure 1 has two transitions per machine.
4. The number of inputs per transition that are states in other machines. Figure 1 has two such inputs: $(A2, B2)$.
5. The number of unique *consumable* messages that can be passed between machines. Figure 1 has one such message: m.
6. The number of inputs per transition that are consumable messages. Figure 1 uses m as input in one transition.
7. The number of outputs per transition that are consumable messages. In Figure 1, m appears as an output in one transition.

3   Nondeterminism

To model nondeterminism in this approach, we will assume that the LURCH1 inference engine is being used to process the FSMs. To use LURCH1, models in different representations are partially evaluated into variant of a directed and-or graph. Conceptually, this graph is copied for N time ticks and the outputs generated at time $i - 1$ become inputs for time i. At runtime, LURCH1 maintains a *frontier* for the search. When a node is popped off the frontier, it is discarded if it contradicts an assertion made at the same time. Otherwise, the node is added to the list of assertions.

LURCH1's nondeterministic nature arises from how the search proceeds after a new assertion is made. If all the pre-conditions of the descendants of the new assertions have been asserted then these descendants are added to the frontier *at a random position*. As a result, what is asserted at each run of LURCH1 can differ. For example, if the node for x and $\neg x$ are both reachable from inputs, they will be added to the frontier in some random order. If x gets popped first, then the node x will be asserted and the node $\neg x$ will be blocked. But if the node $\neg x$ gets popped first, then the node $\neg x$ will be believed and the node x will be blocked.

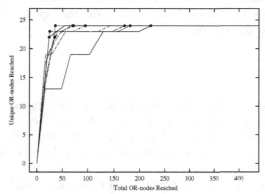

Random search results for model of Dekker's solution to the two-process mutual exclusion problem (the model comes from Holzmann [4]). Dots show when an error added to the model is found by the search. The error is found in every case.

Fig. 2. Random search of AND-OR graphs representing FSM models is effective in finding errors.

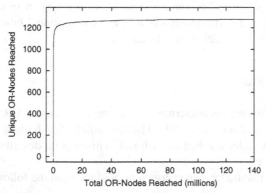

Random search results for a very large randomly generated FSM model, for which the set of FSMs being studied would require at most 2.65×10^{178} states.

Fig. 3. Random search of AND-OR graphs is scalable to very large models.

The random search of LURCH1 is theoretically incomplete but, in practice, it is surprisingly effective. For example, Figure 2 (from Menzies et.al. [8]) shows ten trials with a LURCH1 search over a model of Dekker's solution to the two-process mutual exclusion problem (the original model comes from Holzmann [4]). The dots represent an error added to the model and found quickly by random search in all ten trials. LURCH1 is very simple, yet can handle searches much larger than many model checkers. For example, Figure 3 shows random search results for a very large FSM model. The composite FSM representing all interleavings of the individual machines in the Figure 3 model would require at most 2.65×10^{178} states. This is well beyond the capability of model checking technology (10^{120} states according to [3]).

4   Testability

The claim of this paper is that it is possible to identify agent properties that predict for "testability". This section describes our definition of "testability".

Note the *plateau* shape of Figure 2 and Figure 3. If some method can increase the height of that plateau, then that method would have increased the chances the odds of finding a defect.

This definition of increased "testability" is a reasonable model-based extension of standard testability definitions. According to the IEEE Glossary of Software Engineering Terminology [1], testability is defined as "the degree to which a system of components facilitates the establishment of test criteria and the performance of tests to determine whether those criteria have been met". Voas and Miller [9], and later Bertolino and Stringini [2] clarify this definitions, arguing that testability is "the probability that the program will fail under test if it contains at least one fault". If LURCH1 quickly reveals many unique reachable nodes in the model quickly and if some of these nodes contain faulty logic, then those faults must be exposed.

Note that when the search reaches a plateau, there are no guarantees provided about failure free field operation. But, unvisited nodes in the system model are difficult to reach in the operational environment too, hence the operational failure probability due to testable design of the model does not increase.

5   Model Mutator

In the study shown below, a nondeterministic inference process (LURCH1) was run over 15,000 FSMs generated semi-randomly. The testability of each run was assessed via the percentage of FSM nodes reached in each run. This section describes how the 15,000 FSMs were generated.

Each FSM had parameter values drawn at random from the following ranges:

1. 2–20 individual FSMs.
2. 4–486 states (states within all within machines).
3. 0–272 transitions per machine.
4. 0–737 transition inputs that are states in other machines.
5. 0–20 unique consumable messages.

6. 0–647 transition inputs that are consumable messages.
7. 0–719 transition outputs that are consumable messages.

These parameters where selected to ensure that FSMs from real-world specifications fell within the above ranges (for details of those real-world models, see [8]).

The FSM generation process not truly random. Several *sanity checks* were imposed to block the generation of bizarre FSMs:

- The *current state* and *next state* must come from the machine in which the transition is defined and must not match.
- Inputs that are states must come from *other* machines, and none may be mutually exclusive (the transition could never occur if it required mutually exclusive inputs).
- The set of inputs that are messages from other machines contains no duplicates.
- The set of outputs that are messages to other machines contains no duplicates.

6 Data Mining

Having generated 15,000 outputs, some data mining technology is required to extract the essential features of all those runs. The data miner used in this paper was the TAR2 *treatment learner* [6]. This is a non-standard data miner, so we take care to fully introduce it here.

The premise of treatment learning, and the reason why we use it, is that the learnt theory must be *minimal*. TAR2 was an experiment in generating the essential minimal differences between classes. To understand the algorithm, consider the log of golf playing behavior seen in Figure 4. In that log, we only play *lots* of golf in $\frac{6}{5+3+6} = 43\%$ of cases. To improve our game, we might search for conditions that increases our golfing frequency. Two such conditions are shown in the WHERE test of the select statements in Figure 4. In the case of outlook=overcast, we play *lots* of golf all the time. In the case of humidity $\leq$ 90, we only play *lots* of golf in 20% of cases. So one way to play lots of golf would be to select a vacation location where it was always overcast. While on holidays, one thing to watch for is the humidity: if it rises over 90%, then our frequent golf games are threatened.

The tests in the WHERE clause of the select statements in Figure 4 is a *treatment*. Classes in treatment learning get a score and the learner uses this to assess the class frequencies resulting from *applying a treatment* (i.e. using them in a WHERE clause). In normal mode, TAR2 does *controller learning* that finds a treatment which selects for better classes and reject worse classes By reversing the scoring function, treatment learning can also select for the worse classes and reject the better classes. This mode is called *monitor learning* since it finds the thing we should most watch for. In the golf example, *outlook = 'overcast'* was the controller and $humidity \geq 90$ was the monitor.

TAR2 automatically explores a very large space of possible treatments. TAR2's configuration file lets an analyst specify a search for the best treatment using conjunctions of size 1,2,3,4, etc. Since TAR2's search is elaborate, an analyst can automatically find the *best* and *worst* possible situation within a data set. For example, in the golf example, TAR2 explored all the attribute ranges of Figure 4 to learn that the *best* situation was *outlook = 'overcast'* and worst possible situation was $humidity \geq 90$.

TAR2 also comes with a *N-way cross validation* tool that checks the validity of a select statement. In this process, a training set is divided into N buckets. For each bucket in turn, a treatment is learned on the other $N - 1$ buckets then tested on the bucket put aside. A treatment is preferred if it is *stable*; i.e. works in the majority of all N turns.

Theoretically, TAR2 is intractable since there are an exponential number of possible attribute ranges to explore. TAR2 culls the space of possible attribute ranges using a heuristic *confidence1* measure that selects attribute ranges that are more frequent in good classes than in poorer classes (for full details, see [7]). The use of *confidence1* has been quite successful: TAR2's theoretically intractable nature has yet to be of practical concern.

outlook	temp(°F)	humidity	windy?	class
sunny	*85*	*86*	*false*	*none*
sunny	*80*	*90*	*true*	*none*
sunny	*72*	*95*	*false*	*none*
rain	*65*	*70*	*true*	*none*
rain	*71*	*96*	*true*	*none*
rain	*70*	*96*	*false*	*some*
rain	*68*	*80*	*false*	*some*
rain	*75*	*80*	*false*	*some*
sunny	*69*	*70*	*false*	*lots*
sunny	*75*	*70*	*true*	*lots*
overcast	*83*	*88*	*false*	*lots*
overcast	*64*	*65*	*true*	*lots*
overcast	*72*	*90*	*true*	*lots*
overcast	*81*	*75*	*false*	*lots*

input:

```
SELECT class          SELECT class          SELECT class
FROM golf             FROM golf             FROM golf
                      WHERE                 WHERE
                      outlook = 'overcast'  humidity >= 90
```

output:

```
none none none        lots lots lots       none none none
none none some        lots                  some lots
some some lots
lots lots lots
lots lots
```

distributions:

legend: □ none ▦ some ■ lots

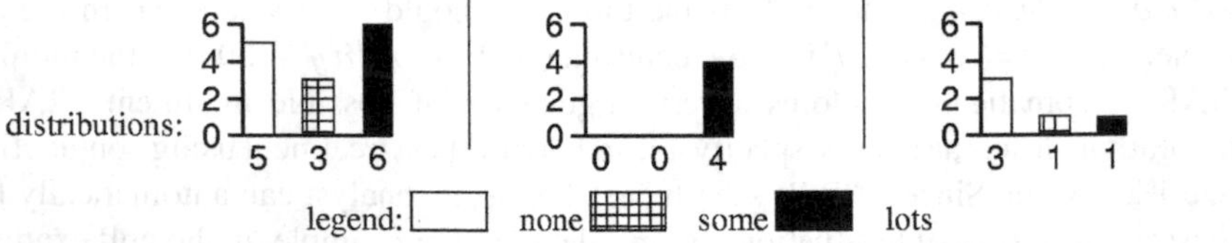

Fig. 4. Class distributions selected by different conditions.

7   Experiments

We now have all the pieces required for our study. The model mutator can generate many FSMs, LURCH1 can nondeterministically execute them, and TAR2 can find the FSM features that change testability (plateau height).

Figure 5 shows a summary of LURCH1 executing over 15,000 semi-randomly generated models. The top histogram summarizes *time-to-plateau* results, e.g., *time-to-plateau* for approximately 375 models was 0 ($< 1\times$ graph size). The average value was about $208\times$ graph size. The right side of the plot shows that, for a few models, nearly 2,500 $\times$ the size of the graph was processed before a plateau was reached. This may seem like a lot, but compared to the exponential size of the composite FSM exhaustively searched by a model checker, a factor of 2,500 is insignificant. The bottom part of Figure 5 is a histogram summarizing search *plateau height* for our 15,000 semi-randomly generated

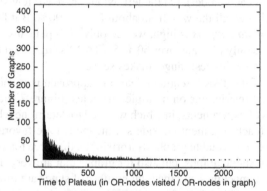

Average time-to-plateau = 208.0 × NAYO size (NAYO size is polynomial in the size of FSM model input).

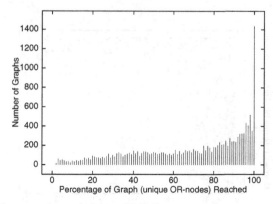

Average plateau height = 69.39%.

Fig. 5. Summary of time-to-plateau (top) and plateau height (bottom) results for 15,000 models.

models. The average value was about 70%, with a significant number of models showing much lower plateaus.

The top part of Figure 5 indicates that plateaus were reached quickly for nearly all models, whether high or low plateaus. So the key distinction, in terms of testability, is plateau height. We would like to how FSM models yielding high search plateaus are different from FSM models yielding low search plateaus. Specifically, what ranges of the attributes listed above (number of machines, number of states, etc.) characterize the models with high plateaus represented by the right side of the bottom histogram in Figure 5?

In our first simple experiment we used TAR2 to determine what single attribute, and what range of that attribute, could most significantly constrain our models to high plateaus (just like the very simple TAR2 golf example in the previous section, where we found that restricting *outlook* to *overcast* led to *lots* of golf). TAR2 suggested the following treatment: restrict *state inputs* to its highest range (590–737). To understand what that means, consider Figure 6, which shows the number of *state inputs* vs. plateau height (with a dot for each model). On the left, where there are few *state inputs*, we see plateau height distributed all the way from about 5% to 100%. But further to the right, where the number of *state inputs* is high, we see only high plateaus—once *state inputs* exceeds 1,000 we see only plateaus over 60%. So TAR2's suggested treatment, that we restrict *state inputs* to the highest range, makes sense.

The real power of the TAR2 treatment learning approach is in more complex treatments, which suggest restrictions on multiple attributes. Figure 7 shows a summary of results from a series of experiments, in which we tried to determine which combinations of attribute ranges (each treatment considers 4 attributes) are favorable for testability and which give us very untestable graphs. Surprisingly, the three top parameters are low for not only highly testable graphs, but also for graphs that are very difficult to test (the number of finite-state machines and the total number of states are more significant than the total number of transitions). So if we restrict our sample to simpler models (fewer machines, fewer states, fewer transitions) the testability results are polarized.

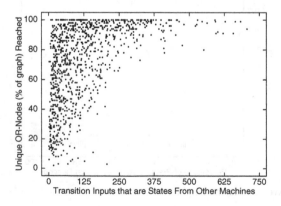

Fig. 6. The number of transition inputs that are states from other machines vs. plateau height.

The bottom half of Figure 7 shows which attributes have the greatest affect on testability, given that the top three are held low. The most significant attribute is *state inputs,* followed by *message inputs* and *message outputs.* To verify the result from TAR2, we need to make sure that the treatments learned apply generally, not just to the data from the original experiment. Figure 8 shows a comparison of plateau height (our indicator of testability) for the original data (left) and a new 10,000 input models (right) generated using TAR2's recommendation of what treatment most improves plateau height; i.e.

1. 2–5 FSMs.
2. 4–49 states.
3. 0–43 transitions.
4. 0–247 transition inputs that are states from other machines.
5. 0–10 unique consumable messages.
6. 0–229 transition inputs that are consumable messages.
7. 0–241 transition outputs that are consumable messages.

←— Better Treatments

Machines	lowest (2–4)	lowest	lowest
States	lowest (4–49)	lowest	lowest
Transitions	low (0–109)	low	low
State Inputs	high (443–737)		
Messages Message Inputs	(not significant) high (389–647)		
Message Outputs			high (432–719)

Worse Treatments —→

Machines	lowest (2–4)	lowest	lowest
States	lowest (4–49)	lowest	lowest
Transitions	lowest (0–54)	lowest	lowest
State Inputs			lowest (0–147)
Messages Message Inputs	(not significant) lowest (0–129)		
Message Outputs	lowest (0–143)		

Fig. 7. Best and worst treatments learned by TAR2.

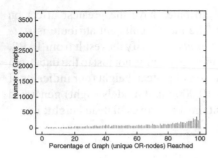 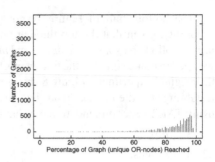

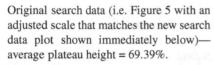

Original search data (i.e. Figure 5 with an adjusted scale that matches the new search data plot shown immediately below)— average plateau height = 69.39%.

Search data for input models generated according to TAR2's suggestions—average plateau height = 91.34%.

Fig. 8. Comparison of plateau height for original search data (top) and new data based on TAR2's suggested treatments.

Figure 8 shows that we can meet the goal specified in the introduction. It is possible to learn parameters of an FSM that significantly improve FSM testability. In this case the improvement was a change in the average plateau height from 69% to 91%.

8   Discussion

In the case of FSMs via a nondeterministic algorithm and assessed via plateau height, we have applied our analysis method to automatically learn the features that most effect FSM testability via model mutators and TAR2.

We believe that this method would generalize to other representations and other definitions of testability. The only essential requirement for such a study is the availability of an automatic oracle of success. With such an oracle available, then mutation plus treatment learning can find model features that select for successful runs.

Another possibility that arises from this work is that we can identify design parameters that make our nondeterministic FSM-based agents *more* or *less* testable. For example, given two implementations of the same requirement, we could favor the implementation that results in a more testable system. That is, we can *design for testability*, even for nondeterministic agents.

References

1. IEEE glossary of software engineering terminology, ANSI/IEEE standard 610.12, 1990.
2. L. S. A. Bertolino. On the use of tesability measures for dependability assessment. *IEEE Transactions on Software Engineering*, 22(2):97–108, 1996.
3. E. Clarke, Orna Grumberg, and Doron A. Peled. *Model Checking*. MIT Press, Cambridge, MA, 1999.

4. Gerard J. Holzmann. Basic SPIN Manual. Available at
   http://cm.bell-labs.com/cm/cs/what/spin/Man/Manual.htm.
5. N. Leveson. *Safeware System Safety And Computers*. Addison-Wesley, 1995.
6. T. Menzies and Y. Hu. Constraining discussions in requirements engineering. In *First International Workshop on Model-based Requirements Engineering*, 2001. Available from
   http://menzies.us/pdf/01lesstalk.pdf.
7. T. Menzies and Y. Hu. Agents in a wild world. In C. Rouff, editor, *Formal Approaches to Agent-Based Systems, book chapter*, 2002. Available from
   http://menzies.us/pdf/01agents.pdf.
8. T. Menzies, D. Owen, and B. Cukic. Saturation effects in testing of formal models. In *ISSRE 2002*, 2002. Available from
   http://menzies.us/pdf/02sat.pdf.
9. J. Voas and K. Miller. Software testability: The new verification. *IEEE Software*, pages 17–28, May 1995. Available from
   http://www.cigital.com/papers/download/ieeesoftware95.ps.

Taking Intelligent Agents to the Battlefield

Jeffrey Hicks, Richard Flanagan, Plamen Petrov, and Alexander Stoyen

21ˢᵗ Century Systems, Inc. 12152 Windsor Hall Way
Herndon VA 20170-2359 USA
{jeff, rich, plamen, alex}@21csi.com
http://www.21csi.com

Abstract. The battlefield is a place of violence ruled by uncertainty. Timely knowledge of what's happening around a soldier can mean the difference between life and death. The goals of an enhanced mobile infantry are becoming a reality through innovative progress by the U.S. Army's 21st Century Land Warrior (LW) program. However, the current system does not provide a "head up" display capability like that provided by today's avionics. When the soldier employs the weapon, he should see objects easily distinguishable as friendly or not, as well as enemy locations. The Eyekon project is an intelligent agent-based decision support system hosted on the soldier's wearable computer. Eyekon will use the LW network to provide a perspective view in the weapon sight. This will naturally draw the warrior to the most desirable target. There are many performance and human factors issues to address before the concept can be used in lethal situations.

1   Introduction

In October 1993, the U.S. Army got a wake up call when a small raid developed into a major fire fight that claimed the lives of 18 U.S. Army Rangers and Delta Force soldiers and another 77 wounded. The battlefield, whether in a town or in open terrain is a place of extreme violence, chaos and ruled by uncertainty ("the fog of war") [1]. In the pursuit of the Al-Qa'ida, will there be another Mogadishu? The U.S. Army's 21st Century Land Warrior program is outfitting the future soldier with advanced weapon sights and wearable components with computational capabilities and linking the soldiers through voice and data communication networks. However, the current Land Warrior system does not provide a "heads up" display (HUD) like the capability that avionics provides to fighter pilots. Fighter pilots can see targets out the cockpit window while reading vital targeting data from the avionics display.

   In comparison, the weapon sight picture that the Land Warrior sees provides the image of the scene and a wealth of information about the weapon but does not provide battlefield situational information in the weapons sight picture at the same time. What is needed is a capability that, when the Soldier shoulders his weapon and looks through his aiming sights, he sees objects easily distinguishable as friendly or not, as

M.G. Hinchey et al. (Eds.): FAABS 2002, LNAI 2699, pp. 220–232, 2003.
© Springer-Verlag Berlin Heidelberg 2003

well as enemy locations along his current heading on a basic map schematic. In other words, what's missing is intuitive situational awareness for the Soldier *immersed* in the situation *while* it is happening.   The goals of an enhanced mobile infantry as expressed in Heinlein's timeless *Starship Troopers* is becoming a reality today through the innovative progress being made by the U.S. Army's Land Warrior Program.

> *If you load a mud foot down with a lot of gadgets that he has to watch, somebody a lot more simply equipped--say with a stone ax---will sneak up and bash his head in while he is trying to read a vernier."*
>
> ---Robert Heinlein, <u>Starship Troopers</u>

In order to provide the dismounted U.S. Army infantry soldier with 21st Century battlefield dominance, weapon systems must be optimized not only minimize the total weight carried by the Soldier *but also minimize the cognitive overload.* Too much data in the display data and the soldier rapidly is overwhelmed with "data," not vital situational information. If a fighter pilot's HUD displays too much information, the battle is lost before it starts. The same applies to the dismounted infantry soldier; too much information in the sight and the soldier becomes battle causality due to missed dangerous threat. These weapon systems are required to meet the tactical battlefield environmental characteristics including delivery by parachute while worn by the Soldier. They must be self-contained, man-packed and battery-powered since maximum efficiency without outside help is a must. Required systems must not rely on any fixed infrastructure to meet the operational performance requirements.

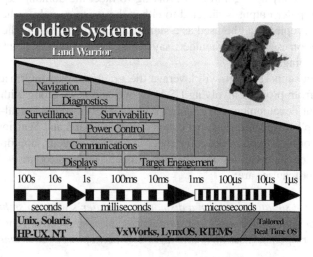

Fig. 1. Requirements for Soldier Systems

As shown in Figure 1, Soldier Systems have explicit real-time processing requirements in the Joint Technical Architecture-Army [2]. Of particular note, target engagement is the most stringent. There are many competing requirements for the Soldier systems. The "ideal" system would be weightless, run on no power, and provide instantaneous accurate solutions without requiring any training. In addition, real-time performance not only requires timely solutions that responds to battlespace stimuli but also indicates that processing operations must be executed in a repeatable, predictable, and deterministic timeframe.

2 Augmented Reality

Augmented reality (AR) technology provides the user with superimposed information that can be seen in the real world; we supplement it. Ideally, it would seem to the user that the real and virtual objects coexisted. Alignment of the superimposed information is critical. Just a few pixels off and the "augmentation" becomes a nuisance. Add latency and confusion results for the user. What is AR good for? Basically, applications of this technology use the virtual objects to aid the user's understanding of his environment. AR improves the perception of the natural world by adding to our senses via computer-generated information visual graphics, sounds, smells or tactical sensations. Televised football games use SporTVision's first-down line superimposed over the game scene to increase the viewing audience awareness.

Eyekon involves the design of a user interface and is a subset of AR of visual enhancements applied to the Land Warrior concept. Our concept is aimed not at the current configuration (LW System 1.0) but next version since it would be too costly to add a requirement into the current design and there are limitations in the weapon sight capability. Our study configuration is evolving to meet the domain requirements Figure 1. The computer output is directed to either the weapon sight or helmet mounted eyepiece. The eyepiece can be used as a situation map display or as the weapon sight when the weapon is held off shoulder; say when the weapon is pointed around the corner of a building.

The decision support design will leverage the graphical user interface development methodology from projects involving USA, USAF and USN along with our real-time Assistive Agent development environment (AEDGE™) to provide real-time software for a "heads-up" weapon aiming application. With proper Land Warrior visualization and host environment requirements for specific Soldier's needs, appropriate planning for software development for the Eyekon concept and prototype will commence. Eyekon concept features are:

*Superimpose situation icons on a dismounted Soldier's weapon sight
*Improve situation awareness by rating threats in a perspective view
*Maximize responsiveness and minimize weight and power requirements

The technical objective to investigate the applicability of software components that overlay smart icons, named Eyekon, to the dismounted soldier's individual weapon sight. Eyekon provides objects for the graphical user interface of friendly and enemy positions in the weapon sight when the dismounted Soldier employs the weapon. Eyekon is an intelligent agent-based decision support system hosted on a wearable computer with an available database and updates via radio links. The output of Eyekon is fed directly to the soldier's display. Display examples are a hands-free device (HFD), weapon-aiming devices that could be installed on the existing M16 rifle, the M4 carbine, the future Objective Individual Combat Weapon (OICW), or helmet-mounted display (HMD). Eyekon would support not only weapon aiming but also would display combat identification of friendly soldier's response to interrogation devices, help direct fires by highlighting target areas, or augment the direct view using a see-through HMD. The developed software components must conform to the Joint Technical Architecture-Army. This is a vital requirement for enhancing concepts such as interoperability, cost avoidance, and force multiplier due to fielded asset commonality.

The Eyekon concept is comprised of a baseline set of display symbols and an optional set of functions that enhance the display. The use of the options depends the reported usefulness through customer feedback. The proposed implementation minimizes cognitive workload and requires minimal training.

The baseline implementation of Eyekon functions using LW wearable computer host and using Land Warrior database, network queries, and computing host provide perspective-view icons overlaid on weapon sight display. We will use size and brightness for perspective. The decision aid provides the individual soldier a more in-depth situational awareness with decision graphics (e.g., rated targets by most dangerous, steering arrow, ROE issues, team status). Steering arrow points to next priority target, if outside of view, then arrow points in direction of acute angle and the arrow length is proportional to angle magnitude. Rules of Engagement (ROE) can help soldier in situations where escalation responses are changing. Team status provides what the team's real-time situation (e.g., rounds remaining, water, casualties). An extended version is to provide support at the team level. Given LW computing performance capabilities, processing speed, memory capacity, and network bandwidth, Eyekon would support a new type of team interaction: self-organizing behavior. See for example, the article from US Army War College [3]. The Team with LW capability and Eyekon Option 2 divides recon and target areas as a self-organizing team. It is very robust because the enemy cannot "take out" the leader. The Team is very adaptable and responsive to changing battlefield conditions. It swarms the battlefield and instantly responds to the unfolding event, in part due to the capability of Eyekon *In-the-situation* awareness.

3 Technical Approach

The technical approach is to investigate and analyze dismounted land warrior interface requirements that increase situation awareness from present practice. It will determine a set of Land Warrior system visualization requirements and metrics, to perform a functional analysis and develop a software plan, to adapt 21st Century System's AEDGE™ software and to host it on a soldier's wearable system. The "heads-up" situation awareness is first defined as when the soldier shoulders the weapon and looks though the weapon aiming sight; a HFD. Alternate "heads-up" are: (1) being able to use the weapon sight off the weapon, such as to look around a building corner without being exposed, (2) a helmet-mounted display (HMD) consisting an eye-piece that fits over one eye (not see-through), and (3) a HMD with see-through eyepiece. User interface requirements and related resource requirements investigation areas that will be addressed, for day, twilight or night operations are: (1) Heading of the using Soldier, (2) Position of all friendly units and Soldiers, (3) Enemy threat locations, if available by Army digital Tactical Internet, (4) Weapons orientation of friendly Soldiers, (5) Identification of individual Soldier and aggregate units and (6) Ready status of individual Soldiers in terms of ammunition, water and health.

Data requirements via situational reports fed continuously by the Soldiers will also be investigated. The automated reports and Eyekon data provide the situational awareness of the team to a Soldier without having the entire unit stop and take a formal report and expose themselves to enemy counter-attack by losing momentum. In addition, for military operations in urban terrain (MOUT) or possibly close-quarters battle (CQB) where non-combatants are in the are of operations ("no-shoot" targets mixed with known threats), the study will investigate display requirements to depict friendly locations even if behind a wall in building or in a cave by superimposing an Eyekon over their relative positions through the weapons sight.

Another requirement is that Eyekon must perform in the host environment, that is, be rugged to handle the warrior mission. Host system processing, networking and data storage characteristics are continuing to advance. Wearable system technology advances continue in many application areas such as for the military's Land Warrior Program and USSOCOM projects. Industries always want worker's productivity to increase. Wearable computers, combined with wireless technology, allow art dealers to examine artifacts on location and instantly compare with electronic library high-resolution photographs. Another area is working in tight quarters, such as in commercial aerospace application where a flight-line technician has direct access to all technical orders while working in the cramped areas (e.g., electronics bay of the aircraft. The point-of-departure Eyekon concept is shown in Figure 2. As concept matures, the baseline is expected to change. The point-of-departure provides a reference for which to compare candidate concepts. Data is provided to Eyekon via the LW's database. Eyekon provides an overlay of friendly and enemy icons positioned on the weapon sight video. Position accuracy is dependent on database data accuracy. Agents maintain Eyekon updates as weapon sight is moved through angles. It is comprised of a baseline set and an optional set of functions. The use of the options depends the reported usefulness through customer feedback.

A point-of departure for the Eyekon baseline is to develop symbols using data from the LW database. Determine the soldier kinematics such as present position, heading and rate of change, weapon pointing (compass, tilt and rate of change) and possibly head pointing then determine kill box for the weapon's range and kinematic state. Agents will query database and Internet for target position reports of friendly, enemy & neutral in or near the kill box and develop standard object display icons for position reports and track. An intelligent agent will adjust the standard icons for perspective view objects (smart icons). The perspective view is based on identity and distance.

The icon's display attributes such as color, brightness and size will also be adjusted for time of day to account for vision changes due to daylight, twilight or darkness. It will also adjust weapon sight display based on sight magnification, heading, tilt and angular rates. It will register for weapon sight and movement, and then display icons.

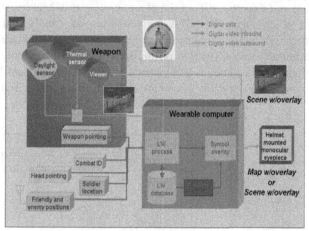

Fig. 2. Eyekon Concept

LW provides guidance for assessment (via criteria weighting) or the override of the assessment function. The assessment determines most dangerous threats based upon threat vulnerability. The vulnerability calculation determines LOS distance and the threat's weapon type using probability of hit and probability of kill values from the LW database. It adjusts the perspective view of the icons based on assessed threat values, ROE and current level of escalation. It will provide a steering arrow that will point to the next priority target(s). That is, if next target is inside the current field of view (FOV), then arrow points to maximum threat icon. However, if next target is outside of current FOV, then arrow points in shortest direction (left or right) and the arrow length is proportional to angular magnitude. A control deadband would remove pointing ambiguity if the enemy were directly behind. Eyekon decision aids will take advantage of the fact that the team is networked via LW Network and Tactical Network. The networked team is technically capable of being a team that is self-organizing and non-hierarchical. An example in the literature is New York City. The populace is feed every day. Yet, no one is in charge of feeding the inhabitants. No one organization is responsible for ordering, scheduling, delivering or expediting food. It works through self-organizing commerce. This is not the current way that the U.S. Army, or any army or any national military organization works today. As the thrust for information access is pushed down to lower and lower echelon levels, ultimately every soldier will be able to access any information available at any time. This widespread access has the potential for new, unheard-of organization schemes to emerge. See for example *The Real Military Revolution* [3]. The Team with this capability and Eyekon Option 2 divide up recon and target areas as a self-organizing team. It is very robust because the enemy cannot "take out" the leader. The Team is very adaptable and re-sponsive to changing battlefield conditions. It swarms the battlefield.

The concept for a set of point-of departure (POD) symbols will be reviewed with subject matter experts and trades against the POD set will be made. A follow-on study, using subject matter experts, will consist of a cognitive task analysis (CTA) performed by a cognitive psychologist. The CTA study will consider individual and team inter-actions. Metrics will be used to quantify symbol layout, selections and symbol attrib-utes. Though initial work is focused on the individual and the individuals interface, team interactions will become more important as use of the Tactical Internet and LW Network increases. The friendly situation is shown in the lower right portion of the weapon sight.

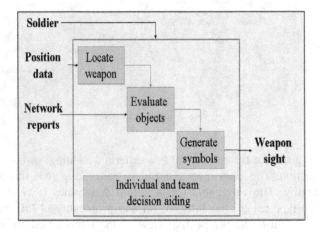

Fig. 3. Eyekon Functionality

For the baseline, a requirements analysis will develop the top-level functions for the Eyekon concept and be presented as a functional flow diagram. The functions are shown in Figure 3.

It defines four functions. The first function is "Locate weapon" and sets the stage for the display of the area sector – just where is the soldier in the area and where is the weapon (sight) pointing and how is it changing. As depicted at the top in the figure the LW, interacting with Eyekon functions, may change criteria weightings if the database information accuracy changes or if the weapon that the sight is attached changes. Implementation depends upon selection of options. With the soldier and weapon posi-tion now known, Eyekon might send out queries on the LW network for situation reports within the weapon range. Periodic report updates and aperiodic queries feed Eyekon object evaluation. LW database objects are identified as friend, foe, neutral or unknown and located within the FOV. The decision aiding then scales according to leader criteria and threat level.

4 Application of AEDGE™

We take a pragmatic approach to intelligent agents, as we apply our experience delivering agent technology to other domains (team decision support, software systems synthesis). Our agents are autonomously running software components, which monitor, analyze, and advise human users. Such agents will add great utility to the platoon. Agents provide choices and evaluate the performance of users "on the fly" to give valuable feedback to the participants. We propose two classes of agents in our tool suite.

4.1 Agent Types

The first class is comprised of *human-assistant* agents. A human assistant agent provides concrete advice to humans who are participating in the session. Such assistant agents could be useful both in the learning process as well as in the content development and evaluation processes. If a trainee is making an incorrect choice at a critical point in the exercise on which the correctness of the rest is dependent, an agent can provide a second chance or additional clues for the concrete situation, thus highly increasing the educational value for the trainee. Human assistant agents both react to human requests and provide advice without being prompted for it, if, they determine that help and guidance is needed. Human assistant agents are one of the contributions of this work.

Coordinators and arbitrators of distributed decisions populate the second class of agents. Even when individual agent and human decisions are based on team-level, global knowledge (which may or may not be the case, depending on the nature of a decision or knowledge available to a human or an agent), it is normal to expect conflicts and also temporal discrepancies. Agents of the third kind try alleviating such conflicts, advising agents and humans (including, agents of the second kind) how to adjust these decisions and re-enter a more stable situation, while still not sacrificing their (conflicting) objectives. Examples of conflicts include multiple users requesting modification of a single simulation object (e.g. a route way point or an infiltration zone) at the same time, or a user attempting to switch the nature or the pace of an exercise while in a team mode with other participants. Agents of the third kind too are a major contribution of this work.

The need for a standardized common infrastructure has lead 21CSI to design an environment where both agents and simulated entities (or representations of real-world assets) are represented as first-class objects capable of interacting with each other. 21CSI's extensible multi-component Decision Support Systems (DSS) architecture, known as AEDGE™, is a standardized Commercial Off the Shelf (COTS), DII COE compliant agent architecture that enables complex DSS to be developed as an expansion of the AEDGE™ core functionality.

The Eyekon-AEDGE™ study interface is shown in Figure 4. The developer is provided a set of overlay controls, the circle "A", and a set of scenario controls, "B". The picture is a video capture of an experimental site. The overlay controls direct either video feed to the screen or brings up a 2D map (simulating the warrior's HMD). In this setup five people are positioned with three to the front of the observer with a video camera and two behind. We are undertaking to build a common reference framework and a test-bed environment for integrated simulation and agent-based decision support. In a simulation that feeds Eyekon the people with initial headings begin walking and the observer rotates the camera. The kernel of the architecture consists of four core and five extender components. These define the internal structures, dataflow, and interface to the architecture.

Fig. 4. Initial Set Up with Video Only

AEDGE™ defines Agents, Entities, Avatars and their interactions with each other and with external sources of information. This standardized architecture allows additional components, such as service-specific DSS tools, to be efficiently built upon the core functionality. Common interfaces and data structures can be exported to interested parties who wish to extend the architecture with new components, agents, servers, or clients. When the core AEDGE™ components developed by 21CSI are bundled with customer-specific components in an integrated environment, a clean separation of those components, through APIs, is provided. Distributed components communicate via Services. Services are an abstract and network-friendly representation of functions, implemented by AEDGE™ components. The Service object is a data storage and transport mechanism for a service request. The request includes the class and the type of the service, an optional sub-type and a list of parameters. Return values for services are provided via ServiceResult objects, which encapsulate a service-success code and the actual return value.

Shown in Figure 5, the developer has selected the video with Eyekon overlay during a simulation run. Note that around the screen is information on weapon position ("C" for weapon elevation, "D" for azimuth or compass and "F" for GPS location. In the screen area are friendly positions are noted by a blue box, threats by a red diamond. Tracks developed by updated position reports are given an identification number such as 1301 for the friendly and 1302 for the threat.

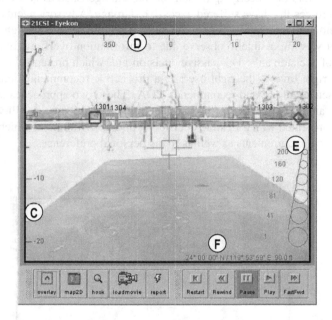

Fig. 5. Video with Eyekon Overlay

4.2 Assisting Situational Awareness

Maintaining situational awareness both in training and in operational environment is the single most important element for achieving the mission objectives as well as for improving the training process. In the present and especially in the future reality of a digital battlefield, the inflow of information from sensors, intelligence reports and damage assessment most certainly will overwhelm the soldier as a decision-maker and will obscure the tactical picture. A high level of situational awareness is maintained by introducing *monitoring and advisory agents*. The purpose of the monitoring agents is to subscribe to specific data-flows, to observe and analyze their trends and to raise flags in case the tactical situation has changed significantly. Information fusion techniques will be applied to correlate data from different sources in order to increase the certainty of the tactical picture. Advisory agents occupy the next level in the information processing hierarchy – they subscribe to the information provided by the monitoring agents and react to situational changes by re-evaluating the threats posed to our forces and the risks associated with the mission.

Figure 6 is a result of the decision aiding process where track 1302 has been selected or "hooked". Hooked refers to target selected from either the map or sight picture and tracked. The "G" points to the target (1302) and has a box around it to denote that special attention is to be given to this object. Object is identified, in lower left corner of the screen, "H", as a human and is a hostile target. Advisory agents then communicate with human user (via specialized user interfaces) to alert him of the changed risks and the underlying reason for that change, such as new enemy detected, or friendly forces that have suffered excessive damage. Advisory agents can focus the user's attention to a particular area of the tactical picture or can highlight a trend in the picture that was impossible to observe due to information overflow. Eyekon provides two types of decision aids: 1) a passive decision aid, which presents the right information at the right time to the right user; 2) a pro-active recommendation agent, which provides tactical advice and recommends COA. These two approaches are often complimentary and thus, their combined application provides greater utility. In addition, the user is presented with a flexible decision support environment, which adapts to the current tactical requirements as well as to his personal preferences.

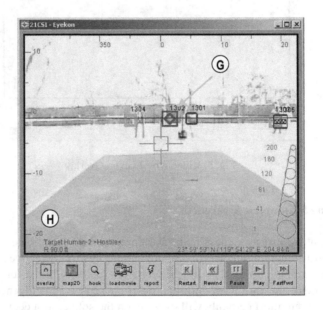

Fig. 6. Target Selected

The passive decision aid is based on the monitoring and advisory agents and their ability to analyze the enormous amounts of incoming information and highlight important changes. The agents do not interact directly with the user, but rather sit in the background and monitor the development of the tactical picture. Once the picture changes, the advisory agents dynamically reconfigure the user display to show these changes and the predictions for future effects. For example the monitoring agents may detect movement of the enemy forces at the left flank. This movement will initially trigger re-evaluation of the threat based on the enemy's new positions and simultane-ously will invoke a heuristic predictor of the enemy's future positions and intentions.

The displayed information (enemy movement route at the left flank and future po-sitions) will depend on the likelihood of this change affecting adversely our current operations. As a result the new threat and projected future threat areas will be shifted toward the left flank. The dynamic reconfiguration based on heuristic threat estimation goes beyond improving the situational awareness of the user. This capability provides the commander with clues as to what his next action should be. In the pro-active deci-sion aid, a class of recommendation agents is used to provide explicit COA recom-mendations. These agents are based on the human-role-playing and the human-assistant agents described earlier. While the role-playing agents are capable of fol-lowing orders and reacting to the changing environment, the human-assistant agents are more analytical and are able to use trend and rule-based cause-effect analyses. Combining these agent capabilities with a dynamic alternative generator and utility function evaluator provides powerful real-time decision support.

Essentially, we view the process of decision-making support as general resource allocation (a system consists of tasks, which require resources (sensors, processors, humans, information, and trucks...) with functional and non-functional properties. The system's goal is to recommend to the human decision maker, or implement automated decisions, to allocate resources, subject to the conflicting objectives and constraints, in the best possible way (there is possibly significant competition for the resources). This allocation process differs in level of detail only, across different stages of combat control process. Failures result from poor allocation choices. Given the general growth of the problem space the process has to consider heuristics and approximate "best effort" strategies (exact allocation is computationally prohibitive) must be used. The study provides a slate of heuristics, which can be called explicitly by the user, or by the system under general instructions given by the user. These will include commonly available and "home-grown": genetic, neural net, projection, greedy, and other meth-ods for designing and developing large-scale, complex software. Three-modi operandi will be supported: search (entire space is considered per iteration), construction (a fixed number of objects are considered per iteration), and hybrid (the heuristic relies on a strategy/user to switch modes; e.g. first, do a quick global search, then optimize-construct a local region...).

5 Conclusion

Eyekon will directly enhance the warrior's lethality by quickly and intuitively locating targets in the weapon sight. It will also reduce the warriors' vulnerability by aiding in the designation of most dangerous threat and identifying teammates. The result is an AR system using intelligent agents to superimpose smart icons (Eyekon) on the real world weapon sight picture. The team decision aid function of Eyekon can provide the team leader and the team with a method of designating and assigning targets to indi-vidual (networked) soldiers in a very flexible robust self-organizing environment.

The work to date is still in feasibility concept design to influence the LW program. The next step is to develop a prototype for evaluation by the LW program or similar systems.

References

1. "The Battle Book", Major John Sutherland, Infantry, R.A., Byrrd Enterprises, Inc. 1999.
2. Joint Technical Architecture-Army, 5.0 (JTA v1.0)
3. T.K Adams, "The Real Military Revolution", *Parameters*, Autumn 2000.
4. Hicks, J. D., Stoyen, A. D., Zhu, Q. "Intelligent Agent-Based Software Architecture for Combat Performance under Overwhelming Information Inflow and Uncertainty," Proc. of the Seventh IEEE International Conf. on Complex Computer Systems, ICECCS'2001, Skovde, Sweden, June 2001.
5. Petrov, P. V., Stoyen, A. D. "An Intelligent-Agent Based Decision Support System for a Complex Command and Control Application," Proceedings of the Sixth IEEE International Conference on Complex Computer Systems, ICECCS'2000, Tokyo, Japan, September 2000.
6. Petrov, P. V. "Applications of Agent Architectures to Decision Support in Distributed Simulation and Training Systems," Dissertation Thesis. New Jersey Institute of Technology, Newark, NJ, May 2000.
7. Petrov, P. V., Stoyen, A. D., Hicks, J. D., Myers, G. "21st Century Systems, Inc.'s Agent Enabled Decision Guide Environment (AEDGE™)," IAT 2001 Maebahsi, Japan, October 2001.

Naval Applications of Secure Multi-agent Technology

Ramesh Bharadwaj

Center for High Assurance Computer Systems
Naval Research Laboratory
Washington DC, 20375
ramesh@itd.nrl.navy.mil

Agents and multi-agent systems (MAS) are increasingly being viewed as *the* enabling technology for successful development and deployment of future Naval Command and Control systems. A recent Department of Defense report to Congress [1] identifies the lack of secure, robust connectivity and interoperability as one of the major impediments to progress in Network Centric Warfare. Among the requirements for the Navy's command and information infrastructure are flexibility, modular system design, fast and easy reconfiguration, and information assurance. Secure agents are becoming an important paradigm in a software engineer's toolchest because it is believed that agents provide the necessary agility, efficiency, and survivability necessary for building a secure and survivable information grid.

Not only is robust connectivity important, but it is also imperative for the Information Network infrastructure to provide commanders with a situational awareness of their assets in the information battle-space and, in addition, to deny adversaries access to this information. For the vision of Network Centric Warfare to become a reality, the DoD, the Navy, and the Marine Corps require a network infrastructure for disseminating mission-critical information in a secure and timely manner. Another important requirement is rapid reconfigurability of the networked battle-space to satisfy the needs of new missions. Also needed at the user level is programmability of the underlying application, such as a distributed mission planning system or a network centric C^2 for combat application, with a rapid turnaround time. Therefore, there is growing awareness within the defense and R&D communities that developing the next generation of sensor-rich, massively distributed, and autonomous systems will require a total paradigm shift in terms of the capabilities, processes, and architectures used to mitigate threats, plug vulnerabilities, and provide countermeasures. It is envisaged that agent technology will provide the necessary infrastructure for achieving the desired degree of trust and survivability in the context of rapidly changing mission needs.

References

1. *Network Centric Warfare*, Department of Defense Report to Congress, July 2001.

M.G. Hinchey et al. (Eds.): 'FAABS 2002, LNAI 2699, p. 235, 2003.

Challenges Arising from Applications

Charles Pecheur

RIACS / NASA Ames

The Application: Health Maintenance for a Next-Gen Space Shuttle

NASA is investigating automated and integrated technologies for monitoring the health of future space shuttles and their ground support equipment. This application field, known as Integrated Vehicle Health Management (IVHM), is being developed in by the aerospace industry under the auspices of NASA's Space Launch Initiative (SLI) program. The proposed IVHM system includes advanced software technologies such as model-based diagnosis using NASA's Livingstone system. This holds the promise of automating the diagnosis across a number of subsystem components and possible scenarios that is not tractable for more conventional diagnosis techniques. On the flip side, however, it also raises multiple technical challenges, both related to the diagnosis techniques themselves and to their verification and validation (V&V) for flight qualification.

We define and discuss three of these challenges here. These challenges do not call for innovative research results so much as for maturation of of existing advanced technologies. Our point is to expose the gap between promising research prototypes and verifiably dependable products that qualify for safety-critical applications such as space vehicles. In other words, we are looking over tech transfer challenges.

Challenge 1: Model-Based IVHM

Conventional health monitoring and diagnosis techniques rely on an explicit description of the mapping from observable effects to the faults that may induce them—this mapping can be hardwired in the logic of a program or, in more elaborate systems, provided as a set of rules. As the system becomes larger and more complex, developing, debugging and maintaining these sets of rules becomes unmanageable.

The challenge consists of using logic reasoning to infer the mapping from a model of the system being observed. This approach, known as model-based diagnosis, is hardly new; indeed, NASA's Livingstone system has even been premiered in space in 1999 as part of the Deep-Space One mission. Nevertheless, more progress is still needed in order to achieve model-based diagnosis systems that:

- can be applied to large, complex systems,
- can deal with continuous, non-linear, noisy signals,
- provide diagnosis within a limited, predictable response time,
- use reasonable amounts of scarce computing resources.

M.G. Hinchey et al. (Eds.): 'FAABS 2002, LNAI 2699, pp. 236–238, 2003.

Challenge 2: Flight-Qualified Agent Systems

The second challenge is to develop advanced agent-based software in such a way that it can be qualified and used for flight. This means not only using rigorous and disciplined development and verification steps to make sure that the software has the desired level of dependability and conformance to its specifications, but also doing so in a convincing and well-documented way, so that the relevant authorities (FAA for civil aviation, NASA for U.S. space missions) will approve and adopt it.

A large part of the challenge lies in infusing the new technologies into existing software engineering processes and practices. In particular, one has to comply with standards, such as ISO/IEEE 12207 or DO-178B, which codify these processes. This can be an awkward fit at places, as those processes and standards are oriented towards traditional imperative-style programming languages such as Fortran, Ada or C. For example, widely used structural code coverage metrics are not adequate for data-centric systems such as model-based reasoning; some form of model coverage would be much more appropriate.

Finally, one cannot over-stress the resistance to adoption of innovation in flight software, for understandable risk reduction concerns. Few space mission managers will want to be the first adopter of a new technology that has never been previously demonstrated in flight. This justifies the need for technology validation programs and missions, whose main purpose is to give a first chance to innovative technologies to show their worthiness and reliability.

Challenge 3: Flight-Qualified Formal Methods

As discussed above, advanced agent-based approaches address a much richer and broader range of possible situations, which makes their verification considerably harder. Advanced verification techniques, based on formal approaches such as model checking, are necessary to achieve the desired level of assurance. The next challenge, then, is to have those techniques themselves, and the results they produce, accepted as part of the V&V process. The issues are similar to those exposed in the second challenge: infusion in legacy software processes, practices and standards; adaptation of traditional (test-based) paradigms; adoption by mission deciders.

Another important aspect is usability: developers of flight software should be able to understand and use these techniques with a reasonable amount of training—not a Ph.D. in computer science. Automation should be maximized, both in performing the verification and in developing the necessary formal models and specifications on which it is performed. Verification should be integrated with the rest of the development environment and be able to import and export information from and to other activities.

Last but no least, the quality of the verification tools themselves must be addressed, under two different facets. First, one must assess how good those methods are in principle: whether they provide firm guarantees or strong confidence, how much they cover (especially compared to testing), whether they may report spurious errors (false negatives) or miss real ones (false negatives). Quantitative metrics, rather than notional arguments, are highly preferable. Second, one must demonstrate that the actual tool being used correctly and reliably implement those principles—in other terms, give V&V results on the V&V tools. This second aspect can be mitigated upon as long as the verification tools are only used to find errors as part of the development phase (debugging), but becomes critical once these tools are used in the quality assurance phase on the final product (certification).

Agents Applied to Autonomous Vehicles

Craig Schlenoff

National Institute of Standards and Technology, Stop 8230
100 Bureau Drive, Gaithersburg, MD 20899
craig.schlenoff@nist.gov

In order to make an unmanned vehicle drive truly autonomously, many different software components are needed. Each of these components is tasked with providing a particular function that is necessary to accomplish the ultimate goal of autonomous driving. Typical functions include perception, sensory processing, world modeling, planning, route following, behavior generation and value judgment. Each component can be seen as an individual agent, and the entire system can be viewed as an agent architecture. The agent architecture that is the focus of this paper is the RCS Control System (RCS) [1] developed in the Intelligent Systems Division at the National Institute of Standards and Technology (NIST).

As with many agent architectures, one of the major challenges is how to completely and accurately exchange pertinent information among different agents. Although each agent has a specific set of actions to perform, all of the agents are jointly working towards a common goals, namely, autonomous driving. As such, one agent often relies on information that may reside in other agents. Some types of information that one agent may need from another agent are:

Requesting Agent	Receiving Agent	Information Type
World Modeling	Perception	What are the objects that reside in the environment?
World Modeling	Sensory Processing	What are the pertinent characteristics of objects in the environment?
Planning	World Modeling	What can be inferred about the motion of objects in the environment (e.g., the goal of the object)?
Planning	Behavior Generation	How can the overall goal of the vehicle be decomposed into actionable items?
Planning	Value Judgment	Did the planner identify all possible plans to accomplish the stated goal?
Planning	Value Judgment	Did the chosen plan truly accomplish the stated goal?

One approach to ensuring complete and unambiguous communication among different agents is to develop a formal ontology of the concepts that need to be exchanged in the

M.G. Hinchey et al. (Eds.): FAABS 2002, LNAI 2699, pp. 239–240, 2003.

realm of autonomous driving.[1] An ontology is different than other types of interchange specification in that it focuses exclusively on the semantics or the meaning of the concepts instead of placing the focus on the syntax that is used to represent the concepts. Efforts have already begun at NIST in developing such an ontology, with initial emphasis focusing on formally encoding the "rules of the road" based upon the Driver Education Task Analysis: Instructional Objectives document [3] developed by the Human Resources Research Organization for the Department of Transportation.

The ontology is represented in the Knowledge Interchange Format (KIF) [4]. An example of a KIF axiom is included below.

If the force on the car prior to an occurrence of the accelerate activity is ?acc, then the force on the car after the occurrence is increased by the amount ?increment.
```
(forall (?car ?acc ?occ ?increment)
    (=>        (and  (occurrence_of ?occ (accelerate ?car ?increment))
                     (prior (force ?car ?acc) ?occ))
          (holds (force ?car (+ ?acc ?increment)) ?occ)))
```
Even with the ontology developed, there are still numerous challenges that need to be addressed, including:

o   How important is reusability, and how do we decide which parts of the ontology should be reused in other applications and which parts are situation specific?
o   Are ontologies and agents useful in representing low-level data, such as the pixel-level data that is the output of perception systems? If ontologies are useful at this level, how do you represent this type of data?
o   What language should be used to communicate between agents? Although the data may be represented in ontologies, there still need to be a communication/query language to pass the data between agents.
o   What other types of information should be unambiguously defined in the ontology besides driving activities and the "rules of the road"?

References

1. Albus, J., "4-D/RCS: A Reference Model Architecture for Demo III," NISTIR 5994, Gaithersburg, MD, March 1997.
2. Gage, Douglas, Information Processing Technology Office – Mobile Autonomous Mobile Software http://www.darpa.mil/ipto/research/mars/. Last Viewed May 30 2002.
3. McKnight, A.J. and A.G. Hundt. 1971. *Driver Education Task Analysis: Instructional Objectives*. Human Resources Research Organization.
4. Genesereth M., Fikes R. 1992. Knowledge Interchange Format. Stanford Logic Report Logic-92-1, Stanford Univ. http://logic.stanford.edu/kif/kif.html.

---

[1] This work is being performed under the auspices of the DARPA-funded MARS project. [2]

Using XML for Interprocess Communications in a Space Situational Awareness and Control Application

Stuart Aldridge, Alexander Stoyen, Jeffrey Hicks, and Plamen Petrov

21st Century Systems, Inc. 12152 Windsor Hall Way
Herndon VA 20170-2359 USA
{stuart, alex, jeff, plamen}@21csi.com
http://www.21csi.com

Abstract. As various militaries progress toward a network-centric environment, their dependency upon space assets is expected to grow exponentially. It is important for the commander to be aware of the dispositions and movements in this fourth medium. The success of terrestrial forces requires comprehensive space situational awareness (SSA). 21st Century Systems, Inc. is essentially developing a SSA and decision support application that, with proper inputs, will provide an integrated space picture. We call this concept, SituSpace. The visualization uses two and three dimensional depictions to provide the watchstander with rapid situational awareness. SituSpace employs intelligent software agents to provide timely alerts and cogent recommendations. The intelligent agents apply the user's ROE, situation, resources, etc. to rapidly derive actionable recommendations to accelerate the decision loop. The SituSpace concept gains synergy from combining two complementary ideas: using a metalanguage as the medium of storage and interprocess communication and a modular publish-subscribe software architecture.

1 Overview

As militaries progress towards the network-centric environment, their dependency upon space assets to meet their force enhancement (C4, weather, navigation, intelligence, surveillance, etc.) requirements is expected to grow exponentially. This trend is not only for U.S. forces, but the forces of their potential adversaries, as well. With so many mission critical assets parked in various orbit types above the theater, it is important for the commander and his staff to be operationally aware of activities in this fourth medium, space. The theater commander's battlespace awareness must now extend many miles above the earth's surface into this arena.

Indeed, the task of space control is rapidly becoming a necessity. The success of terrestrial forces requires a comprehensive space situational awareness (SSA) and, very soon, will necessitate a space control capability. 21st Century Systems, Inc. is essentially developing an SSA and decision support client application that provides an integrated space picture capable of being used in the space control arena. We call this

M.G. Hinchey et al. (Eds.): FAABS 2002, LNAI 2699, pp. 241–253, 2003.

concept, SituSpace. The visualization uses two dimensional and three dimensional depictions to provide the theater and space force C2 watchstander with rapid, intuitive situational awareness. SituSpace will also employ intelligent software agent technology to provide timely alerts and cogent recommendations. The intelligent agents will apply the user's rules of engagement, situation, resources, and more to rapidly derive actionable recommendations in order to accelerate the decision loop of the C2 watchstander. With the proper inputs, this application will provide a single integrated space picture (SISP) for many C2 users.

Any foray into monitoring the space environment runs into two early challenges. Immediately, there are a great number of objects in orbit and that number is growing. These objects range from operating satellites to derelicts and debris. And there is a growing diversity in the cadre of watchstanders interested in SSA. The first challenge is how to prevent this abundance of objects from overwhelming the user and system. The second challenge is how to develop a system that meets the needs of as many of these users as possible.

The SituSpace concept gains synergy from the combining of two complementary ideas. First is the use of a metalanguage as the medium of storage and interprocess communication (IPC). A metalanguage, such as Extensible Markup Language (XML), provides for interoperability, flexibility, and multilevel abstraction in the handling and passing of data elements. The second source of inherent value in the SituSpace concept is the use of a modular publish-subscribe software architecture which supports intelligent agents. This has allowed us to model and to display synthetic environments with remarkable ease.

This Small Business Innovative Research (SBIR) project has completed its first phase and a proof-of-concept prototype was delivered. This proof-of-concept prototype was further enhanced in the option portion of the first phase. The next two-year-long phase is slated to enhance the decision support aspect and to add terrestrial and extraterrestrial weather into the visualization. This project is supported by the U.S. Army's Space and Missile Defense Command (SMDC).

2   Space Teems with Life

Even if we consider only objects in close earth orbit and larger than a particular size, there are still a great number of objects. The USAF tracks more than 8,000 objects in orbit around the earth. Most are debris, such spent rocket bodies, but a large number are operating satellites, both U.S. and foreign, military and civilian [1]. And any SSA software application must be able to handle this number of objects (from a performance standpoint), yet be able to filter through the clutter in order to provide rapid situational awareness. The SituSpace project attempts to do just that.

2.1 Storage and Distribution

One linchpin of the SituSpace effort is the use of a metalanguage to perform activities such as data aggregation from disparate sources, distribution of serializable objects, and display of space object data. XML is the preferred technology in many information-transfer scenarios because of its ability to encode information in a way that is easy to read, process, and generate. Indeed, the Joint Technical Architecture (JTA) referenced XML for document interchange. The JTA stated, "XML allows domain specific markup languages and customized, application-specific markup languages to be defined through the use of application profiles using application-specific tagged data items. This allows XML tags to be used to represent concepts at multiple levels of abstraction, facilitate metadata searches, provide direct access to data described by the metadata, and provide information as to how to obtain data that is not available directly on-line. Finally, XML allows new capabilities to be defined and delivered dynamically" [2].

The burning question of this research is "Can XML be used to represent a number of space objects in a software application?" The answer to this question is a qualified "yes." In this particular application, XML would play a role in the representation/storage of the space objects and in the transfer of space object information in a distributed system.

Metalanguages are languages to describe other languages and objects. They have a great deal of flexibility. But there is a cost associated with this flexibility in the form of verbosity. The tags that are used to make the data portable also add to the processing time and network bandwidth.

```
<XML ID="identifier">
<space-object>
    <intldesignator>YYYYNNNABC</intldesignator>
    <designation>dmsp_2</designation>
    <coe>
        <eccentricity>0.2</eccentricity>
        <raan>090.23</raan>
        <argofperigee>35.234567</argofperigee>
        <inclination>23.23987654</inclination>
        <epoch>35.234567</epoch>
        <meananom-
aly>123.23954</meananomaly>
    </coe>
    <mission>
        <operator>NPOESS</operator>
    <mission-
type>force_enhancement</missiontype>
    <missionde-
tail>environmental_monitoring</missiondetail>
    <sensor>
        <sensortype>visible</sensortype>
        <fieldofview>120</fieldofview>
    </sensor>
    <sensor>
        <sensortype>infrared</sensortype>
        <fieldofview>150</fieldofview>
    </sensor>
    </mission>
<weight>2545</weight>
```

Fig. 1. Rudimentary XML Space Object

The XML object in Figure 1 has approximately 70% tag characters (highlighted) versus 30% actual data characters. Just as overhead associated with headers in network communications is referred to as header tax, I would characterize this as a "tag tax."

This "tag tax" would not be as challenging an issue were it not for the number of objects that will be involved in this application. The sheer number of space objects makes the data element inclusion decision and the naming decision very significant. There is a tradeoff in performance for each additional element of information.

The issue of the transfer of space object information in a distributed system appears to an issue that can be overcome. In corporate America, the most significant use of XML is for data transfer among businesses to replace older, more expensive EDI systems [3]. Once again, the issue of the "tag tax" must be dealt with. David Hayes, in "The Potential of XML," stated "The XML metadata in the form of data tags creates a transmission overhead. The metadata imposes an added burden on network capacity and processing to parse the message." Mr. Hayes also offered insight into addressing this issue, "Data compression, local computation and manipulation of data, intelligent communication of knowledge as opposed to raw data, and granular updates are mechanisms that mitigate the network load penalty." [4]

2.2 Clutter Management

The plethora of objects in orbit presents another challenge to providing intuitive SSA. The display, either two dimensional or three dimensional (or both) must strike a delicate balance between providing data and overwhelming the watchstander. Too little data and the watchstander doesn't get an accurate depiction. Too much data and the watchstander "can't see the forest for the trees" or the flood of data delays understanding. Figure 2 below shows the inherent clutter associated with a two dimensional display of only 200 objects.

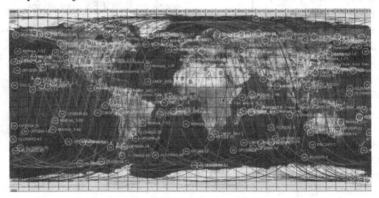

Fig. 2. Cluttered screen with only 200 objects

There are several ways to gain control of the clutter. One such method is to allow the watchstander to define the parameters of the objects that he/she is interested in viewing in the display. The watchstander would select the categories and types of the objects of interest. This is done by filtering out those objects that do not meet these criteria. One advantage to this method is the user can tailor what is displayed to those objects associated with his/her mission. A disadvantage is the watchstander can induce clutter through ineffective filtering by trying to see too much. A typical filtering mechanism is shown in Figure 3.

A second, more effective method of controlling the clutter is to use intelligent software agents to aid in the filtering and decluttering process. This works in two ways. Intelligent software agents can be used to "coach" the user through the filtering process in order to reduce the chances of over-filtering and under-filtering. It goes without saying that the watchstander has override authority over the software agent. The software agents can also assist in real time by highlighting objects of interest to the watchstander. Using watchstander input, the software agents can be "trained" to alert the watchstander and to highlight an object of interest when it appears or acts in a particular manner. The watchstander has

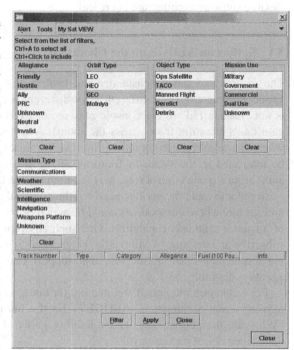

Fig. 3. SituSpace Filter Storyboard

the option to retain the highlight in order to more rapidly acquire the object in future use or to remove the highlight if the object is no longer of interest.

3 Handling Diversity

While it is traditional for military commands with a space charter to desire a space picture that provides SSA, most military and government entities have come to the conclusion that activities in space (both manmade and otherwise) can have an impact on operations. The average military unit, becoming dependent on force enhancement capabilities provided from orbit (navigation, intelligence, meteorological, etc.), has a vested interest in the space situation. A simple example from a requirements document for a Navy surface combatant:

> *CVNX shall be able to develop, maintain, and display consoli-*
> *dated situational awareness including integrated air/space picture,*
> *integrated ground picture and integrated maritime picture including*
> *subsurface for any area a carrier could be assigned."*
> *(from ORD for Future Aircraft Carrier, CVNX, 23Feb2000)*

Thus, there is an increasing diversity in the watchstander desiring SSA. In order to meet the challenging needs of this growing and evolving user segment, a mature, flexible software architecture is critical.

3.1 Getting an AEDGE on the Challenge

The diversity of the watchstander and his/her environment means a SSA software application must operate differently for different watchstanders. A watchstander who is not "handcuffed" to the console may require verbal alerts from the application (to gain one's attention from across the room). Another may operate in an environment where that would not be practical (i.e., due to noise). Another watchstander may only be interested in the swath or footprint of the satellite's payload on the earth, while another, in a space control role, may be interested in the space environment.

In order to meet the various needs of the potential user base, we required a software architecture where components could be added or removed seamlessly (like in the case of a speech synthesis capability). One such environment is one employing a publish-subscribe architecture. Additionally, since various watchstanders have differing alerting requirements, an architecture that support easy tailoring of intelligent software agents is desirable.

For a common integrated architecture for our application, we choose to use 21CSI's existing agent architecture, AEDGE™. So the burning question of the moment is, "What are the performance and reliability gains of AEDGE™ over a more mature distributed object technology?"

AEDGE can roughly be classified as middleware built on top of distributed object-oriented technology (so far based on Java, with a number of extensions) with native support for agents, extensible data representations and flexible user interfaces. AEDGE is a robust, high-performance, flexible framework, designed specifically for building agent-based near-real-time decision support systems. In order to explain the benefits of this approach, let us review the underlying and preceding technologies.

In the paradigm of object-oriented programming (OOP) languages, distributed computing is usually supported by language extensions for distributed objects. While standard OOP languages are quite powerful in defining control and data structures for single processors, most of them do not feature mechanisms for defining and implementing various object distribution models. Thus, with the development of networked and distributed computing, various extensions and models were developed. Object Management Group (OMG)'s Common Object Request Broker Architecture (CORBA) is now considered a standard object distribution model. CORBA defines object location and method invocation services for remote (as well as local) objects, which supports transparent distributed interactions. Multiple implementations of CORBA and other Object Request Brokers (ORBs) exist, for a variety of languages and operating systems. CORBA's advantages of transparency and wide interoperability come at a high price of considerable overhead and relatively low (and unpredictable) performance, partially due to inefficient implementations and partially to CORBA's inherent architectural complexity.

Microsoft introduced its own approach to distributed object oriented computing – the Distributed Component Object Model (DCOM) – an extension of COM, which defines services and interactions with remote COM objects. While DCOM addresses some of the performance issues, its availability for platforms other than Windows/PC is limited. The model is inherently dependent on Microsoft-specific implementation of features and is thus hard to analyze with external tools.

Sun Microsystems's Java was designed and built as an advanced network-friendly OOP language with built-in possibilities for extensions. Java's version of distributed object support, the Remote Method Invocation (RMI), borrows from the ORB model and from the older, well-understood Remote Procedure Call (RPC) model. RMI provides remote object location services and a skeleton-stub implementation of RPC. It is more efficient, more flexible, but less programmer-friendly than CORBA or DCOM.

AEDGE is developed as an object-oriented paradigm. Its basic data units are objects, which are capable of writing themselves to a stream and reading themselves back from a stream (i.e. they are serializable, in the Java jargon). In addition, these generic AEDGE data objects support introspection during run-time, which enables the user to peek into any of them and even change their structure, on the fly. This presents tremendous capabilities in terms of system maintainability and robustness – for instance, the operator of an AEDGE-based system can isolate part of the system, while another part takes over the suspended functions, then modify data structures, rules, even expressions and conditions, then safely bring the modified services back, all while the system is still operating (note that no shutdown, reboot, recompile or even linking and restarting was required). Thus, AEDGE implements a flexible and powerful distributed object model, based on existing services (CORBA or RMI where available) or on its own XML-based services over TCP/IP sockets, where required.

In AEDGE, agents are represented through the common serializable framework of objects. This means that agents are mobile by design (they can serialize themselves, transmit themselves as "data" in a message and the AEDGE environment will reinstantiate and initialize them on the receiving side). The user is free to specify when, where and how the agents are to migrate from one AEDGE node to another. An agent can even "bootstrap" the AEDGE environment on a fresh node, provided the necessary system permissions and basic services (such as RMI or CORBA) are present. With that in mind, the AEDGE agents are designed with an inherent balance between flexibility and performance. While the user has the power to alter, redesign and create new agents, the internal execution model is still based on language primitives, which are compiled in one form or another (Java byte-code or native code), which enables the framework to maintain the requirement for high performance much better than purely interpretive or rule-based systems.

Several research communities have modeled distributed computing by studying communication and coordination mechanisms among autonomous software entities, or Agents. Agent-based computing focuses on the interaction mechanisms among agents, which permit a rich set of coordinated activities. Effective models of interaction require the following basic capabilities: 1) a transport mechanism to convey messages in an asynchronous fashion, 2) an interaction protocol, defining the available types of communications and their semantics, 3) a content language providing the base for composition of requests and their interpretation, and 4) an agreed-upon set of shared vocabulary and meaning of concepts (often called on ontology). The most common foundation technology used for such agent-based architectures is the Knowledge Query Manipulation Language (KQML) [5]. KQML specifies interaction protocols by defining symbolic performatives to represent information about the purpose of a communication. Since it uses a standardized representation of conversational interactions, KQML is limited by its reliance on a fixed set of atomic performatives. Arriving at just the right set of performatives in the ontology has been a major hurdle in this and other approaches.

Another approach to implementing the fundamental capabilities for Agent-based computing is structuring the agent's activities around the concepts of Belief, Desire, and Intention (BDI) [6]. While BDI's emphasis on a higher level of abstraction has been important in giving direction to work on agent-based systems, its applicability may be limited by the structural requirements posed on individual agents. BDI makes stronger assumptions about the knowledge availability and processing within agents, which induces difficulties in operating with largely-legacy systems.

The Open Agent Architecture (OAA) [7] also provides a framework for Agent-based computing. OAA focuses on a balanced set of objectives, including efficient interoperation, autonomy, coordination, flexibility and extensibility. The architecture incorporates a promising set of new technologies, though it is still under development. Practical applications of OAA will require improvement in scalability and robustness, as well as the construction of new development, testing and profiling tools.

The AEDGE architecture uses an amalgam of these approaches in a way that maximizes flexibility while not compromising performance. AEDGE's framework does rely on a finite number of primitives (or data abstractions), however it does not limit or constrain those primitives – the data framework can change and grow even after the AEDGE-based system has been deployed, even while online. The domain specific knowledge in the system is encoded and preserved in the AEDGE agents. Rules and number-crunching algorithms can be imported from databases and libraries, while the agents know how to access those via bridges and interfaces. AEDGE defines a number of standard database and data format bridges, though we recognize that we cannot possibly provide a complete set of converters, access protocols and interfaces. This is why AEDGE has been designed to support extensions that will convert new unknown data formats to AEDGE's framework structures that are known to its agents.

3.2 Publish-Subscribe for Flexibility

As mentioned above, the ability to easily add or remove sophisticated software components is a must for a SSA application. The needs of the diverse user base drive the necessity to tailor the overall application with differing services. And, it would be cost prohibitive if the software had to be rewritten in each case.

In the AEDGE architecture, components communicate among each other via the Service Provider/Service Requester Protocol (SPSR). Service providers are components that implement an algorithm or need to share their data (data sources). Service requesters are the components that need a function performed for them by some other component or need to import data from another component. Both service requesters and service providers implement remote interfaces, which enables such components to communicate over a TCP/IP network. The remote interface implementation is currently based on Java RMI (remote method invocation, a type of simplified ORB service), though the Architecture is not dependent on this implementation.

The SPSR protocol is based on three data objects: Service, ServiceResult and Message. The Service object encapsulates the class, the type, the required quality of service (QoS) and the parameters of a service request. The ServiceResult object provides a reference to the original service, a return code (success or failure), a return object (String, Recommendation, etc), and an actual received QoS. Messages provide a way of service providers to advertise the availability of new services and to notify subscribers of new data available.

Service provider components register their location and the services they provide with a Component Registry, which is responsible for tracking and maintaining service provider information current. Service requesters lookup service provider information from the Component Registry and then establish a direct connection with the providers they wish to engage. A service request (either blocking or non-blocking) is sent from the service requestor to the service provider. The provider then replies (immediately or at some future time) with a ServiceResult.

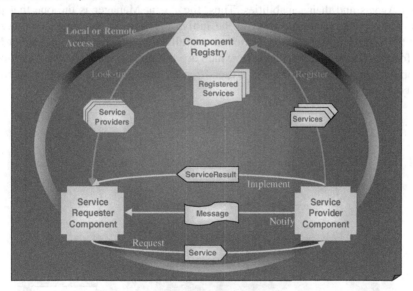

Fig. 4. SPSR Protocol Diagram

3.3 Tailored to Suit

As mentioned previously, the diversity of watchstanders and missions means meeting a diversity of need. One watchstander may be interested in force enhancements satellites and their impact on terrestrial operations while another may be tasked with maintaining awareness in the space realm itself (as in the space control mission). Each involves monitoring many of the same on-orbit assets, but requires specific, distinct alerting and recommendations. From a software standpoint, this implies the same types of intelligent software agents with specifically tailored differences. This is another reason we went with the AEDGE COTS product.

Agents in AEDGE are specialized components that generate recommendations either in response to a user inquiry or spontaneously, according to their function. Agents are usually organized in agent communities, unified under an Agent Manager component, which is responsible for invoking and synchronizing individual agents.

The Agent Manager interacts with agents via the SPSR protocol, while users (through UIs) interact with the Agent Manager through more user-friendly Inquiry/Recommendation exchange protocol (IREP). The users can query the agent manager by sending context information (entities, geo-references, target information, etc.) and specific requests for recommendations. The query is internally translated to service requests and sent to the Agent Manager. The users are not limited to the IREP – they can use any query representation, such as SQL queries, as long as they can be internally converted to service requests.

Upon receiving a user-level query, the Agent Manager selects and invokes the appropriate agents to perform the desired tasks. The Agent Manager has a table of registered Agents and their capabilities. Thus, the Agent Manager is the one that partitions the problem, sends sub-tasks to the individual Agents, and later combines and deconflicts to reach the solution. After an overall solution is reached, the Agent Manager forms a set of recommendations, which are returned to the User via a ServiceResult object. In essence the IREP is a user-friendly protocol build on top of the SPSR protocol.

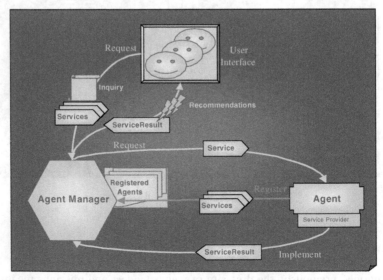

Fig. 5. Agent Components over AEDGE Services

The interactions among agents and the Agent Manager are solely based on the SPSR protocol, as these are optimized for efficiency and not necessarily for user-friendliness. Figure 6 demonstrates four different modes of User/Agent-Manager/Agent interactions, described below.

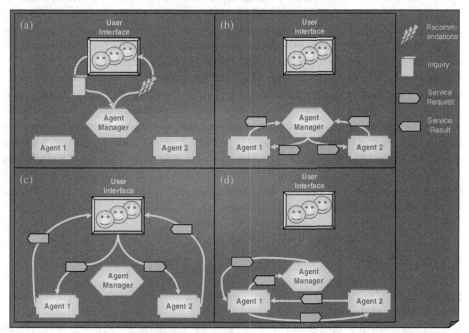

Fig. 6. Different modes of agent interactions: (a) User to Agent Manager; (b) Agent Manager to individual agents; (c) User bypasses Agent Manager; and (d) Agent-Direct interaction

User to Agent Manager Interactions. Essentially the user sends an inquiry to the Agent Manager, based on the user's current needs and query representation language. The inquiry may consist of a task description (e.g. "Check Fuel 1022" or "Check Range 1022 from 1021"), and optionally a context update, such as platforms, targets, geo-references etc. The inquiry is internally serialized and translated into service requests, which are then sent to the Agent Manager via the SPSR protocol. After the Agent Manager performs the requested tasks, it sends a reply in the form of a set of recommendations. Recommendations are core objects in AEDGE's framework, which represent desired actions and commands. Recommendations may be produced by both Agent Managers and users and are interpreted by Entities to form tasks and orders. In this case Recommendations are generated by the Agent Manager and sent for approval to the User.

Agent Manager to Individual Agents. In this interaction the Agent Manager partitions the task to subtasks for the individual agents, registered under the Manager. Subtasks are then sent to the agents via the SPSR protocol, encapsulated in Service objects. After the individual agents arrive at a solution they respond to the Agent Manager with ServiceResult objects, which are interpreted by the Manager. The Agent manager performs synchronization and deconfliction of the individual agents' results to ensure that the user will receive a coherent set of recommendations (in case individual agents had provided conflicting information).

User bypasses Agent Manager. The user can interface directly with the individual agents, using the SPSR protocol. If the user process can locate the Service Provider of an agent (via a Component Manager where that agent is registered), the user can send service requests directly to the agent and listen for the ServiceResult object in the reply. This places the burden of locating and interfacing with the agent's service provider on the user, but it provides more flexibility and faster response.

Agent-Direct interaction. Agents can communicate with each other indirectly (through the Agent Manager) or directly, via the SPSR protocol. The Requester agent looks up other agents' service providers from any component manager (including the Agent Manager) and can then send service requests to other individual agents. The Provider Agent handles the service request just like it would handle a request from the Agent Manager. The Requester agent needs to be able to handle the ServiceResult returned by the Provider. Agent-direct interaction provides the flexibility of extending the agent community that belongs to an Agent Manager without having to modify the login of the Manager itself.

4 The Future

Since Phase I of this project clearly demonstrated technical feasibility of the SituSpace concept, the next step is to take the concept "out of the laboratory" and demonstrate it in the field using real operators [8]. The Phase II SituSpace application, using inputs from the actual watchstanders slated to use this type of application, will be tailored to provide intuitive space situational awareness and effective decision support for those operators. The Phase II SituSpace application will be extended to integrate atmospheric data (both terrestrial and extraterrestrial). And, in Phase II, we will elicit feedback from the users in order to produce superior information vice superior data. We will continue to focus on SituSpace's critical elements: intuitive visualization and efficacious decision support. [9]

First and foremost, the SituSpace application must be tailored to the needs of the users ... the watchstanders who will use this decision support system to perform their tasks more intelligently. A true decision support system should allow the user to think at the higher level by presenting information (vice data), by "handling" the innocuous details, and by allowing the user to address the complex, human-in-the-loop decisions with confidence. Thus, the first step is to obtain watchstander input as to what the system should do for them.

Secondly, SituSpace will be extended to incorporate environmental effects, both terrestrial and extraterrestrial. The user should be kept apprised of the effects earthbound weather has on mission accomplishment and the effects space weather anomalies have on on-orbit assets.

Lastly, it's one thing to detect, predict, and react to a situation. But, a true decision support system would also provide information as to the possible effect of the actions. This is known as Level 3 fusion and this is derived from applying the parameters of the situation to information typically maintained in a database (troop dispositions, population densities, etc.). SituSpace will be extended to incorporate this type of functionality, as it applies to the user.

References

1. D. Atkinson, "USAF Battlelab to Improve Satellite Detection, Defense Weekly 10 August 1998
2. Department of Defense Joint Technical Architecture Version 2.0, 26 May 1998
3. Ahmad Abualsamid, "A Metalanguage For the Ages," Network Computing, April 3, 2000
4. D. Hayes, "The Potential of XML," Space and Missile Defense Technical Center Paper, 18 Dec 2000
5. Y. Labrou and T. Finin. A Proposal for a New KQML Specification. Technical Report TR CS-97-03, Computer Science and Electrical Engineering Department, University of Maryland Baltimore County, Baltimore, MD, 1997
6. A. Rao and M. Georgeff. "Modeling rational agents within a BDI-architecture." Proceedings of Knowledge Representation and Reasoning, p. 473--484, 1991
7. D. L. Martin, A. J. Cheyer, D. B. Morgan. The Open Agent Architecture: A Framework for Building Distributed Software Systems, 1998
8. S. Aldridge, "SituSpace-Space Battlespace Awareness Application," Phase I Final Technical Report to US Army Space and Missile Defense Command, August 2002
9. S. Aldridge, "SituSpace-Space Battlespace Awareness Application," Phase I Option Final Technical Report to US Army Space and Missile Defense Command, January 2003

Asimov's Laws: Current Progress

Diana F. Gordon-Spears

Department of Computer Science
University of Wyoming
Laramie, WY 82071
dspears@cs.uwyo.edu

Commercial and military decision-makers frequently express concerns about fully autonomous agents. There is an inherent distrust of anything intelligent not under human control. What can we, as agent researchers, do to alleviate these concerns? Ethically, we should have a sense of responsibility regarding the types of artifacts that we release into society. Isaac Asimov, the science fiction writer, addressed such issues in his Laws of Robotics [1].

Although one might disagree with the precise laws invented by Asimov, most of us agree that some kind of behavioral restrictions should be placed on agents. But how do we provide these behavioral assurances? I contend that agent safety should evolve in parallel with AI. We could begin with primitive safety measures – to provide assurances on the current (relatively primitive) agent technology. As agent technology evolves to ever more sophisticated levels, the assurance technology would *co*-evolve along with it. Granted, assurances will never be perfect, but that should not imply that we abandon such concerns altogether. After all, human ethics is far from being perfect; however the ethical code that *does* exist in human society serves a useful purpose in maintaining civilization. Therefore, some AI researchers are working toward implementing the first part of Asimov's first law. Rephrased in more modern terms, the focus of these efforts is the law: *"An agent should not cause harm."* The purpose of my panel presentation is to summarize what has been accomplished thus far in this regard.

The first publication to recognize the need for this law was that of Weld and Etzioni [15]. This paper's main concern was a "Call to Arms: Before we release autonomous agents into real-world environments, we need some credible and computationally tractable means of making them obey Asimov's First Law." The technical contribution of Weld and Etzioni was a modification to an automatic plan generation process. This modification guarantees that plans will achieve their goals, but that they will also not violate certain safety or tidiness constraints. Pynadath and Tambe followed up several years later on this work with a paper that provides a much more complete integration of safety constraints into planning [12].

I also continued the work of Weld and Etzioni, but my focus was more on how to address *adaptive* agents, i.e., how to apply formal verification to agents that learn [5]. Some of the results in [5] define constraint-preserving learning methods, while others focus on efficient re-verification after learning. This early work has since been extended [4], and also rephrased within a control theoretic framework [6]. The latter research was done in collaboration with Kiriakos Kiriakidis. Owre

M.G. Hinchey et al. (Eds.): 'FAABS 2002, LNAI 2699, pp. 257–259, 2003.

et al. [8] also extended the work of [5], by addressing the issue of how to preserve constraints after determinization.

There are also a number of approaches to agent safety that are substantially different from the line of research adopted by Weld and Etzioni in [15]. Let us consider some of these approaches. First of all, there is a body of relevant research on planning that focuses on preserving plan completeness, rather than correctness (which is the focus of all the research mentioned above). A good example is Mike Barley's Ph.D. thesis [3] on how to learn search control rules without decreasing coverage. Barley's thesis subsequently led to a joint publication with Hans Guesgen on this topic [2]. Also, Barley and Guesgen co-chaired a AAAI-02 Spring Symposium on "Safe Learning Agents." This symposium featured a wide variety of related work. For example, Shapiro and Shachter presented a paper on how to align a user's concerns with an agent's learning reward [10], Musliner talked about timeliness in a mission-critical context [7], and Perkins and Barto presented a Lyapunov design for safe reinforcement learning [9]. There is also a body of research that adopts a more macro-level perspective to agent safety. Two examples of this approach are that of Shoham and Tennenholz, who provide social laws (such as traffic laws) for artificial agent societies [11], and Spears and Gordon, who provide physics laws to ensure proper robot formations [13].

It should be noted that although the FAABS'00 and FAABS'02 workshops were not explicitly addressing agent behavioral assurance laws, the papers published in these proceedings are, in fact, quite applicable to the topic! By furthering progress in the field of formal methods for agent-based systems, the FAABS workshops are providing a significant body of literature on which the "safe agents" community can build.

What I have described here is only a beginning. The methods are still in the early stages of development, and many gaps remain to be filled. In the long run, as our agents become "super-intelligent machines," or "SIMS" [14], I believe we need a more multi-faceted approach. For example, I think that we need a combination of:

- A set of ethics for our agents
- External social laws that capture this code of ethics
- Law enforcement (reward/punishment)
- Internal "emotions" or "sensations" (pleasure/pain)
- Internal methods for agent self-regulation, i.e., the ability to operationalize/interpret the laws and self-verify that they are obeyed to the best of an agent's knowledge

With regulations analogous to those in human society, it is hoped that agent technology will be more broadly accepted.

Acknowledgements. My son, Joseph, inspired my research in this direction. He also made useful contributions to the ideas in this panel discussion.

References

1. Asimov, I. (1942). Runaround. *Astounding Science Fiction.*
2. Barley, M. & Guesgen, H. (2002). Towards safe learning agents. *Proceedings of the AAAI'02 Workshop on "Safe Learning Agents".*
3. Barley, M. (1996). Model-based refinement of search heuristics. *Ph.D. thesis, Rutgers University.*
4. Gordon, D. (2000). Asimovian adaptive agents. *Journal of Artificial Intelligence Research, 13,* pages 95–153.
5. Gordon, D. (1998). Well-behaved Borgs, Bolos and Berserkers. *Proceedings of the Fifteenth International Conference on Machine Learning,* pages 224–232.
6. Kiriakidis, K. & Gordon, D. (2001). Supervision of multiple-robot systems. *Proceedings of the American Control Conference.*
7. Musliner, D. (2002). Safe learning in mission-critical domains: Time is of the essence. *Proceedings of the AAAI'02 Workshop on "Safe Learning Agents".*
8. Owre, S., Ruess, H., Rushby, J., & Shankar, N. (2000). Formal approaches to agent-based systems with SAL. *Proceedings of FAABS'00.*
9. Perkins, T. & Barto, A. (2002). *Proceedings of the AAAI'02 Workshop on "Safe Learning Agents".*
10. Shapiro, D. & Shachter, R. (2002). User-agent value alignment. *Proceedings of the AAAI'02 Workshop on "Safe Learning Agents".*
11. Shoham, Y. & Tennenholz, M. (1995). On social laws for artificial agent societies: Off-line design. *Artificial Intelligence 73(1-2),* pages 231–252.
12. Pynadath, D. & Tambe, M. (2001). Revisiting Asimov's First Law: A response to the Call to Arms. *Proceedings of ATAL'01,* pages 307–320.
13. Spears, W. & Gordon, D. (1999). Using artificial physics to control agents. *Proceedings of ICIIS'99,* pages 281–288.
14. Turney, P. (1991). Controlling super-intelligent machines. *Canadian Artificial Intelligence 27,* pages 3–35.
15. Weld, D. & Etzioni, O. (1994). The First Law of Robotics. *Proceedings of the Twelfth National Conference on Artificial Intelligence,* pages 1042–1047. AAAI Press.

Asimov's Laws

James P. Hogan

POB 30031
Pensacola, FL 32503-1031
jim@jamesphogan.com

To be honest, I was never that excited about Asimov's famous Laws of Robotics. They struck me as one of those things that people repeat but have never really thought through – a bit like that dictum of Sherlock Holmes that you come across everywhere: "When you've eliminated the impossible, then what's left must be the truth." Well, it just doesn't follow. When you've eliminated the impossible, then what's left is the possible. Reality is seldom so obliging that when you've ruled out fairies, magic, and Martians, one neat and tidy answer is left as the solution to the problem. Almost invariably you end up with several equally plausible alternatives to choose from. What's left includes the truth. Real police work, and real science, begin where Homes leaves off.

The debates we hear about Asimov's Laws – and, indeed, for the most part the stories themselves – typically hinge around possible ambiguities and undecidable interpretations of what the laws mean, which can vary from hilarious to fatal. Thus we get the familiar kinds of dilemma of not knowing whether action or inaction is more likely to result in somebody's getting hurt, or having to weigh one life against another when there's no other way out. And yes, these can be complex issues that have been causing even us humans trouble enough for thousands of years. In fact, I sometimes suspect that part of Asimov's motive in creating these stories was to draw attention to the defects in some of the heady predictions being heard from the Artificial Intelligence community around the early sixties, such as fluent translation of natural languages being five years away at the most, and full all-round human cognitive capability by the end of the century. However, true as all this might be, the real problem, I would submit, goes far deeper. The issues that figure at this level all examine consequences of applying the laws. That is to say, it's assumed that what the law means is clear enough, and the complications arise when trying to put it into practice. But sweeping generalizations that might be easy for humans to comprehend can be notoriously difficult to capture and convey in the precise, formal syntax necessary to program a machine. Precisely this has been one of the major problems bedeviling AI work for the last fifty years, and as far as I'm aware that remains pretty much still the case today. Let's take Asimov's First Law as an illustration: "A Robot shall not injure a human being, nor by inaction allow a human being to come to harm." Clear enough to us; but getting the idea across to a robot runs into trouble right there. Since it has no innate knowledge of what "harm" means or of what causes it, it will have to be told. And since the symbolic system that forms the basis of its programming language

M.G. Hinchey et al. (Eds.): 'FAABS 2002, LNAI 2699, pp. 260–263, 2003.
© Springer-Verlag Berlin Heidelberg 2003

is deductive in nature not inductive, it has no way to "get the idea" from a few given examples. So the only way is to spell everything out explicitly.

So we start by telling it that one way humans come to "harm" is by being hit by hard, fast-moving objects. And since "hard" and "object" and "fast-moving" in themselves convey nothing, we supply a list of cases ranging from a bullet to a Mac truck. We think we've covered that one until the robot lets Johnny ride his bike into a wall because we didn't specify that "moving" is relative; and then it watches unconcernedly while Johnny walks off the roof. Then, when we've told it about all the things that are "hot," and it won't let me unpack the skillet I've brought home from the store, we have to get across that skillets off the stove are okay, or on the stove when the stove isn't lit, but even then the handle is okay. . . . But you've already "got the idea." We very quickly run into an exponential explosion that after a few branching levels becomes totally unmanageable. As John McCarthy succinctly put it, "General rules apply, except when they don't." The natural human language in which the law is expressed, is used in completely the opposite way to the artificial languages we employ for communicating with machines. Humans use language to supply only that information which we suppose is not obvious. But to a machine– absolutely literal-minded–nothing is obvious. Its entire reality is described by what it has been given explicitly. Nothing else exists.

This is fine for the kinds of applications for which computers were developed in the first place, such as business and engineering analysis, theorem proving, logical problem solving, where solutions are required to be rigorously, deductively correct. Here, you want the system to be fragile so that errors will immediately reveal themselves. But as was seen repeatedly in the history of AI research, the properties that enable machines to excel in areas where humans perform poorly make them ill-suited to tasks like end-to-end vision processing, motion coordination in 3-D space, and natural language comprehension (as opposed to recognition) that even young children perform easily and naturally. What we do superbly well, and they don't, is make those huge inductive leaps by which we "get the message," or "see the big picture." And that's as it should be, since the business of life that we are in depends not on deriving rigorous proofs that are useless if not 100 percent right, but in making bets that are 90 percent right 90 percent of the time–and hoping that the ones we get wrong won't be any of the big ones. We see this in the uncanny human ability to recognize patterns: to see "likeness" in the most unlikely places and extract commonality from the most obscure comparisons. Take elephants, for instance. Imagine a photograph of an elephant in a jungle; a Walt Disney cartoon elephant; an elephant dashed out in a few deft brush strokes on a coffee mug; a brass table leg cast as an elephant; an elephant-styled umbrella stand, and a dog-chewed fluffy elephant with an ear, a leg, and half its trunk missing in the children's toy box. There's nothing comparable in any of them that you could specify to an image processing program, or list as attributes for our robot, diligently trying to make sense of this induction business. Yet we unhesitatingly extract a property of "elephantness" from all of them, and then are able to recognize it in things like a carved ebony bookend, a plastic toothbrush handle, and pattern on a pair of socks. We have no real idea how we do it ourselves, so how can we specify it as a list of instructions to a machine? Marvin Minsky tells me that there is still no program anywhere that can reliably distinguish an image of a dog from one of a cat. Similarly, we see the same letter A, say, in all the styles and typefaces it could be represented in from Roman, Gothic, solid-block renderings, and copperplate through to balloon-like surreals on an art poster; or conversely, we recognize the commonality of style in all 26 letters of the same set although no two are the same, in the kind of way we see family likeness in a face.

The same faculty is seen in our use of analogy and metaphor. Some analogies are straightforward and direct, such as likening an electrical circuit to a hydraulic system. But they rapidly become obscure to the point where the similarity that's being alluded to, while we recognize it unconsciously, can take a bit of thought to put into words. Take the hackneyed political metaphor that refers to the "ship of state." Why is the state like a ship? A ship has a sharp and a round end, floats on the water, is typically made of steel, propelled by engines, etc. etc. The state is a geographical area with towns, factories, road and rail networks, a history, customs, and traditions. Our robot dutifully inputs gigabytes of related raw data and remains none the wiser. What it was supposed to latch onto, of course, was the concept of people progressing under the stewardship of a captain and crew to a desired destination, the progress in one case being through physical space, in the other toward an improved political condition. How do you write the rules for telling a machine to see that and ignore everything else? It doesn't help that what it's supposed to see and what it's supposed to ignore are not fixed, but depend totally on circumstances. Before it can decide to see or ignore anything, the robot first has to be able to identify what's relevant. From the torrent of information that pours in ceaselessly through the senses, humans are able to zoom in instantly on the aspects that suit the situation and needs of the moment. Looking at the same objective reality, we can see very different things in different situations. The properties of interest in asking what's "like" even something as simple as a piece of paper depend on whether we want to write a message, kindle a fire, wedge a wobbly table leg, or crumple it into a ball to throw to get someone's attention. Once again, how do you write the rules?

Humans can communicate with each other in this way because we have all had the same experience of forming our perceptions and associations in the same universe of physical space, populated by the same objects, and growing up in the same cultural environment. In short, shared world knowledge. This is what we take for granted when dealing with each other. It's the reason why our natural languages are used to communicate merely that which we don't assume to be obvious. And what we take for granted as being obvious turns out to be colossal indeed. This was recognized early on, and the answer widely agreed as being "learning programs." But while easy to talk about, what's being implied here is something matching the stupendous general-learning potential that comes with every newborn human infant, and just how to go about it is still far from clear. So Doug Lenat, who has always shown a proclivity for rolling his sleeves up and doing something while everyone else is talking, embarked on a project to implant world knowledge by hand–a process he calls "education by brain surgery." His team have been working on "CYC," at Cycorp Corporation in Texas, for some years now. Their approach is to take sources in the form of pieces of text encountered in life: novels, picture captions, advertising copy, textbooks, whatever, and ask the question, What did the writer of this assume the reader already knew? And then to construct that net of relationships. The hope is that this collection of information will reach a point of "semantic convergence," where the various items connect up and become mutually reinforcing to the point of mimicking the kind of background knowledge that a human typically brings to bear on dealing with life. The envisaged end-product could be thought of as a "common-sense chip" that would become as indispensable in any computer one day as a character processor is today. Opinions vary within the AI community as to whether or not it's the way to go, but everyone seems to be awaiting the outcome with interest.

I mention it here because it illustrates perfectly the problem that I've been talking about. Examples of the things that the machine needed to be specifically told, because it wasn't immediately obvious, included: You have to be awake to eat. You cannot remember things that haven't happened yet. A piece of peanut butter cut in half is two pieces of peanut butter, but a table cut in half is not two tables. One of the earliest samples of text used was the sentence, "Napoleon died on the island of St. Helena. Wellington was sad." Eleven words. The meaning pretty clear to anyone of average intelligence and education. It took the CYC programmers three months to encode the background knowledge that the writer presumed the reader shared. Perhaps this approach will lead to artificial world knowledge in the form of a hierarchy of special-purpose agents forming the lower regions of a higher-level, coordinating "consciousness." Or it could be that the way toward human-like abilities doesn't lie with the manipulation of formal symbol systems at all. It might entail a different form of physics from that which underlies today's computer architecture.

I'm thinking here of something possibly in the direction of holography, which exhibits many of the properties of "ruggedness" and failure tolerance that we associate with real biological systems in the real world. Unlike with a photograph, if a piece of a hologram is removed, the complete image will still be reconstructed from the rest, albeit somewhat degraded. And here's a remarkable property. If you make a hologram of a printed page, it appears as a dark rectangle. Now make a separate hologram of the letter E, say. If you superpose the two holograms, a bright spot will show at every point on the page where the letter E appears. And the more closely each E resembles the E that the hologram was made from, the brighter its corresponding spot will be. Instantly extracting a degree of "likeness." It's got that feeling about it of doing things the way minds do. So, in conclusion, Asimov's laws being meaningfully comprehended and interpreted by machines? Wonderful material for science-fiction, yes. And to be frank, that's where I see it remaining for some considerable time to come.

On Laws of Robotics

Yoji Kondo

NASA Goddard Space Flight Center
Greenbelt, MD
kondo@stars.gsfc.nasa.gov

Discussions of *any* and *all* conceivable 'Behavioral Laws for Agents (Robots)' would be a topic appropriate for several conferences. Since the panel (on which I am to serve) lasts only an hour and a half, I am assuming in what follows below that the theme for this panel would be Asimov's Three Laws of Robotics.

Regarding Asimov's First Law – A robot may not injure a human being, or, through inaction, allow a human being to come to harm – I am not sure whether or not even intelligent human beings are capable of obeying this law when they are willing and wanting to do so. It is often not so easy to know in advance what will or will not harm a human being. Even something as straight forward as an air-bag in an automobile can sometimes inflate itself accidentally, causing injuries to those in the car and sometimes to those outside. I don't know of many simple safety devices to protect human lives that are really fail-safe in this sense.

If we do not always know what will or will not harm human beings, how do we design a device or a robot that will protect us? Are we limiting ourselves here to simple (relatively) straight forward situations, such as an elevator free-falling fifty stories or a mid-air collision of two airplanes? Even the second case would not necessarily be a simple problem involving only two airplanes.

The Second Law – A robot obey orders given it by human beings, except where orders would conflict with the First Law – would be comparatively easy to enforce, except the part where the compliance with the First Law is involved. For example, if a police officer were to use a deadly (robotic) weapon to protect a citizen from a gun-toting mugger about to kill a law-abiding citizen, how does the robotic weapon resolve its conflicting requirements that it should not harm a human being but should not, through inaction, allow a human being to come to harm? How would it know which life to protect or *not* to take?

The Third Law – A robot must protect its own existence as long as such protection does not conflict with the First or Second law – would similarly be not so difficult to design into robots except where the compliance with the First Law is relevant.

Compliance with Asimov's Three Laws of Robotics would consist of two basic elements. (A) Robot's ability to judge what, if any, robotic laws are about to be infringed upon or invoked, and analyze the situation for proper action – or inaction as the case may be. (B) Robot's ability to do whatever it takes to comply with the robotic laws. Of the above two, (A) appears to be the more difficult of the two tasks as it could involve complex decision making.

Problems would appear to arise whenever or wherever the compliance with the First Law becomes an issue. We have robotic hardware and software that

M.G. Hinchey et al. (Eds.): 'FAABS 2002, LNAI 2699, pp. 264–265, 2003.

usually do what they are supposed to do. Engineers try to design these devices to comply with the First Law (although it is not called as such in daily life), whenever conflicting and confusing issues are sufficiently straight forward for resolution. Perhaps, we should first consider those cases where the conflict resolution is fairly simple and straight forward, and should then move on to instances where potential conflicts become increasingly complex. We shall see if we can suggest approaches toward resolving such issues. We might then consider what other laws we might need to make robots safe for the human race (if that is our ultimate objective). We probably wouldn't want to repeat the scenario of the movie "The Terminator" or the threat of HAL in "Space 2001".

Examples of relatively simple 'robotic' systems for discussion might include: surface and air transportation systems, burglar alarms and automatic home defense systems, discriminating telephone monitoring devices with built-in responses, vital-sign-monitoring and life-support systems in hospitals, various weapons for police and military purposes. We might even talk about the fully vocalized computer system on Star Ship Enterprise (which is presumably located at the Universal Studio in Hollywood).

Post-Workshop Thoughts: Designing a robot's 'brain', programming it, and giving it appropriate instructions are all complex undertakings. Giving instructions will be no easy task even if we had the technology to design a super-brain equipped with all necessary software (which we do not have, as yet).

If instructions are given in computer codes (as in the case of relatively primitive robots such as those we have already in use for some limited purposes) or verbally, they can be given only in terms of abstract symbols. Words are really symbols that are used to describe the world. Mathematical symbols used in science and engineering are also designed to correspond to the actual physical universe. However, those words or mathematical symbols do not – cannot – represent the real universe completely, although we try very hard to do so, succeeding adequately sometimes.

We human beings have to make decisions or choices from incomplete sets of data, often making intuitive leaps to cover the gaps in the data. Those who are capable of taking correct intuitive leaps will succeed; those who are not will fail. One of the important questions in designing robots that will follow the Laws of Robotics is whether or not we will be able to equip our robots with an ability to make intuitive leaps when necessary.

Another important issue might be whether or not we wish to equip the robot with an ability to learn from their experiences. [We already do so, in a very limited sense, in designing some automated devices.]

If we successfully develop a robot that can make intuitive leaps and learn from experiences, we may have created a being that may not be controlled by its 'masters' (meaning 'us') and may even reproduce better versions of itself. The creation of truly thinking, autonomous robot is a great technological challenge but its consequences might be difficult to predict, as has been foreshadowed in various science fiction novels and movies.

Challenges Arising from Applications of Agent-Based Systems

Walt Truszkowski

Senior Technologist
Code 588, NASA – Goddard Space Flight Center, 301-286-8821
walt.truszkowski@nasa.gov

Abstract. This paper, based on an Applications Panel presentation, briefly introduces and discusses several agent-based applications, currently being investigated at Goddard, and then identifies some issues that have formal methods implications.

1 Applications

The applications to be discussed are: Ontology Negotiation, Perspectives, Reusable Agent Repository, and Spectral Analysis Automation. All of these applications are agent-based applications.

1.1 Ontology Negotiation

Consider the following figure. There are two heterogeneous information sources each mediated by an agent. The sources are heterogeneous in the sense that they have differing schemas and use different terminology (ontology) to guide the user to his/her wanted information. The sources are agent mediated in the sense that the agents know the source's structure and terminology used and assist the user in obtaining desired information (i.e., in satisfying the user's query). Assume further that the agents need to collaborate because the desired information involves both information sources.

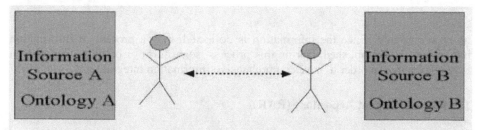

These two agents need to collaborate in supporting a request for information that involves access to both information sources

M.G. Hinchey et al. (Eds.): FAABS 2002, LNAI 2699, pp. 269–273, 2003.

In the process of collaborating the agents may need to reconcile terminological differences arising from the fact that the information sources are heterogeneous with respect to information source ontologies. The process of ontology negotiation [1] allows the agents, through a dialog process, to resolve the ontological differences and proceed to satisfy, in a collaborative fashion, the user's query.

1.2 Perspectives

Another aspect of ontology management can be seen when considering the concept of "perspectives" [2]. The following figure illustrates the major features of our current research in the area of perspectives. The idea is to collect information on an object of interest from several different points-of-view where each point-of-view is supported by

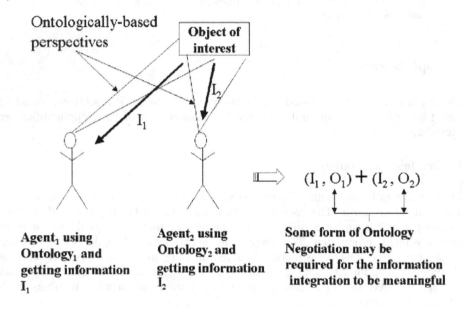

its own ontology. Once the information is collected, then a process of information integration is accomplished. During this process, some form of ontology negotiation may be required in order to have comprehensive information integration.

1.3 Reusable Agent Repository (RAR)

Over the past several years prototypes of agent communities, for supporting the automation of ground system command and control functions, have been developed. Once a community of agents had been developed for a particular control center function for a particular mission, the question arose: "what can be reused when considering the generation of an agent community for a similar function for a different mission and control enter?". The following figure illustrates an overall strategy for using a repository of existing agents and agent communities when trying to satisfy new mission requirements.

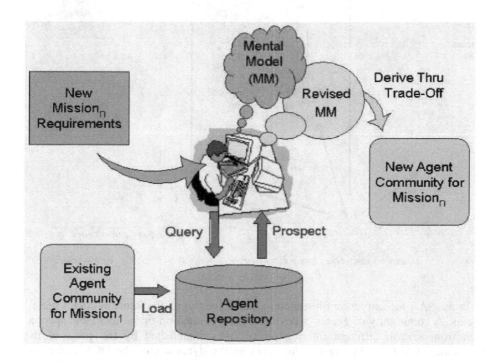

The Reusable Agent Repository (RAR) [3] application is trying to realize a workable infrastructure and interaction/interface mechanisms to support the reuse of agent-based assets.

1.4 Spectral Analysis Automation (SAA)

The final application considered is the Spectral Analysis Automation (SAA) [4] application. The major objective of the SAA activity is to develop a system that is capable of filtering spectral data and making the selected data available for a complete spectral analysis processing. In particular, we are pursuing a goal-driven data filtering capability that assesses observations for their relevance to mission goals. This type of data filtering will eventually find its way onboard a spacecraft and the filtering will result in less demand for restricted download capabilities and enable onboard or in-situ science event detection and response.

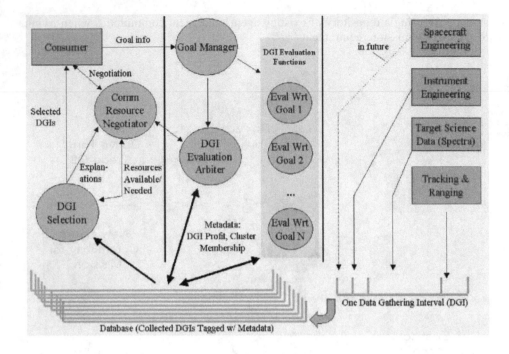

In the SAA infrastructure illustrated in the above figure, the items in circles are all agents. A community of agents is devoted to the evaluation of the available spectral data from several different filtering perspectives established by the goals of the Consumer. The Goal Manager agent oversees the dynamics of the DGI Evaluation community of agents. There is a DGI Evaluation arbiter agent which reconciles the decisions of the DGI Evaluation agents. The Communication Resource Negotiator agent helps to provide requested communication resources and the DGI Selection agent is responsible for selecting and packing DGI's into a transmission to the Consumer within available communication resources. The Consumer provides for new filtering goals by creating an agents which embodies the new goals and causing the agents to migrate to the DGI Evaluation community under the control of the Goal Manager agent.

2 Implications for Formal Methods

All of the above-cited applications use agent technology for the intelligent access and management of data and information. The RAR and SAA applications also involve dynamic agent community behaviors and agent creation concepts.

Some of the issues that are associated with the described applications are:
(from an intelligent information management perspective)
- how can the syntactic, semantic and pragmatic aspects of an information object be integrated into a truly usable construct?

- what kind of information algebra can be established to support such things as information correctness checking , information integration, etc.?
- how can automatic ontology generation and maintenance be effectively realized?
- how can "concepts" be formally defined and manipulated?

(from an agent and a multi-agent system perspective)
- how can the dynamics of an agent community be formally modeled?
- how can capabilities like adaptation to a changing environment and learning be formally modeled?
- how can agent creation be facilitated?

Although these issues have been studied for some time, easy-to-use formal methods, leading to proofs of completeness and correctness and addressing these highly dynamic issues, still need to be further developed and applied. This is a challenge for formal methods.

3 Conclusions

Work on the above mentioned applications is proceeding. The implications of this work for future NASA systems and missions, in such areas as intelligent information access and management, and mission autonomy, are considerable. Having ready mechanisms to address completeness and correctness questions would be a major advancement in the on-going applied agent technology work.

Acknowledgements. The author wishes to acknowledge Dr. Sidney Bailin, Dr. Victoria Yoon, Dr. Pam Clark, Dr. Mike Rilee, Jay Karlin, and Tim McClanahan for their major contributions to the applications cited in this paper.

References

1. "Ontology Negotiation between intelligent information agents", Sidney Bailin, Walt Truszkowski, The Knowledge Engineering Review, Vol. 17:1, 2002
2. "Perspectives: An analysis of Multiple Viewpoints in Agent-Based Systems", Sidney Bailin, Walt Truszkowski, AAAI Spring Symposium, Stanford University, 2003
3. "Reusable Agent Repository", Victoria Yoon, Jay Karlin, Internal GSFC Report, 2002
4. "Agent-based Spectral Analysis Automation (SAA) for On-board Science Data Processing", Walt Truszkowski, Sidney Bailin, FLAIRS 2003, May 2003

Tools and Education towards Formal Methods Practice

John-Jules C. Meyer

Utrecht University
Institute of Information and Computing Sciences
Intelligent Systems Group
P.O. Box 80.089
3508 TB Utrecht, The Netherlands

1   My Background

To put my position on the panel theme in perspective, I first will give a sketch of my own background and that of my group in Utrecht. Currently I'm a full professor of artificial intelligence, and our group in Utrecht is mainly focused on agent technology in a broad sense: we are looking at theoretical/logical foundations (agent logics) as well as ways of realizing agents (by means of agent programming languages and agent-oriented software engineering) as well as applications (such as cognitive robotics and agent-mediated electronic commerce, electronic institutions). I hold a Master's degree in Mathematics and a PhD in (Theoretical) Computer Science via a thesis on the semantics of programming languages (Amsterdam, 1985). After my PhD I turned to the area of (modal) logics for AI and later to agent theories.

In the past our group has done much work on logics for AI. During the last years research of the group has been centered increasingly around the theoretical foundations and realisation of intelligent agents. The former deals with the logical description of (the behaviour of) agents, and in particular their informational (including reasoning), motivational and social attitudes, while the latter concerns the realisation of agents by means of programming languages. Subsidiary problems concern some typical AI problems concerning knowledge representation as well as reasoning and inference methods in AI such as commonsense reasoning, including belief revision and argumentation, model-based (diagnostic) reasoning and reasoning within the legal domain. Also these problems should be regarded as agent-related: they concern knowledge representation and reasoning methods to be used by intelligent agents. More recently we are also looking at applications of agent technology in e.g. robotics, knowledge management and e-commerce.

The methods used range from (modal) logic to game theory and argumentation theory, from speech act theory to machine learning techniques. Furthermore, with regard to the realisation of agents dedicated (so-called agent-oriented) programming languages are used, for the formal aspects of which we employ techniques from 'traditional' programming theory and the theory of concurrent programming, such as structured operational semantics by means of transition systems and techniques and concepts from process algebra (which is rather novel

M.G. Hinchey et al. (Eds.): 'FAABS 2002, LNAI 2699, pp. 274–279, 2003.

for the field of AI). So, although perhaps some 6 years ago we mainly based our work on (modal) logical techniques, we have turned this around: agents are our main concern and we are increasingly eclectic with respect to methods and techniques: we use what we need. Presumably the area of agent technology is so intrinsically diverse that not one method/technique suffices to treat the subject properly.

I personally think it is very important and needed to bridge the gap between agent theory and practice that researchers like Rao & Georgeff already noticed. Our approach to overcoming the gap between agent specification and realization follows the lines of tradition in 'ordinary' programming: distinguish between a (logical) specification (assertion) language and a (procedural) programming language. We have devised a number of agent programming languages, or rather perhaps 'libraries' of programming constructs (3APL, ACPL, GOAL, GrAPL), to write agent programs, each with an emphasis on a particular aspect, with the intention to eventually integrate these into one comprehensive and 'real' (multi-)agent programming language, in which the most important features of agency should be incorporated. One of these languages, 3APL, developed by Hindriks et al., is particularly suited for programming BDI-like agents by means of a mixture of constructs from imperative and logic programming. This language contains constructs involving beliefs and (procedural) goals. From our range of languages/libraries, this language is developed the furthest, both theoretically and implementation-wise, and is taken to be the platform on which we want to develop a 'real' agent programming languages. Till now we have preliminary implementations of 3APL in C++, JAVA and Haskell. ACPL, developed by Van Eijk et al., contains constructs for communication, based on speech act theory, but given a formal semantics using process-algebraic concepts and techniques, with which one can program agents that coordinate and negotiate. It is intended to provide for a basis for e-commerce-like applications where agents have to follow certain communication protocols. GOAL (Hindriks et al.) is a language with declarative goals ('goals-to-be' rather than the procedural 'goals-to-do' that are present in 3APL). GrAPL (De Vries et al.) contains constructs for initiating group activity (group coordination, distributed planning and execution of tasks). This 'library' is expected to be of use for situations where agents must coordinate desires, goals and tasks within an agent society.

The idea is to have assertion languages associated with these programming languages in which specification and verification of agent programs can be done, much in the same vain as in traditional software engineering. However, of course in order to be useful these assertion languages should also contain sufficient expressiveness to express the BDI-like notions that are used in the programming languages. So here a kind of mix is needed of formal methods from 'traditional' software engineering and formal methods from AI and knowledge representation. Typically one could think of temporal or Hoare logics augmented with BDI modalities. For (fragments of) the languages 3APL and GOAL we have already obtained first versions of such assertion languages. We have started a PhD project to investigate this further, and hope to benefit from the work done in the semantics and formal methods in concurrency and object-oriented languages in which there is considerable expertise within the group.

Of course, the availability of such assertion languages is only a first step towards what one can call agent-oriented software engineering. A very important line of our research comprises the further development of the agent language 3APL and a method(ology) for programming in this language. In the past we have also done work on formal methods for concurrent and object-oriented programming together with semi-automated reasoning tools for verification like HOL and PVS. In a nationally funded project we are developing the programming language 3APL further, on the one hand by extending the language with extra features (like communication), on the other by providing a method(ology) to aid the 3APL programmer and the tools associated with this. We are also aiming at a good interface with JAVA so that our language may be widely used, at least in principle. As an application we want to be able to program advanced ('cognitive') robots by means of the language 3APL. We have already some preliminary results on this by a master's student of ours, but this needs a lot more research. One of the major problems is a principled solution to symbol grounding. We have good contacts with the Toronto group headed by Hector Levesque that is doing related work by using the language CONGOLOG based on the situation calculus.

We also work on a specification method for multi-agent systems and agent societies, more in general. Here the main issue is to obtain systems in which there is a balance between the autonomy of the individual agents and the well behaving of the system as a whole. Norms, rules and contracts play a role here, and we have preliminary results for a model for designing these societies and a (temporal deontic) logic to reason about the behaviour of these agent societies (and their correctness with respect to desired behaviour). Also thenotion of an electronic institution to control the agents within a society/community plays an important role.

2   What Are Formal Methods?

Before embarking on the task of answering the difficult questions of the panel discussion, I like to point out that the very meaning of formal methods needs some discussion, since sspecially the word 'formal' has multiple meanings. Literally 'formal' means 'relating to form', and formal reasoning like in logic pertains to the reasoning on the basis of the form only (by means of formulas in a calculus). So here we may think of a logical calculus with axioms and proof rules. But, of course, also a program written in some programming language is formal in this strict sense. However, there is also a more liberal meaning of 'formal', which is 'according to a very ordered, organized style or method' (cf. Collins Cobuild English Language Dictionary). This use of 'formal ' one normally encounters when one is talking about a formal definition or proof in mathematics. This is mostly not done in a strict logical calculus, but in natural language, as precise as possible. Also a so-called formal semantics of a (logical or programming) language is mostly written in a mathematical style, using set theory and mathematical functions, for example, and is not formal in the strict sense above.

Although programs written in some programming language are formal (in the strict sense) and thus very precise objects, their behavior when interpreted is so complex that it needs analysis to prove properties of that behavior that are not evident. For this we use formal methods. What I mean with formal methods here is formal reasoning methods for reasoning about (in this case agent-based) programs. This formal reasoning may be formal in the sense of mathematical, but also of course formal in the strict sense, i.e. within some logical calculus/system, which may also be provided with automated reasoning tools.

3 The Questions

3.1 How Can We Make Formal Methods Easier to Use without Reducing Their Effectiveness?

I believe the question that should be answered first is for whom the formal methods are intended: for the end user, the application software engineer, or the system developer. This makes a big difference as to the constraints on user-friendliness of the formal methods, since system developers can afford to become experts in their favorite methods.

3.2 How Can We Better Insert Formal Methods into the Software Engineering Process So It Becomes a Natural Part of the Process?

This is an important question with regard to seeing to it that formal methods are really used! My famous fellow countryman, the late Edsger W. Dijkstra, promoted the idea of developing/synthesizing the correctness proof together with the program itself. This is very hard in practice, and requires a lot of skill on the part of the programmer. Perhaps this is too hard. However, I do believe that in order to be able to use formal methods for devising agent-based systems it is imperative that these formal methods and the programs that constitute/realize these systems must have a conceptual basis in common. What I mean by this is that, for instance, the specification logics used and the programming languages that one employs are close in the sense that they refer to the same (agent-related) notions. So, for example, if one uses a logic that uses BDI-notions also the programming language should be able to express these and vice versa. Although from a PR point of view I understand those AOSE researchers that maintain that agent-oriented specification methods and languages can/must be used to specify *any* software system written in *any* programming language, I really believe this is a bridge too far, at least for now. Rather I believe in matching specification logics / methods / tools to (agent-oriented) programming languages like 3APL. This is exactly what our group is trying to do. Of course, an alternative way of getting a better (or even the ultimate) match is to use specifications that are executable themselves, like the METATEM people in Liverpool are doing. I think this is also an interesting road, but the very requirement of the logical specification having to be executable puts big restrictions on the logic at hand, and possibly means that one cannot use too intricate agent-related concepts / aspects in the language...

3.3   Can We Insert Formal Methods into Tools That Are Already Being Used So People Do Not Have to Change Their Processes?

I think we should try to make use of methods and tools that are already there (although adaption may be needed to cater for the typical agent-related aspects), and don't start from scratch to develop these methods and tools. This is both beneficial for the development time of these methods and the possible acceptability by users of these methods. So, our view is that first of all familiar logical systems for correctness such as temporal and dynamic logics should be used, and, moreover, tools like semi-automated reasoning and model-checking methods from traditional software engineering should be adopted (or adapted).

3.4   Can We Insert Formal Methods into Tools or Processes So People Don't Even Know They Are There But Still Reap the Benefits?

When I think of tools for verification, probably model-checking is easier to use than automated reasoning methods like HOL and PVS. For the latter a lot of knowledge is needed concerning the (semantics of the) language at hand as well as about reasoning tactics. Indeed in the realm of concurrency I know of several projects in which it took PhD's a number of months to prove the correctness of distributed algorithms that were not even that sophisticated! While model-checking is more like a 'push-button' technology (once it has been fully implemented).

3.5   How Can We Better Educate People about the Importance of Formal Methods and What They Can Do for People?

I think that it is important to stress the importance of formal methods by showing their use in software that is used in life-critical or otherwise very costly situations. Probably NASA may provide good examples of these, now already or in the near future. But, of course also some medical software should be really full-proof. We also need to stress that not every piece of software needs a formal proof of correctness. On the one hand this is infeasible (since formal verification is a laborious enterprise) and on the other hand most software can work adequately without full-proof correctness since in practice it can very well be worked with by means of a trial and error approach.

3.6   How Can We Better Educate People on How to Use Formal Methods So They Are Comfortable Using Them?

Students in computer science and AI generally do not like formal methods. That is a fact of life. However, some things should be learned, also when these things are not just fun. Of course, one may help students to overcome their dislike of formal methods by giving interesting examples and using software tools so that it is not just (literally) Greek to them, but at the end of the day one has to learn certain basics of formal methods. (Just as civil engineers need a basic knowledge of mathematics such as calculus etc.) So, expose students to formal methods (even if they do not like it)!

4   Conclusion

I believe formal methods are crucial for getting reliable systems, and in particular and *a fortiori* this holds for getting reliable agent-based systems. Therefore, I really welcome the FAABS initiative. However, a lot of work still has to be done: we are just starting to investigate formal methods for these systems, mostly inspired by and adapted from 'traditional' methods for software systems. It is important to note though, that these methods themselves are also research objects, and we should not expect that every formal method that is devised will be practical in the sense that it can directly be used for constructing real systems. The long history of formal methods within mainstream computer science and software engineering also witnesses this. But this is a normal thing in science. We can only hope that some of the methods to be devised will be useful...

Evaluating Agent-Based Modeling as a Tool for Economists

Margo Bergman

Department of Economics, 204 McElhinney Hall
University of Houston, Houston, TX 77204
margotanne@email.com

1 Introduction

Agent-Based Modeling has the capability to become a very powerful tool in economics, but in order to achieve this will require a great deal of effort on the part of its current practitioners. Economics at its core studies people and their actions. This is inherently difficult to do since the motivation of people is not always discernible. A method by which the variety of human behavior could be mimicked, thus providing insight into the process of decision-making that underlies the behaviors, would be invaluable to researchers. Agent-based modeling is such a method. In situations where analytical methods are not sufficient to answer the questions posed, agent-based modeling can be used to obtain solutions to interesting problems, and assess their robustness. However, until the majority of economists accept agent-based modeling as a legitimate tool, the adequacy of the results will remain in question. Certainly one area that will have to be addressed in order to expand the potential of agent-based modeling in economics is sheer exposure. However, more important to its acceptance will be advancements in the cohesiveness of the discipline. The purpose of this note is to present a series of question that must be answered before agent-based modeling can become accepted as a powerful economic tool.

1.1 Previous Literature

A recent survey article on the uses of agent-based modeling in economics spanned 31 pages and cited 110 papers [1]. Determining all the possible roads that one can take when creating and using agents is impossible. It is analogous to the field of econometrics. The permutations of using econometric tools are myriad. However, they all build off of the same basic toolbox that every economics graduate student learns. Some choose to study the various interesting details of the process itself, exploring new territories and refining old ones. But every economist is expected to know and be able to utilize a few simple regression models. The same can be possible for agent-based modeling. In order for this to happen, several things need to occur. The knowledge of agent-based modeling needs to become a part of the basic set of classes an economist is taught. Just as first-year students have a course in econometrics, they should have a course in agent-based modeling. This course should

M.G. Hinchey et al. (Eds.): FAABS 2002, LNAI 2699, pp. 283–285, 2003.
© Springer-Verlag Berlin Heidelberg 2003

cover the fundamentals of what agents are and how they can be used. To make this possible, the following questions must be answered in order to achieve the goal of transmitting the basics of this method to a large variety of students.

2 Questions

1)   What characteristics do agents have in common? In order for agent-based modeling to be established a definition of agent, or at the very least a consistent set of definitions, must be agreed upon. Currently the term agent can be applied to anything from a Cellular Automaton [2], which has a very basic structure and very little decision making power, to a Internet Bot, who will traverse the web and shop for you [3]. The characteristics that these different agents have in common must be determined so that their uses can be defined.

2)   Where does an agent live? This refers to mathematical properties of the spaces in which agents interact. Do they live on a torus, or donut-shaped, world [4], or do they form elaborate networks [5]. Which problems are the different environments most suited to solving? How can this be determined?

3)   What does an agent do? Agents are used to solve all sorts of problems, such as questions in artificial intelligence, game theory, organizational behavior, optimal search, and many others [4]. Creating a reference guide for the functions agents can perform is essential to helping answer this question and would help maintain order within the system.

4)   How does an agent learn, if it learns at all? This is possibly the most explored region of agent-based modeling. It is a two-fold question, in that agents need to learn, and in return, they can test different models of learning. However, a method to choose which learning style, if any, should be utilized it not yet available.

5)   How do I create an agent? This is likely the most important, yet least understood, area of agent-based modeling. A simple step-by-step process to creating an agent must be available before any researcher would be willing to accept agent as tools. Just as econometrics and theory have basic starting points, so too must agent-based modeling. Already there exist software programs, such as RePast and Ascape, to assist in agent-based modeling in the same way that SAS or RATS does for econometrics. However training in these programs is limited.

3 Conclusion

In order for agent-based modeling to gain the credibility in the mainstream of economics that it deserves much work needs to be done. A key step will be gaining the respect of editors and referees of the top-ranked journals such as the *American Economics Review*, *Econometrica*, *Journal of Political Economics* and *Quarterly Journal of Economics*. Of the 110 papers cited in the survey article mentioned above, only five were published in any of these journals, two from more than five years ago and the other three from more than ten[1]. Clearly the majority of economists has not embraced these very powerful techniques. This respect will be gained when the questions listed above have been answered and the value of a method by which very complex, and until recently unsolvable, problems can at last be analyzed is realized. Held in the hands of the people who use agent-based modeling to study a vast assortment of concepts and theories are the tools that could revolutionize the thinking of this field, and surely others as well. However, the danger of becoming a fancy parlor trick turned passing fad is very real. In order for any tool to become viable it must be accepted, and to some degree understood, not by those who use it regularly, but rather by those who don't.

References

1. Tesfatsion, Leigh. "Agent-Based Computational Economics: Growing Economies from the Ground-Up." ISU Working Paper No.1 March, 2002.
2. Wolfram, S. *Cellular Automata and Complexity.* Addison-Wesley,1994
3. www.bottechnology.com June 2002
4. Epstein, Joshua and Axtell, Robert. *Growing Artificial Societies: Social Science from the Bottom Up.* Brookings Institution Press & MIT Press, 1996.
5. Galstyan, Aram and Lerman, Kristina (2002) " Adaptive Boolean Networks and Minority Games with Time-Dependent Capacities," to appear in *Physical Review E Rapid Communications.*
6. Weiss, Gerhard. Multiagent Systems: *A Modern Approach to Distributed Artificial Intelligence.* The MIT Press, 1999.

---

[1] Arifovic, J. "The behavior of the exchange rate in the genetic algorithm and experimental economics" *Journal of Political Economy* 104 1996; Arthur, W.B. "On designing economic agents that behave like human agents: a behavioral approach to bounded rationality" *American Economic Review* 81, 1991; Gode, D.K. and Sunder, S. "Allocative efficiency of markets with zero-intelligence traders: Markets as a partial substitute for individual rationality" *Journal of Political Economy* 101, 1993; Kandori, M Mailath, G. and Rob, R. "Learning, mutation, and long-run equilibria in games" *Econometrica* 61, 1993; Krugman, P. "Complex landscapes in economic geography" *American Economic Review Papers and Proceedings*, 84, 1994.

Modeling Traffic Control through Deterrent Agents

Michel Rudnianski [1] and Hélène Bestougeff [2]

[1]University of Reims, ARESAD, 39 bis Avenue Paul Doumer , 75116 Paris –France
`Michel.Rudnianski@wanadoo.fr`
[2]CODATA – Boulevard Montmorency, 75016 Paris – France
`hbest@magic.fr`

Abstract. Multi Agents Systems (MAS) technology is used to build Urban Traffic Control (UTC) systems based on traffic lights regulation. Congestion avoidance is analyzed and simulated through modeling the network as a *game of deterrence*, as previously done in the analysis of communication and workflow networks.

1 Introduction

Urbanization growth results in worsening urban traffic conditions. Therefore, Urban Traffic Control (UTC) is of utmost importance, since it simultaneously lowers economic and environmental costs.
A road system consists of roads infrastructure, and the traffic control system that operates it.
Building new roads pays if the system is used at its maximum capacity. If not, a UTC should be designed, that ensures full use of the existing capacity, through not only simulation and control of the existing network, but also optimal design of potentially required extensions of the former.

A number of simulation tools have been developed, like CORSIM, CONTRAM, CORFLO, PARAMICS, many based on queuing theory, with problems of computational performance, model accuracy and integrating management and information, due to the network size. [8]

Multi Agents Systems technology (MAS) is a promising alternative with respect to distributed systems: MAS are fitted to complexity problems usually found in large systems.
We consider here a traffic light based UTC, the traffic light set being a MAS. The congestion avoidance approach through modeling the network as a game of deterrence, already used in communication and workflow networks [1, 6, 7], is here applied to UTC.

M.G. Hinchey et al. (Eds.): FAABS 2002, LNAI 2699, pp. 286–289, 2003.

2 Network Modeling and Control Algorithm

A crossroad includes a set of incoming and outgoing flow directions pairs (the *nodes*), such that if traffic may theoretically flow from the former to the latter, the pair is associated with a traffic light.

At time t, the binary pair $(a_{ij}(t), b_{ij}(t))$ tells if node i may send vehicles to node j, and j may receive vehicles from i.

The set of pairs $(a_{ij}(t), b_{ij}(t))$ for all nodes i and j of a given level (traffic network or crossroad) defines a *matrix*, representing the state of the system, controlled by the game of deterrence where player Row (R) and player Column (C) select incoming and outgoing directions respectively

Under usual circumstances, incoming directions can always emit and so traffic flow only depends on the capacity of outgoing directions,. The same goes for the game solutions.

If an outgoing direction j can receive vehicles from any adjacent incoming direction, any pair including j may be associated with a green light, while traffic may enter from outside the network.

If no such pair exists, then no traffic is allowed to enter from outside the network, while one or several direction pairs are selected to "force" the traffic throughout the network.

3 Network Example: One Way / One Lane Traffic

Let us consider an horizontal street (H street) with right bound traffic intersecting a vertical street (V street) with upward bound traffic. At the crossroad cars can turn. The crossroad matrix is given on table 1, where the subscripts S and T stand for "straight" and "turn" respectively.

Table 1.

	r_{VS}	r_{VT}	r_{VS}	r_{VT}
e_{VS}	$(1,b_{VS})$	$(1,1)$	$(1,1)$	$(1,1)$
e_{VT}	$(1,1)$	$(1,b_{VT})$	$(1,1)$	$(1,1)$
e_{HS}	$(1,1)$	$(1,1)$	$(1,b_{HS})$	$(1,1)$
e_{HT}	$(1,1)$	$(1,1)$	$(1,1)$	$(1,b_{HT})$

Security conditions imply that the 4-tuplets $(b_{VS}, b_{VT}, b_{HS}, b_{HT})$ can only take the 8 following values :

(0,0,0,0) ; (0,0,0,1) ; (0,0,1,0) ; (0,0,1,1) ; (0,1,0,0) ; (0,1,0,1); (1,0,0,0) ; (1,1,0,0)
Based on this crossroad, we then build a network of 4 horizontal and 4 vertical inter-secting streets, with opposite traffic directions on two consecutive horizontal or verti-cal streets, and simulate it through a two module simulation program :

– A model of a sixteen crossroad network designed by using the Vensim™ lan-guage. The figure below shows a four traffic light crossroad model, where the flow follows a Poisson distribution, each traffic lane is associated with a given capacity, and turns are assigned a given percentage of the total flow.
– A C++ control program, giving the value (red or green) of each light of the 16 crossroads. At each tick of the clock, the value of the different capacity storage is tested in order to build the game matrix.. From the game solutions the lights will be set to green or red with respect to the control algorithm.

When simulation is run with the "Simulate" button (see figure 1), congestion occurs, while it doesn't with the "Simulate with Deterrence Game Control" one, using the control algorithm.

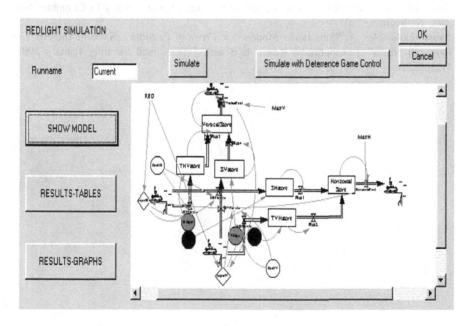

Fig. 1.

References

1. H.Bestougeff, M. Rudnianski : "Games of deterrence and satisficing models applied to business process modelling" Proceedings AAAI Spring Symposium, Stanford 1998.
2. K. Erol " A Study of Agent Based Traffic Simulation" Final Report, US DOT, 1998
3. J.M. Fernandes, E. Oliveira, "TraMas : Traffic Control through Behaviour Based Multi-Agent Systems"; Proceedings of The Fourth International Conference On the Practical Application of Intelligent Agents and Multi-Agent Technology, pp. 457–458, London, April 1999
4. G.F. Newell "Properties of Vehicle Actuated Signals : 1. One Way-Streets" Transportation Science, 3, pp. 30–52, 1969
5. M. Rudnianski, "Multipolar Deterrence in a Dynamic Environment" IEEE Systems, Man and Cybernetics 1995, vol 5, pp 4279–4285.
6. M. Rudnianski, H. Bestougeff, "Modeling Task and Teams through Game Theoretical Agent", Proceedings of the Workshop on Theoretical Agents, Springer Verlag, Lecture Notes in Computer Science, 1871, pp. 235–249 series, Berlin 2001
7. M. Rudnianski, H. Bestougeff, "Congestion Control in Multi-Agent Systems through Dynamic Games of Deterrence", in Proceedings of the Nasa First Workshop on Formal Approaches to Agent Based Systems, Springer-Verlag, Lecture Notes in Computer Science, forthcoming 2003.
8. Skarbadonis, May A, "Simulation Models for Freeway Corridors; State of the Art and Research Needs" Transportation Research Board, 77th Annual meeting, January 1998, Washington

Towards a Formal Representation of Driving Behaviors [*]

Craig Schlenoff[1] and Michael Gruninger[2]

[1] National Institute of Standards and Technology, Stop 8230
100 Bureau Drive, Gaithersburg, MD 20899
craig.schlenoff@nist.gov
[2] University of Maryland, College Park
College Park, MD 20742
gruning@cme.nist.gov

1 Introduction

To successfully perform their required tasks, intelligent information agents require accurate and meaningful communication and integration among other agents and information resources. However, the applications and infrastructure of information technology are rife with heterogeneity at many levels. This paper explores applying formal ontologies to address the challenges faced in developing and applying autonomous agents for the purpose of driving unmanned vehicles. Specifically, we are developing a formal ontology to encapsulate the rules of on-road driving, facilitating the ability for an autonomous vehicle to drive on a busy street while following the "rules of the road". This ontology will constitute a major component of the internal knowledge representation within the Real-Time Control System (RCS) [1], which is the architecture that will control the unmanned vehicle.

2 The On-Road Driving Ontology

The ontology focuses upon behaviors for an initial baseline, on-road, autonomous driving capability based on a document capturing driver task descriptions developed for the Department of Transportation (NTIS PB197325) [3]. This document contains a comprehensive inventory of the behaviors involved in operating an automobile, along with the rated criticalities of these behaviors. The task descriptions are organized in terms of the situations that give rise to the behaviors.

For each of the behaviors in the ontology, a vocabulary of task commands and a hierarchy of behavior generation processes are being developed that can accept those

---

[*] This work is being performed under the auspices of the DARPA-funded MARS project [2]. The technology goal of the MARS program is to understand and satisfactorily address the key challenges to the realization of reusable software for autonomous mobile system.

M.G. Hinchey et al. (Eds.): FAABS 2002, LNAI 2699, pp. 290–291, 2003.
© Springer-Verlag Berlin Heidelberg 2003

task commands. For a small selected set of behaviors, an in-depth study is being performed of behavior generation processes that decompose the behavior into a sequence of lower level task/behaviors that are expressed in a state-graph formalism at each level of the hierarchy. Specifically, a hierarchy of behavior generating processes is being defined with planning horizons from 50 ms to 100 minutes.

The MARS ontology is represented in the Knowledge Interchange Format (KIF) [4]. An example of a KIF axioms represented in the MARS ontology is included below.

If the force on the car prior to an occurrence of the accelerate activity is ?acc, then the force on the car after the occurrence is increased by the amount ?increment.
(forall (?car ?acc ?occ ?increment)
      (=>   (and   (occurrence_of ?occ (**accelerate** ?car ?increment))
                      (prior (**force** ?car ?acc) ?occ))
        (holds (*force* ?car (+ ?acc ?increment)) ?occ)))

3 Conclusion

The introduction of symbolic data, and more specifically, ontologies, is breaking new ground in the world of autonomous vehicles. There are so many challenges in this field that most researchers are so caught up in the lower levels of the control hierarchy (i.e., not crashing into the static obstacles in front of you), that few, if any, have explored introducing symbolic data. However, the introduction of ontologies has the potential to provide significant value to this field that has up-to-now not been recognized.

Many challenges remain to be addressed, such as the issues related to the integration of symbolic information with lower level map-based and image data. The integration of these two types of information is essential to ensure that all components of the architecture communicate properly, and that all available information is used to make the best decisions possible.

References

1. Albus, J., "4-D/RCS: A Reference Model Architecture for Demo III," NISTIR 5994, Gaithersburg, MD, March 1997.
2. Gage, Douglas, Information Processing Technology Office – Mobile Autonomous Mobile Software http://www.darpa.mil/ipto/research/mars/. Last Viewed May 30 2002.
3. McKnight, A.J. and A.G. Hundt. 1971. *Driver Education Task Analysis: Instructional Objectives*. Human Resources Research Organization.
4. Genesereth M., Fikes R. 1992. Knowledge Interchange Format. Stanford Logic Report Logic-92-1, Stanford Univ. http://logic.stanford.edu/kif/kif.html.

Formal Analysis of an Agent-Based Medical Diagnosis Confirmation System

(Extended Abstract)

Alexander Hoole[1], Issa Traore[2], and Michael Liu Yanguo[2]

[1] Microdev Engineering Corp.
4521 Durling Pl.
Victoria, B.C. V8N 4Y9
alex@microdevtraining.com
[2] University of Victoria
Department of Electrical and
Computer Engineering
PO Box 3055 STN CSC
Victoria BC V8W 3P6
Canada
itraore@ece.uvic.ca

One of the most challenging issues nowadays in the software community is the development of systems providing a certain level of quality at reasonable cost and time delay. This is reflected in the fact that many important application areas such as aeronautics, nuclear energy, telecommunication or medical applications require a high level of reliability and safety. A cost reduction and increased reliability policy requires adopting rigorous methodologies at the earlier phases of the development process where it is cheaper to fix the deficiencies that may arise. Rigorous and precise development can be achieved using formal methods. The use of formal methods in software development improves the insight into and understanding of requirements, help clarify the customer's requirements by highlighting or avoiding contradictions and ambiguities in the specifications, enables rigorous verification of specifications and their software implementations. In spite of these benefits, the utilization of formal methods in industry is relatively restricted, due primarily, among other reasons, to the esoterism and lack of friendliness of the formalisms, and the lack of industrial tool support and so on.

In this respect, in order to facilitate the use of formal methods and their reasoning mechanisms, we have developed an integrated platform called the precise UML Development Environment (PrUDE)[1] that supports the rigorous validation and verification (V&V) of Unified Modeling Language (UML) models [1].

The purpose of this paper is to report on a case study of an agent-based medical diagnosis confirmation system application. The case study involves solving one facet of a larger medical diagnosis assistance system using mobile agents. The main goal of the application is to respond to a need for doctors to accurately diagnose patients medical conditions based on the symptoms, history, and investigation detected during medical examinations. The system allows a doctor

---

[1] PrUDE can be downloaded from http://www.isot.ece.uvic.ca

M.G. Hinchey et al. (Eds.): 'FAABS 2002, LNAI 2699, pp. 292–293, 2003.
© Springer-Verlag Berlin Heidelberg 2003

to enter in the symptoms, history, and investigation data of a patient (through a GUI) and have a system compare these symptoms against medical records (files, databases, data stores, data warehouses, etc.) at hospitals, academic institutions, clinics, and other repositories around the globe. The system then, after comparison, returns a record set of cases that are similar to the initially input patient information. The returned cases can then be analyzed by additional components to find patterns that may not appear under initial scrutiny (using data mining). Through this process, doctors would be able to detect medical conditions based on the experience of medical evidence discovered around the globe. Doctors would then be able to perform, among others, the following tasks: analyze data sets to determine which other cases are truly comparable; resolve which relevant instances had successful treatment; and contact doctors who applied the treatment to compare notes. These steps will help to ensure a more successful and accurate treatment of a patient's condition.

The primary reasons behind the use of agents in this application is that they provide several features that make them ideal for information retrieval and resources optimization in distributed environments. During execution there are initially agents for retrieval of information from remote data stores, other agents for searching and sorting result Sets, and lastly, agents for performing datamining on the result set in an attempt to find interesting patterns in the returned data.

The system was designed independently using the UML, and implemented using Java. Then a separate team conducted the V&V using the UML model as input to PrUDE. The Precise UML Development Environment (PrUDE) is an integrated V&V framework for critical systems design. It provides a proprietary formal semantic for UML diagrams [4], expressed in the Prototype Verification System (PVS) [2], which is used as basis for formal analysis. The UML model was fed to the PrUDE toolkit in order to generate corresponding PVS semantics. Then using the PVS semantics we were able to check several interesting properties of the system. The emphasis was put mainly on the properties characterizing the dynamic patterns of interactions within and between agents. The complex reasoning mechanisms and acting patterns of agents are quite often captured by the specification of their dynamic behaviour [3].

References

1. G. Booch, J. Rumbaugh, I. Jacobson, The Unified Modeling Language User Guide, Addison-Wesley, Oct. 1999.
2. Judy Crew, Sam Owre, John Rushby, Natarajan Shankar, Mandayam Srivas, A Tutorial Introduction to PVS, WIFT'95: Workshop on Industrial-Strength Formal Specification Techniques, Boca Raton, Florida, April 1995
3. F. Brazier, B. D. Keplicz, N.R. Jennings, J. Treur, Formal Specification of Multi-Agent Systems: a Real-World Case, 1rst International Conference on Multi-Agent Systems (ICMAS'95), San Francisco, CA, USA, pp. 25–32, 1995.
4. I. Traore, April 2000, An Outline of PVS Semantics for UML Statecharts, Journal of Universal Computer Science (JUCS), Springer Pub. Co., Nov. 2

Agent Programming in Dribble: From Beliefs to Goals with Plans

Birna van Riemsdijk[1], Wiebe van der Hoek[1,2], and John-Jules C. Meyer[1]

[1] Department of Computer Science, Utrecht University, The Netherlands
[2] Department of Computer Science, University of Liverpool, United Kingdom

1 The Context

In research on agents, besides architectures, the areas of agent theories and agent programming languages are distinguished. Theories concern descriptions of (the behaviour of) agents. Agents are often described using logic [8,10]. Concepts that are commonly incorporated in such logics are for instance knowledge, beliefs, desires, intentions, commitments, goals and plans.

To support the practical development of intelligent agents, several programming languages have been introduced that incorporate concepts from agent logics. Firstly, there is a family of languages taking goals as *procedural* (goals to do): whether they are called commitments (Agent-0, [9]), intentions (AgentSpeak(L), [6]), or goals (3APL, [2]) makes little difference: all these notions are structures built from *actions* and therefore similar in nature to *plans*. In a series of papers, it was argued that the languages AgentSpeak(L), Agent-0 and ConGolog (see [1,3,5]) can be reduced to 3APL. At the same time, to reason about 3APL, one could try using a BDI ([7]) or KARO ([11]) like logic, incorporating beliefs and plans. Such logics however also incorporate a *declarative* notion of goals, which was typically missing in 3APL. To bridge this gap, the programming language GOAL was proposed ([4]). This language takes the declarative point of view on goals (goal to be).

2 The Language

The language that we propose in this paper constitutes a *synthesis* between the declarative and the procedural approaches, combining both notions in one and the same programming language. The idea is, that in such a language a more precise mapping with logical specification languages like BDI or KARO can be obtained. To be more specific, we define the language Dribble, in which the declarative and procedural features of the languages GOAL and 3APL are combined. The language 3APL offers the means for *creating and modifying plans* during the execution of the agent. GOAL agents on the other hand do not have planning features, but they do offer the possibility to *use declarative goals* to select actions. The language Dribble thus incorporates beliefs and goals as well as planning features. The idea is, that a Dribble agent should be able to select a plan to reach a goal from where it is at a certain point in time. In order to

M.G. Hinchey et al. (Eds.): 'FAABS 2002, LNAI 2699, pp. 294–295, 2003.

do that, the agent has beliefs, goals and rules to select plans and to create and modify plans.

In [12], the operational semantics of Dribble was defined using a transition system. This transition system defines the possible state changes for an agent. We also sketched a dynamic logic in which one can reason about actions defined in that logic. These actions transform the state of the agent, expressed with a transformation function. The correspondence between state transitions defined by actions in the logic and those defined by the transition system, is proven.

References

1. K. V. Hindriks, F. S. de Boer, W. van der Hoek, and J.-J. Ch. Meyer. A formal embedding of AgentSpeak(L) in 3APL. In G. Antoniou and J. Slaney, editors, *Advanced Topics in Artificial Intelligence*, pages 155–166. Springer, LNAI 1502, 1998.
2. K. V. Hindriks, F. S. de Boer, W. van der Hoek, and J.-J. Ch. Meyer. Agent programming in 3APL. *Int. J. of Autonomous Agents and Multi-Agent Systems*, 2(4):357–401, 1999.
3. K. V. Hindriks, F. S. de Boer, W. van der Hoek, and J.-J. Ch. Meyer. A formal semantics for the core of AGENT-0. In E. Postma and M. Gyssens, editors, *Proceedings of Eleventh Belgium-Netherlands Conference on Artificial Intelligence*, pages 27–34, 1999.
4. K. V. Hindriks, F. S. de Boer, W. van der Hoek, and J.-J. Ch. Meyer. Agent programming with declarative goals. In *Intelligent Agents VI – Proceedings of the 7th International Workshop on Agent Theories, Architectures, and Languages (ATAL'2000)*, Lecture Notes in AI. Springer, Berlin, 2001.
5. K. V. Hindriks, Y. Lespirance, and H. Levesque. A formal embedding of ConGolog in 3APL. In *Proceedings of the 14th European Conference on Artificial Intelligence*, pages 558–562, 2002.
6. A. S. Rao. AgentSpeak(L): BDI agents speak out in a logical computable language. In W. van der Velde and J. Perram, editors, *Agents Breaking Away (LNAI 1038)*, pages 42–55. Springer-Verlag, 1996.
7. A. S. Rao and M. Georgeff. BDI Agents: from theory to practice. In *Proceedings of the First International Conference on Multi-Agent Systems (ICMAS-95)*, pages 312–319, San Francisco, CA, June 1995.
8. A. S. Rao and M. P. Georgeff. Modeling rational agents within a BDI-architecture. In J. Allen, R. Fikes, and E. Sandewall, editors, *Proceedings of the Second International Conference on Principles of Knowledge Representation and Reasoning (KR'91)*, pages 473–484. Morgan Kaufmann, 1991.
9. Y. Shoham. Agent-oriented programming. *Artificial Intelligence*, 60:51–92, 1993.
10. W. van der Hoek, B. van Linder, and J.-J. Ch. Meyer. An integrated modal approach to rational agents. In M. Wooldridge and A. S. Rao, editors, *Foundations of Rational Agency*, Applied Logic Series 14, pages 133–168. Kluwer, Dordrecht, 1998.
11. B. van Linder, W. van der Hoek, and J.-J. Ch. Meyer. Formalizing abilities and opportunities of agents. *Fundamenta Informaticae*, 34(1,2):53–101, 1998.
    M. B. van Riemsdijk, W. van der Hoek, and J.-J. C. Meyer. Agent programming in Dribble: from beliefs to goals with plans. In *Proceedings of AAMAS*, Melbourne, Australia, July 2003.

Author Index

Aldridge, Stuart 241
Arjona, José Luis 79

Bergman, Margo 283
Bestougeff, Hélène 286
Bharadwaj, Ramesh 126, 235
Böhne, Thomas 68

Clark, Keith 162
Corchuelo, Rafael 79
Cukic, Bojan 208

Dignum, Frank 37
Dignum, Virginia 37

Esterline, Albert C. 28, 146

Fisher, Michael 15
Flanagan, Richard 220

Ghidini, Chiara 15
Gordon-Spears, Diana F. 92, 193, 257
Goss, Simon 1
Gruninger, Michael 290

Heinze, Clinton 1
Hicks, Jeffrey 220, 241
Hinchey, Mike 162
Hirsch, Benjamin 15
Hoek, Wiebe van der 294
Hogan, James P. 260
Homaifar, Abdollah 28
Hoole, Alexander 292

Jung, Hyuckchul 103

Kimiaghalam, Bahram 28
Kiriakidis, Kiriakos 92
Kondo, Yoji 264

Łasica, T. 115
Lomuscio, A. 115

Marche, Mikaël 173
Marsella, Stacy 103
Menzies, Tim 1, 208
Meyer, John-Jules C. 37, 274, 294

Nair, Ranjit 103
Nelson, Stacy D. 53

Owen, David 208

Pearce, Adrian 1
Pecheur, Charles 53, 236
Peña, Joaquín 79
Penczek, W. 115
Petrov, Plamen 220, 241

Quemener, Yves-Marie 173

Riemsdijk, Birna van 294
Robinson, Peter J. 162
Rudnianski, Michel 286

Schlenoff, Craig 239, 290
Spears, William M. 193
Stoyen, Alexander 220, 241

Tambe, Milind 103
Traore, Issa 292
Truszkowski, Walt 269

Van Baalen, Jeffrey 68

Weigand, Hans 37

Yanguo, Michael Liu 292

Zappacosta Amboldi, Silvana 133